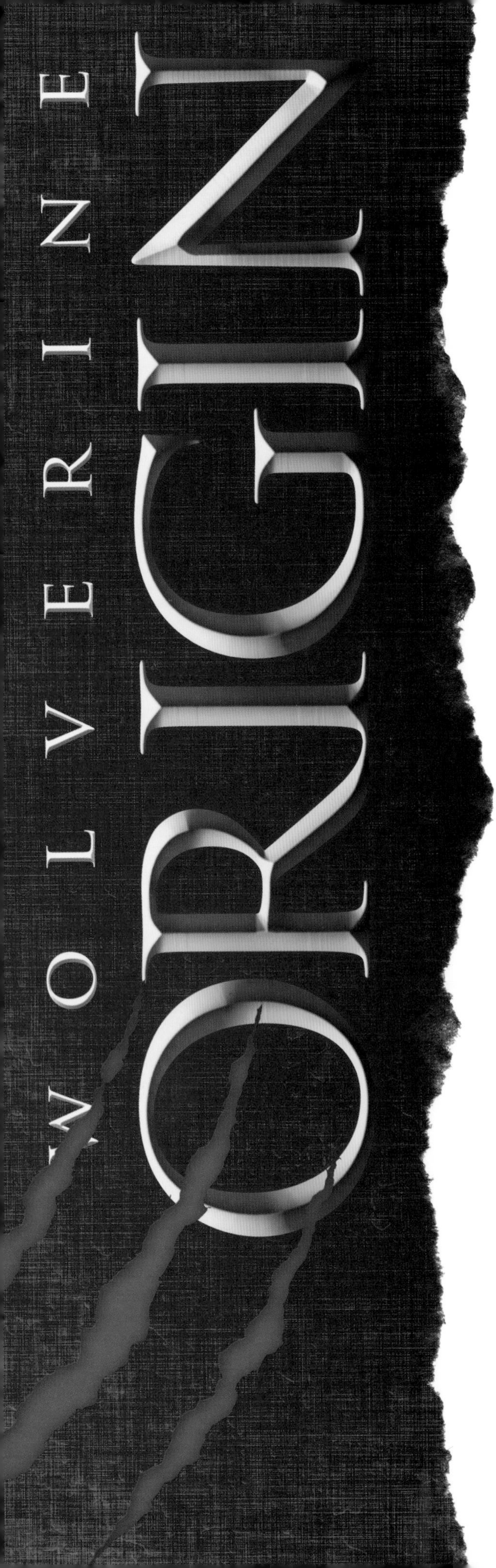
WOLVERINE
ORIGIN

**PLOT**
Bill Jemas, Joe Quesada & Paul Jenkins

**SCRIPT**
Paul Jenkins

**PENCILER**
Andy Kubert

**DIGITAL PAINTER**
Richard Isanove

**LETTERERS**
John Roshell & Comicraft's Wes Abbott, Oscar Gongorra & Saida Temofonte

**COVER ART**
Joe Quesada & Richard Isanove

**ASSISTANT EDITOR**
Mike Raicht

**EDITOR**
Mike Marts

---

**COLLECTION EDITOR**
Mark D. Beazley

**ASSISTANT EDITORS**
Nelson Ribeiro & Alex Starbuck

**EDITOR, SPECIAL PROJECTS**
Jennifer Grünwald

**SENIOR EDITOR, SPECIAL PROJECTS**
Jeff Youngquist

**SVP OF PRINT & DIGITAL PUBLISHING SALES**
David Gabriel

**BOOK DESIGNER**
Rodolfo Muraguchi

**EDITOR IN CHIEF**
Axel Alonso

**CHIEF CREATIVE OFFICER**
Joe Quesada

**PUBLISHER**
Dan Buckley

**EXECUTIVE PRODUCER**
Alan Fine

---

**SPECIAL THANKS TO**
Richard Isanove, Spencer Beck & Chris Allo

---

**WOLVERINE: ORIGIN.** Contains material originally published in magazine form as WOLVERINE: THE ORIGIN #1-6. Second edition. First printing 2013. ISBN# 978-0-7851-8384-6. Published by MARVEL WORLDWIDE, INC., a subsidiary of MARVEL ENTERTAINMENT, LLC. OFFICE OF PUBLICATION: 135 West 50th Street, New York, NY 10020.  **Printed in China**. ALAN FINE, EVP - Office of the President, Marvel Worldwide, Inc. and EVP & CMO Marvel Characters B.V.; DAN BUCKLEY, Publisher & President - Print, Animation & Digital Divisions; JOE QUESADA, Chief Creative Officer; TOM BREVOORT, SVP of Publishing; DAVID BOGART, SVP of Operations & Procurement, Publishing; RUWAN JAYATILLEKE, SVP & Associate Publisher, Publishing; C.B. CEBULSKI, SVP of Creator & Content Development; DAVID GABRIEL, SVP of Print & Digital Publishing Sales; JIM O'KEEFE, VP of Operations & Logistics; DAN CARR, Executive Director of Publishing Technology; SUSAN CRESPI, Editorial Operations Manager; ALEX MORALES, Publishing Operations Manager; STAN LEE, Chairman Emeritus. For information regarding advertising in Marvel Comics or on Marvel.com, please contact Niza Disla, Director of Marvel Partnerships, at ndisla@marvel.com. For Marvel subscription inquiries, please call 800-217-9158. **Manufactured between 2/18/2013 and 4/5/2013 by R.R. DONNELLEY ASIA PRINTING SOLUTIONS, CHINA.**

10 9 8 7 6 5 4 3 2 1

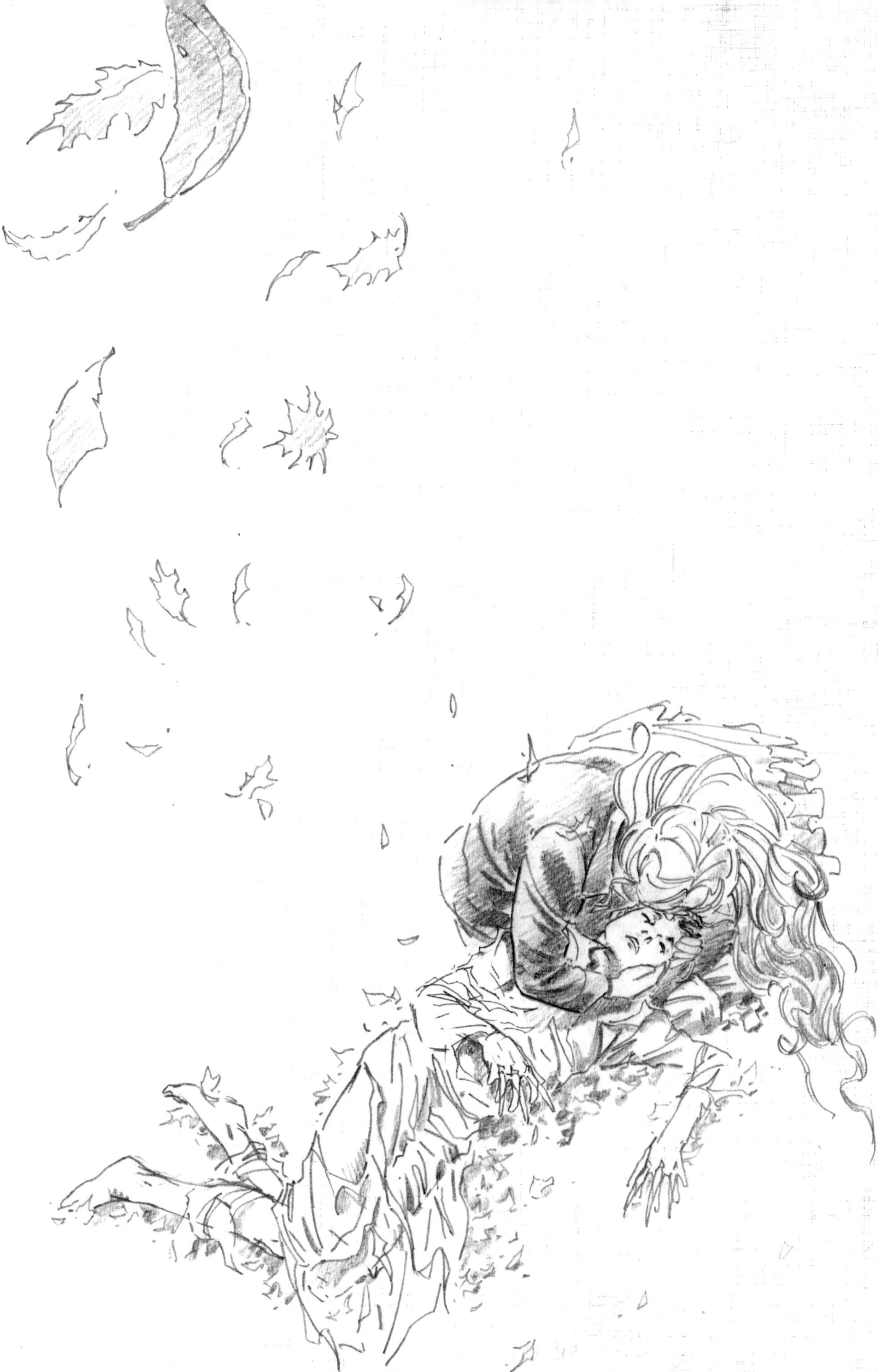

# INTRODUCTION BY TOM DeSANTO

ORIGIN #5 PAGES 2-3 PENCILS BY ANDY KUBERT

"WHAT DO YOU THINK OF THE IDEA OF A LIMITED SERIES TELLING WOLVERINE'S ORIGIN?"

Two words immediately popped into my head... bad idea. That was how my first lunch with Joe Quesada began back in September of 2000. I had just spent the past four years of my life working to bring X-Men to life on the big screen and Wolverine was a big part of me. X-Men was the movie I wanted to make since I was twelve years old and I had assumed the role as the protector of the mythology on the film. But now it wasn't the studio system that was going to screw Logan up but Marvel itself. Nightmare visions of the Spider-Man "Clone Saga" danced through my head.

For the rest of the lunch Joe and I went back and forth debating the pros and cons of finally revealing the greatest mystery of comicdom — the history of Wolverine. I used all the arguments. That it would ruin the mystique of the character, that Logan wouldn't be as tragic a hero if we knew his past, even stooping to "you should let the reader flesh out that mystery in their own head." None of it worked. For as passionate as I was Joe was equally as passionate; and I could see in his eyes that he had already made up his mind, he was going to tell the origin of Logan. At that point I asked him "Why? Why take the chance of damaging the character?" Joe looked me dead in the eye and said, "If anyone is going to tell the origin of Logan, Marvel should do it first, not the movie." You know what? I agreed with him.

At that moment all of my fanboy trepidation turned into excitement, now I wanted to read it. Over eighteen months have passed since that lunch and I've been patiently waiting for all of the issues to come out so I could read ORIGIN at one sitting. I resisted the urge to read it every time a new issue came out, although I broke down and peeked at the artwork and was blown away by the lushness and sweep of the visuals, which owed more to Mark Twain than spandex-clad four color heroes. But I was going to wait. Two days ago I got a call saying that Bill Jemas and Joe Quesada wanted to know if I would write the foreword to the ORIGIN hardcover. Needless to say I feigned indifference and immediately asked if I could get copies of all the issues published and unpublished sent to me overnight. Of course FedEx was a day late. Well, having just finished reading ORIGIN, I think back on Joe's original question, "What do you think of the idea of a limited series telling Wolverine's origin?" and now what pops into my head is ... damn, I wish I had thought of that.

A True Believer Always,

*Tom De Santo*

TOM DeSANTO
EXECUTIVE PRODUCER/ CO-WRITER
X-MEN: THE MOVIE
2002

P.S. — To Messrs. Jenkins, Kubert, Isanove, Jemas, and Quesada: Success belongs to those who take the risk; thanks for taking the risk. But an even bigger thanks for succeeding.

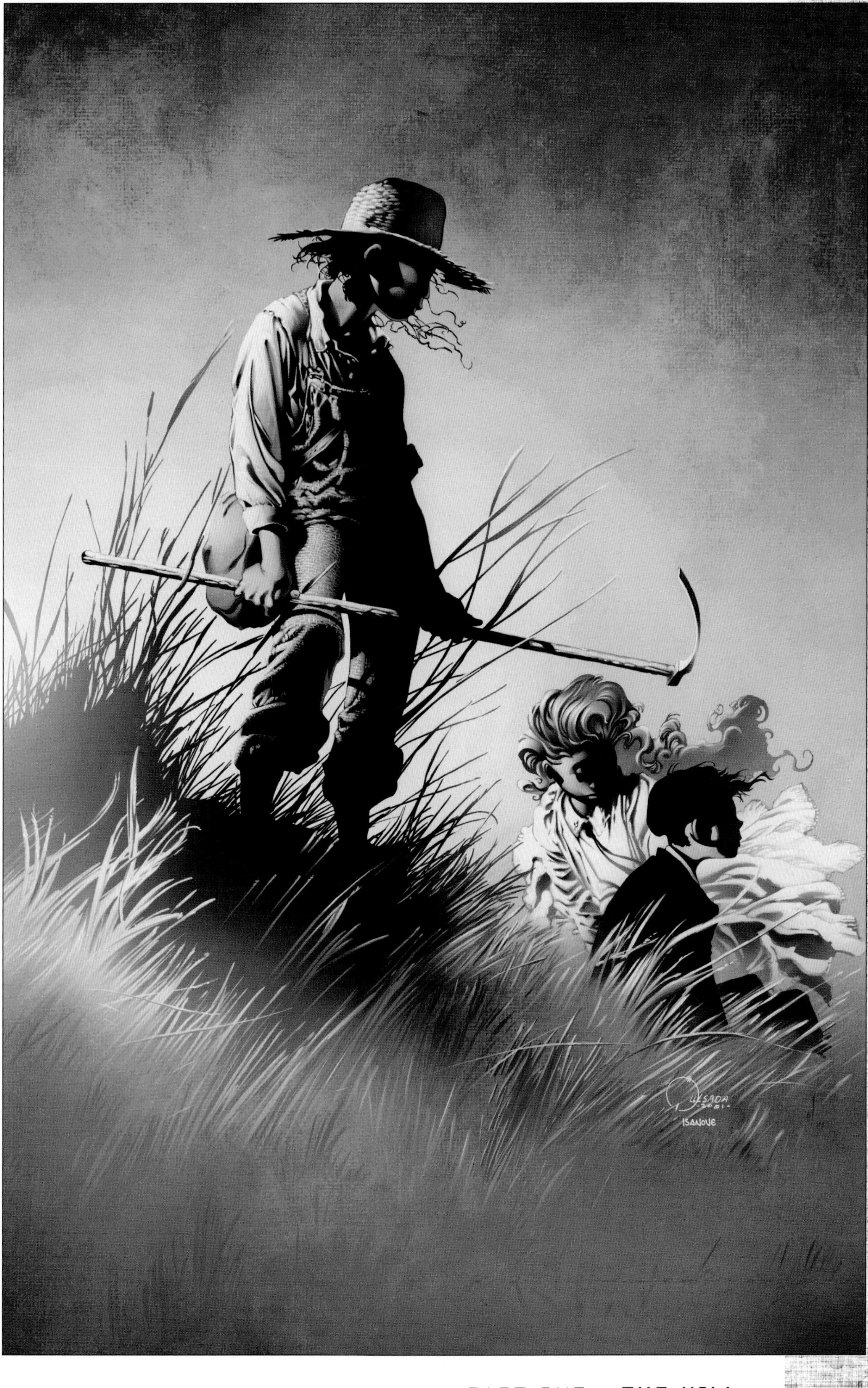
QUESADA 2001
ISANOVE

## PART ONE – **THE HILL**

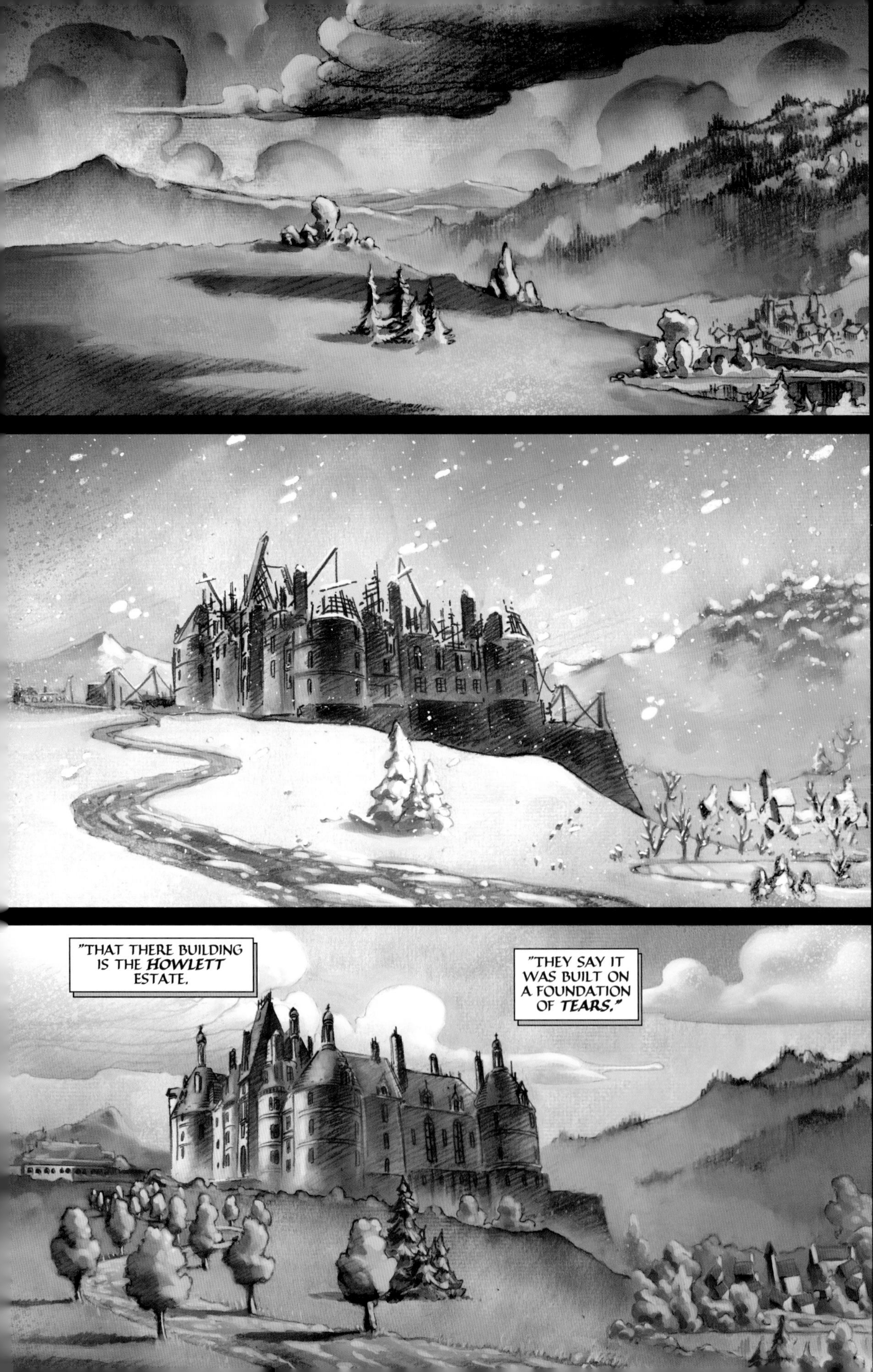
"THAT THERE BUILDING IS THE *HOWLETT* ESTATE.
"THEY SAY IT WAS BUILT ON A FOUNDATION OF *TEARS.*"

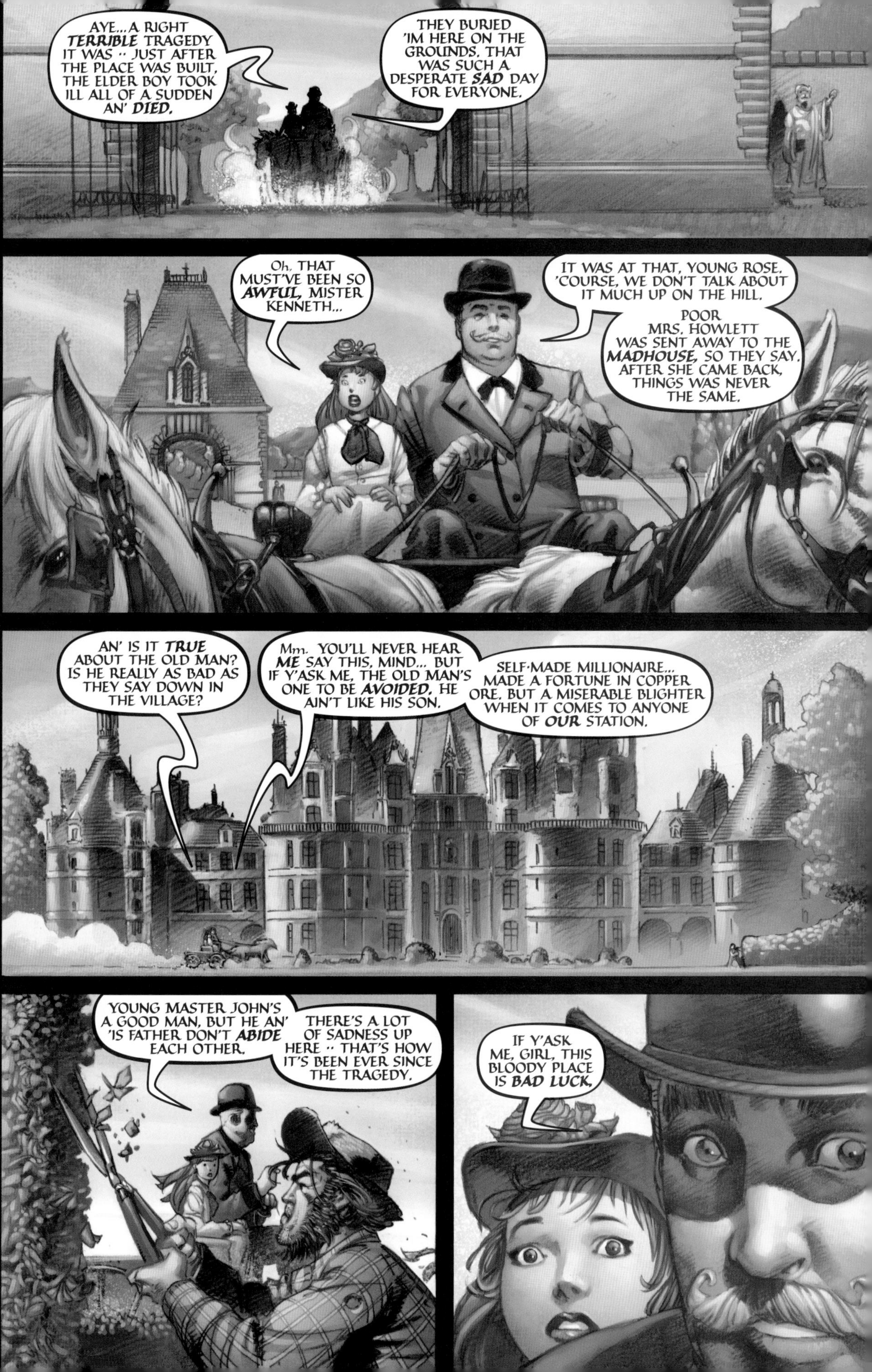
AYE... A RIGHT TERRIBLE TRAGEDY IT WAS -- JUST AFTER THE PLACE WAS BUILT, THE ELDER BOY TOOK ILL ALL OF A SUDDEN AN' DIED.
THEY BURIED 'IM HERE ON THE GROUNDS. THAT WAS SUCH A DESPERATE SAD DAY FOR EVERYONE.
Oh, THAT MUST'VE BEEN SO AWFUL, MISTER KENNETH...
IT WAS AT THAT, YOUNG ROSE. 'COURSE, WE DON'T TALK ABOUT IT MUCH UP ON THE HILL.
POOR MRS. HOWLETT WAS SENT AWAY TO THE MADHOUSE, SO THEY SAY. AFTER SHE CAME BACK, THINGS WAS NEVER THE SAME.
AN' IS IT TRUE ABOUT THE OLD MAN? IS HE REALLY AS BAD AS THEY SAY DOWN IN THE VILLAGE?
Mm. YOU'LL NEVER HEAR ME SAY THIS, MIND... BUT IF Y'ASK ME, THE OLD MAN'S ONE TO BE AVOIDED. HE AIN'T LIKE HIS SON.
SELF-MADE MILLIONAIRE... MADE A FORTUNE IN COPPER ORE. BUT A MISERABLE BLIGHTER WHEN IT COMES TO ANYONE OF OUR STATION.
YOUNG MASTER JOHN'S A GOOD MAN, BUT HE AN' 'IS FATHER DON'T ABIDE EACH OTHER.
THERE'S A LOT OF SADNESS UP HERE -- THAT'S HOW IT'S BEEN EVER SINCE THE TRAGEDY.
IF Y'ASK ME, GIRL, THIS BLOODY PLACE IS BAD LUCK.

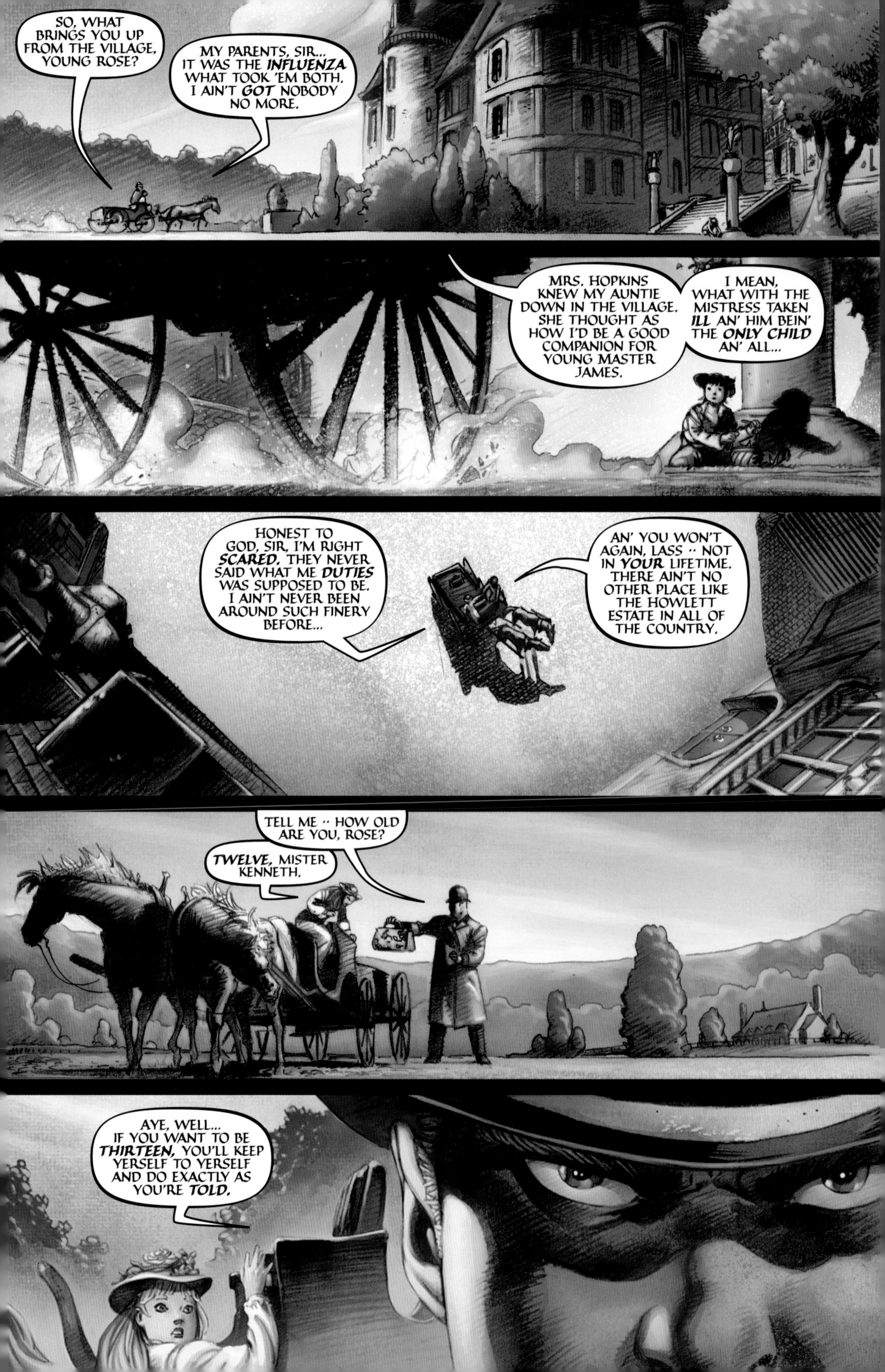
SO, WHAT BRINGS YOU UP FROM THE VILLAGE, YOUNG ROSE?
MY PARENTS, SIR... IT WAS THE *INFLUENZA* WHAT TOOK 'EM BOTH. I AIN'T *GOT* NOBODY NO MORE.
MRS. HOPKINS KNEW MY AUNTIE DOWN IN THE VILLAGE. SHE THOUGHT AS HOW I'D BE A GOOD COMPANION FOR YOUNG MASTER JAMES.
I MEAN, WHAT WITH THE MISTRESS TAKEN *ILL* AN' HIM BEIN' THE *ONLY CHILD* AN' ALL...
HONEST TO GOD, SIR, I'M RIGHT *SCARED.* THEY NEVER SAID WHAT ME *DUTIES* WAS SUPPOSED TO BE. I AIN'T NEVER BEEN AROUND SUCH FINERY BEFORE...
AN' YOU WON'T AGAIN, LASS -- NOT IN *YOUR* LIFETIME. THERE AIN'T NO OTHER PLACE LIKE THE HOWLETT ESTATE IN ALL OF THE COUNTRY.
TELL ME -- HOW OLD ARE YOU, ROSE?
*TWELVE,* MISTER KENNETH.
AYE, WELL... IF YOU WANT TO BE *THIRTEEN,* YOU'LL KEEP YERSELF TO YERSELF AND DO EXACTLY AS YOU'RE *TOLD.*

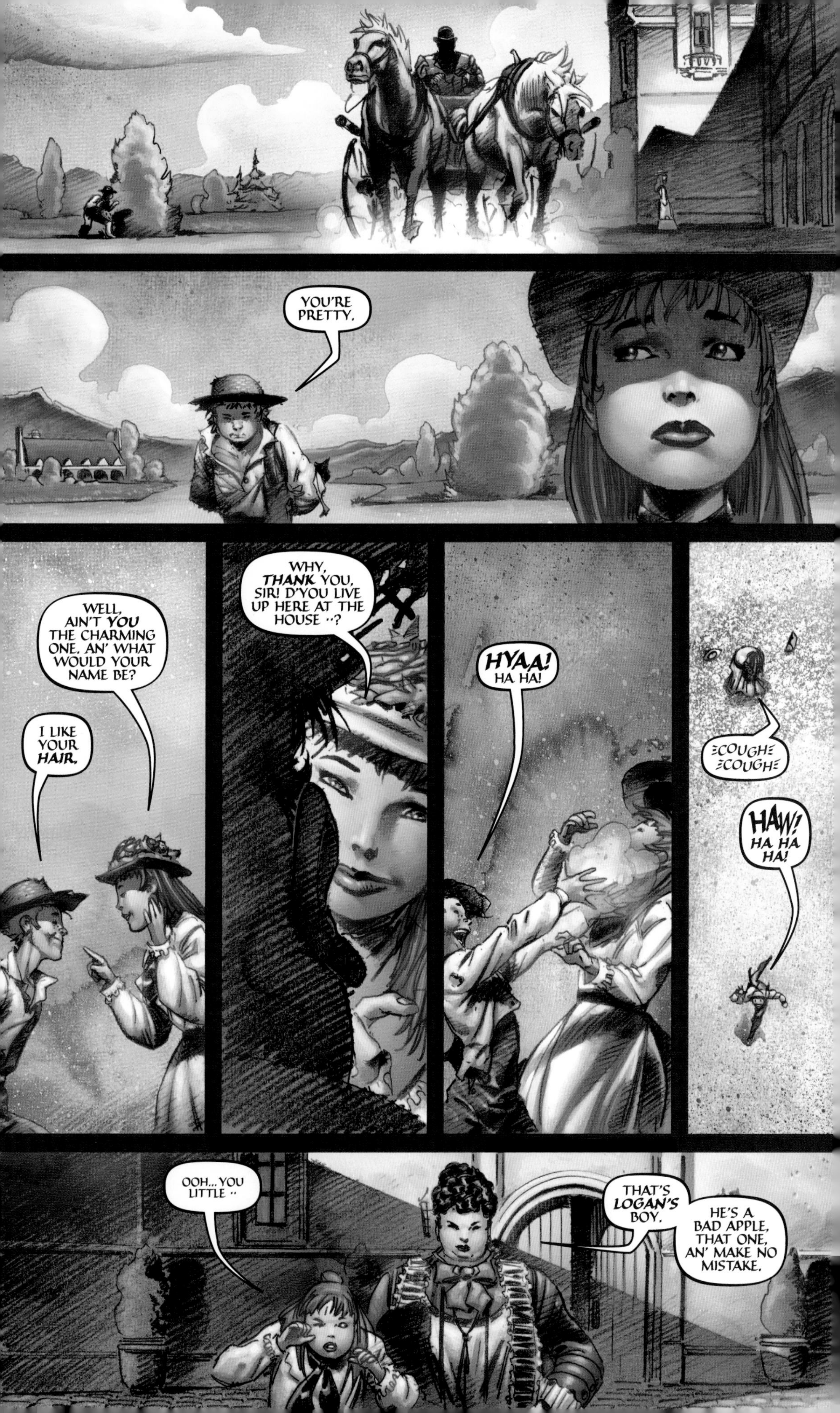

YOU'RE PRETTY.
WELL, AIN'T YOU THE CHARMING ONE. AN' WHAT WOULD YOUR NAME BE?
I LIKE YOUR HAIR.
WHY, THANK YOU, SIR! D'YOU LIVE UP HERE AT THE HOUSE ..?
HYAA! HA HA!
COUGH COUGH
HAW! HA HA HA!
OOH... YOU LITTLE ..
THAT'S LOGAN'S BOY.
HE'S A BAD APPLE, THAT ONE, AN' MAKE NO MISTAKE.

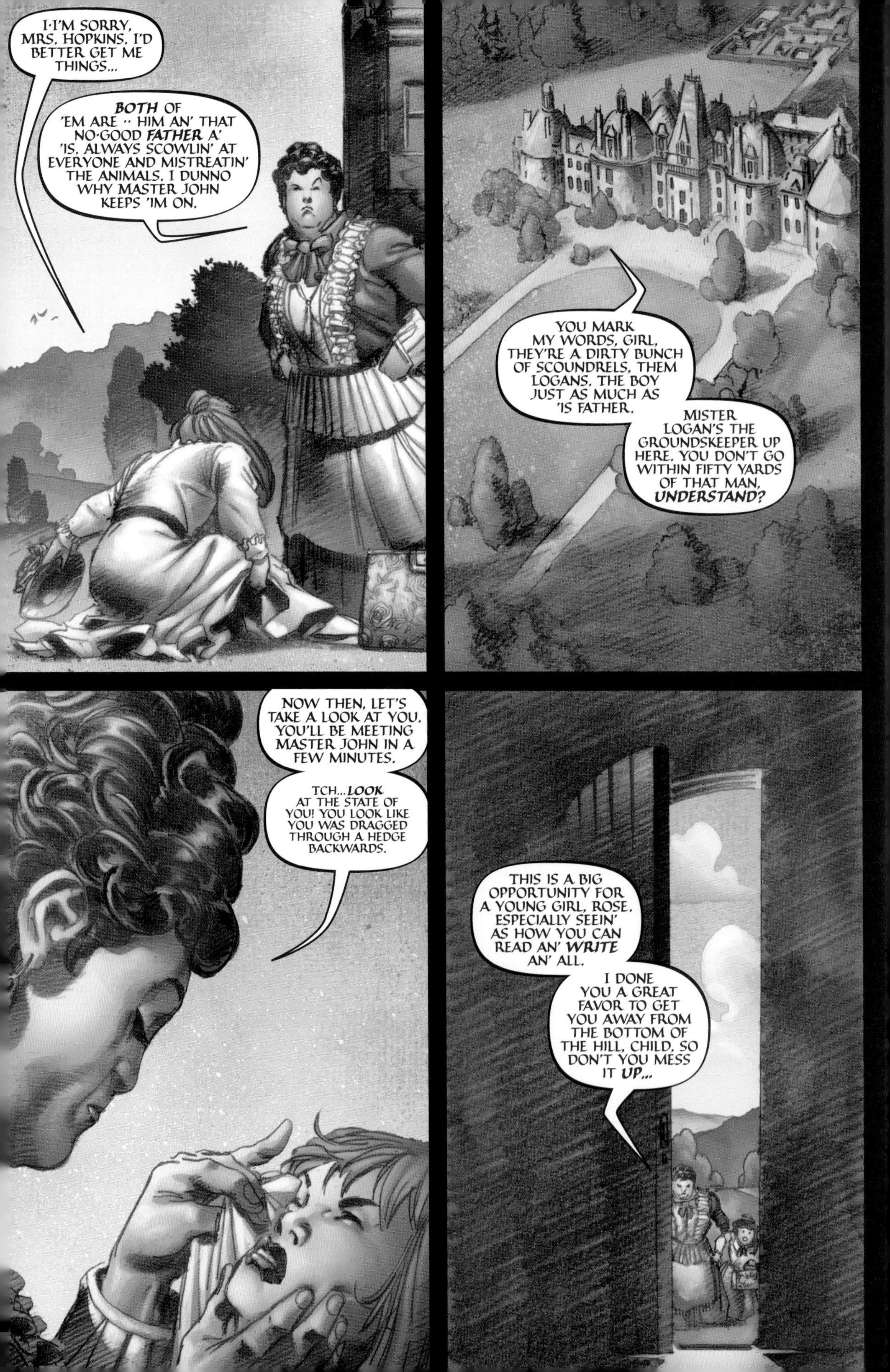
I-I'M SORRY, MRS. HOPKINS. I'D BETTER GET ME THINGS...
BOTH OF 'EM ARE -- HIM AN' THAT NO-GOOD FATHER A' 'IS. ALWAYS SCOWLIN' AT EVERYONE AND MISTREATIN' THE ANIMALS. I DUNNO WHY MASTER JOHN KEEPS 'IM ON.
YOU MARK MY WORDS, GIRL, THEY'RE A DIRTY BUNCH OF SCOUNDRELS, THEM LOGANS. THE BOY JUST AS MUCH AS 'IS FATHER.
MISTER LOGAN'S THE GROUNDSKEEPER UP HERE. YOU DON'T GO WITHIN FIFTY YARDS OF THAT MAN, UNDERSTAND?
NOW THEN, LET'S TAKE A LOOK AT YOU. YOU'LL BE MEETING MASTER JOHN IN A FEW MINUTES.
TCH...LOOK AT THE STATE OF YOU! YOU LOOK LIKE YOU WAS DRAGGED THROUGH A HEDGE BACKWARDS.
THIS IS A BIG OPPORTUNITY FOR A YOUNG GIRL, ROSE, ESPECIALLY SEEIN' AS HOW YOU CAN READ AN' WRITE AN' ALL.
I DONE YOU A GREAT FAVOR TO GET YOU AWAY FROM THE BOTTOM OF THE HILL, CHILD, SO DON'T YOU MESS IT UP...

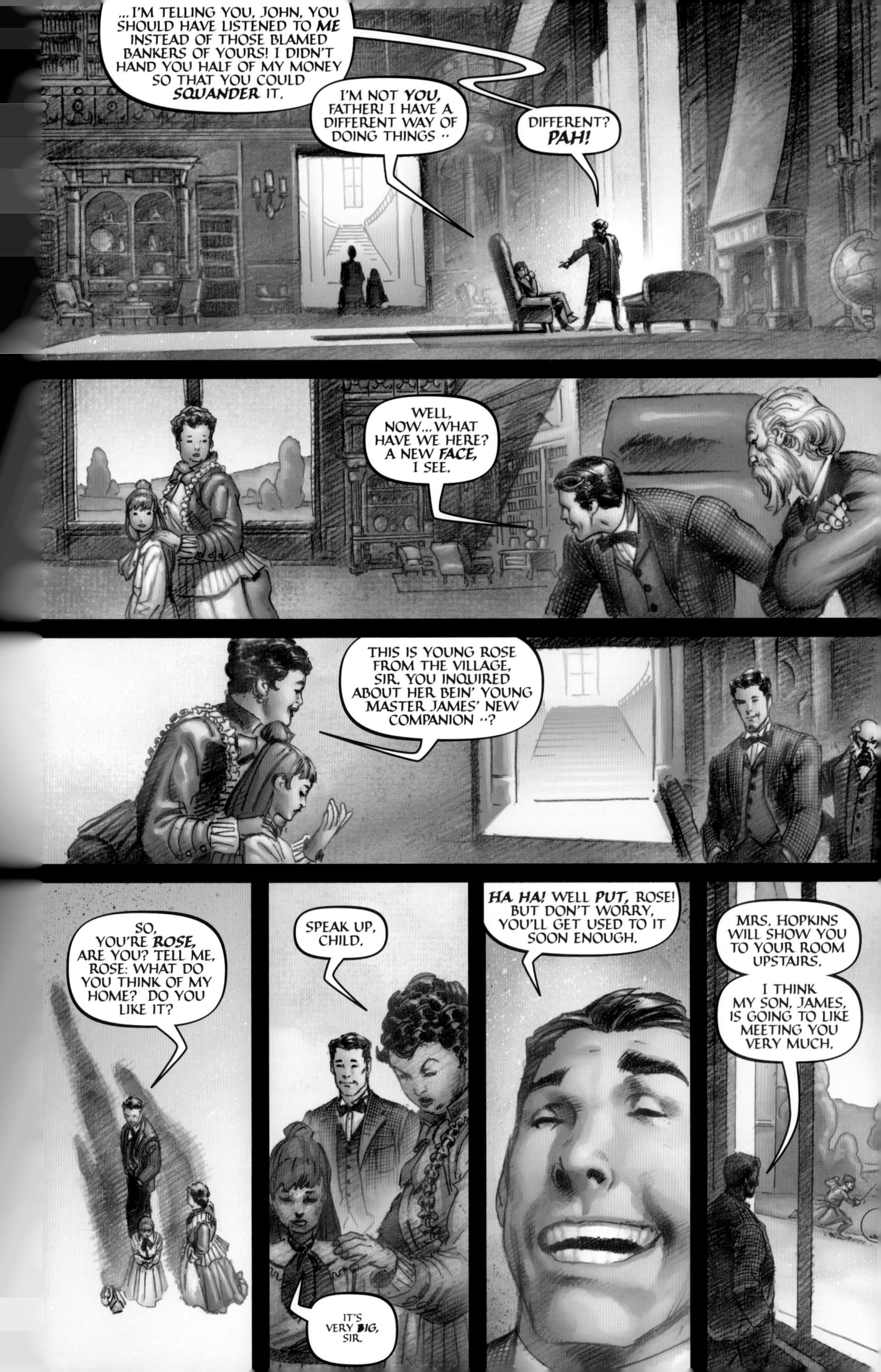
...I'M TELLING YOU, JOHN, YOU SHOULD HAVE LISTENED TO ME INSTEAD OF THOSE BLAMED BANKERS OF YOURS! I DIDN'T HAND YOU HALF OF MY MONEY SO THAT YOU COULD SQUANDER IT.
I'M NOT YOU, FATHER! I HAVE A DIFFERENT WAY OF DOING THINGS ..
DIFFERENT? PAH!
WELL, NOW...WHAT HAVE WE HERE? A NEW FACE, I SEE.
THIS IS YOUNG ROSE FROM THE VILLAGE, SIR. YOU INQUIRED ABOUT HER BEIN' YOUNG MASTER JAMES' NEW COMPANION ..?
SO, YOU'RE ROSE, ARE YOU? TELL ME, ROSE: WHAT DO YOU THINK OF MY HOME? DO YOU LIKE IT?
SPEAK UP, CHILD.
IT'S VERY BIG, SIR.
HA HA! WELL PUT, ROSE! BUT DON'T WORRY, YOU'LL GET USED TO IT SOON ENOUGH.
MRS. HOPKINS WILL SHOW YOU TO YOUR ROOM UPSTAIRS.
I THINK MY SON, JAMES, IS GOING TO LIKE MEETING YOU VERY MUCH.

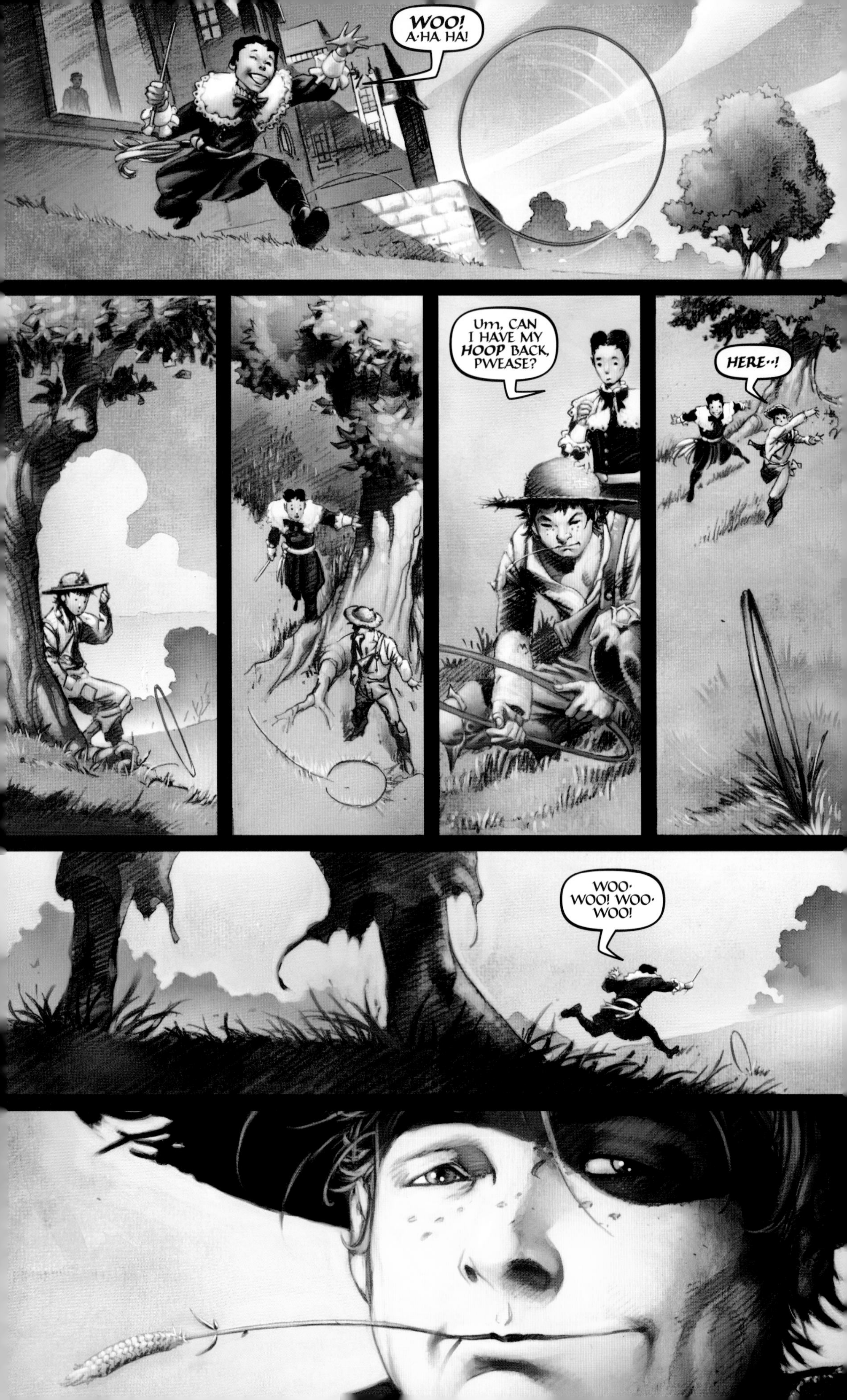
WOO! A-HA HA!
Um, CAN I HAVE MY HOOP BACK, PWEASE?
HERE--!
WOO-WOO! WOO-WOO!

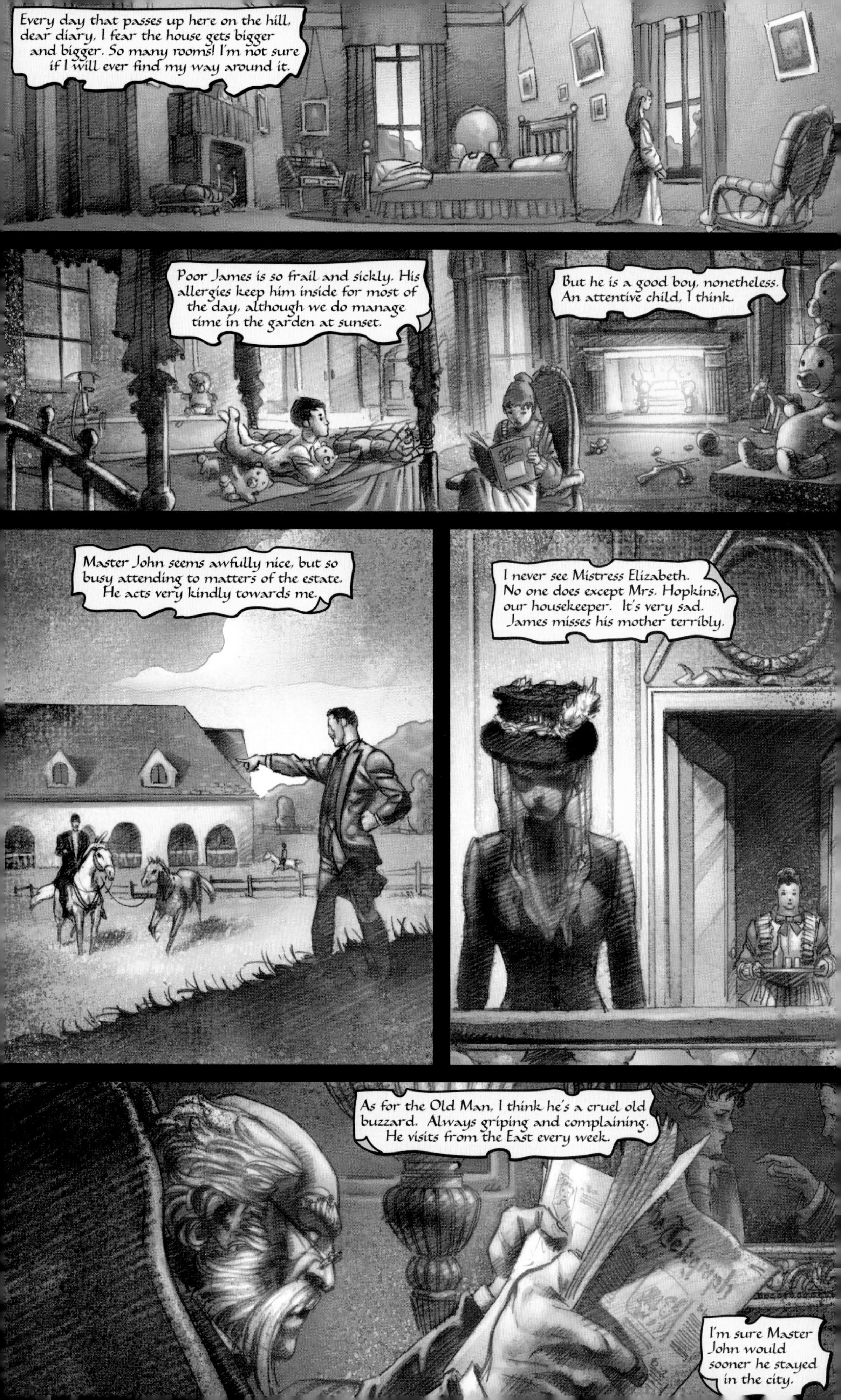
Every day that passes up here on the hill, dear diary, I fear the house gets bigger and bigger. So many rooms! I'm not sure if I will ever find my way around it.
Poor James is so frail and sickly. His allergies keep him inside for most of the day, although we do manage time in the garden at sunset.
But he is a good boy, nonetheless. An attentive child, I think.
Master John seems awfully nice, but so busy attending to matters of the estate. He acts very kindly towards me.
I never see Mistress Elizabeth. No one does except Mrs. Hopkins, our housekeeper. It's very sad. James misses his mother terribly.
As for the Old Man, I think he's a cruel old buzzard. Always griping and complaining. He visits from the East every week.
I'm sure Master John would sooner he stayed in the city.

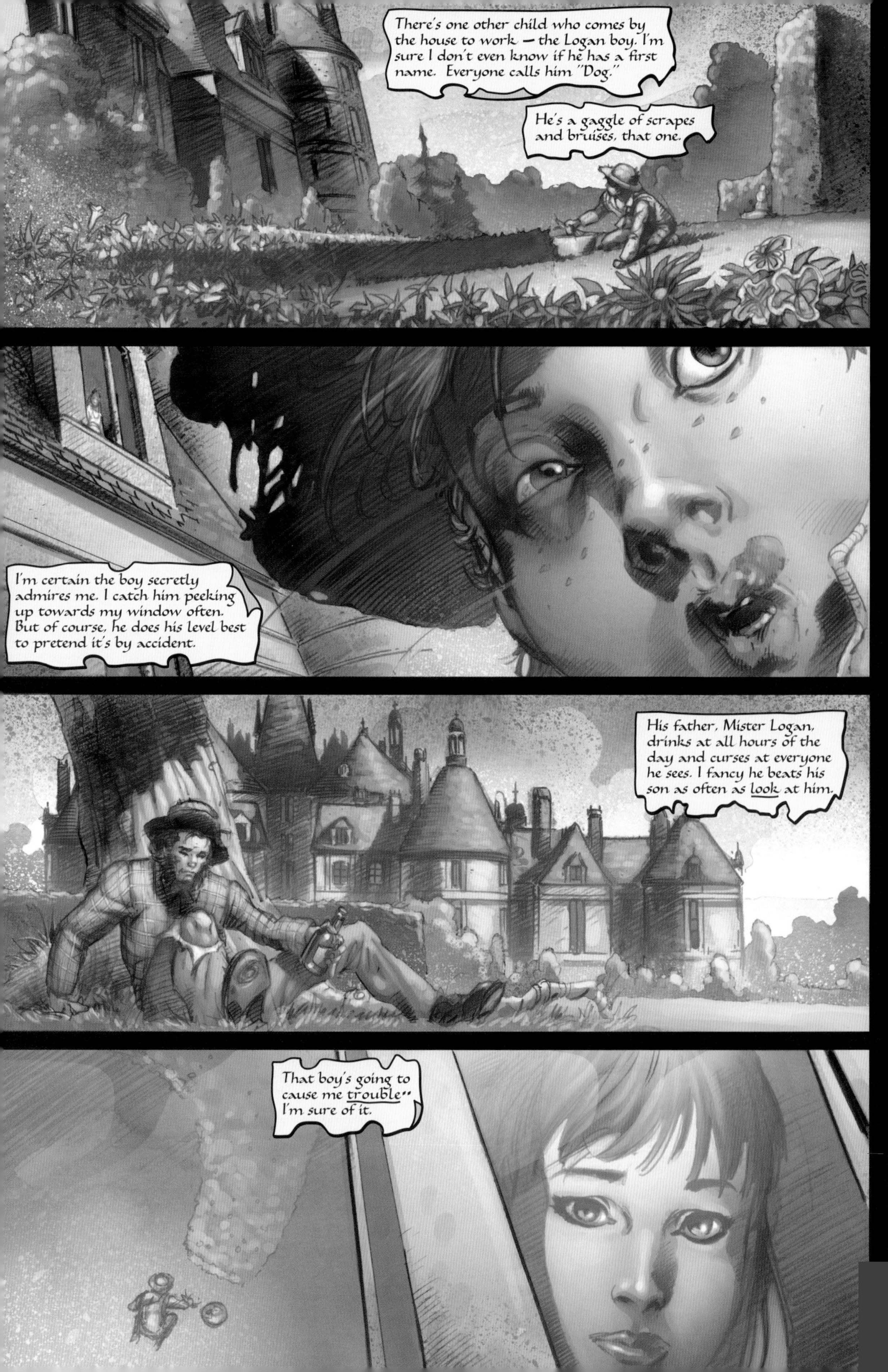
There's one other child who comes by the house to work — the Logan boy. I'm sure I don't even know if he has a first name. Everyone calls him "Dog."
He's a gaggle of scrapes and bruises, that one.
I'm certain the boy secretly admires me. I catch him peeking up towards my window often. But of course, he does his level best to pretend it's by accident.
His father, Mister Logan, drinks at all hours of the day and curses at everyone he sees. I fancy he beats his son as often as look at him.
That boy's going to cause me trouble.. I'm sure of it.

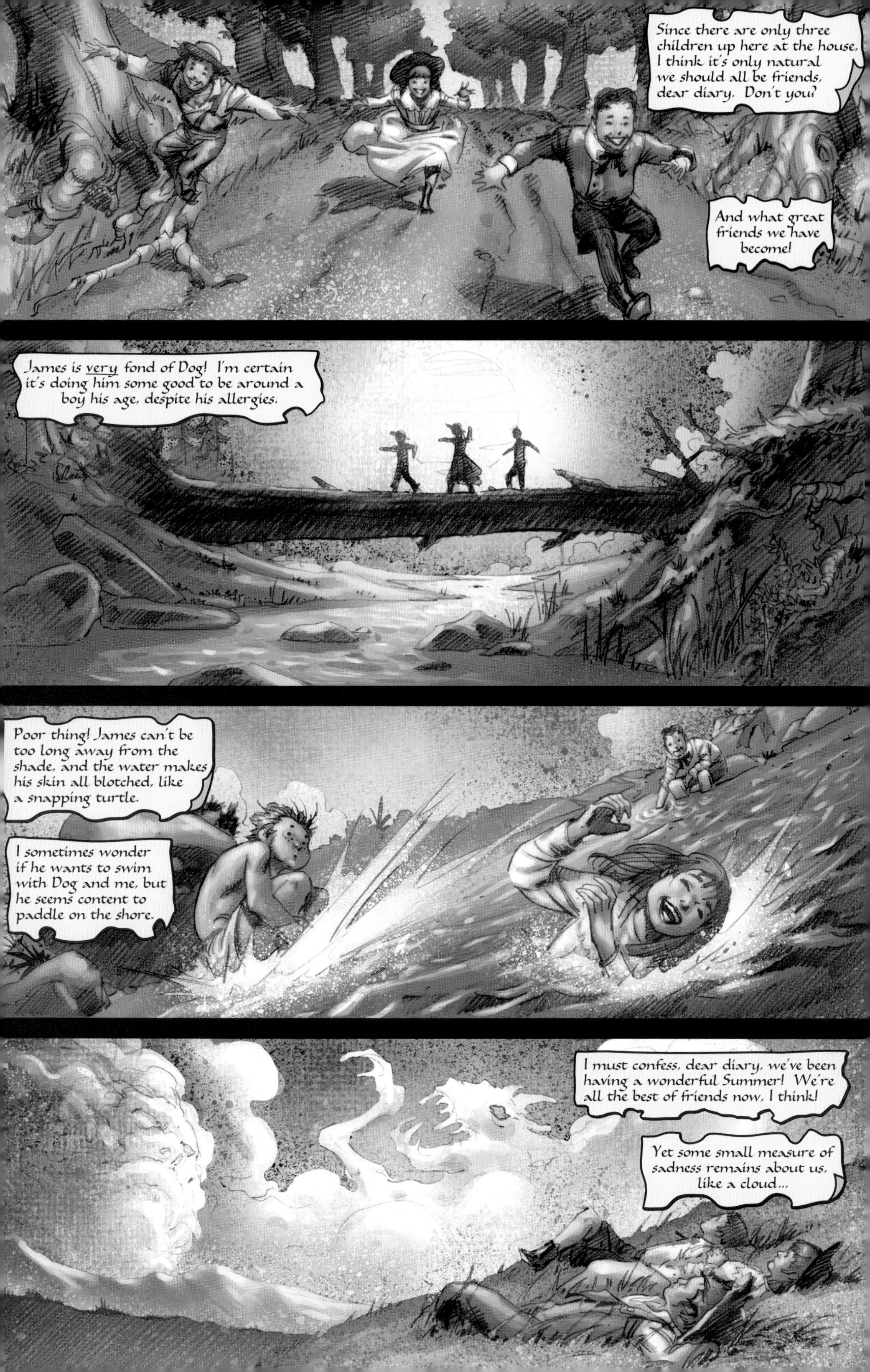
Since there are only three children up here at the house, I think it's only natural we should all be friends, dear diary. Don't you?
And what great friends we have become!
James is very fond of Dog! I'm certain it's doing him some good to be around a boy his age, despite his allergies.
Poor thing! James can't be too long away from the shade, and the water makes his skin all blotched, like a snapping turtle.
I sometimes wonder if he wants to swim with Dog and me, but he seems content to paddle on the shore.
I must confess, dear diary, we've been having a wonderful Summer! We're all the best of friends now, I think!
Yet some small measure of sadness remains about us, like a cloud...

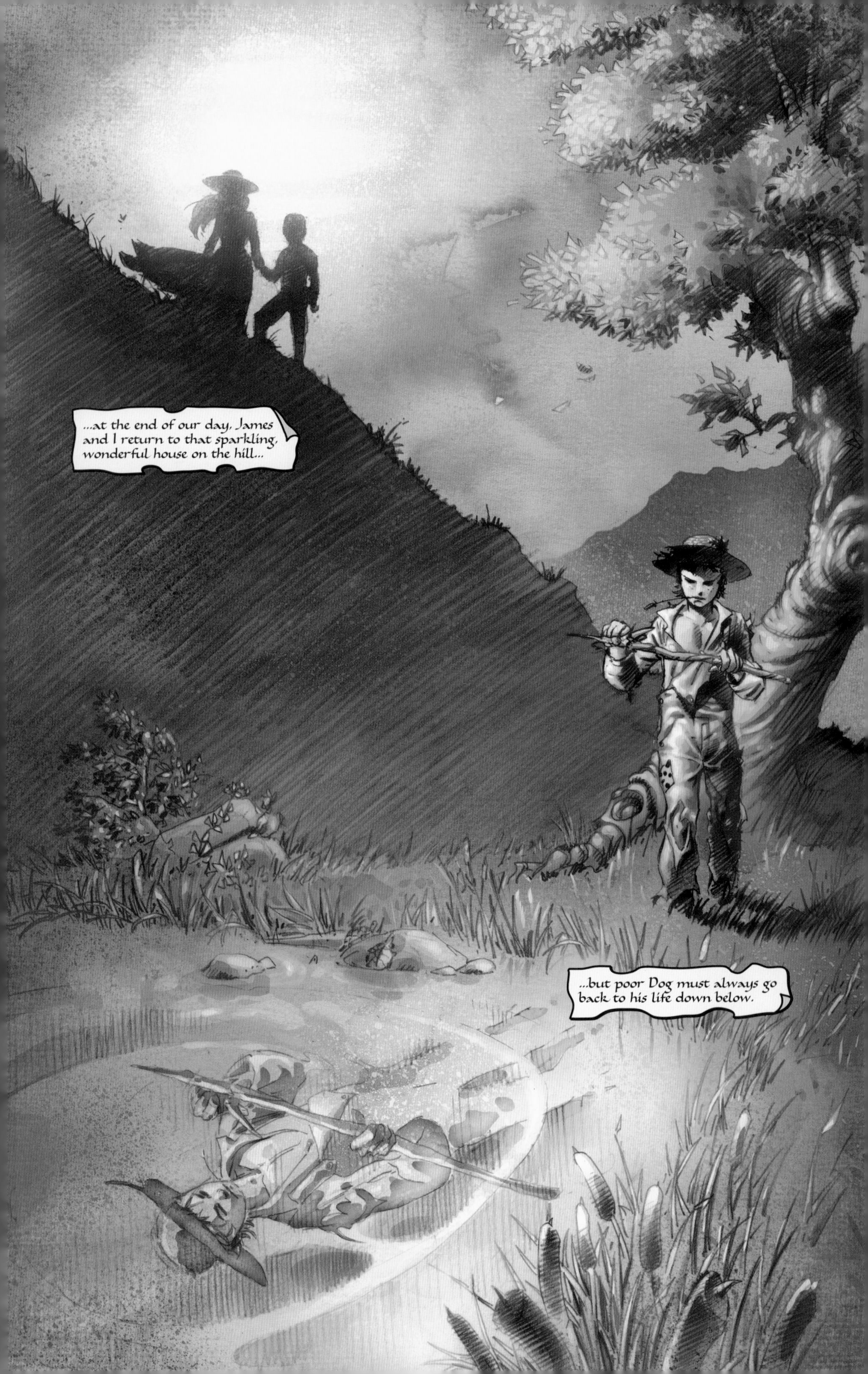
...at the end of our day, James and I return to that sparkling, wonderful house on the hill...
...but poor Dog must always go back to his life down below.

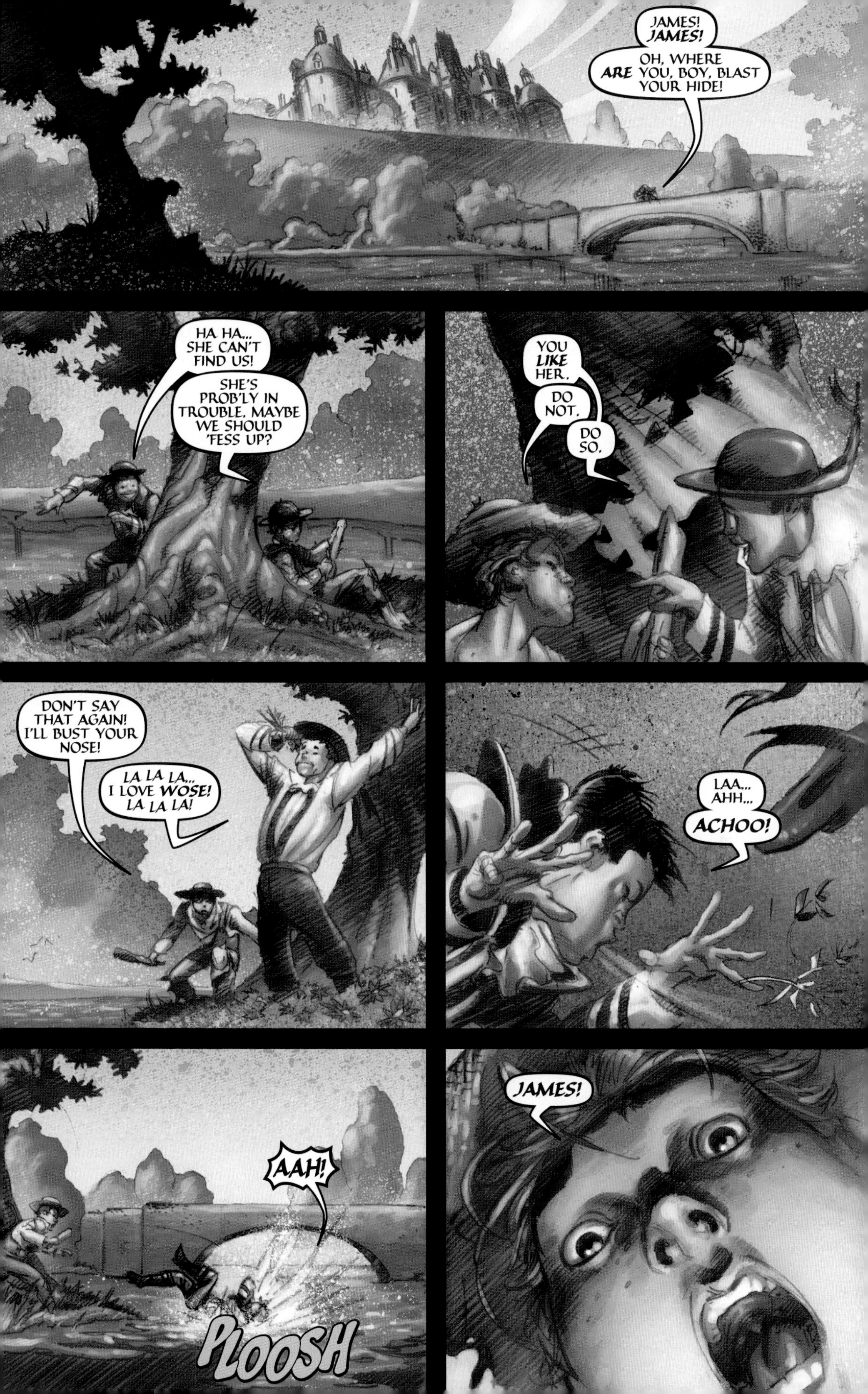
JAMES! JAMES!
OH, WHERE ARE YOU, BOY, BLAST YOUR HIDE!
HA HA... SHE CAN'T FIND US!
SHE'S PROB'LY IN TROUBLE, MAYBE WE SHOULD 'FESS UP?
YOU LIKE HER.
DO NOT.
DO SO.
DON'T SAY THAT AGAIN! I'LL BUST YOUR NOSE!
LA LA LA... I LOVE WOSE! LA LA LA!
LAA... AHH... ACHOO!
AAH!
PLOOSH
JAMES!

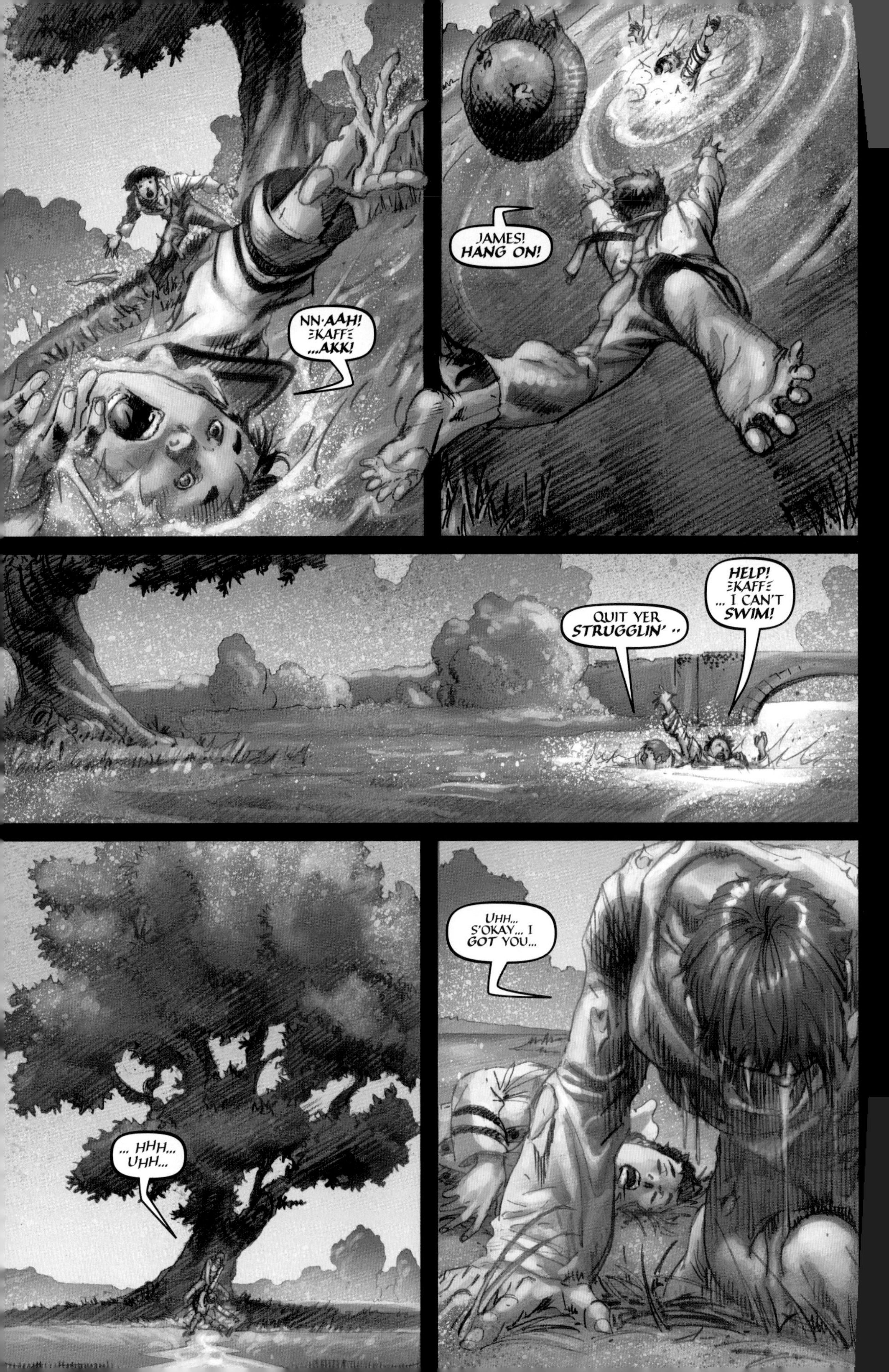
NN·AAH! ≡KAFF≡ ...AKK!
JAMES! HANG ON!
QUIT YER STRUGGLIN' ..
HELP! ≡KAFF≡ ... I CAN'T SWIM!
... HHH... UHH...
UHH... S'OKAY... I GOT YOU...

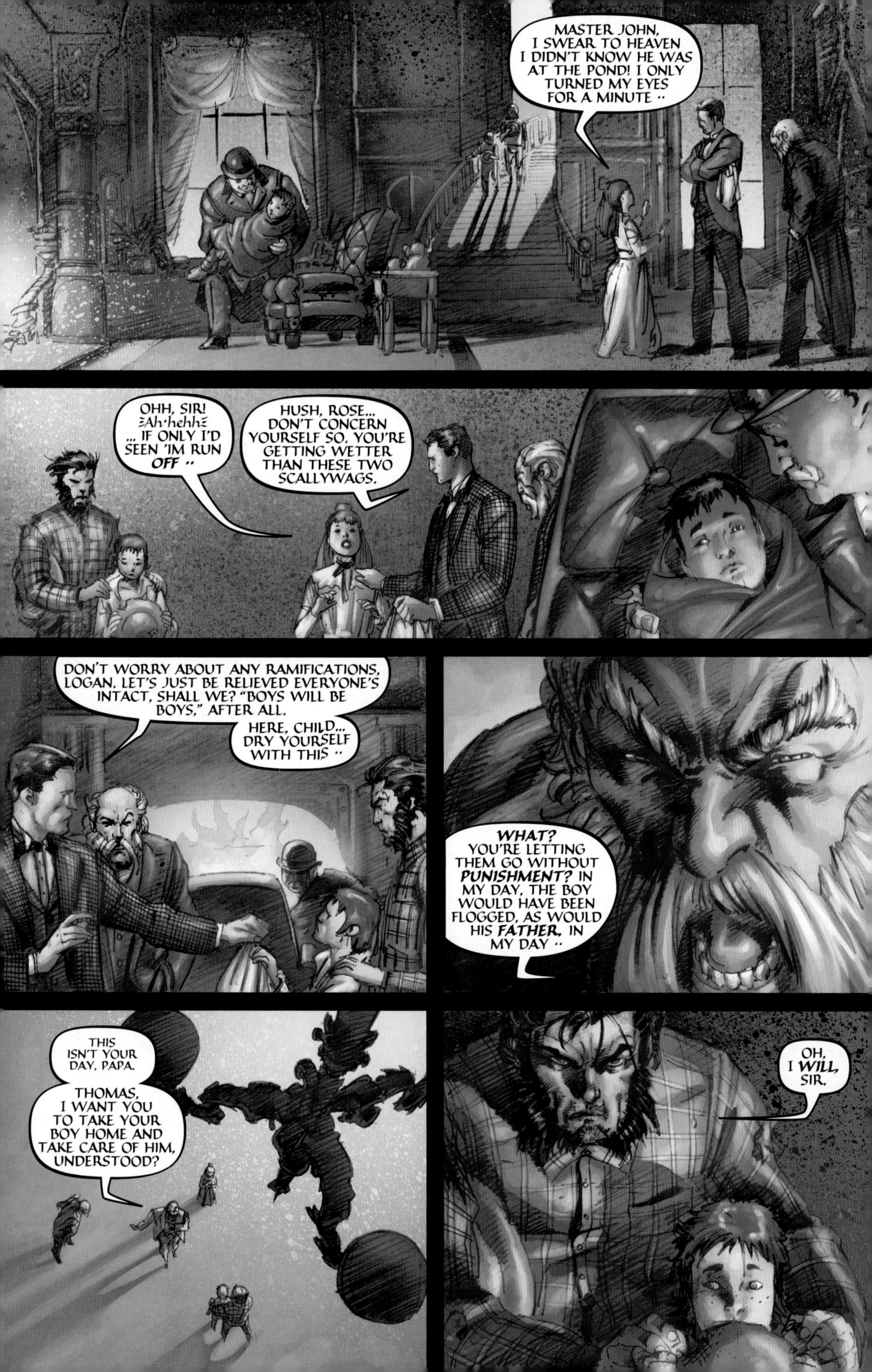
MASTER JOHN, I SWEAR TO HEAVEN I DIDN'T KNOW HE WAS AT THE POND! I ONLY TURNED MY EYES FOR A MINUTE ..
OHH, SIR! Ah-hehh ... IF ONLY I'D SEEN 'IM RUN OFF ..
HUSH, ROSE... DON'T CONCERN YOURSELF SO. YOU'RE GETTING WETTER THAN THESE TWO SCALLYWAGS.
DON'T WORRY ABOUT ANY RAMIFICATIONS, LOGAN. LET'S JUST BE RELIEVED EVERYONE'S INTACT, SHALL WE? "BOYS WILL BE BOYS," AFTER ALL.
HERE, CHILD... DRY YOURSELF WITH THIS ..
WHAT? YOU'RE LETTING THEM GO WITHOUT PUNISHMENT? IN MY DAY, THE BOY WOULD HAVE BEEN FLOGGED, AS WOULD HIS FATHER, IN MY DAY ..
THIS ISN'T YOUR DAY, PAPA.
THOMAS, I WANT YOU TO TAKE YOUR BOY HOME AND TAKE CARE OF HIM, UNDERSTOOD?
OH, I WILL, SIR.

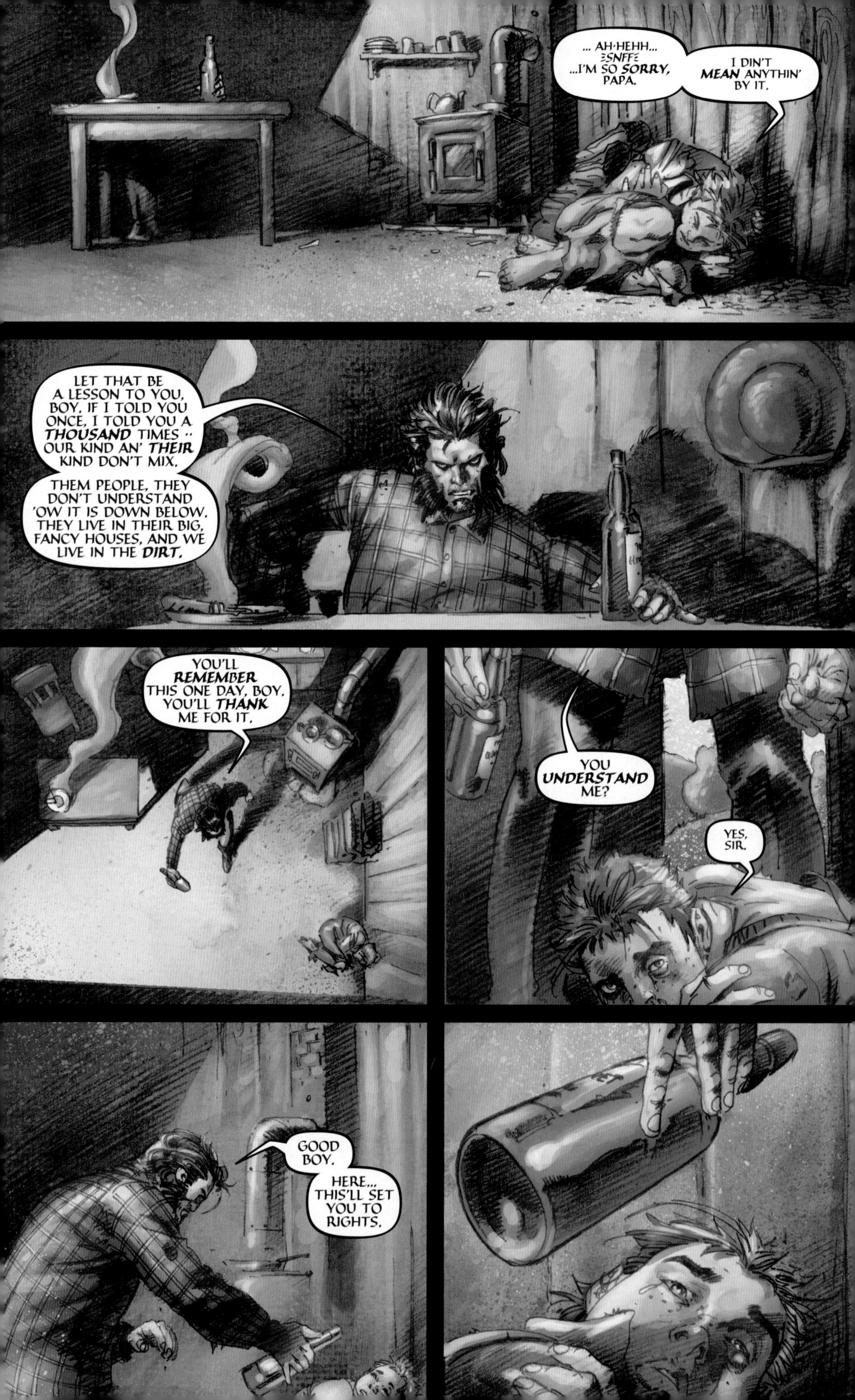
... AH-HEHH... SNFF ...I'M SO SORRY, PAPA.
I DIN'T MEAN ANYTHIN' BY IT.
LET THAT BE A LESSON TO YOU, BOY. IF I TOLD YOU ONCE, I TOLD YOU A THOUSAND TIMES -- OUR KIND AN' THEIR KIND DON'T MIX.
THEM PEOPLE, THEY DON'T UNDERSTAND 'OW IT IS DOWN BELOW. THEY LIVE IN THEIR BIG, FANCY HOUSES, AND WE LIVE IN THE DIRT.
YOU'LL REMEMBER THIS ONE DAY, BOY. YOU'LL THANK ME FOR IT.
YOU UNDERSTAND ME?
YES, SIR.
GOOD BOY.
HERE... THIS'LL SET YOU TO RIGHTS.

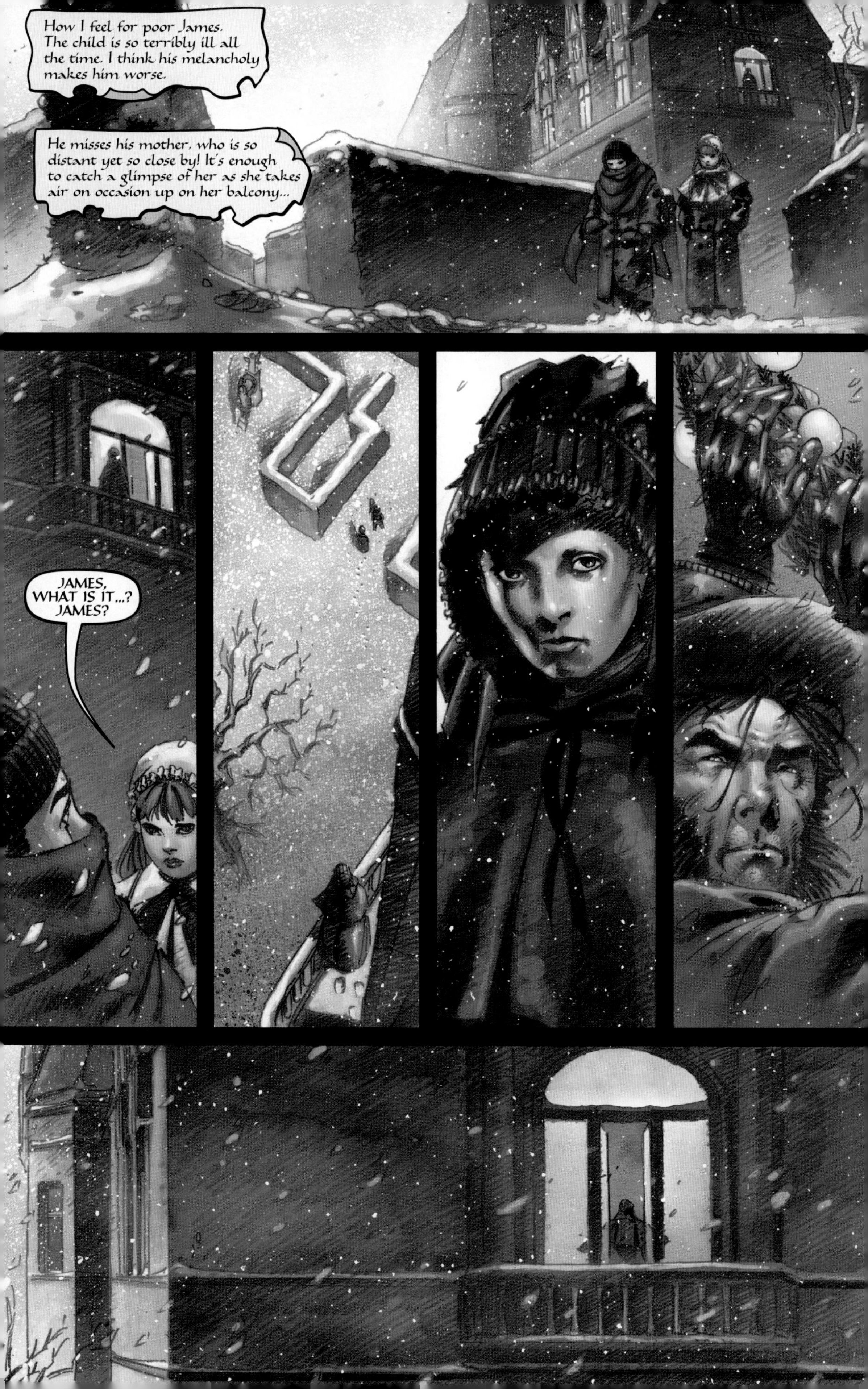
How I feel for poor James. The child is so terribly ill all the time. I think his melancholy makes him worse.
He misses his mother, who is so distant yet so close by! It's enough to catch a glimpse of her as she takes air on occasion up on her balcony...
JAMES, WHAT IS IT...? JAMES?

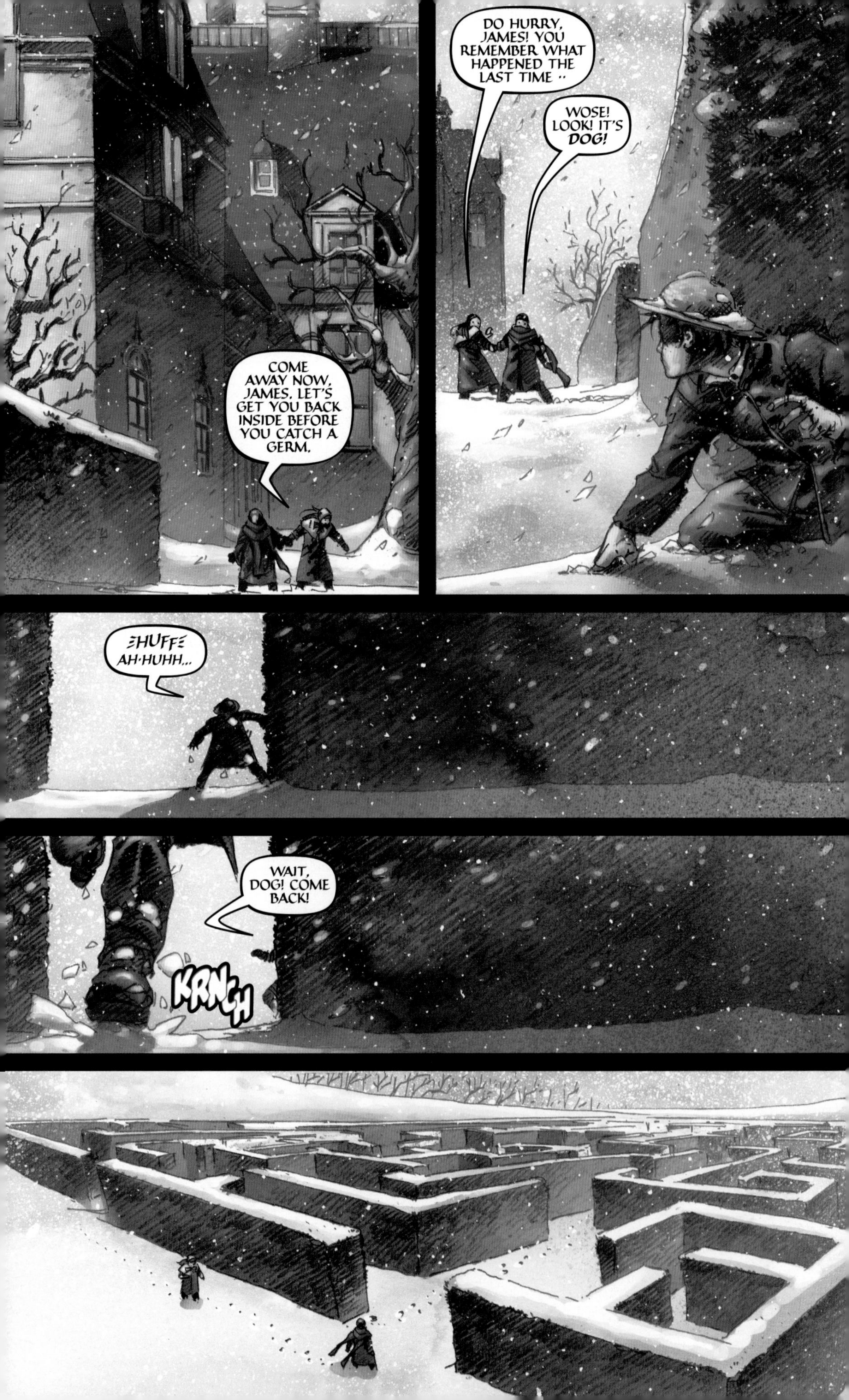
COME AWAY NOW, JAMES. LET'S GET YOU BACK INSIDE BEFORE YOU CATCH A GERM.
DO HURRY, JAMES! YOU REMEMBER WHAT HAPPENED THE LAST TIME ..
WOSE! LOOK! IT'S DOG!
HUFF AH-HUHH...
WAIT, DOG! COME BACK!
KRNCH

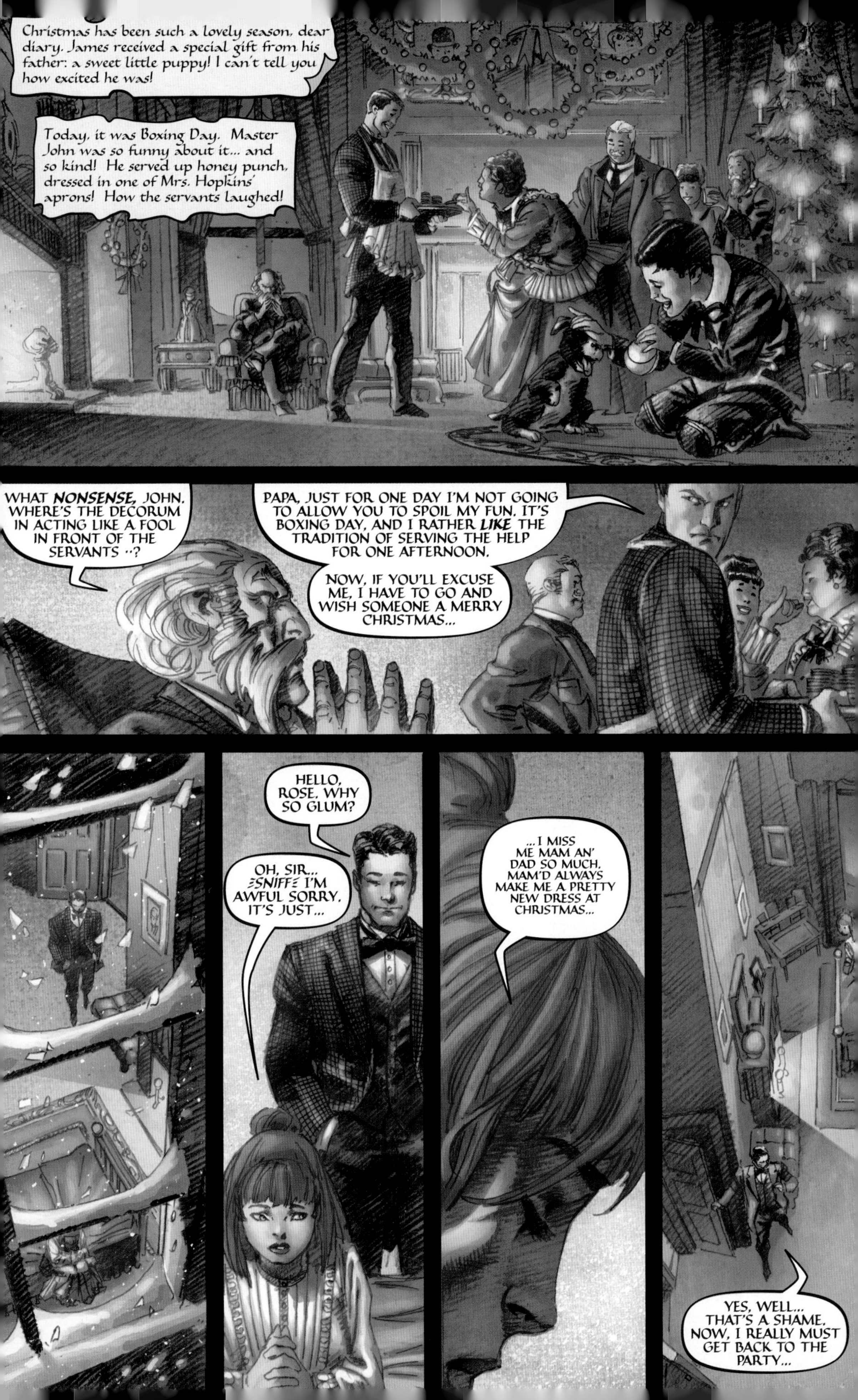
Christmas has been such a lovely season, dear diary. James received a special gift from his father: a sweet little puppy! I can't tell you how excited he was!
Today, it was Boxing Day. Master John was so funny about it... and so kind! He served up honey punch, dressed in one of Mrs. Hopkins' aprons! How the servants laughed!
WHAT NONSENSE, JOHN. WHERE'S THE DECORUM IN ACTING LIKE A FOOL IN FRONT OF THE SERVANTS ..?
PAPA, JUST FOR ONE DAY I'M NOT GOING TO ALLOW YOU TO SPOIL MY FUN. IT'S BOXING DAY, AND I RATHER LIKE THE TRADITION OF SERVING THE HELP FOR ONE AFTERNOON.
NOW, IF YOU'LL EXCUSE ME, I HAVE TO GO AND WISH SOMEONE A MERRY CHRISTMAS...
HELLO, ROSE. WHY SO GLUM?
OH, SIR... SNIFF I'M AWFUL SORRY, IT'S JUST...
...I MISS ME MAM AN' DAD SO MUCH. MAM'D ALWAYS MAKE ME A PRETTY NEW DRESS AT CHRISTMAS...
YES, WELL... THAT'S A SHAME. NOW, I REALLY MUST GET BACK TO THE PARTY...

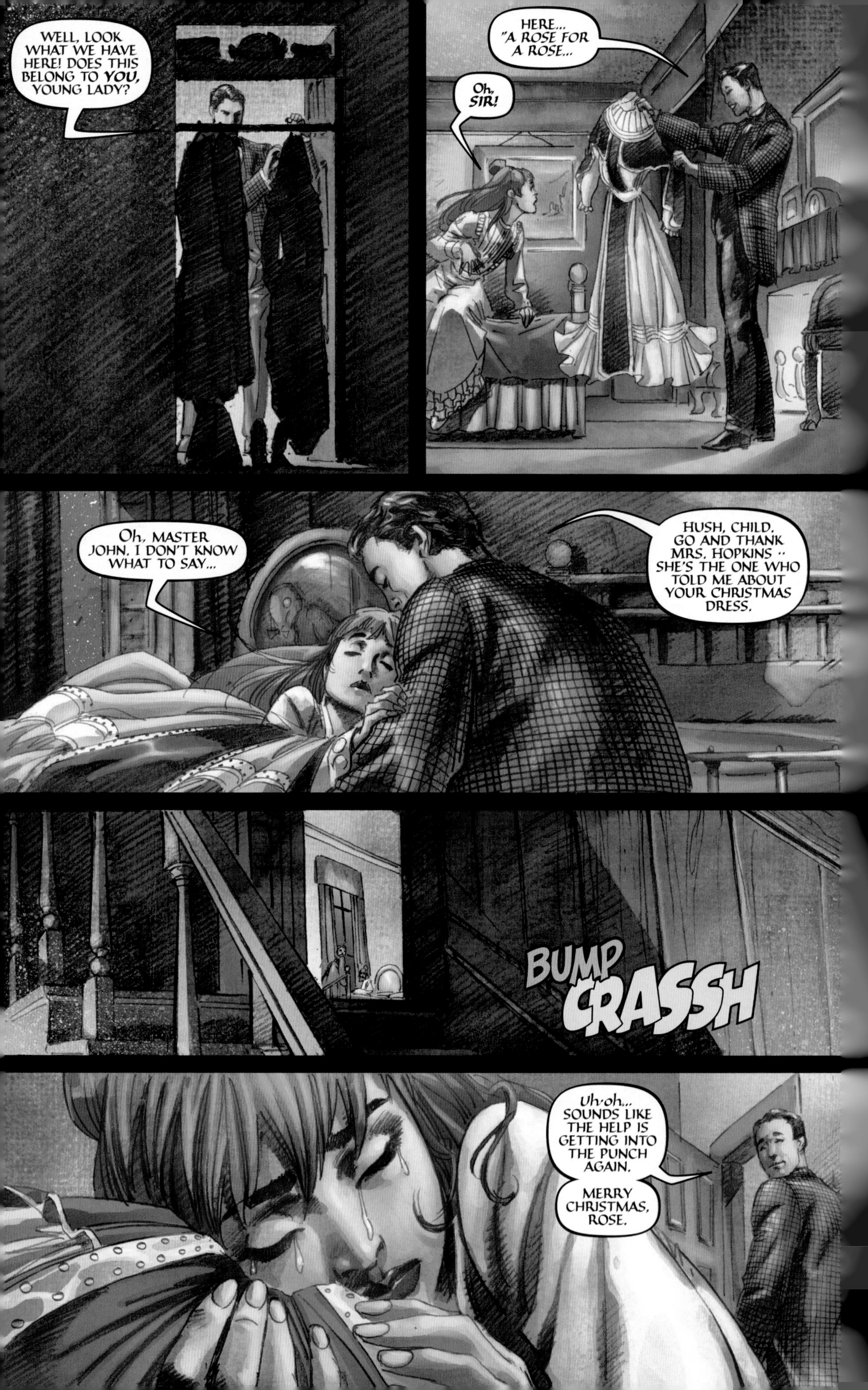
WELL, LOOK WHAT WE HAVE HERE! DOES THIS BELONG TO *YOU*, YOUNG LADY?
HERE... "A ROSE FOR A ROSE...
Oh, *SIR!*
Oh, MASTER JOHN, I DON'T KNOW WHAT TO SAY...
HUSH, CHILD, GO AND THANK MRS. HOPKINS -- SHE'S THE ONE WHO TOLD ME ABOUT YOUR CHRISTMAS DRESS.
BUMP
CRASSH
Uh-oh... SOUNDS LIKE THE HELP IS GETTING INTO THE PUNCH AGAIN.
MERRY CHRISTMAS, ROSE.

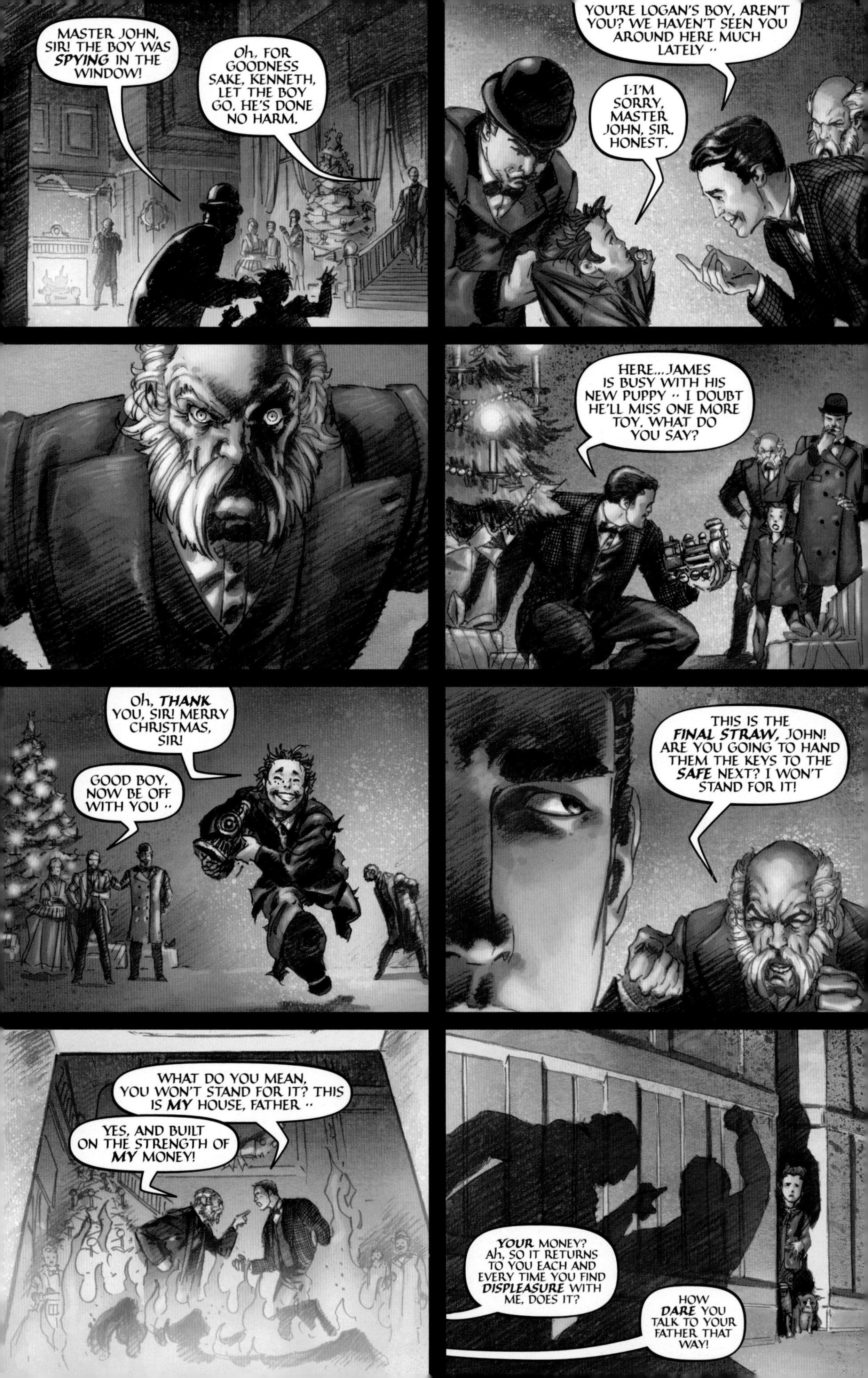
MASTER JOHN, SIR! THE BOY WAS SPYING IN THE WINDOW!
Oh, FOR GOODNESS SAKE, KENNETH, LET THE BOY GO. HE'S DONE NO HARM.
YOU'RE LOGAN'S BOY, AREN'T YOU? WE HAVEN'T SEEN YOU AROUND HERE MUCH LATELY ..
I-I'M SORRY, MASTER JOHN, SIR. HONEST.
HERE... JAMES IS BUSY WITH HIS NEW PUPPY .. I DOUBT HE'LL MISS ONE MORE TOY. WHAT DO YOU SAY?
Oh, THANK YOU, SIR! MERRY CHRISTMAS, SIR!
GOOD BOY. NOW BE OFF WITH YOU ..
THIS IS THE FINAL STRAW, JOHN! ARE YOU GOING TO HAND THEM THE KEYS TO THE SAFE NEXT? I WON'T STAND FOR IT!
WHAT DO YOU MEAN, YOU WON'T STAND FOR IT? THIS IS MY HOUSE, FATHER ..
YES, AND BUILT ON THE STRENGTH OF MY MONEY!
YOUR MONEY? Ah, SO IT RETURNS TO YOU EACH AND EVERY TIME YOU FIND DISPLEASURE WITH ME, DOES IT?
HOW DARE YOU TALK TO YOUR FATHER THAT WAY!

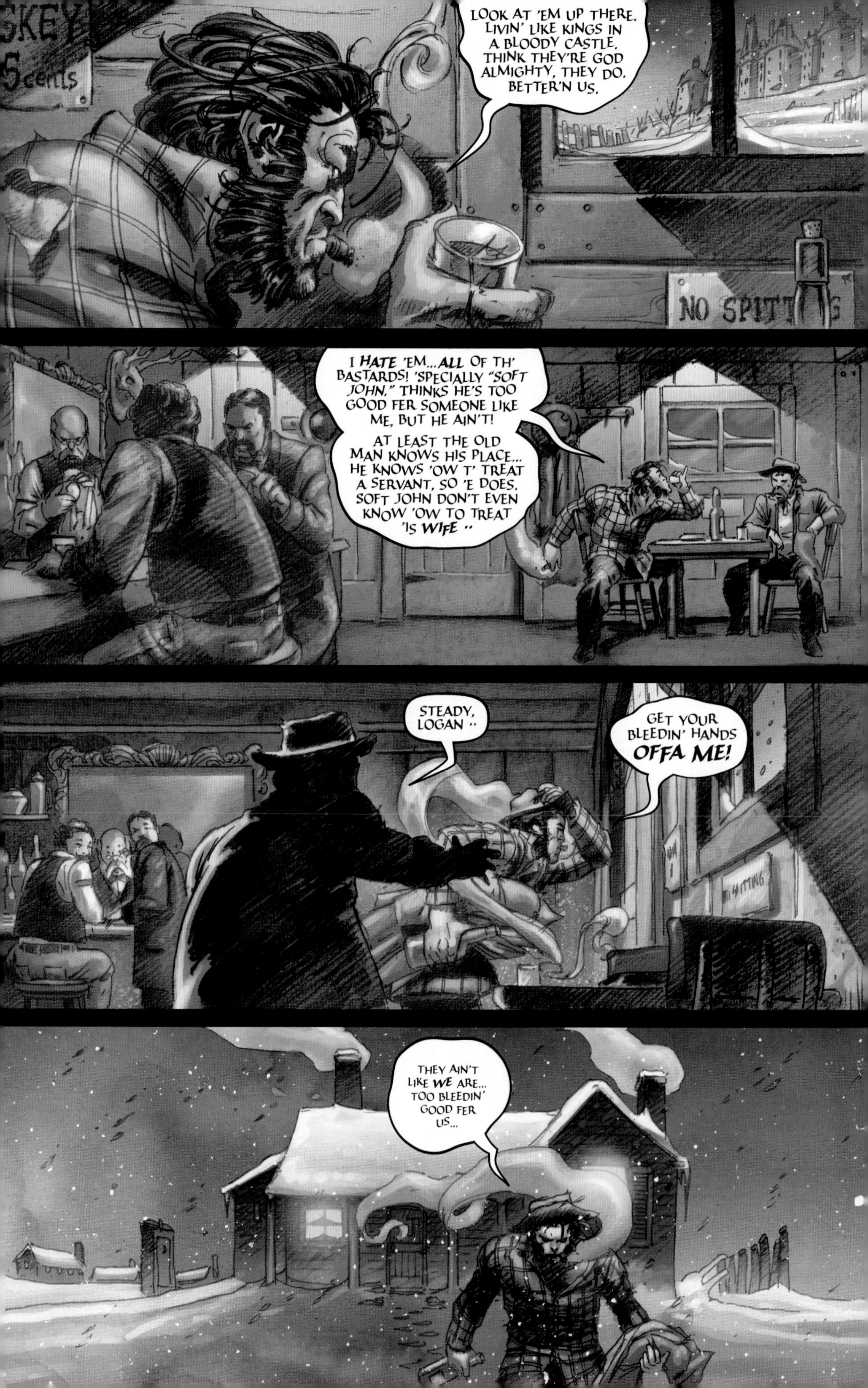
SKEY
5 cents
LOOK AT 'EM UP THERE, LIVIN' LIKE KINGS IN A BLOODY CASTLE, THINK THEY'RE GOD ALMIGHTY, THEY DO. BETTER'N US.
NO SPITT
I HATE 'EM... ALL OF TH' BASTARDS! 'SPECIALLY "SOFT JOHN," THINKS HE'S TOO GOOD FER SOMEONE LIKE ME, BUT HE AIN'T!
AT LEAST THE OLD MAN KNOWS HIS PLACE... HE KNOWS 'OW T' TREAT A SERVANT, SO 'E DOES. SOFT JOHN DON'T EVEN KNOW 'OW TO TREAT 'IS WIFE --
STEADY, LOGAN --
GET YOUR BLEEDIN' HANDS OFFA ME!
THEY AIN'T LIKE WE ARE... TOO BLEEDIN' GOOD FER US...

POPPA! *POPPA!* LOOK WHAT MASTER HOWLETT ··

·· *GAVE* ME.

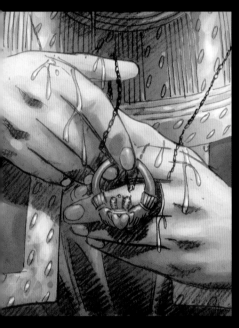

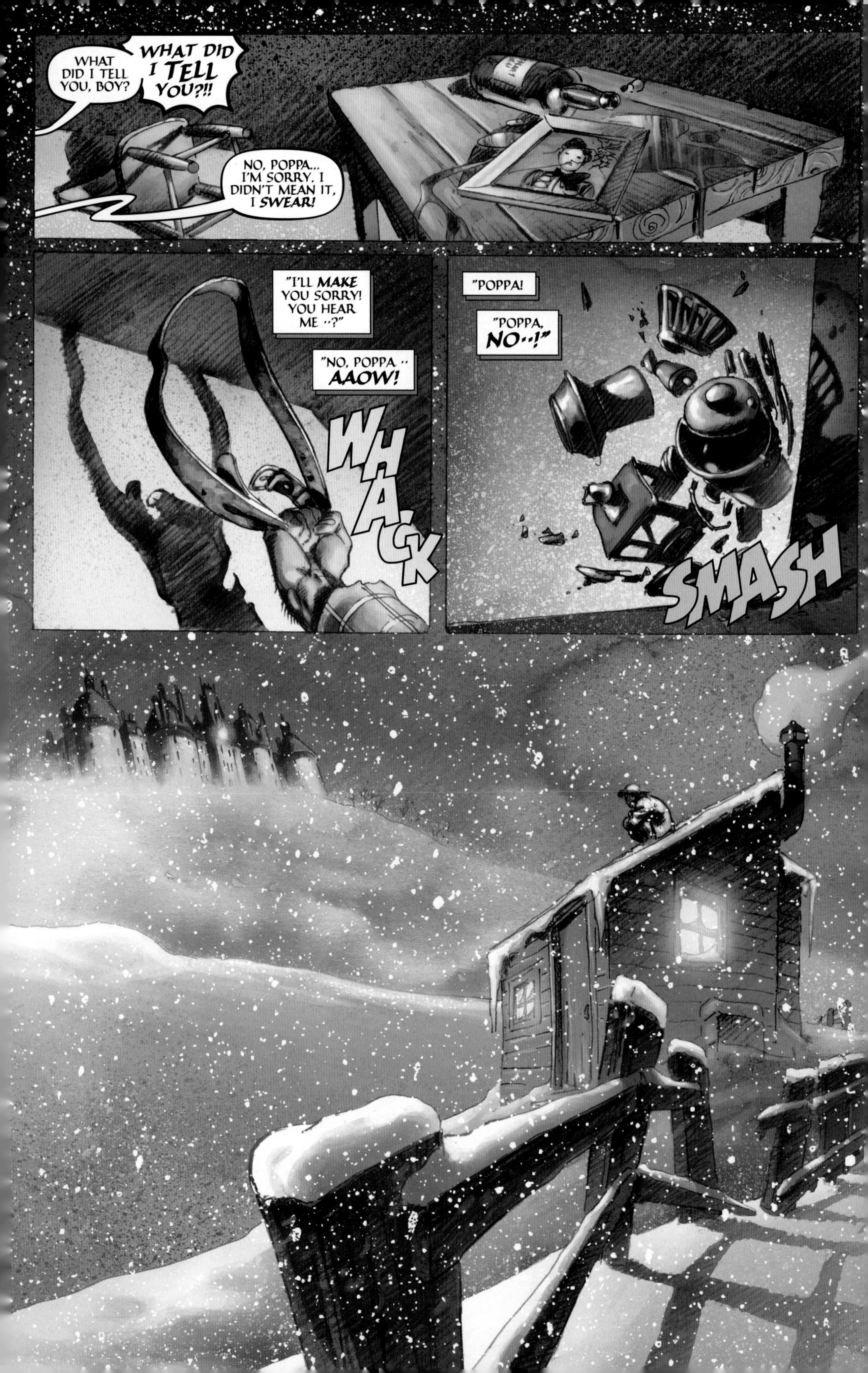
WHAT DID I TELL YOU, BOY?
WHAT DID I TELL YOU?!!
NO, POPPA... I'M SORRY, I DIDN'T MEAN IT, I SWEAR!
"I'LL MAKE YOU SORRY! YOU HEAR ME ..?"
"NO, POPPA .. AAOW!
WHACK
"POPPA!
"POPPA, NO..!"
SMASH

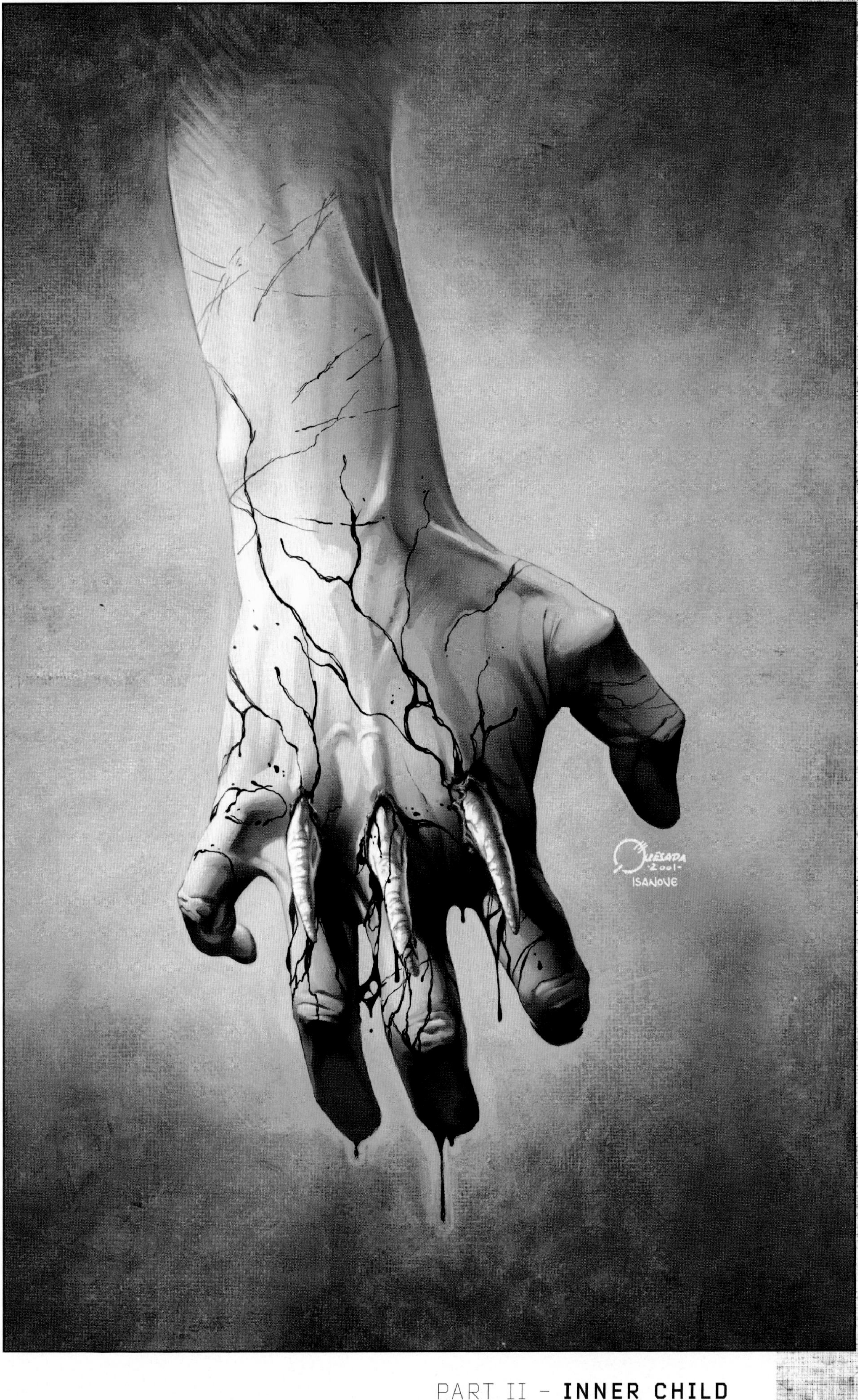
QUESADA
·2001·
ISANOVE

PART II – **INNER CHILD**

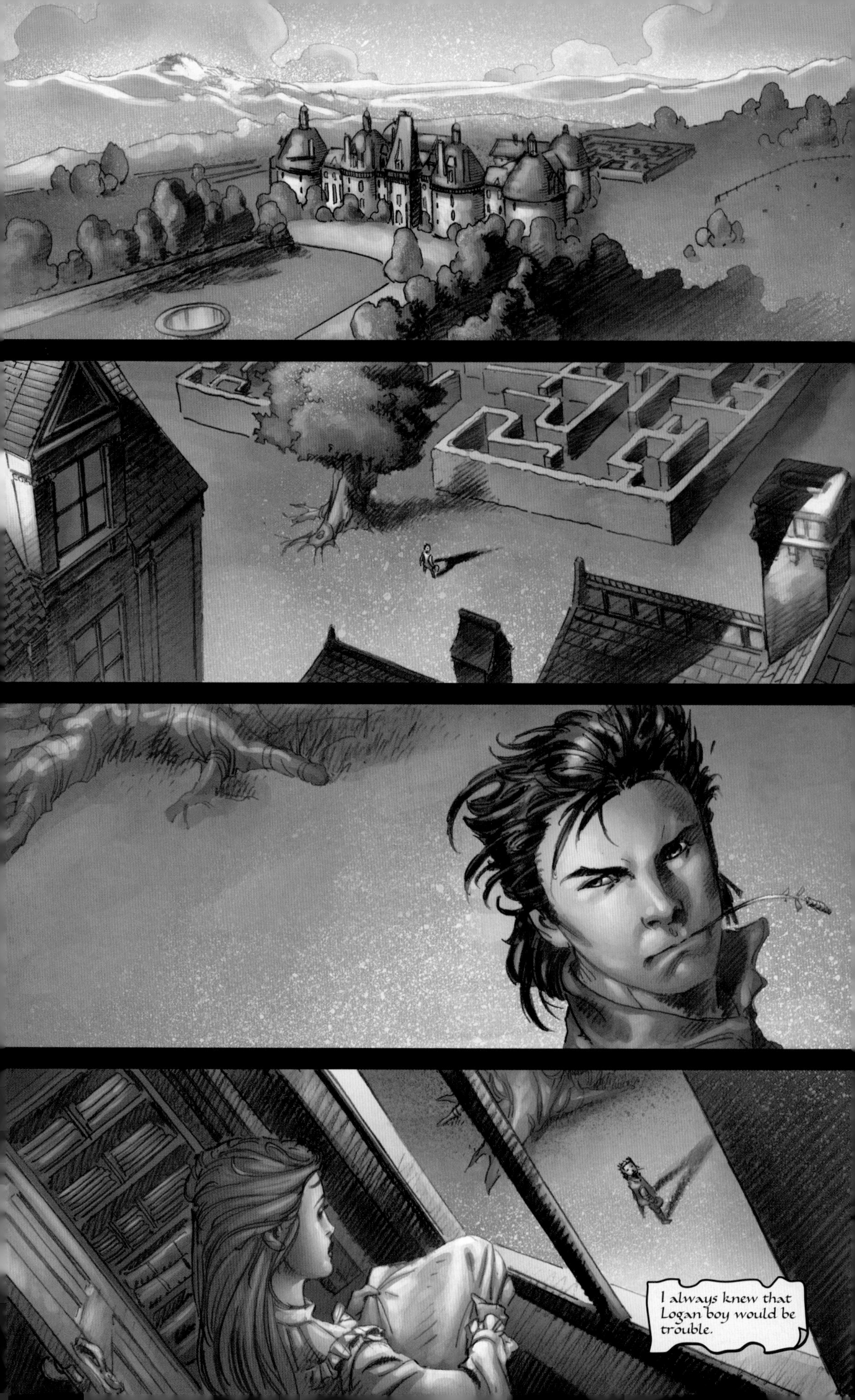
I always knew that Logan boy would be trouble.

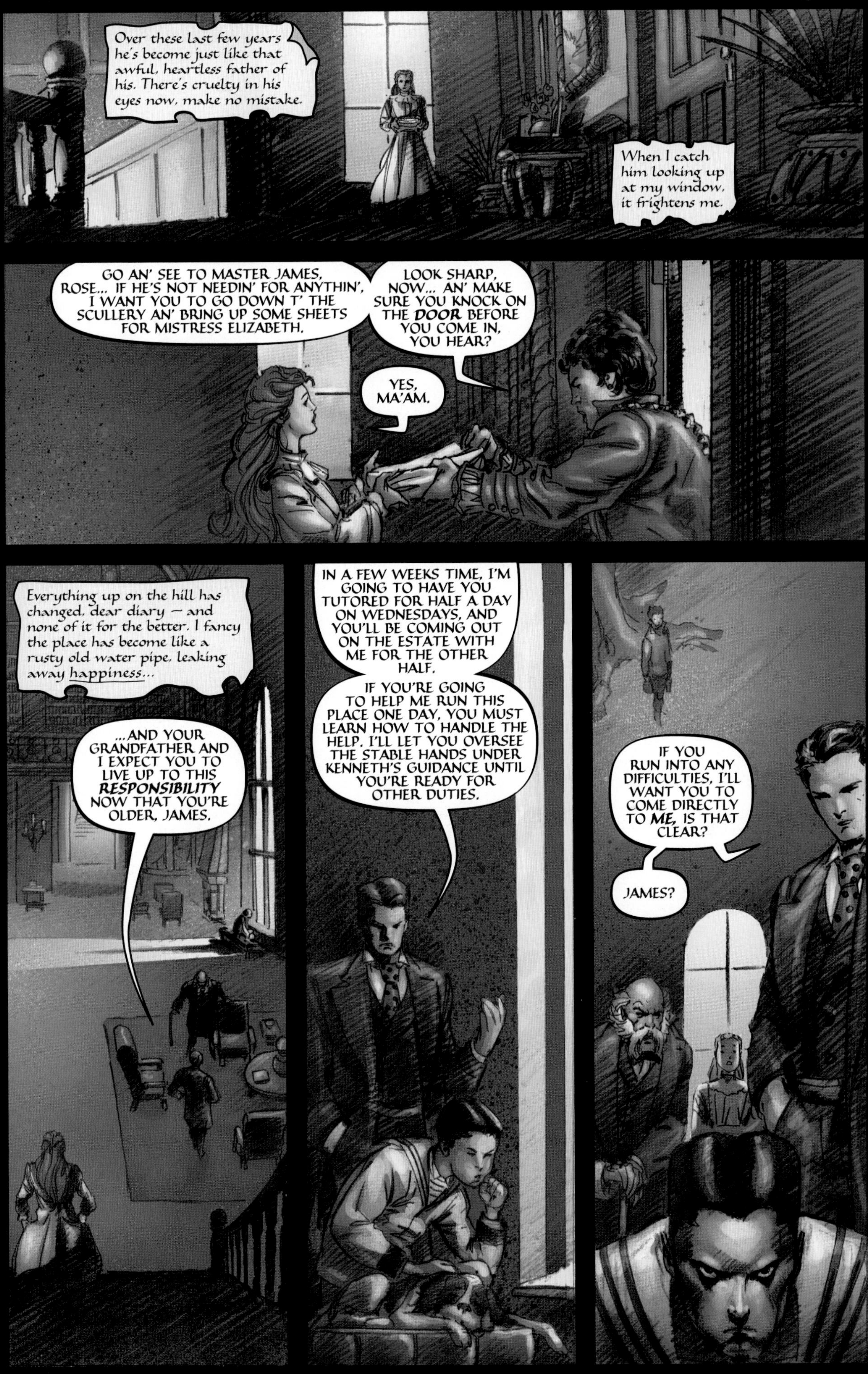
Over these last few years he's become just like that awful, heartless father of his. There's cruelty in his eyes now, make no mistake.
When I catch him looking up at my window, it frightens me.
GO AN' SEE TO MASTER JAMES, ROSE... IF HE'S NOT NEEDIN' FOR ANYTHIN', I WANT YOU TO GO DOWN T' THE SCULLERY AN' BRING UP SOME SHEETS FOR MISTRESS ELIZABETH.
LOOK SHARP, NOW... AN' MAKE SURE YOU KNOCK ON THE DOOR BEFORE YOU COME IN, YOU HEAR?
YES, MA'AM.
Everything up on the hill has changed, dear diary — and none of it for the better. I fancy the place has become like a rusty old water pipe, leaking away happiness...
...AND YOUR GRANDFATHER AND I EXPECT YOU TO LIVE UP TO THIS RESPONSIBILITY NOW THAT YOU'RE OLDER, JAMES.
IN A FEW WEEKS TIME, I'M GOING TO HAVE YOU TUTORED FOR HALF A DAY ON WEDNESDAYS, AND YOU'LL BE COMING OUT ON THE ESTATE WITH ME FOR THE OTHER HALF.
IF YOU'RE GOING TO HELP ME RUN THIS PLACE ONE DAY, YOU MUST LEARN HOW TO HANDLE THE HELP. I'LL LET YOU OVERSEE THE STABLE HANDS UNDER KENNETH'S GUIDANCE UNTIL YOU'RE READY FOR OTHER DUTIES.
IF YOU RUN INTO ANY DIFFICULTIES, I'LL WANT YOU TO COME DIRECTLY TO ME, IS THAT CLEAR?
JAMES?

JAMES, I'M *TALKING* TO YOU, BOY, HAVE YOU REGISTERED EVEN A *SINGLE* WORD I'VE SAID?

YES, PAPA.

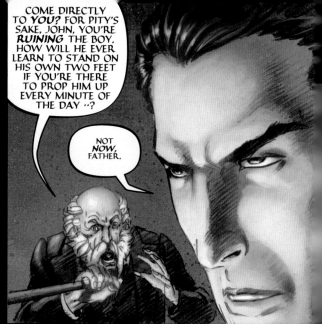

COME DIRECTLY TO *YOU?* FOR PITY'S SAKE, JOHN, YOU'RE *RUINING* THE BOY. HOW WILL HE EVER LEARN TO STAND ON HIS OWN TWO FEET IF YOU'RE THERE TO PROP HIM UP EVERY MINUTE OF THE DAY ··?

NOT *NOW*, FATHER.

DON'T *"NOT NOW"* ME, JOHN HOWLETT! YOU'RE TURNING HIM INTO A LESSER VERSION OF *YOURSELF!* MAYBE YOU'VE FORGOTTEN THAT YOU LOST YOUR *ELDER* CHILD, BUT *I* HAVEN'T, DO YOU REALLY WANT TO LOSE *ANOTHER* ONE?

≡AHEM≡

WHAT DO YOU *WANT*, GIRL? SPIT IT OUT!

IF IT PLEASE YOU, SIR... I WAS SENT DOWN TO ASK AFTER YOUNG MASTER JAMES.

JAMES WILL BE FINE WHERE HE IS FOR THE MOMENT, ROSE. YOU MAY GO ABOUT YOUR DUTIES, THANK YOU.

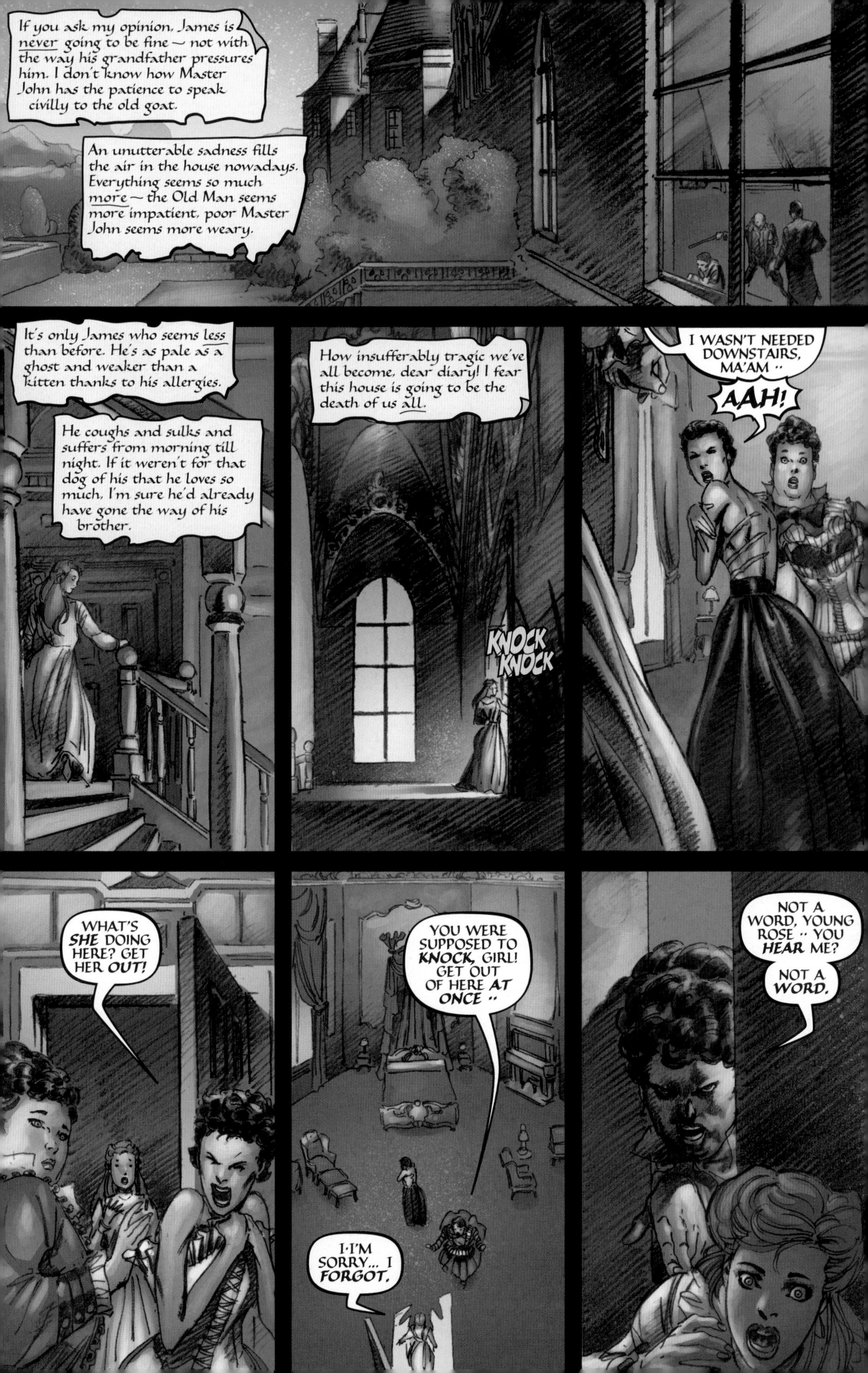
If you ask my opinion, James is never going to be fine — not with the way his grandfather pressures him. I don't know how Master John has the patience to speak civilly to the old goat.
An unutterable sadness fills the air in the house nowadays. Everything seems so much more — the Old Man seems more impatient, poor Master John seems more weary.
It's only James who seems less than before. He's as pale as a ghost and weaker than a kitten thanks to his allergies.
He coughs and sulks and suffers from morning till night. If it weren't for that dog of his that he loves so much, I'm sure he'd already have gone the way of his brother.
How insufferably tragic we've all become, dear diary! I fear this house is going to be the death of us all.
KNOCK KNOCK
I WASN'T NEEDED DOWNSTAIRS, MA'AM ..
AAH!
WHAT'S SHE DOING HERE? GET HER OUT!
YOU WERE SUPPOSED TO KNOCK, GIRL! GET OUT OF HERE AT ONCE ..
I-I'M SORRY... I FORGOT.
NOT A WORD, YOUNG ROSE .. YOU HEAR ME?
NOT A WORD.

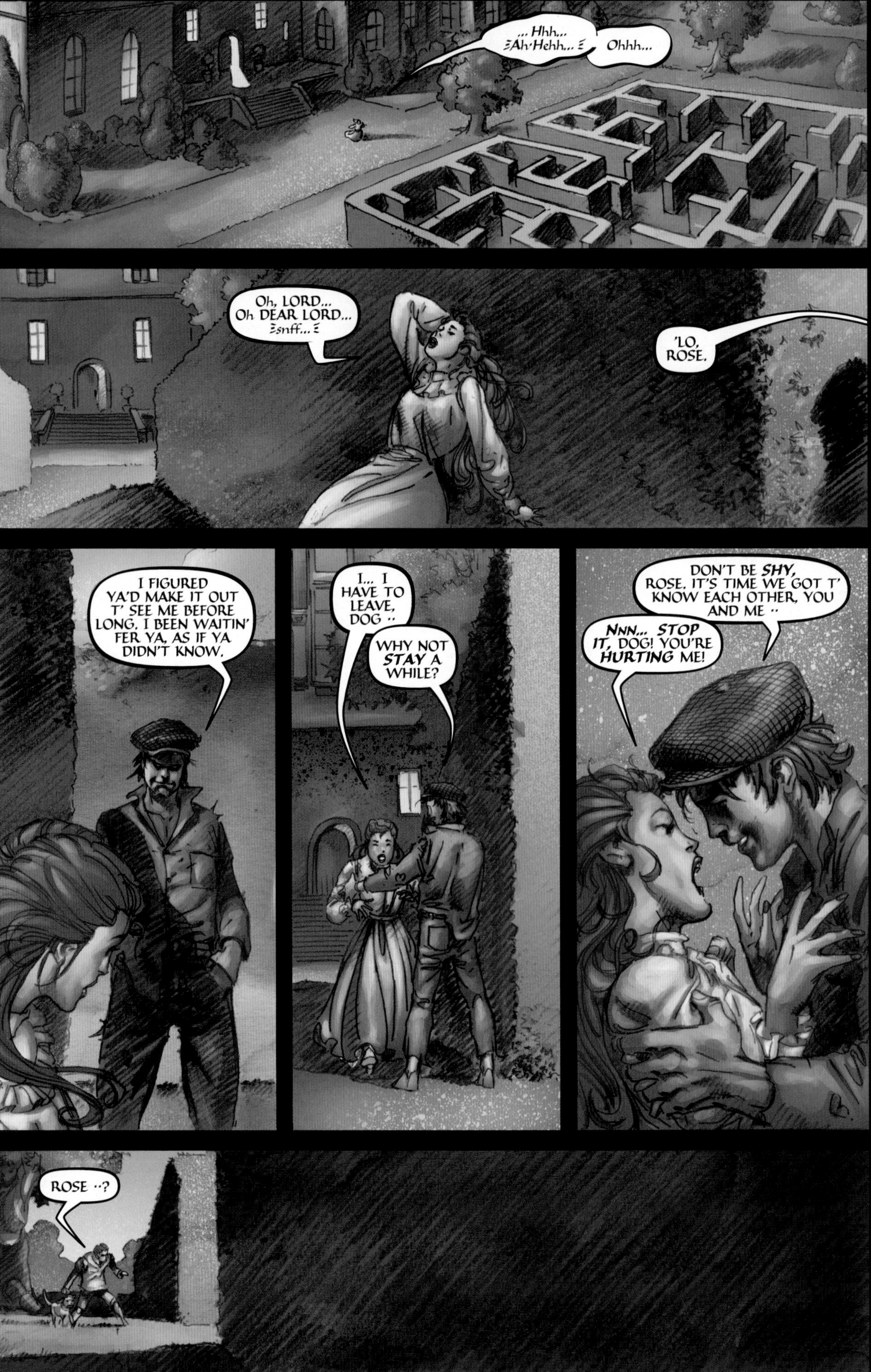

... Hhh... ≷Ah-Hehh...≷ Ohhh...
Oh, LORD... Oh DEAR LORD... ≷snff...≷
'LO, ROSE.
I FIGURED YA'D MAKE IT OUT T' SEE ME BEFORE LONG. I BEEN WAITIN' FER YA, AS IF YA DIDN'T KNOW.
I... I HAVE TO LEAVE, DOG ..
WHY NOT STAY A WHILE?
DON'T BE SHY, ROSE. IT'S TIME WE GOT T' KNOW EACH OTHER, YOU AND ME ..
Nnn... STOP IT, DOG! YOU'RE HURTING ME!
ROSE ..?

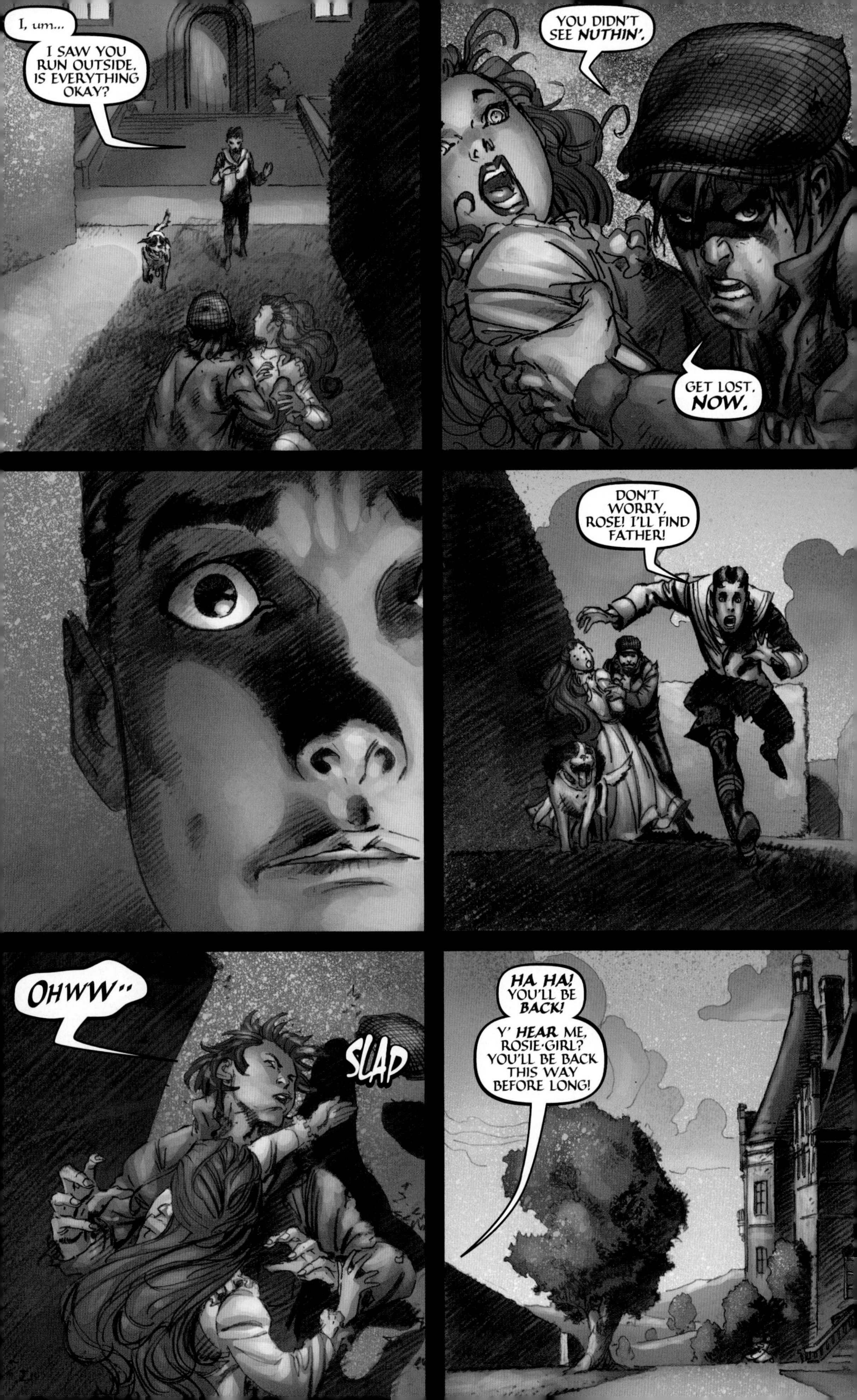
I, um...
I SAW YOU RUN OUTSIDE. IS EVERYTHING OKAY?
YOU DIDN'T SEE NUTHIN'.
GET LOST. NOW.
DON'T WORRY, ROSE! I'LL FIND FATHER!
OHWW..
SLAP
HA HA! YOU'LL BE BACK!
Y' HEAR ME, ROSIE-GIRL? YOU'LL BE BACK THIS WAY BEFORE LONG!

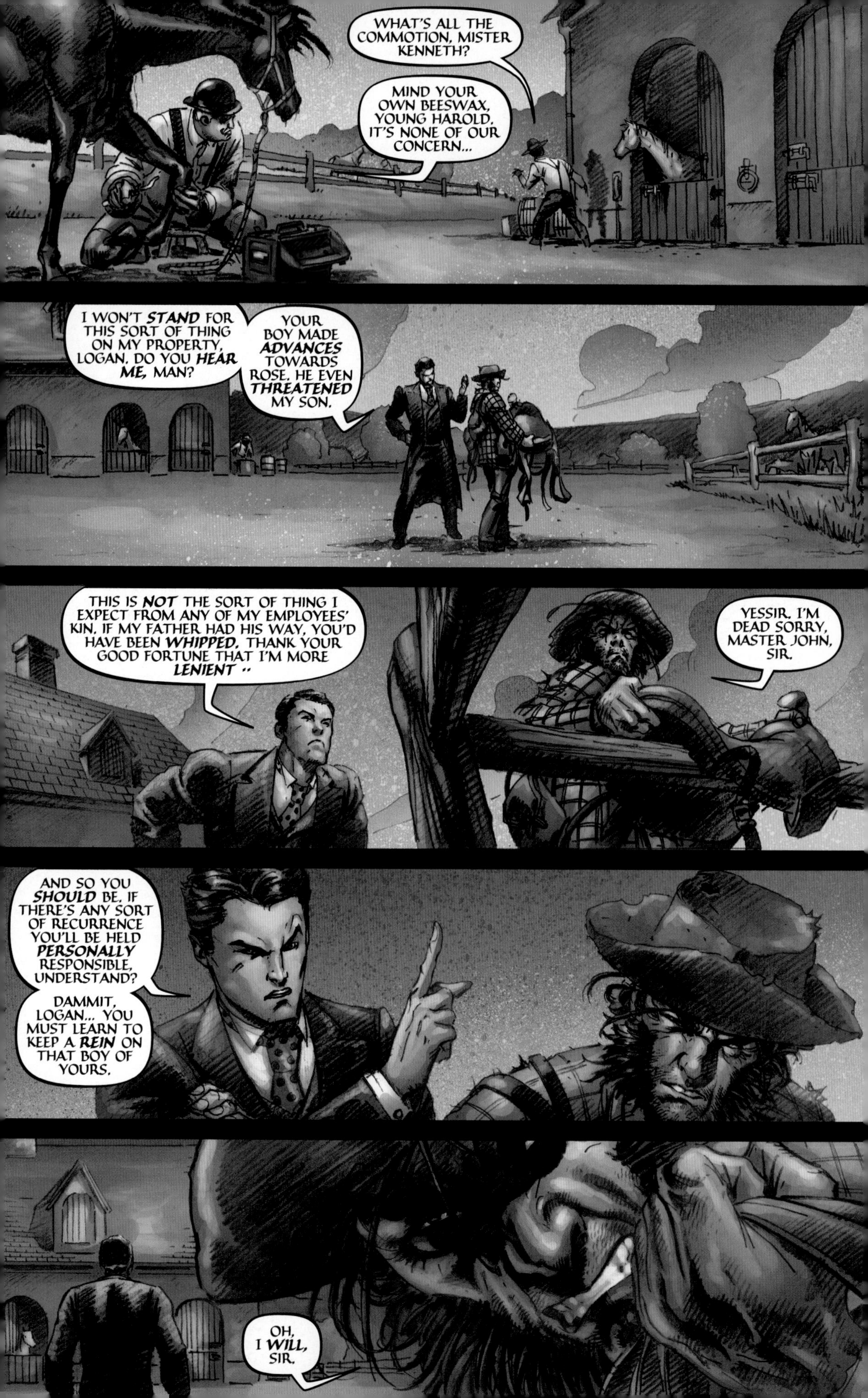
WHAT'S ALL THE COMMOTION, MISTER KENNETH?
MIND YOUR OWN BEESWAX, YOUNG HAROLD, IT'S NONE OF OUR CONCERN...
I WON'T STAND FOR THIS SORT OF THING ON MY PROPERTY, LOGAN, DO YOU HEAR ME, MAN?
YOUR BOY MADE ADVANCES TOWARDS ROSE. HE EVEN THREATENED MY SON.
THIS IS NOT THE SORT OF THING I EXPECT FROM ANY OF MY EMPLOYEES' KIN. IF MY FATHER HAD HIS WAY, YOU'D HAVE BEEN WHIPPED. THANK YOUR GOOD FORTUNE THAT I'M MORE LENIENT --
YESSIR, I'M DEAD SORRY, MASTER JOHN, SIR.
AND SO YOU SHOULD BE. IF THERE'S ANY SORT OF RECURRENCE YOU'LL BE HELD PERSONALLY RESPONSIBLE, UNDERSTAND?
DAMMIT, LOGAN... YOU MUST LEARN TO KEEP A REIN ON THAT BOY OF YOURS.
OH, I WILL, SIR.

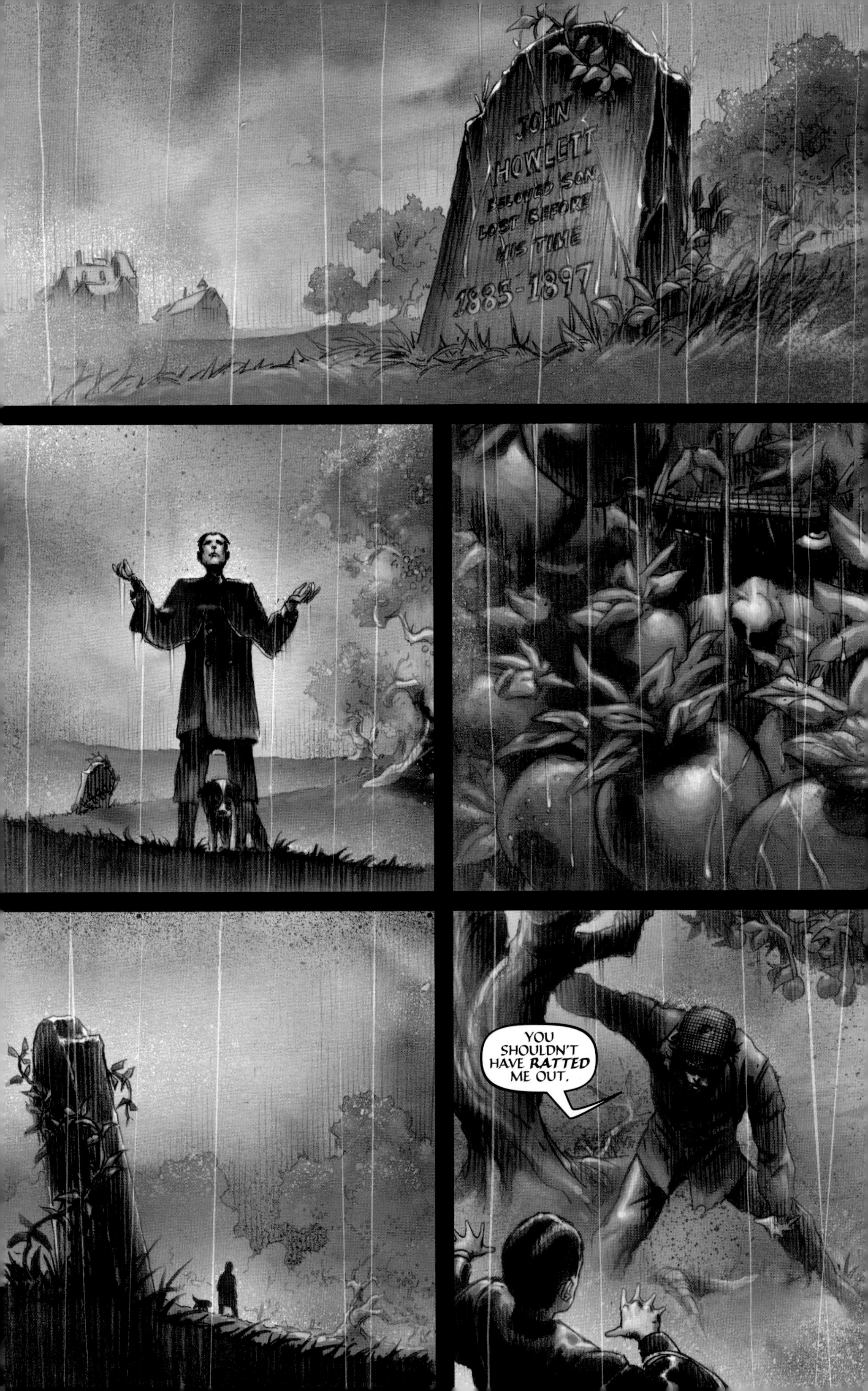
JOHN
HOWLETT
BELOVED SON
LOST BEFORE
HIS TIME
1885-1897
YOU SHOULDN'T HAVE RATTED ME OUT.

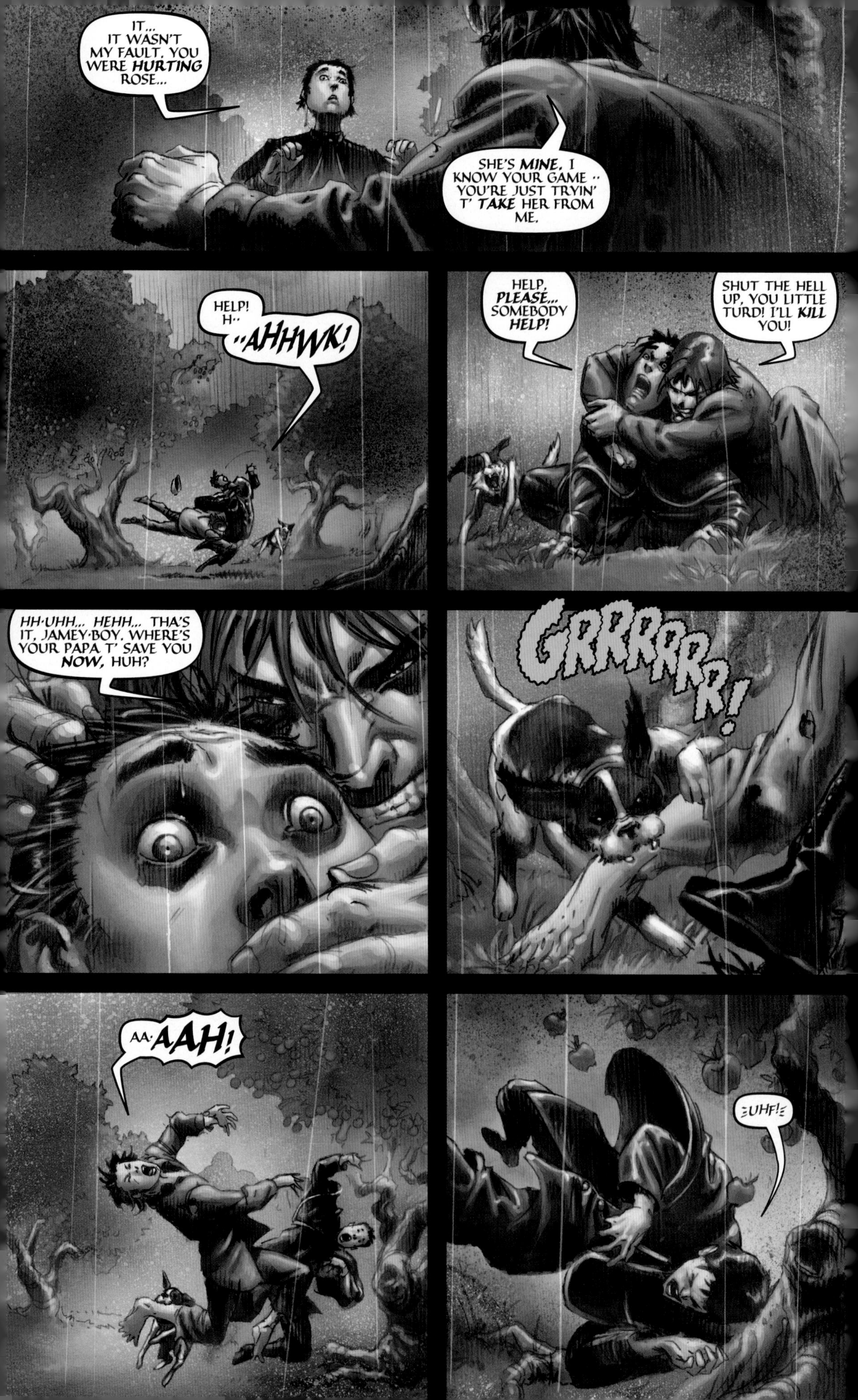
IT... IT WASN'T MY FAULT. YOU WERE HURTING ROSE...
SHE'S MINE. I KNOW YOUR GAME -- YOU'RE JUST TRYIN' T' TAKE HER FROM ME.
HELP! H-- --AHHWK!
HELP, PLEASE... SOMEBODY HELP!
SHUT THE HELL UP, YOU LITTLE TURD! I'LL KILL YOU!
HH-UHH... HEHH... THA'S IT, JAMEY-BOY. WHERE'S YOUR PAPA T' SAVE YOU NOW, HUH?
GRRRRRR!
AA-AAH!
UHF!

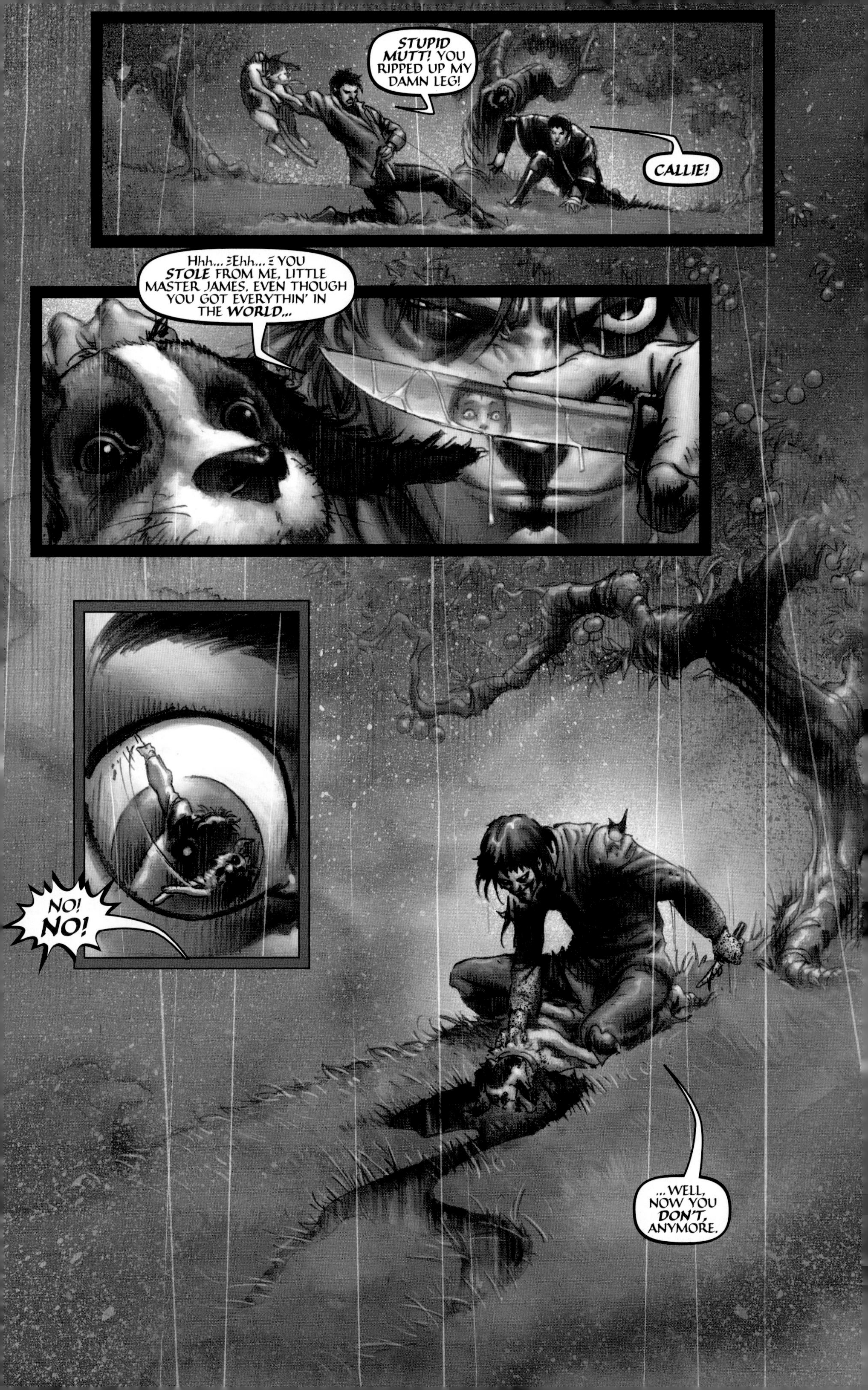
STUPID MUTT! YOU RIPPED UP MY DAMN LEG!
CALLIE!
Hhh... Ehh... YOU STOLE FROM ME, LITTLE MASTER JAMES, EVEN THOUGH YOU GOT EVERYTHIN' IN THE WORLD...
NO! NO!
...WELL, NOW YOU DON'T, ANYMORE.

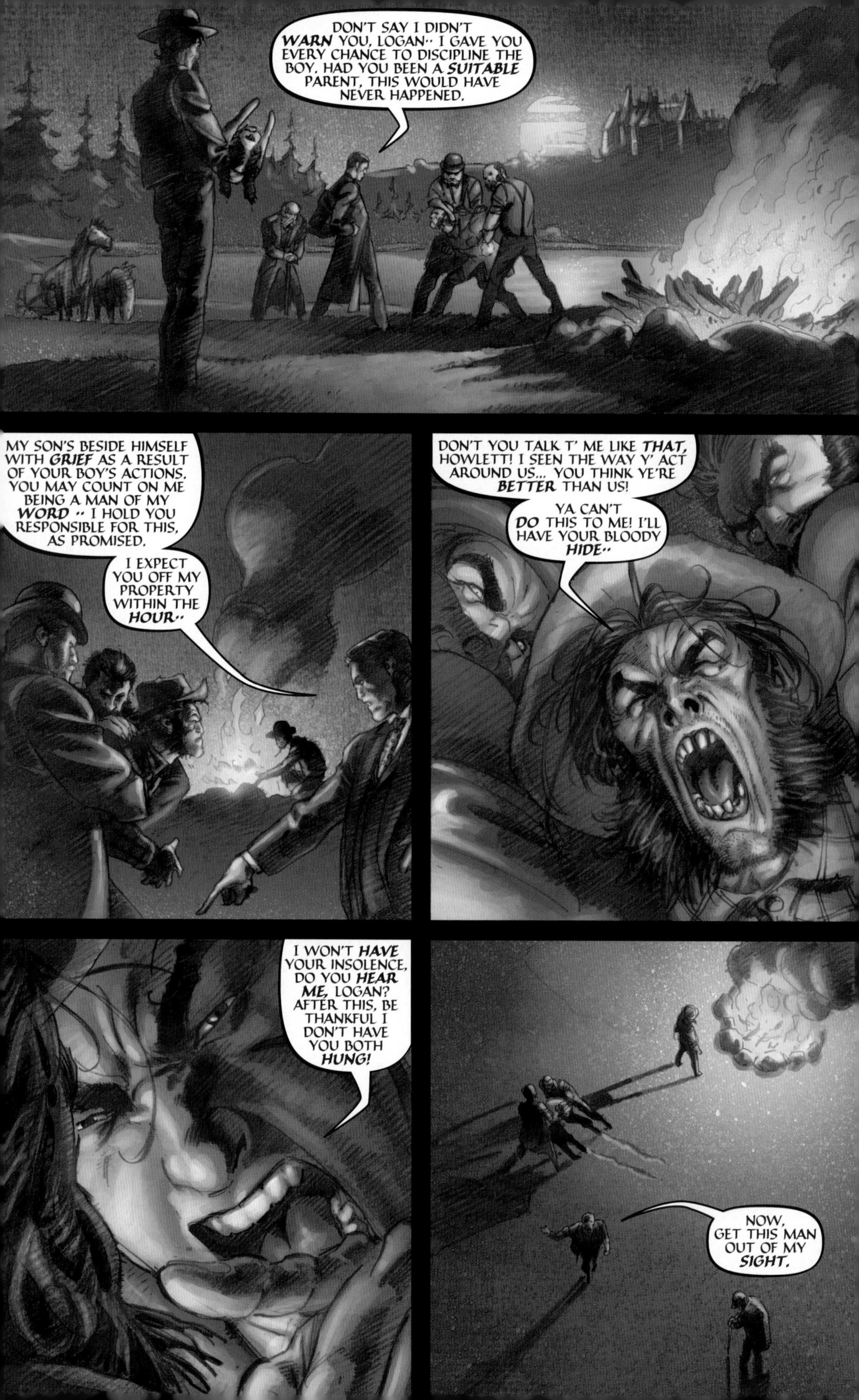
DON'T SAY I DIDN'T WARN YOU, LOGAN·· I GAVE YOU EVERY CHANCE TO DISCIPLINE THE BOY. HAD YOU BEEN A SUITABLE PARENT, THIS WOULD HAVE NEVER HAPPENED.
MY SON'S BESIDE HIMSELF WITH GRIEF AS A RESULT OF YOUR BOY'S ACTIONS. YOU MAY COUNT ON ME BEING A MAN OF MY WORD ·· I HOLD YOU RESPONSIBLE FOR THIS, AS PROMISED.
I EXPECT YOU OFF MY PROPERTY WITHIN THE HOUR··
DON'T YOU TALK T' ME LIKE THAT, HOWLETT! I SEEN THE WAY Y' ACT AROUND US... YOU THINK YE'RE BETTER THAN US!
YA CAN'T DO THIS TO ME! I'LL HAVE YOUR BLOODY HIDE··
I WON'T HAVE YOUR INSOLENCE, DO YOU HEAR ME, LOGAN? AFTER THIS, BE THANKFUL I DON'T HAVE YOU BOTH HUNG!
NOW, GET THIS MAN OUT OF MY SIGHT.

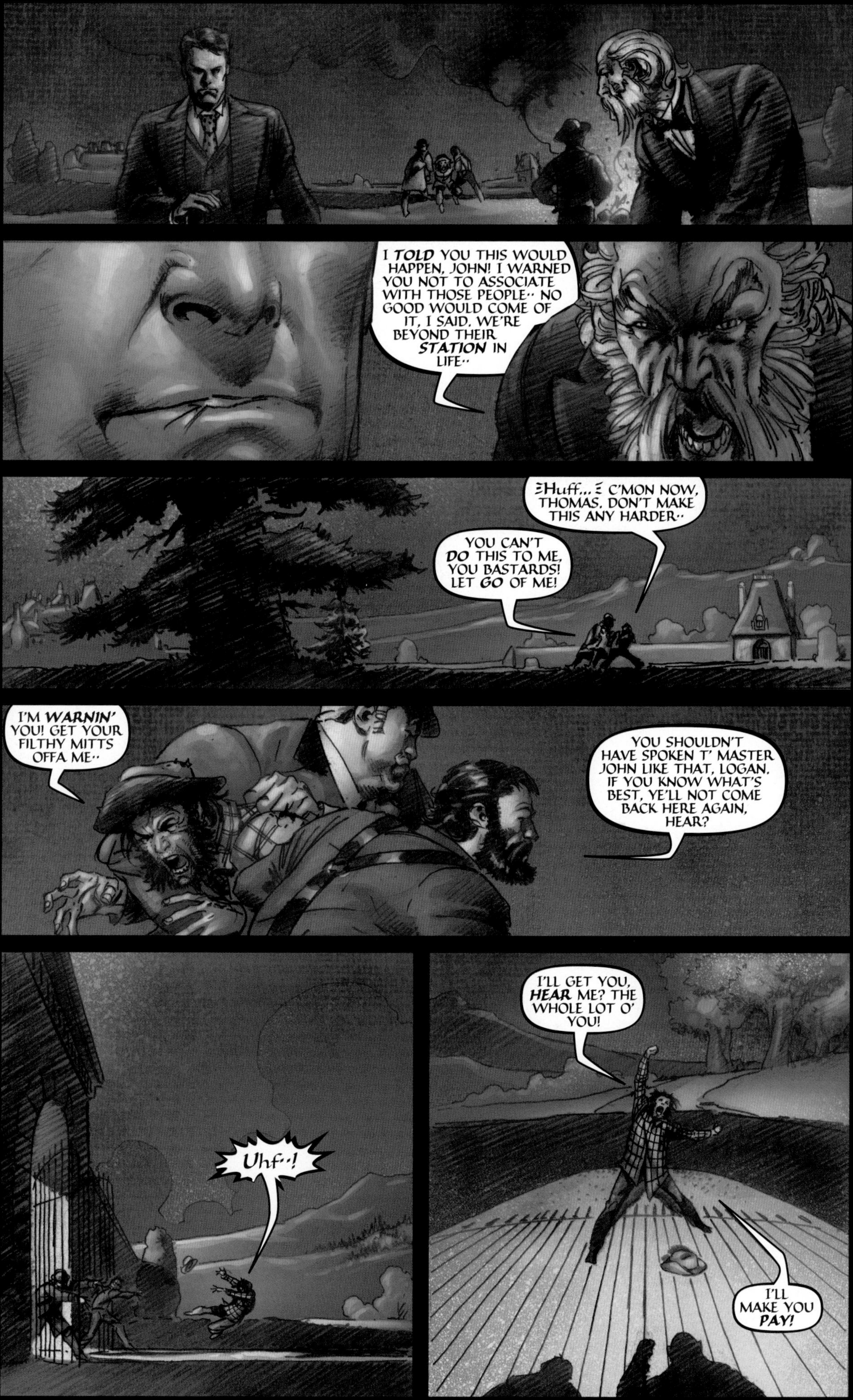
I TOLD YOU THIS WOULD HAPPEN, JOHN! I WARNED YOU NOT TO ASSOCIATE WITH THOSE PEOPLE·· NO GOOD WOULD COME OF IT, I SAID. WE'RE BEYOND THEIR STATION IN LIFE··
Huff... C'MON NOW, THOMAS. DON'T MAKE THIS ANY HARDER··
YOU CAN'T DO THIS TO ME, YOU BASTARDS! LET GO OF ME!
I'M WARNIN' YOU! GET YOUR FILTHY MITTS OFFA ME··
YOU SHOULDN'T HAVE SPOKEN T' MASTER JOHN LIKE THAT, LOGAN. IF YOU KNOW WHAT'S BEST, YE'LL NOT COME BACK HERE AGAIN, HEAR?
Uhf··!
I'LL GET YOU, HEAR ME? THE WHOLE LOT O' YOU!
I'LL MAKE YOU PAY!

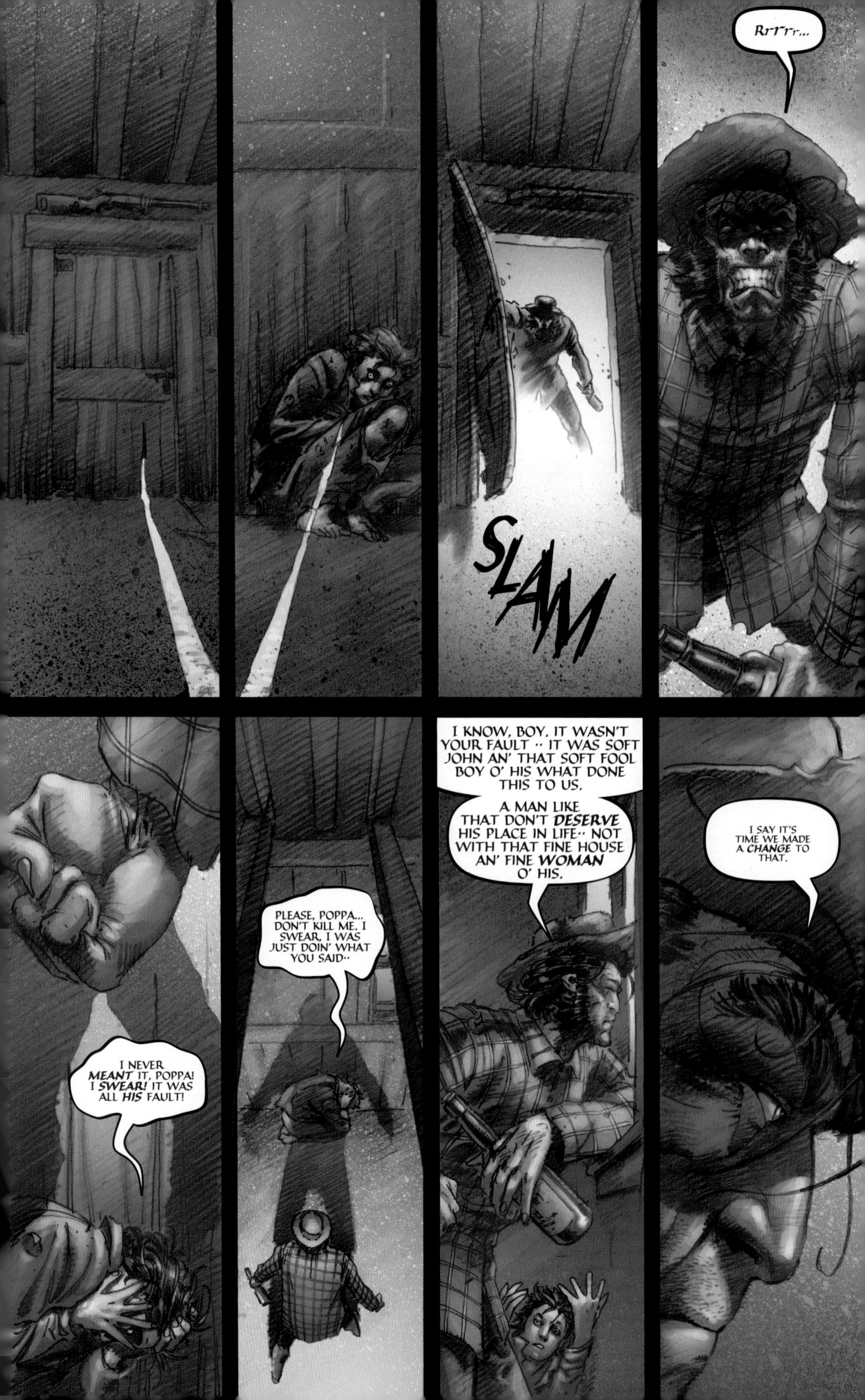
Rrrrr...
SLAM
I NEVER MEANT IT, POPPA! I SWEAR! IT WAS ALL HIS FAULT!
PLEASE, POPPA... DON'T KILL ME. I SWEAR, I WAS JUST DOIN' WHAT YOU SAID..
I KNOW, BOY. IT WASN'T YOUR FAULT .. IT WAS SOFT JOHN AN' THAT SOFT FOOL BOY O' HIS WHAT DONE THIS TO US.
A MAN LIKE THAT DON'T DESERVE HIS PLACE IN LIFE.. NOT WITH THAT FINE HOUSE AN' FINE WOMAN O' HIS.
I SAY IT'S TIME WE MADE A CHANGE TO THAT.

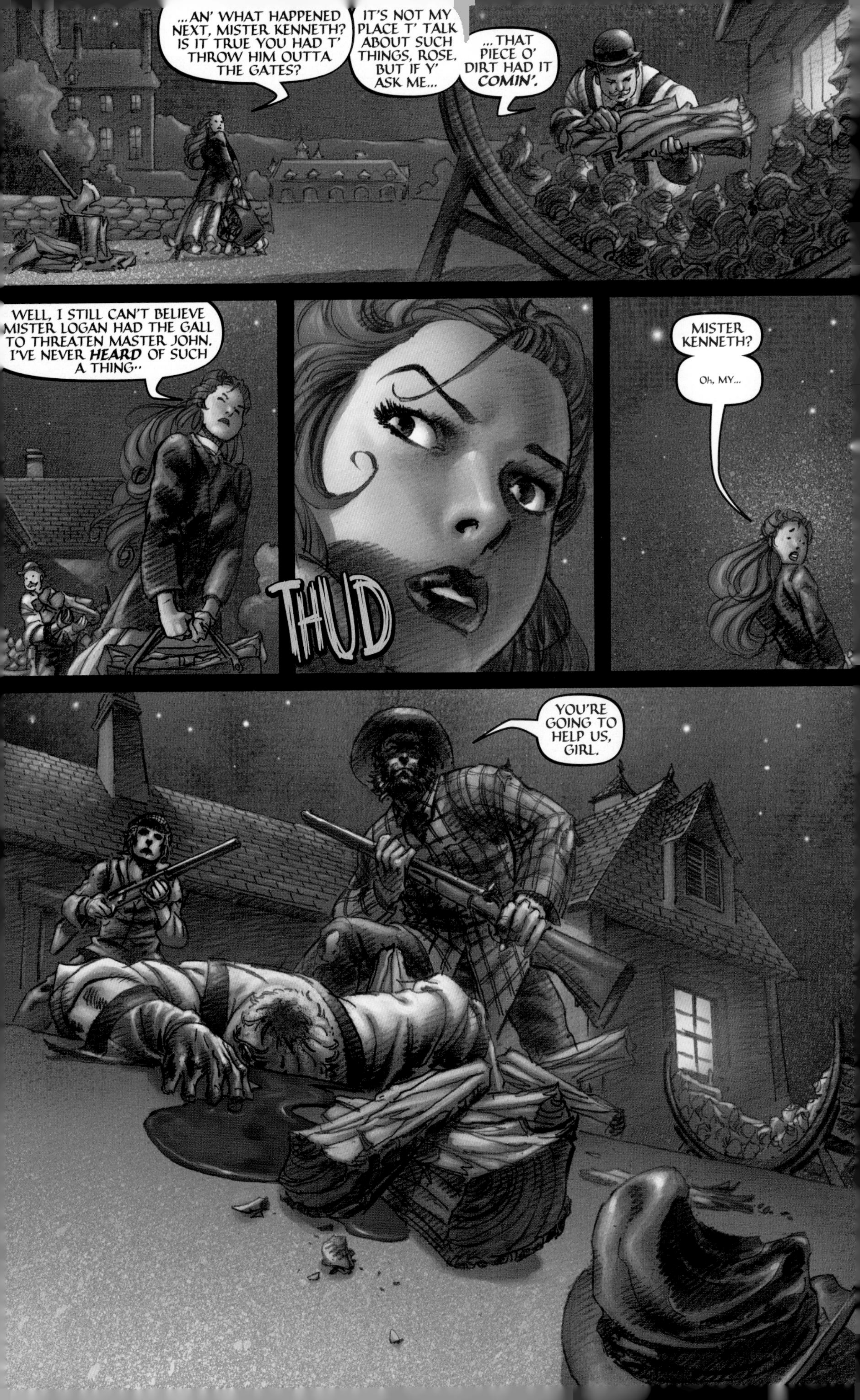
...AN' WHAT HAPPENED NEXT, MISTER KENNETH? IS IT TRUE YOU HAD T' THROW HIM OUTTA THE GATES?
IT'S NOT MY PLACE T' TALK ABOUT SUCH THINGS, ROSE, BUT IF Y' ASK ME...
...THAT PIECE O' DIRT HAD IT COMIN'.
WELL, I STILL CAN'T BELIEVE MISTER LOGAN HAD THE GALL TO THREATEN MASTER JOHN. I'VE NEVER HEARD OF SUCH A THING..
THUD
MISTER KENNETH?
Oh, MY...
YOU'RE GOING TO HELP US, GIRL.

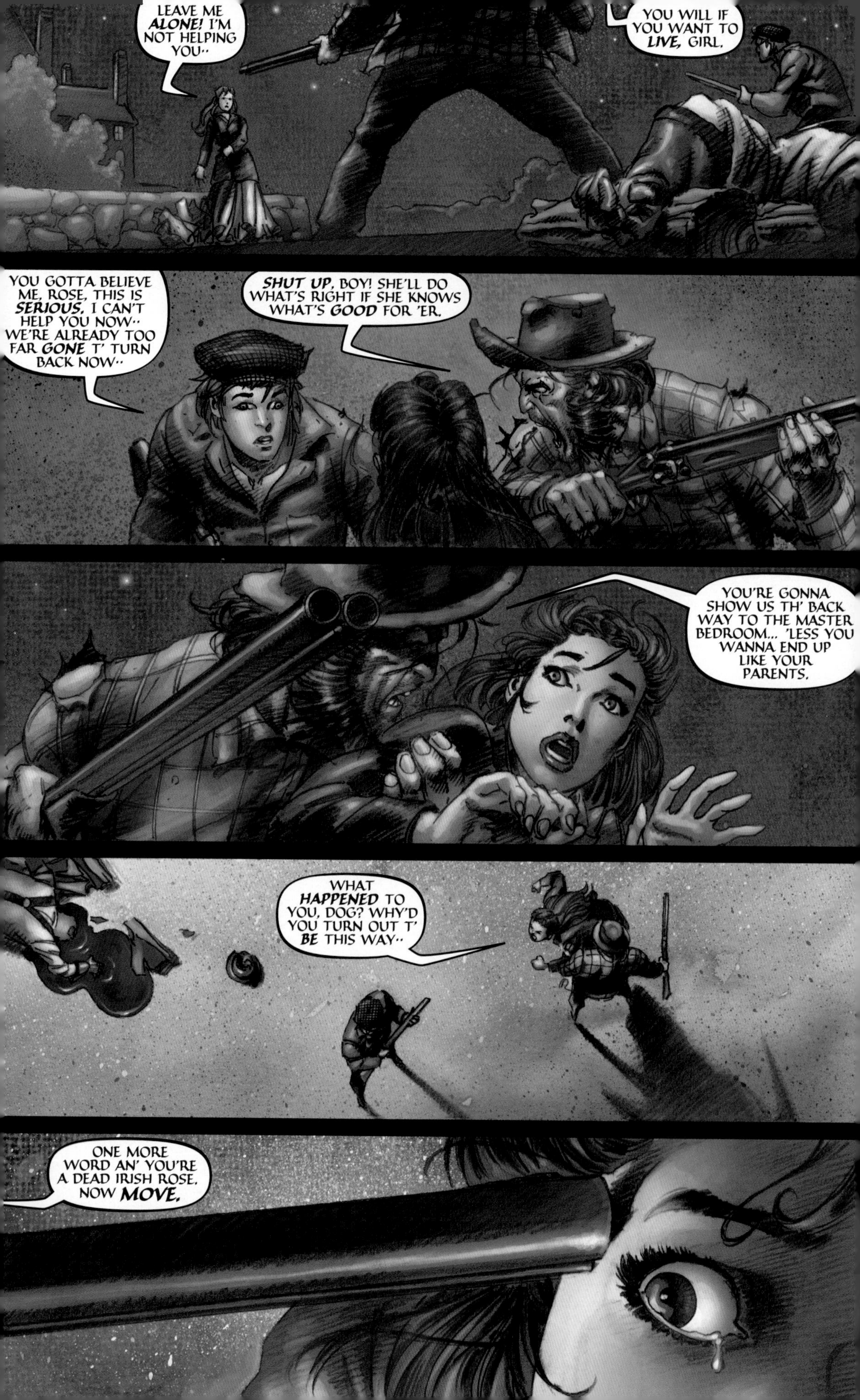
LEAVE ME ALONE! I'M NOT HELPING YOU..
YOU WILL IF YOU WANT TO LIVE, GIRL.
YOU GOTTA BELIEVE ME, ROSE, THIS IS SERIOUS. I CAN'T HELP YOU NOW.. WE'RE ALREADY TOO FAR GONE T' TURN BACK NOW..
SHUT UP, BOY! SHE'LL DO WHAT'S RIGHT IF SHE KNOWS WHAT'S GOOD FOR 'ER.
YOU'RE GONNA SHOW US TH' BACK WAY TO THE MASTER BEDROOM... 'LESS YOU WANNA END UP LIKE YOUR PARENTS.
WHAT HAPPENED TO YOU, DOG? WHY'D YOU TURN OUT T' BE THIS WAY..
ONE MORE WORD AN' YOU'RE A DEAD IRISH ROSE. NOW MOVE.

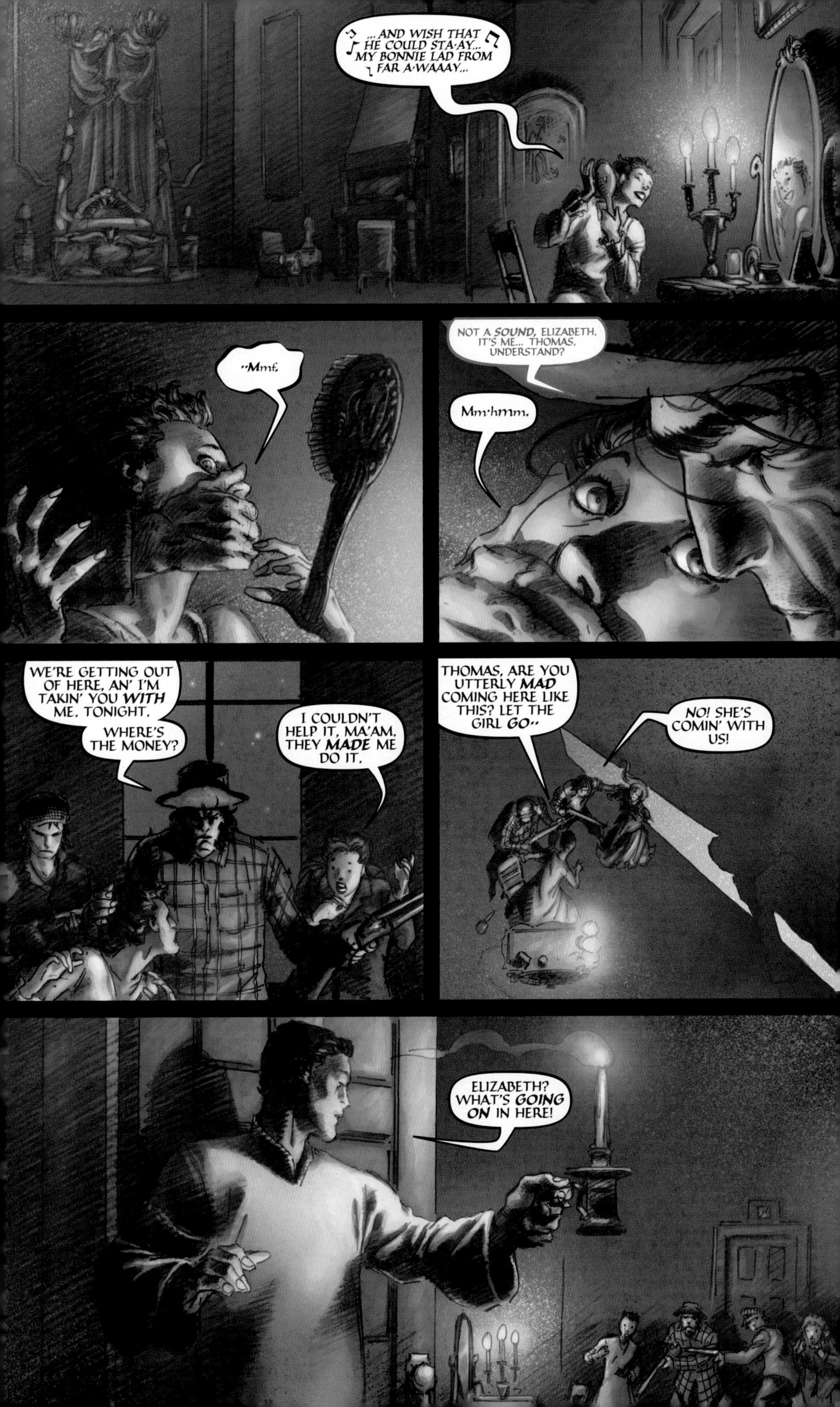
...AND WISH THAT HE COULD STA-AY... MY BONNIE LAD FROM FAR A-WAAAY...
--Mmf.
NOT A SOUND, ELIZABETH. IT'S ME... THOMAS. UNDERSTAND?
Mm-hmm.
WE'RE GETTING OUT OF HERE, AN' I'M TAKIN' YOU WITH ME. TONIGHT.
WHERE'S THE MONEY?
I COULDN'T HELP IT, MA'AM. THEY MADE ME DO IT.
THOMAS, ARE YOU UTTERLY MAD COMING HERE LIKE THIS? LET THE GIRL GO--
NO! SHE'S COMIN' WITH US!
ELIZABETH? WHAT'S GOING ON IN HERE!

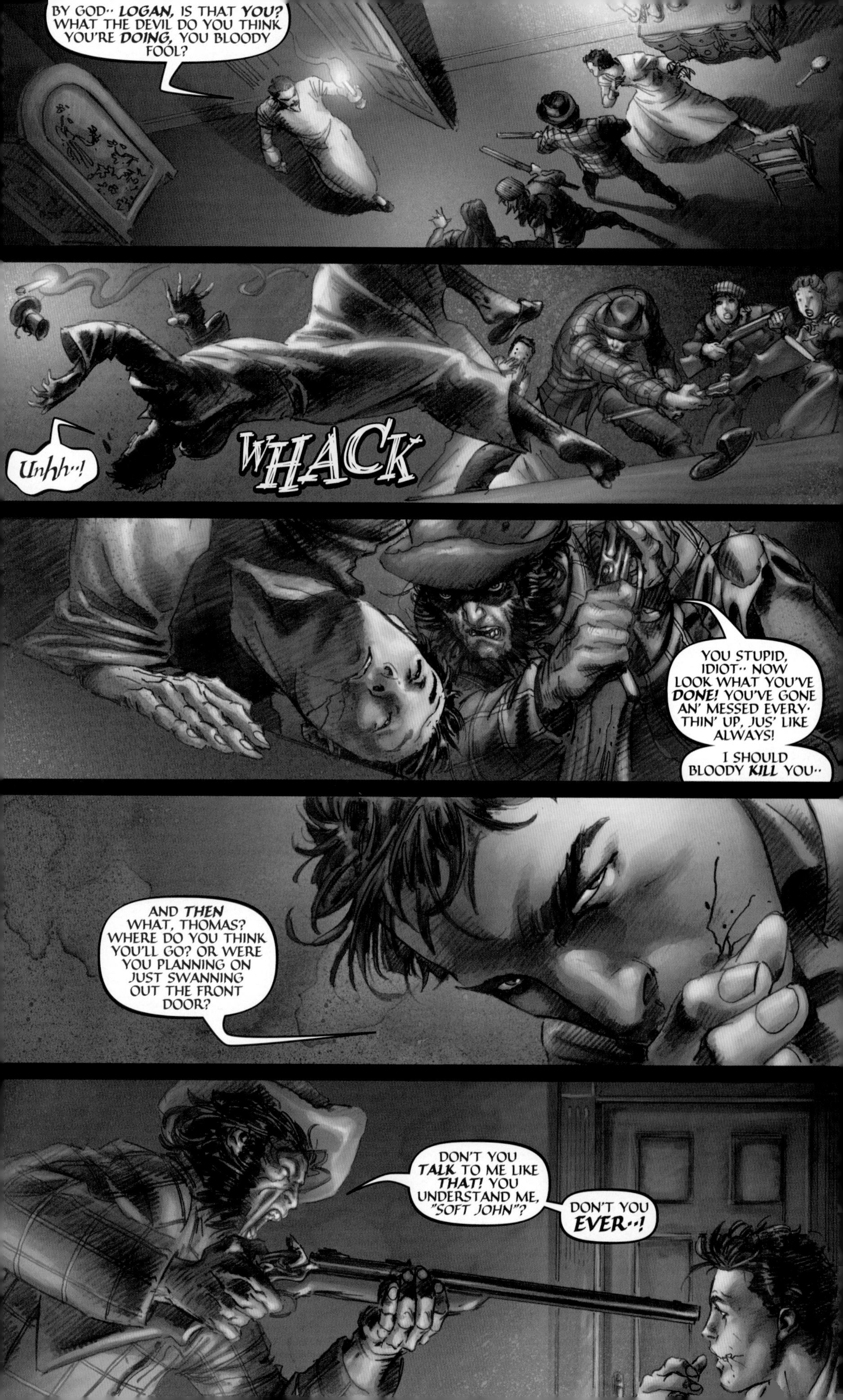

BY GOD·· LOGAN, IS THAT YOU? WHAT THE DEVIL DO YOU THINK YOU'RE DOING, YOU BLOODY FOOL?
Unhh··!
WHACK
YOU STUPID, IDIOT·· NOW LOOK WHAT YOU'VE DONE! YOU'VE GONE AN' MESSED EVERY-THIN' UP, JUS' LIKE ALWAYS!
I SHOULD BLOODY KILL YOU··
AND THEN WHAT, THOMAS? WHERE DO YOU THINK YOU'LL GO? OR WERE YOU PLANNING ON JUST SWANNING OUT THE FRONT DOOR?
DON'T YOU TALK TO ME LIKE THAT! YOU UNDERSTAND ME, "SOFT JOHN"?
DON'T YOU EVER··!

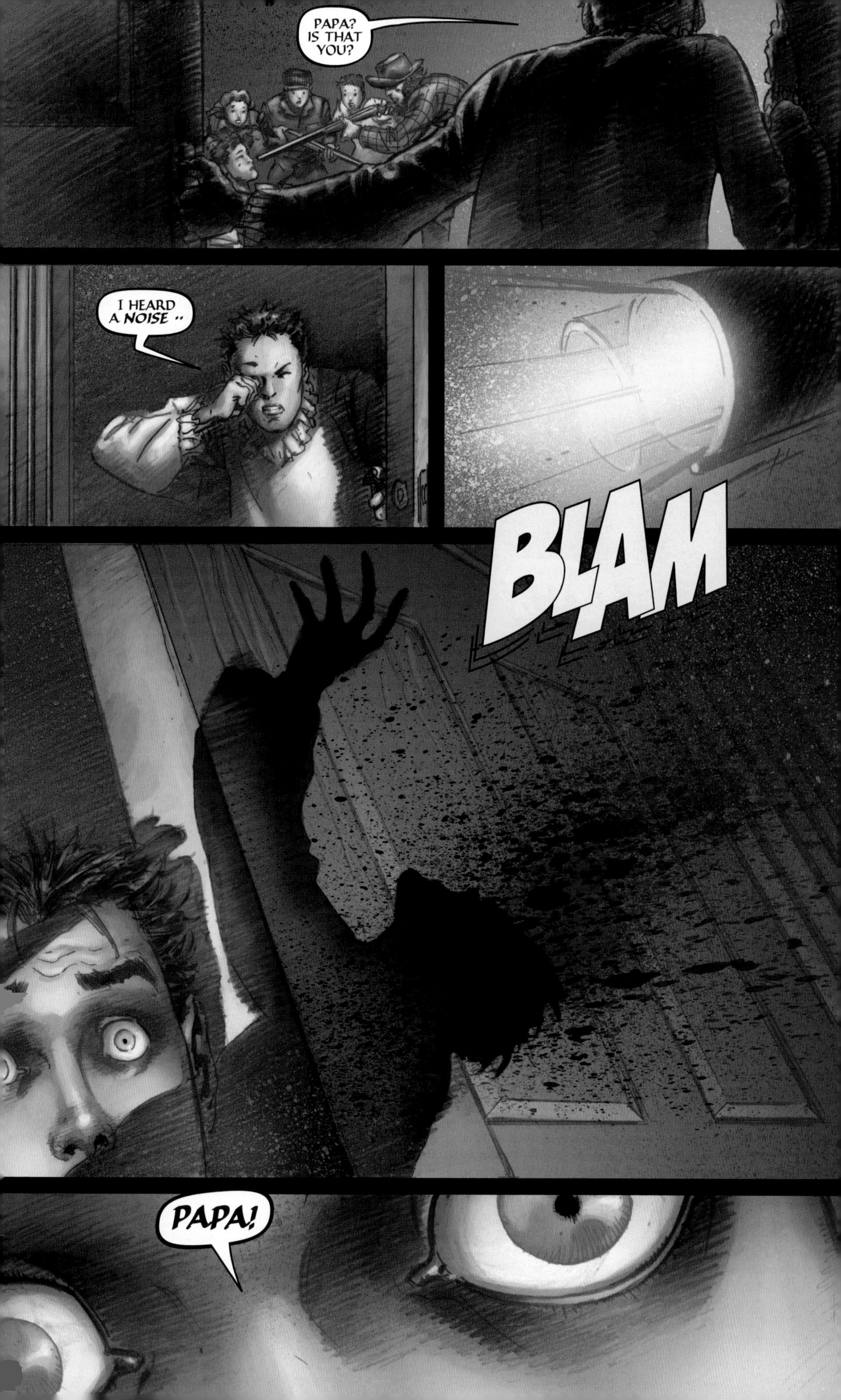
PAPA? IS THAT YOU?
I HEARD A NOISE ..
BLAM
PAPA!

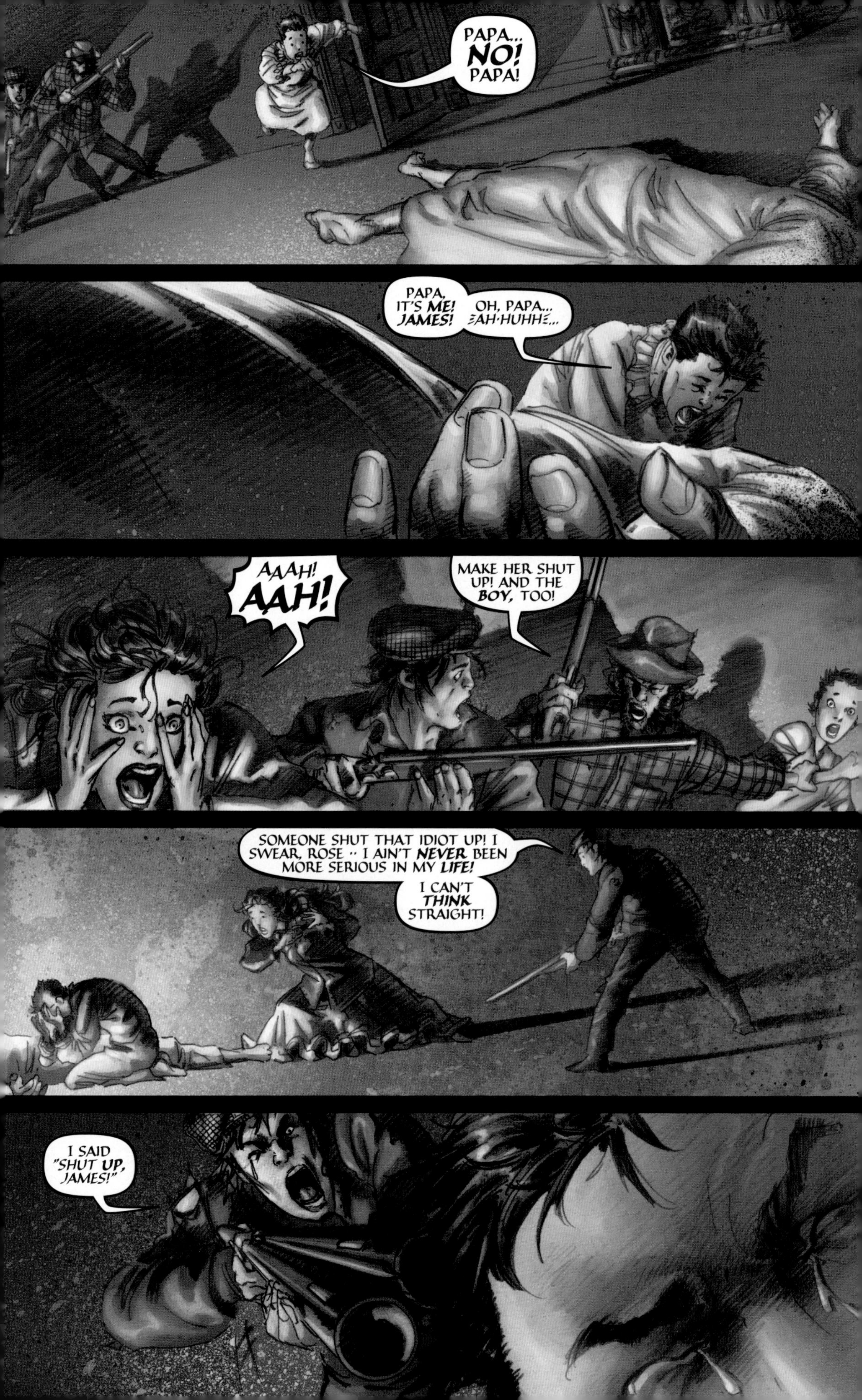
PAPA... NO! PAPA!
PAPA, IT'S ME! JAMES!
OH, PAPA... AH-HUHH...
AAAH! AAH!
MAKE HER SHUT UP! AND THE BOY, TOO!
SOMEONE SHUT THAT IDIOT UP! I SWEAR, ROSE -- I AIN'T NEVER BEEN MORE SERIOUS IN MY LIFE!
I CAN'T THINK STRAIGHT!
I SAID "SHUT UP, JAMES!"

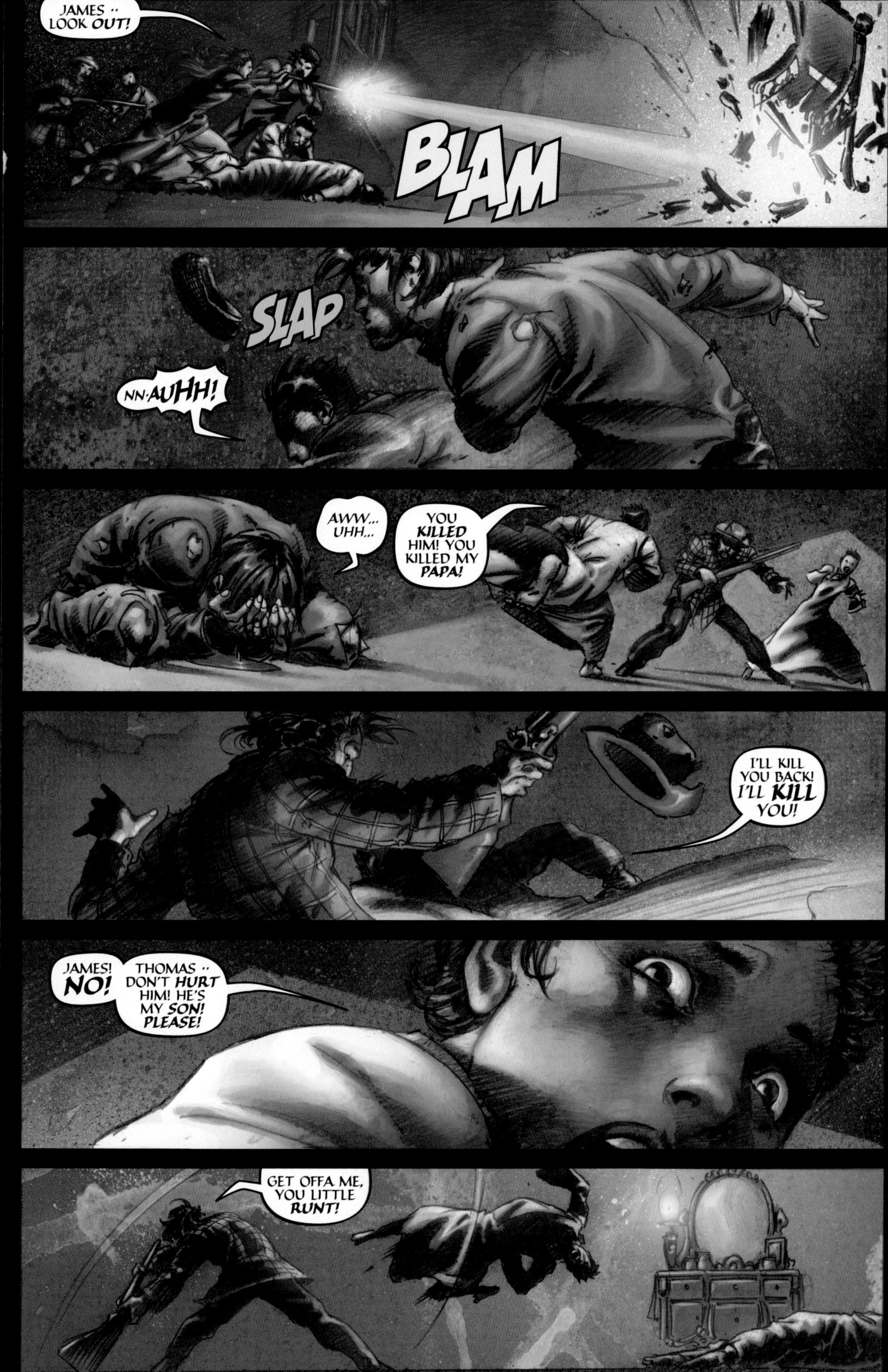
JAMES .. LOOK OUT!
BLAM
SLAP
NN-AUHH!
AWW... UHH...
YOU KILLED HIM! YOU KILLED MY PAPA!
I'LL KILL YOU BACK! I'LL KILL YOU!
JAMES! NO!
THOMAS .. DON'T HURT HIM! HE'S MY SON! PLEASE!
GET OFFA ME, YOU LITTLE RUNT!

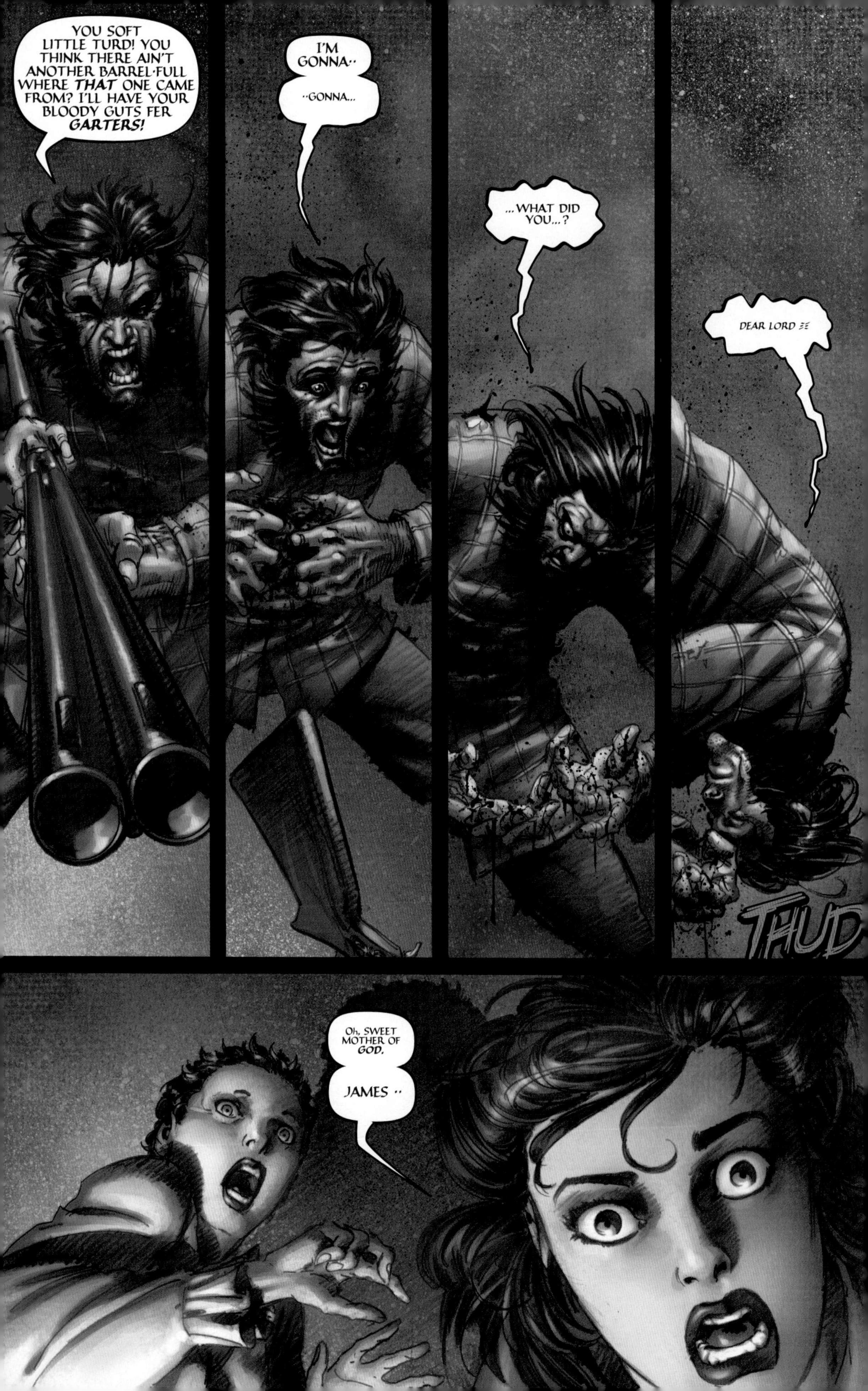
YOU SOFT LITTLE TURD! YOU THINK THERE AIN'T ANOTHER BARREL-FULL WHERE THAT ONE CAME FROM? I'LL HAVE YOUR BLOODY GUTS FER GARTERS!
I'M GONNA..
..GONNA...
...WHAT DID YOU...?
DEAR LORD ==
THUD
Oh, SWEET MOTHER OF GOD,
JAMES ..

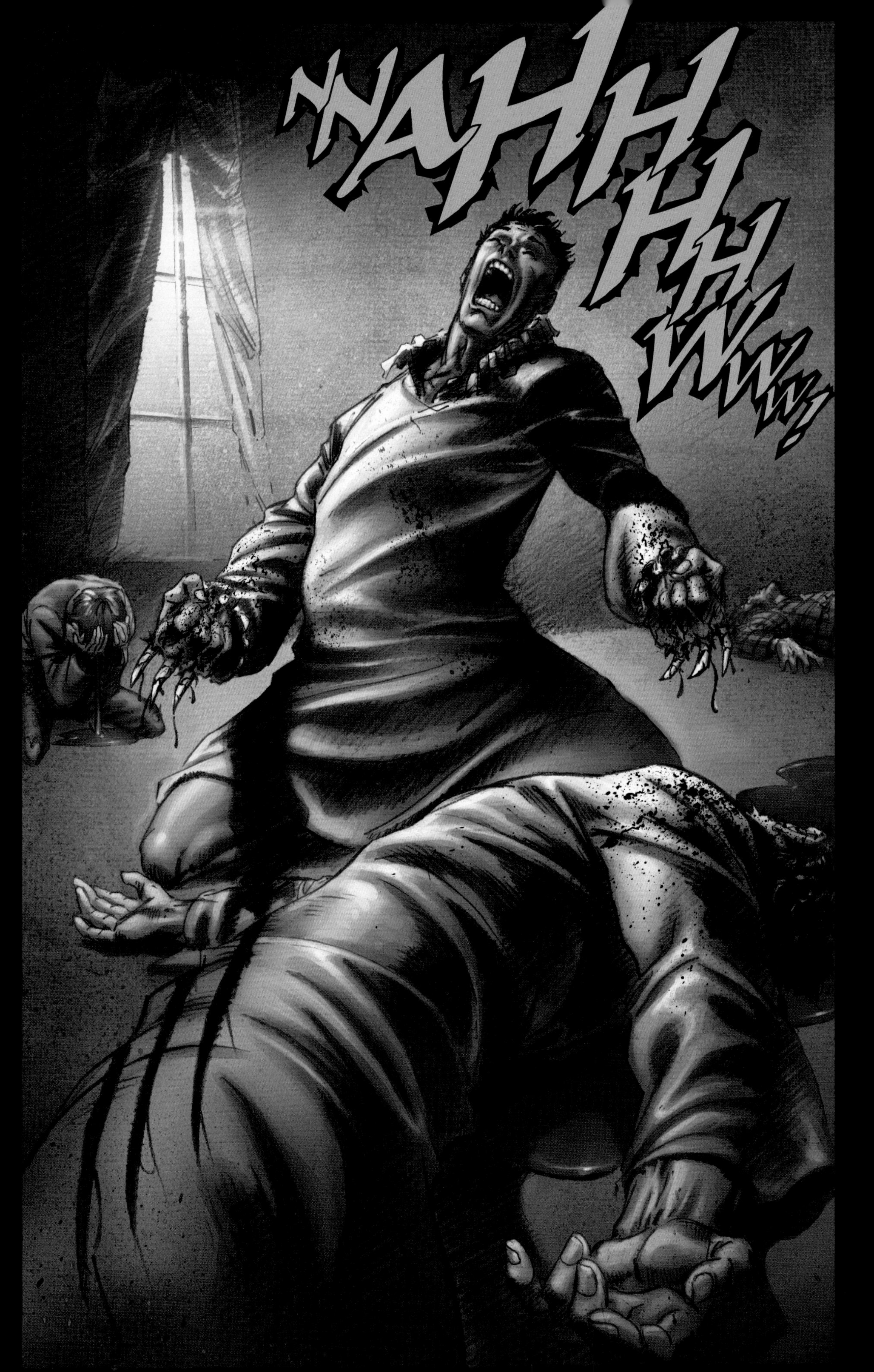
NNAHHHHWW!!

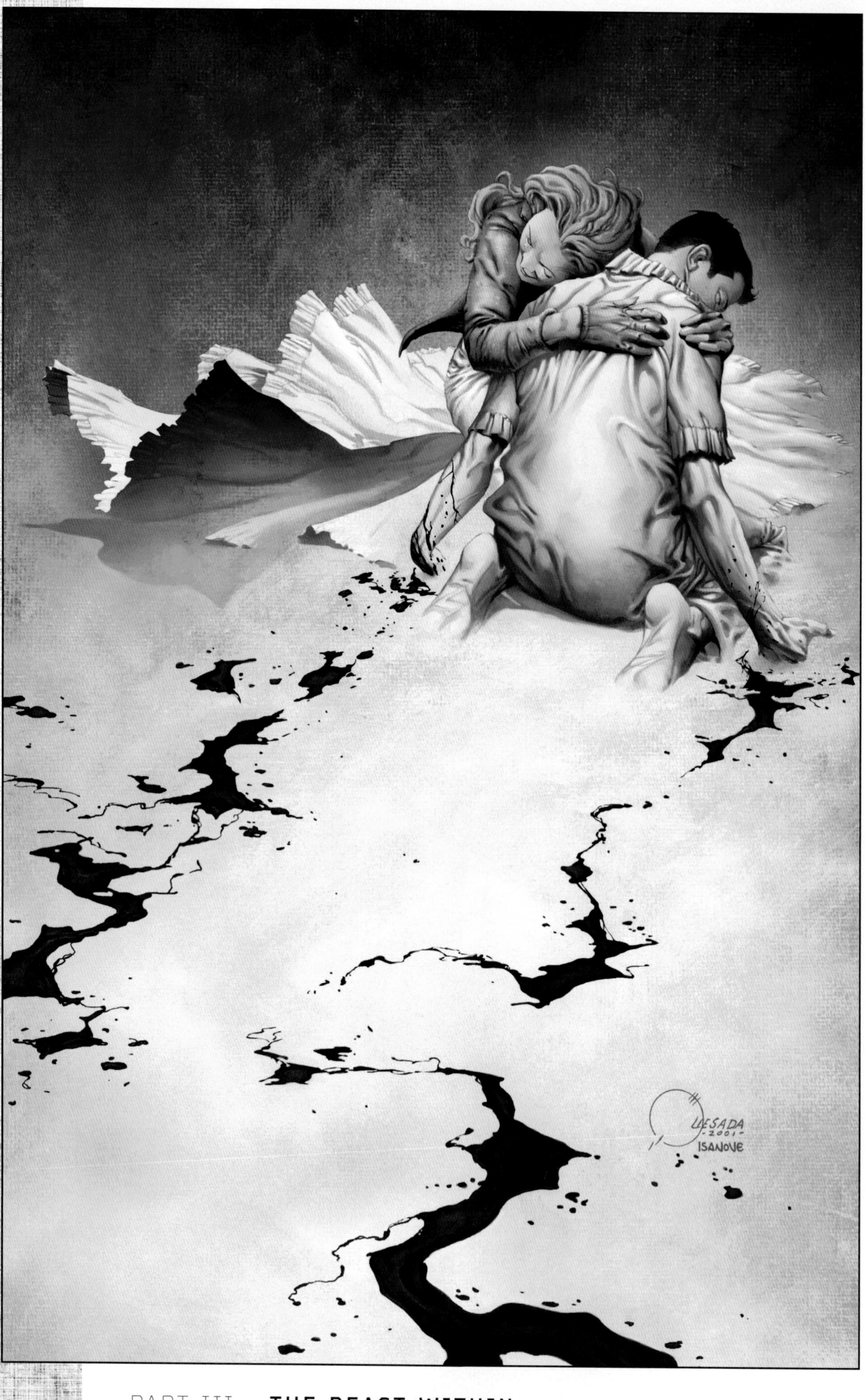
QUESADA
-2001-
ISANOVE

# PART III – THE BEAST WITHIN

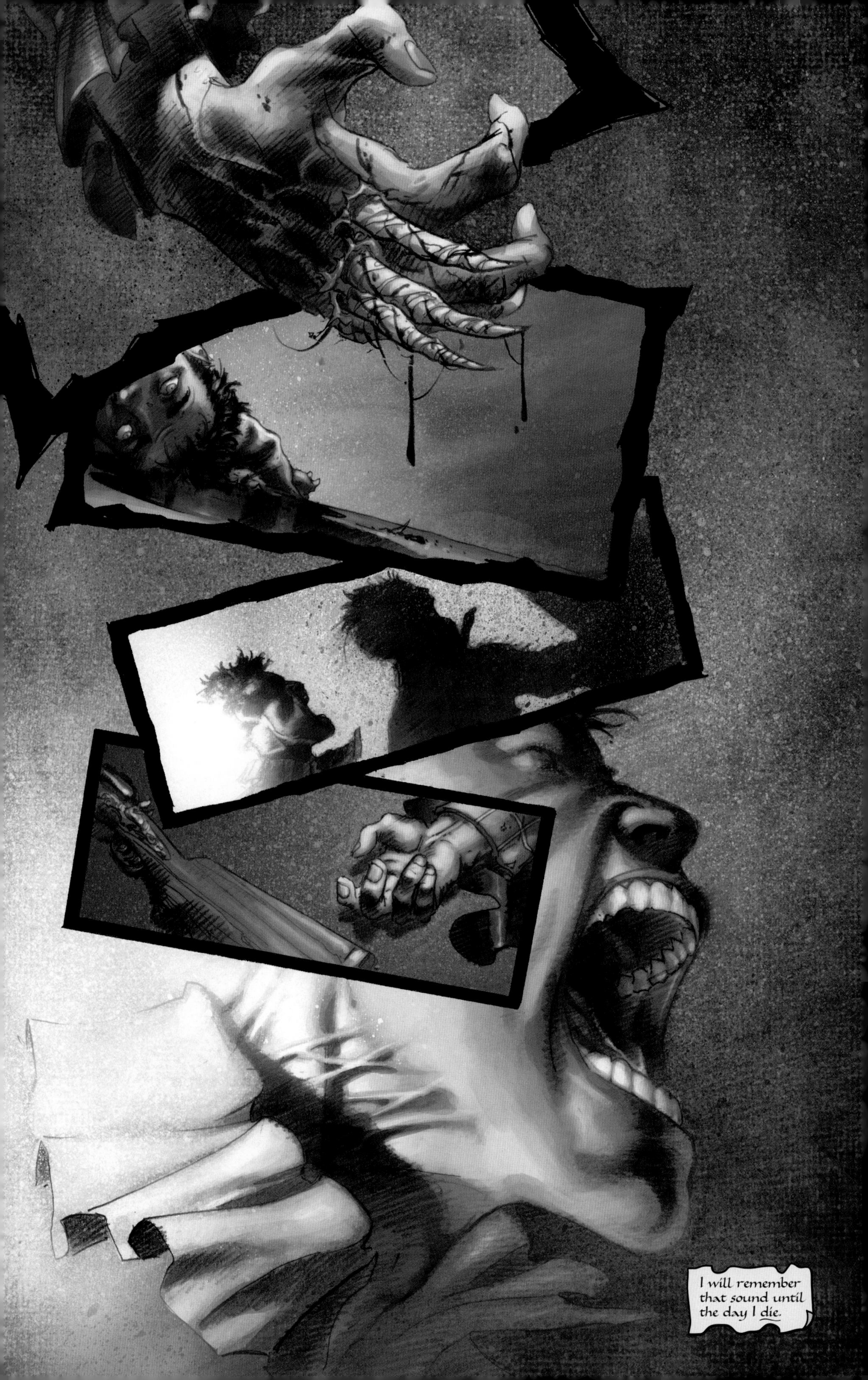
I will remember that sound until the day I die.

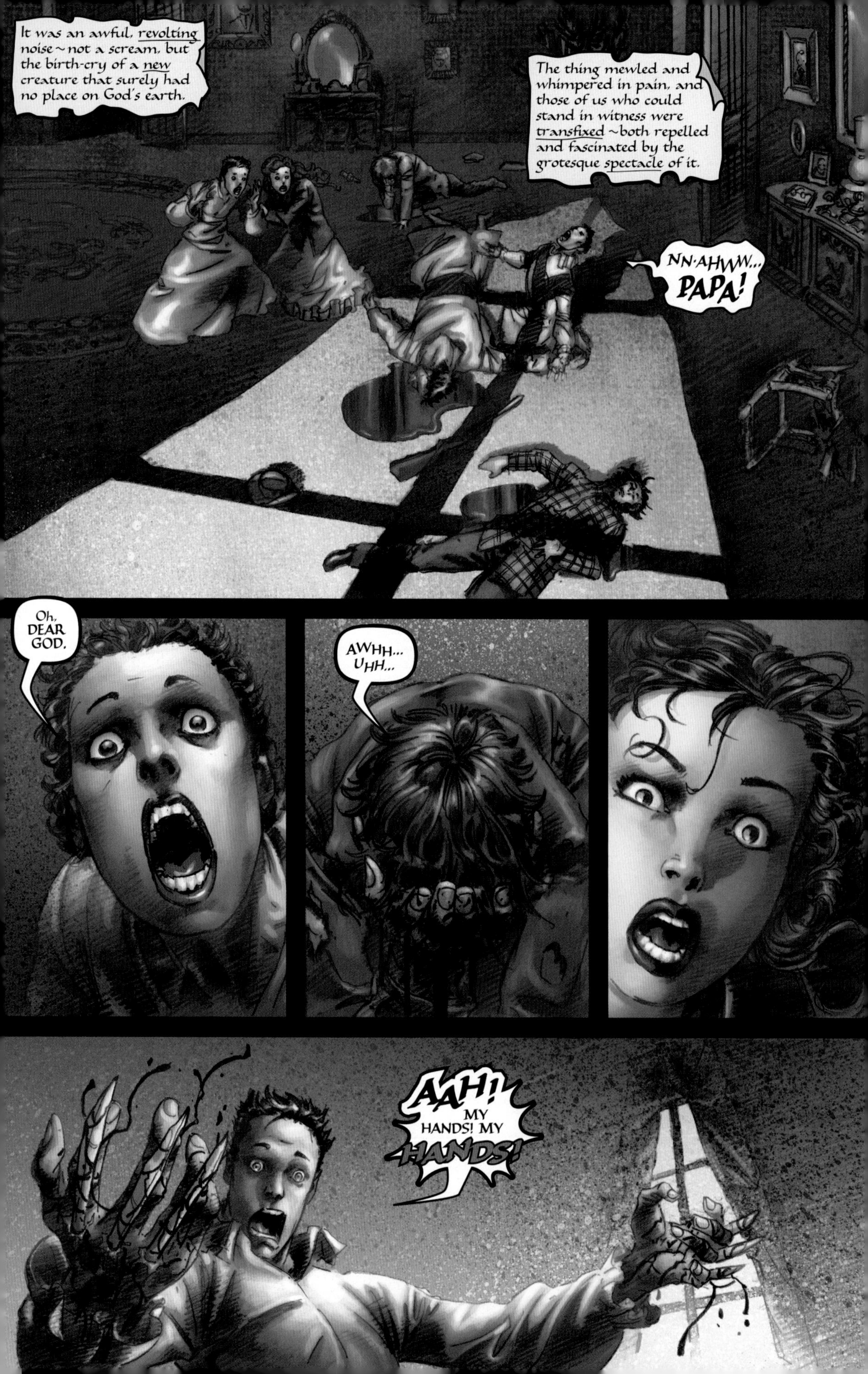
It was an awful, revolting noise ~ not a scream, but the birth-cry of a new creature that surely had no place on God's earth.
The thing mewled and whimpered in pain, and those of us who could stand in witness were transfixed ~ both repelled and fascinated by the grotesque spectacle of it.
NN·AHWW... PAPA!
Oh, DEAR GOD.
AWHH... UHH...
AAH! MY HANDS! MY HANDS!

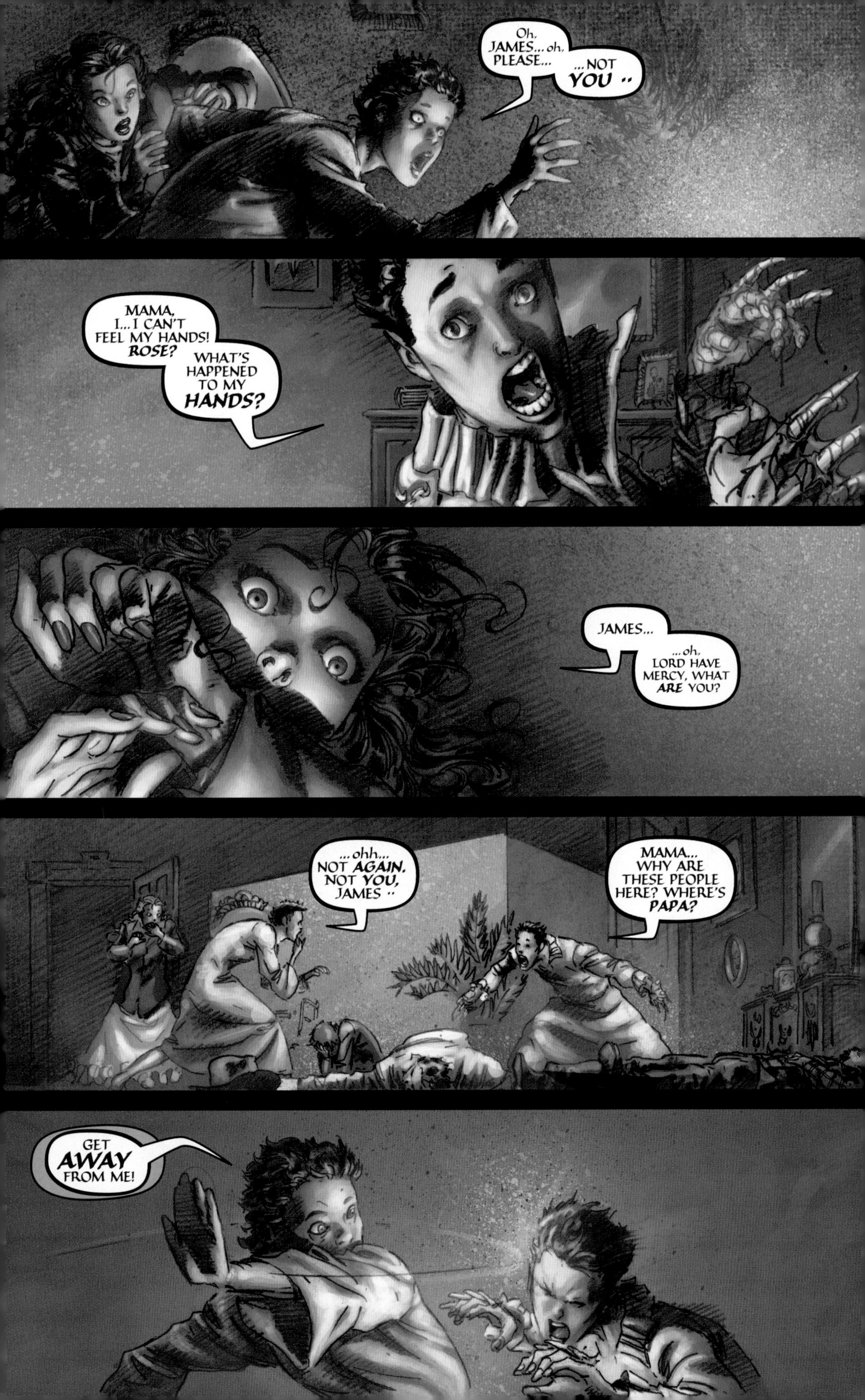

Oh, JAMES... oh, PLEASE...
...NOT YOU ..
MAMA, I... I CAN'T FEEL MY HANDS! ROSE?
WHAT'S HAPPENED TO MY HANDS?
JAMES...
...oh, LORD HAVE MERCY, WHAT ARE YOU?
...ohh... NOT AGAIN. NOT YOU, JAMES ..
MAMA... WHY ARE THESE PEOPLE HERE? WHERE'S PAPA?
GET AWAY FROM ME!

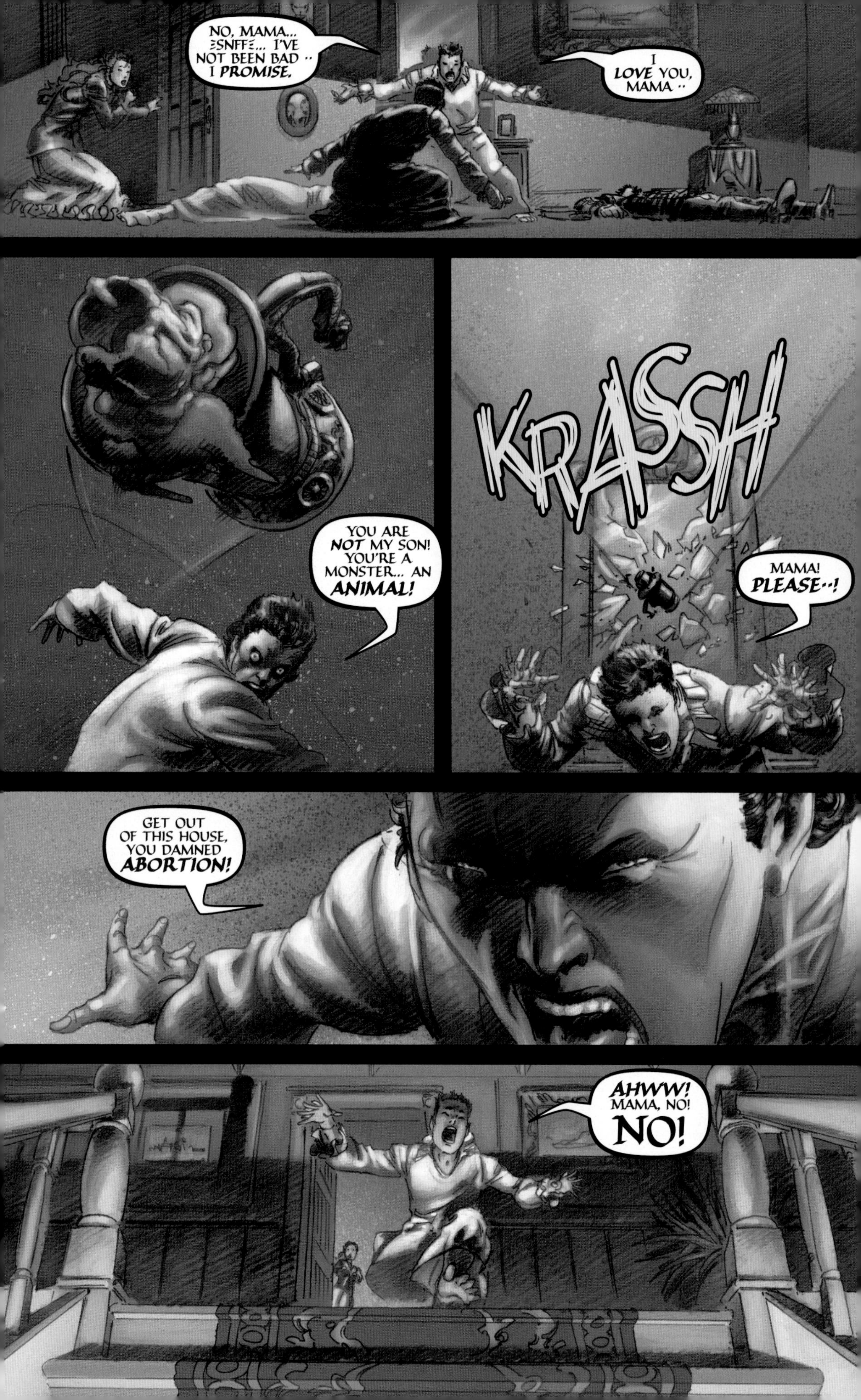
NO, MAMA... SNFF... I'VE NOT BEEN BAD .. I PROMISE.
I LOVE YOU, MAMA ..
YOU ARE NOT MY SON! YOU'RE A MONSTER... AN ANIMAL!
KRASSH
MAMA! PLEASE..!
GET OUT OF THIS HOUSE, YOU DAMNED ABORTION!
AHWW! MAMA, NO! NO!

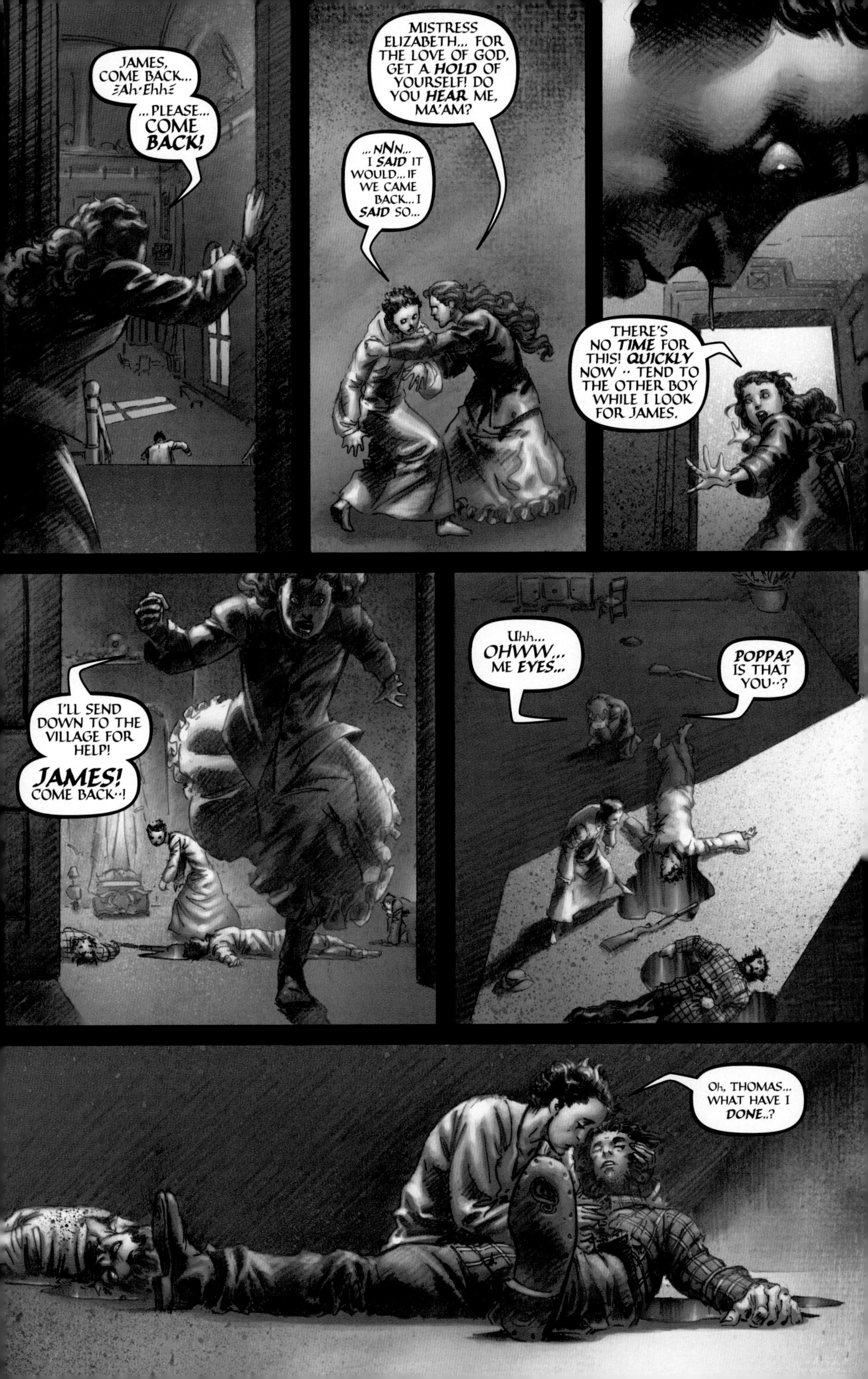
JAMES, COME BACK... ≡Ah·Ehh≡
...PLEASE... COME BACK!
MISTRESS ELIZABETH... FOR THE LOVE OF GOD, GET A HOLD OF YOURSELF! DO YOU HEAR ME, MA'AM?
...NNN... I SAID IT WOULD... IF WE CAME BACK... I SAID SO...
THERE'S NO TIME FOR THIS! QUICKLY NOW ·· TEND TO THE OTHER BOY WHILE I LOOK FOR JAMES.
I'LL SEND DOWN TO THE VILLAGE FOR HELP!
JAMES! COME BACK··!
Uhh... OHWW... ME EYES...
POPPA? IS THAT YOU··?
Oh, THOMAS... WHAT HAVE I DONE..?

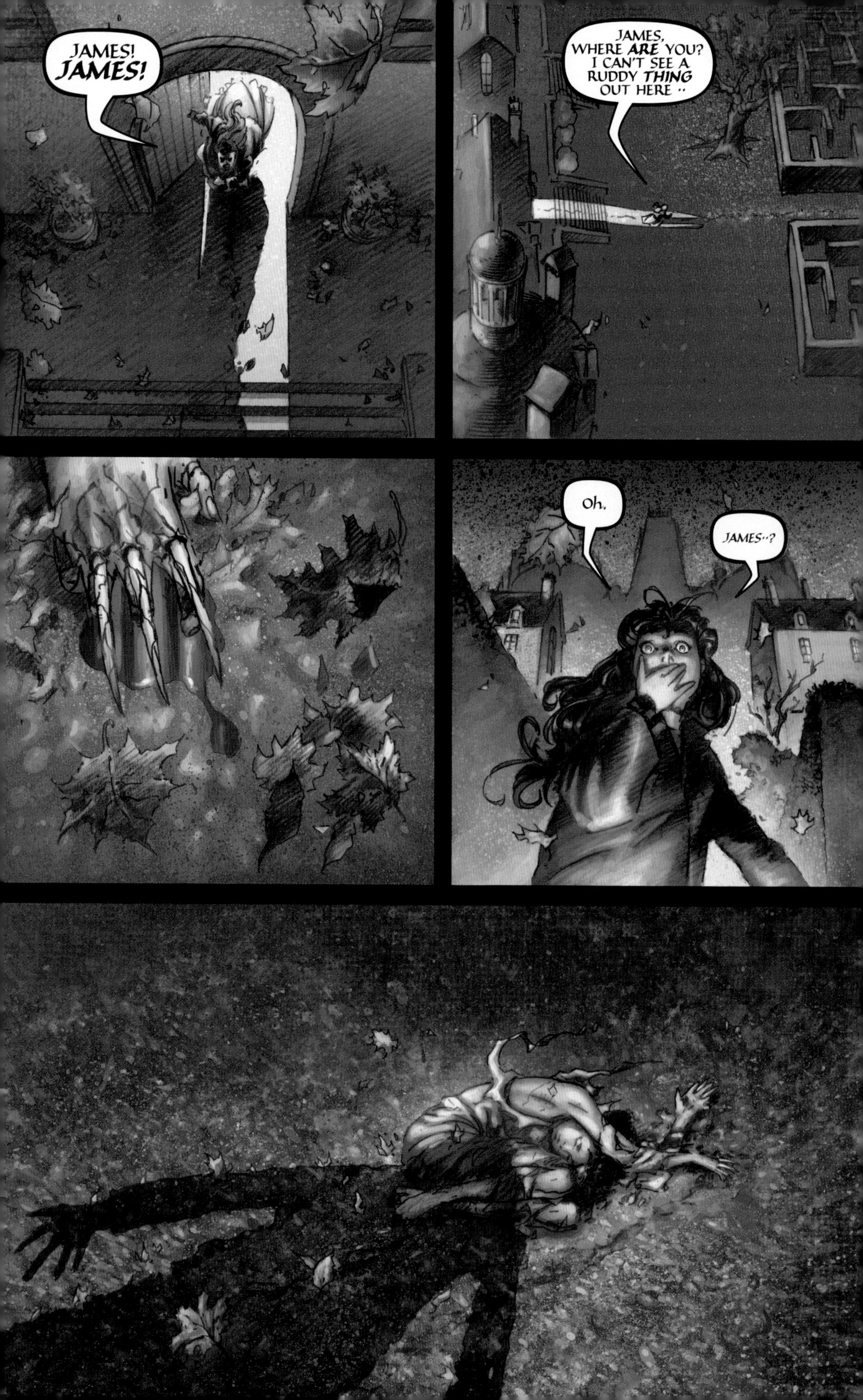
JAMES! JAMES!
JAMES, WHERE ARE YOU? I CAN'T SEE A RUDDY THING OUT HERE ..
Oh.
JAMES..?

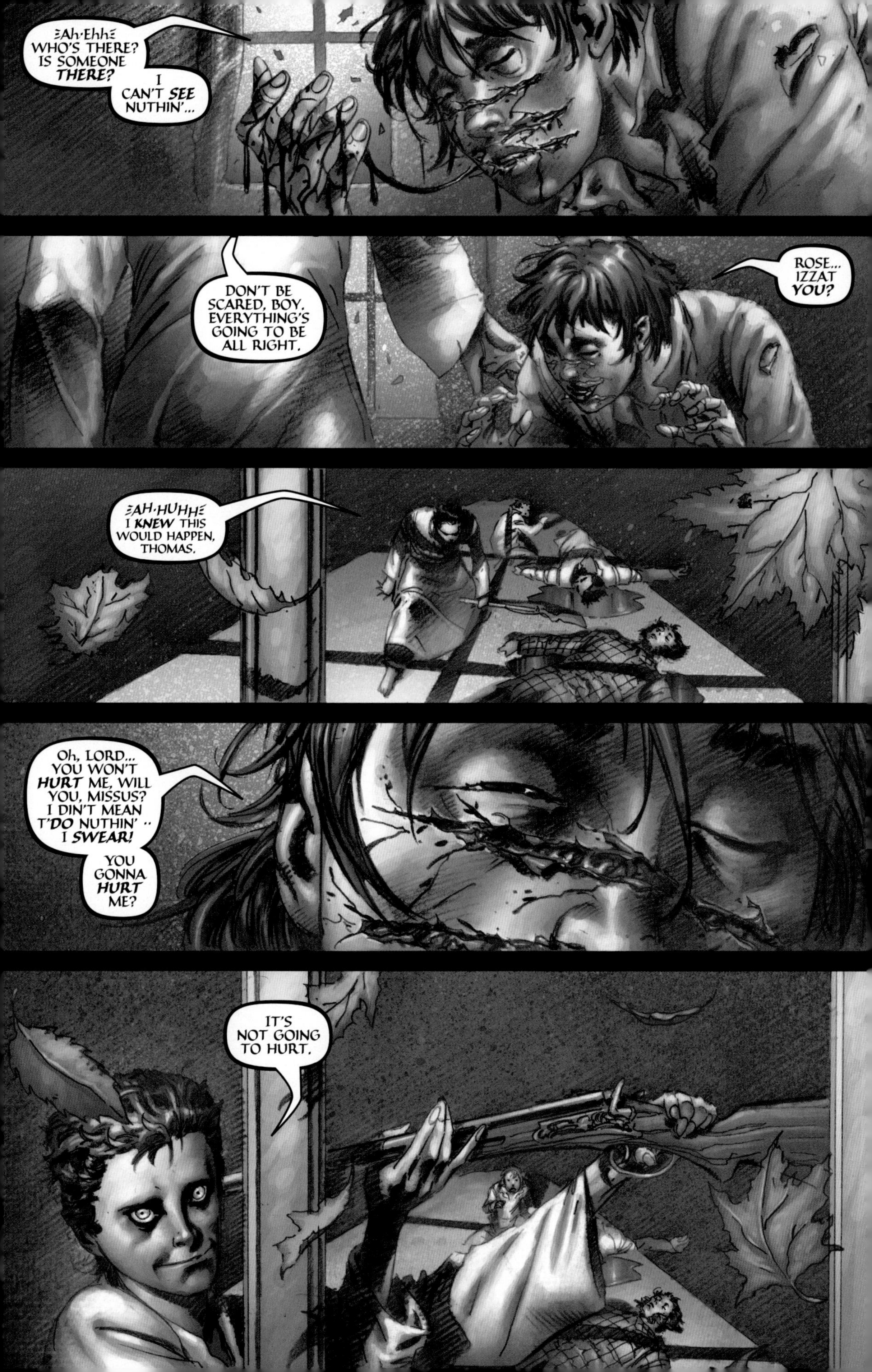

≡Ah·Ehh≡ WHO'S THERE? IS SOMEONE THERE?
I CAN'T SEE NUTHIN'...
DON'T BE SCARED, BOY, EVERYTHING'S GOING TO BE ALL RIGHT.
ROSE... IZZAT YOU?
≡AH·HUHH≡ I KNEW THIS WOULD HAPPEN, THOMAS.
Oh, LORD... YOU WON'T HURT ME, WILL YOU, MISSUS? I DIN'T MEAN T'DO NUTHIN'.. I SWEAR!
YOU GONNA HURT ME?
IT'S NOT GOING TO HURT.

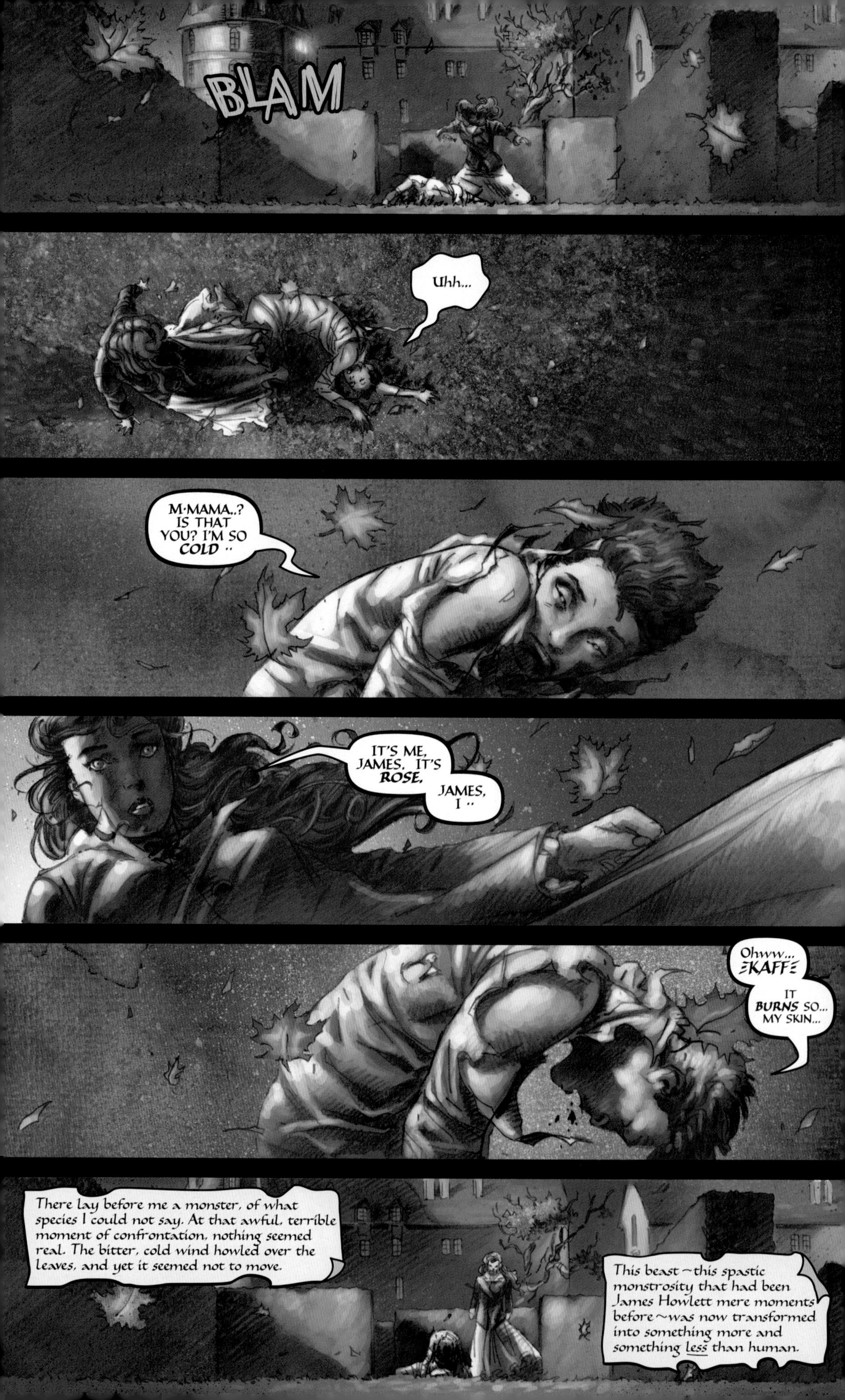
BLAM
Uhh...
M-MAMA..? IS THAT YOU? I'M SO COLD ..
IT'S ME, JAMES. IT'S ROSE.
JAMES, I ..
Ohww... KAFF
IT BURNS SO... MY SKIN...
There lay before me a monster, of what species I could not say. At that awful, terrible moment of confrontation, nothing seemed real. The bitter, cold wind howled over the leaves, and yet it seemed not to move.
This beast ~ this spastic monstrosity that had been James Howlett mere moments before ~ was now transformed into something more and something less than human.

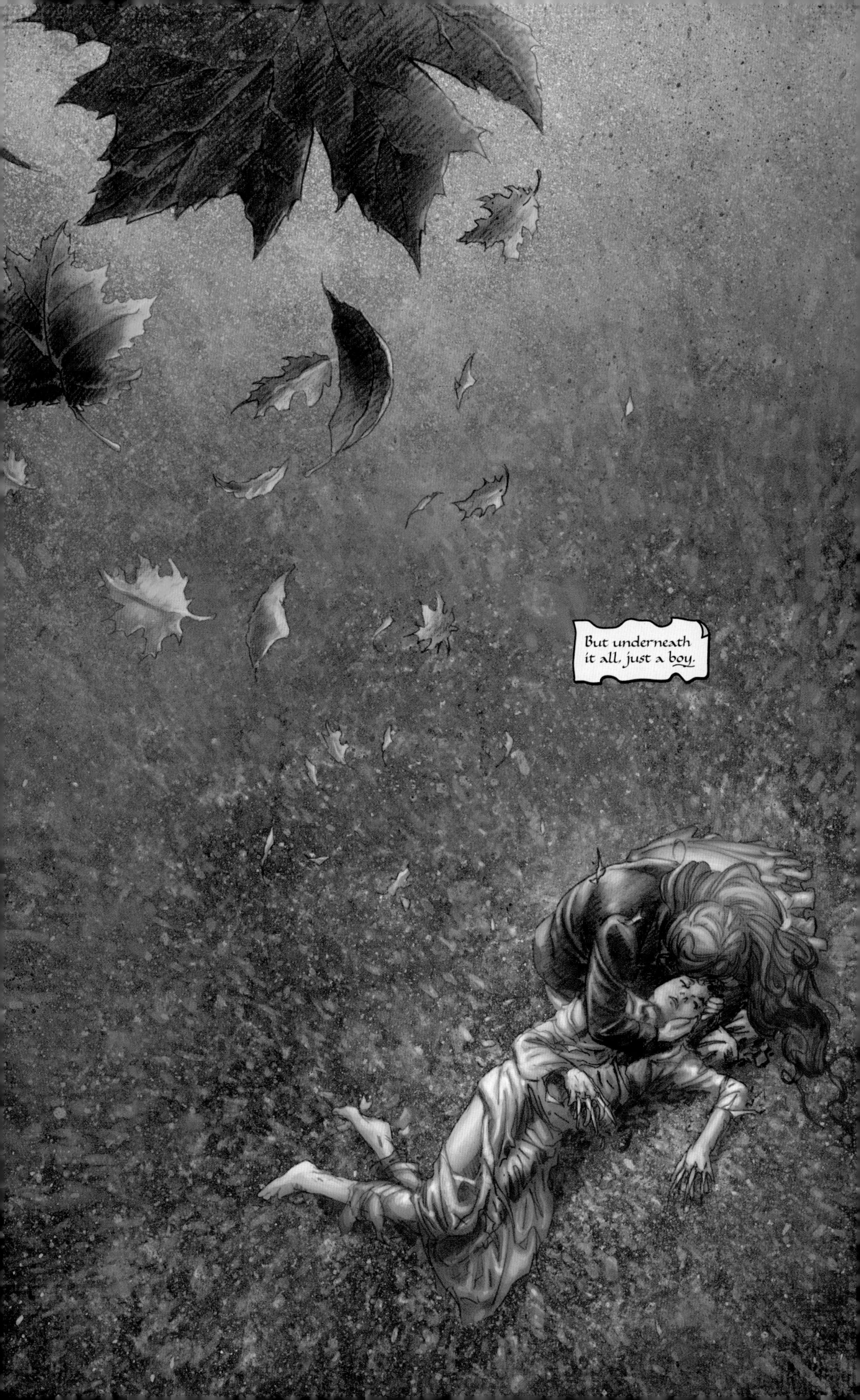
But underneath it all, just a boy.

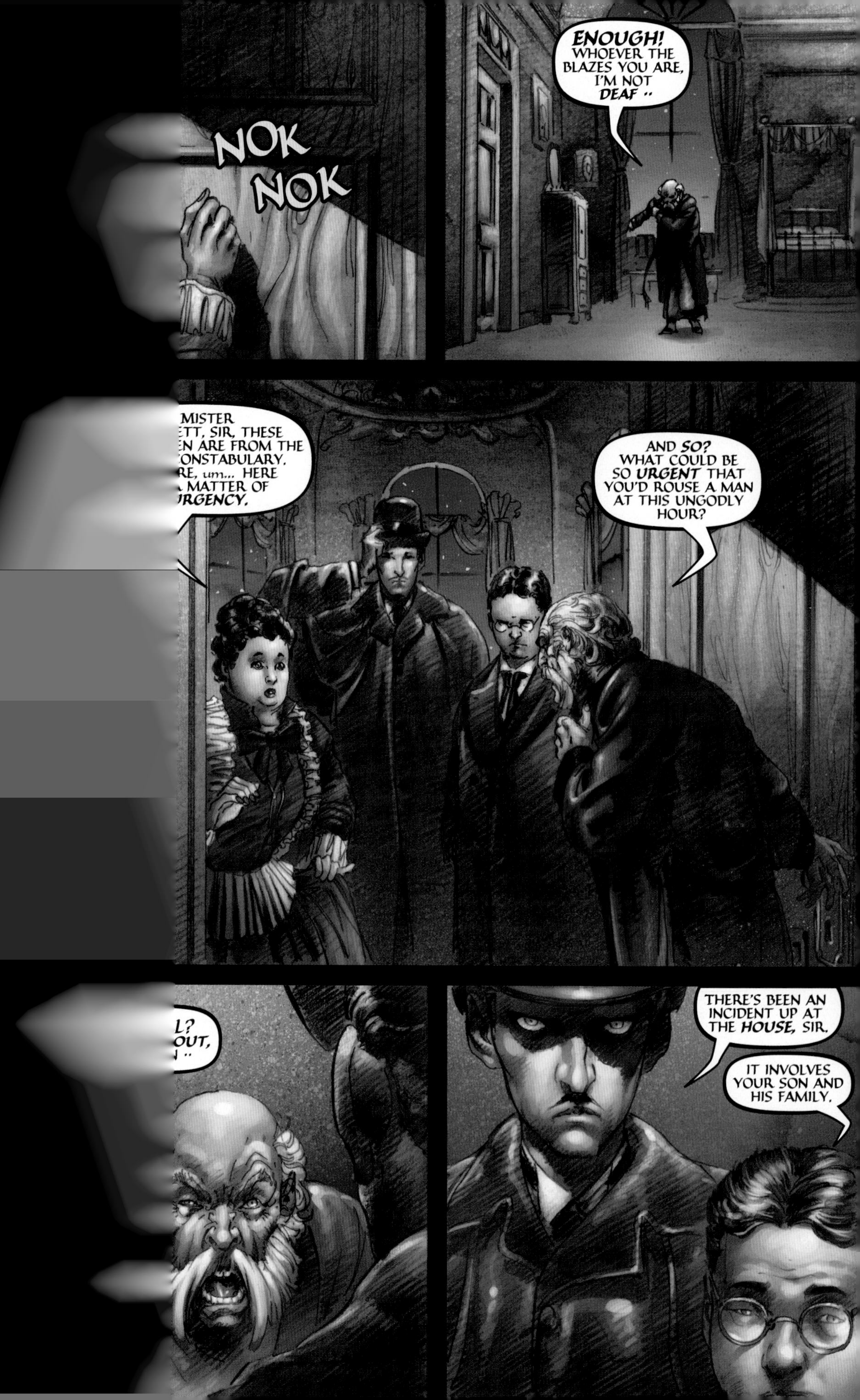
NOK NOK
ENOUGH! WHOEVER THE BLAZES YOU ARE, I'M NOT DEAF ..
MISTER ... SIR, THESE ... ARE FROM THE ... um... HERE ... MATTER OF ...
AND SO? WHAT COULD BE SO URGENT THAT YOU'D ROUSE A MAN AT THIS UNGODLY HOUR?
THERE'S BEEN AN INCIDENT UP AT THE HOUSE, SIR.
IT INVOLVES YOUR SON AND HIS FAMILY.

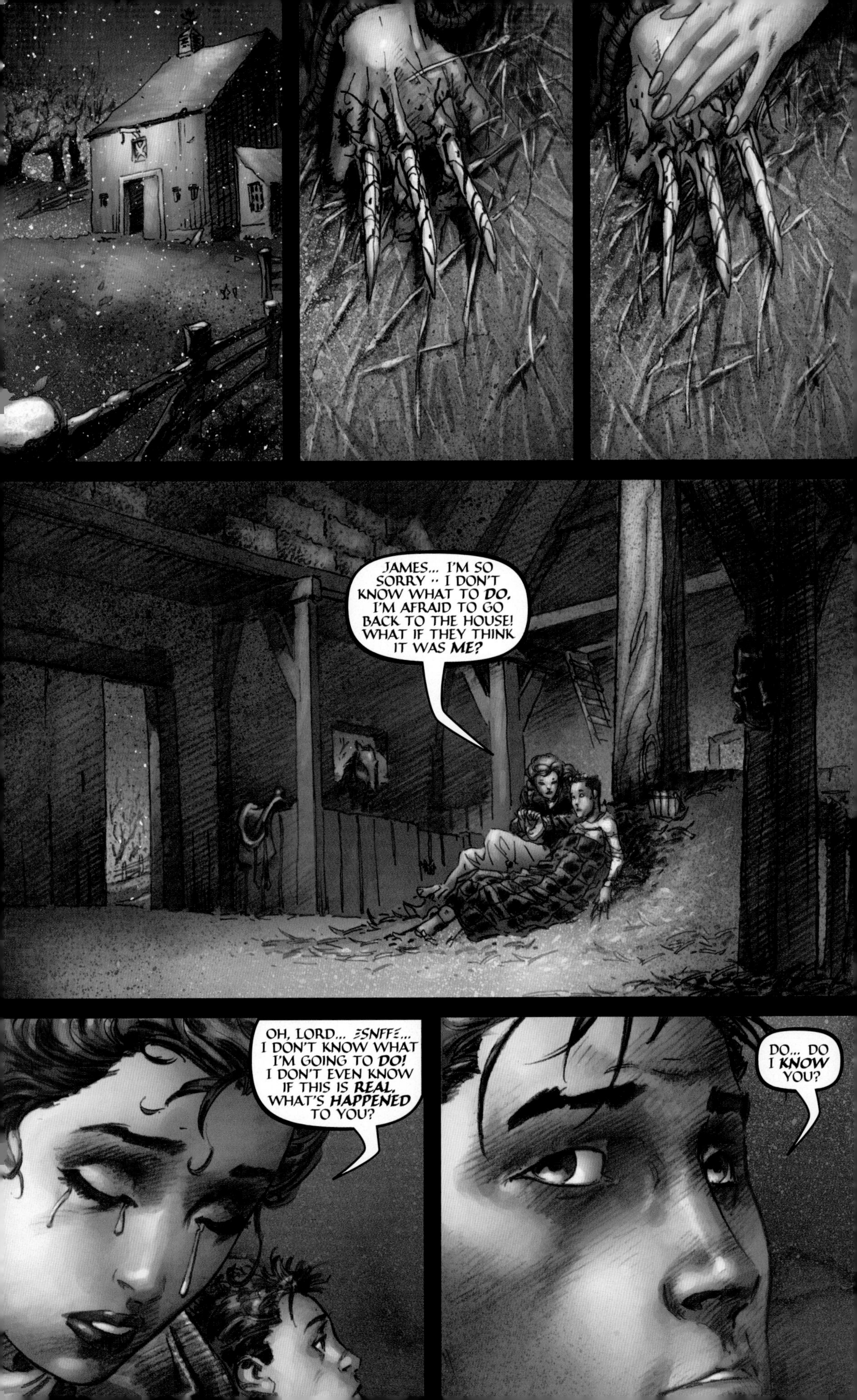
JAMES... I'M SO SORRY -- I DON'T KNOW WHAT TO DO, I'M AFRAID TO GO BACK TO THE HOUSE! WHAT IF THEY THINK IT WAS ME?
OH, LORD... SNFF... I DON'T KNOW WHAT I'M GOING TO DO! I DON'T EVEN KNOW IF THIS IS REAL, WHAT'S HAPPENED TO YOU?
DO... DO I KNOW YOU?

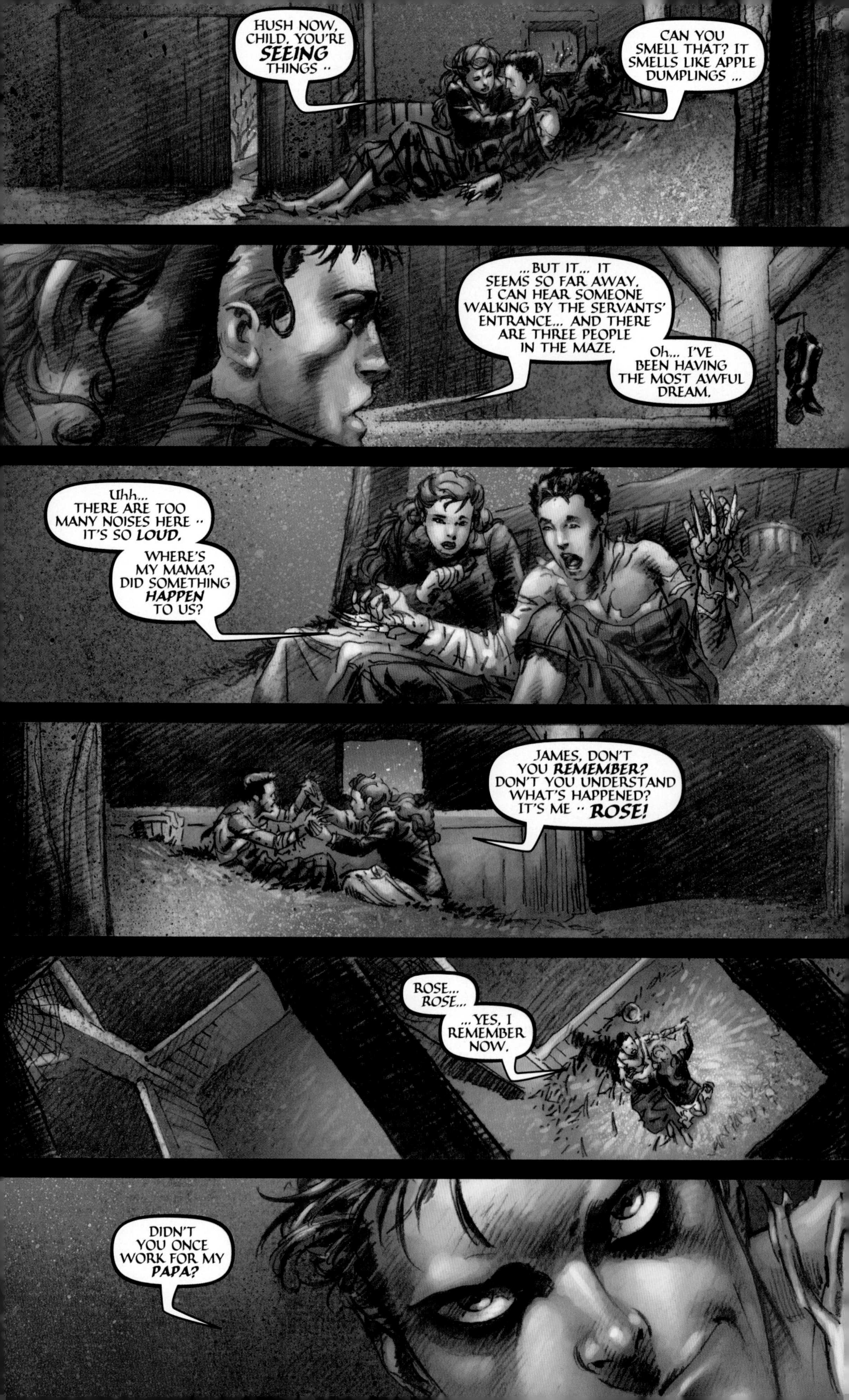
HUSH NOW, CHILD. YOU'RE SEEING THINGS ..
CAN YOU SMELL THAT? IT SMELLS LIKE APPLE DUMPLINGS ...
...BUT IT... IT SEEMS SO FAR AWAY. I CAN HEAR SOMEONE WALKING BY THE SERVANTS' ENTRANCE... AND THERE ARE THREE PEOPLE IN THE MAZE.
Oh... I'VE BEEN HAVING THE MOST AWFUL DREAM.
Uhh... THERE ARE TOO MANY NOISES HERE .. IT'S SO LOUD.
WHERE'S MY MAMA? DID SOMETHING HAPPEN TO US?
JAMES, DON'T YOU REMEMBER? DON'T YOU UNDERSTAND WHAT'S HAPPENED? IT'S ME .. ROSE!
ROSE... ROSE...
...YES, I REMEMBER NOW.
DIDN'T YOU ONCE WORK FOR MY PAPA?

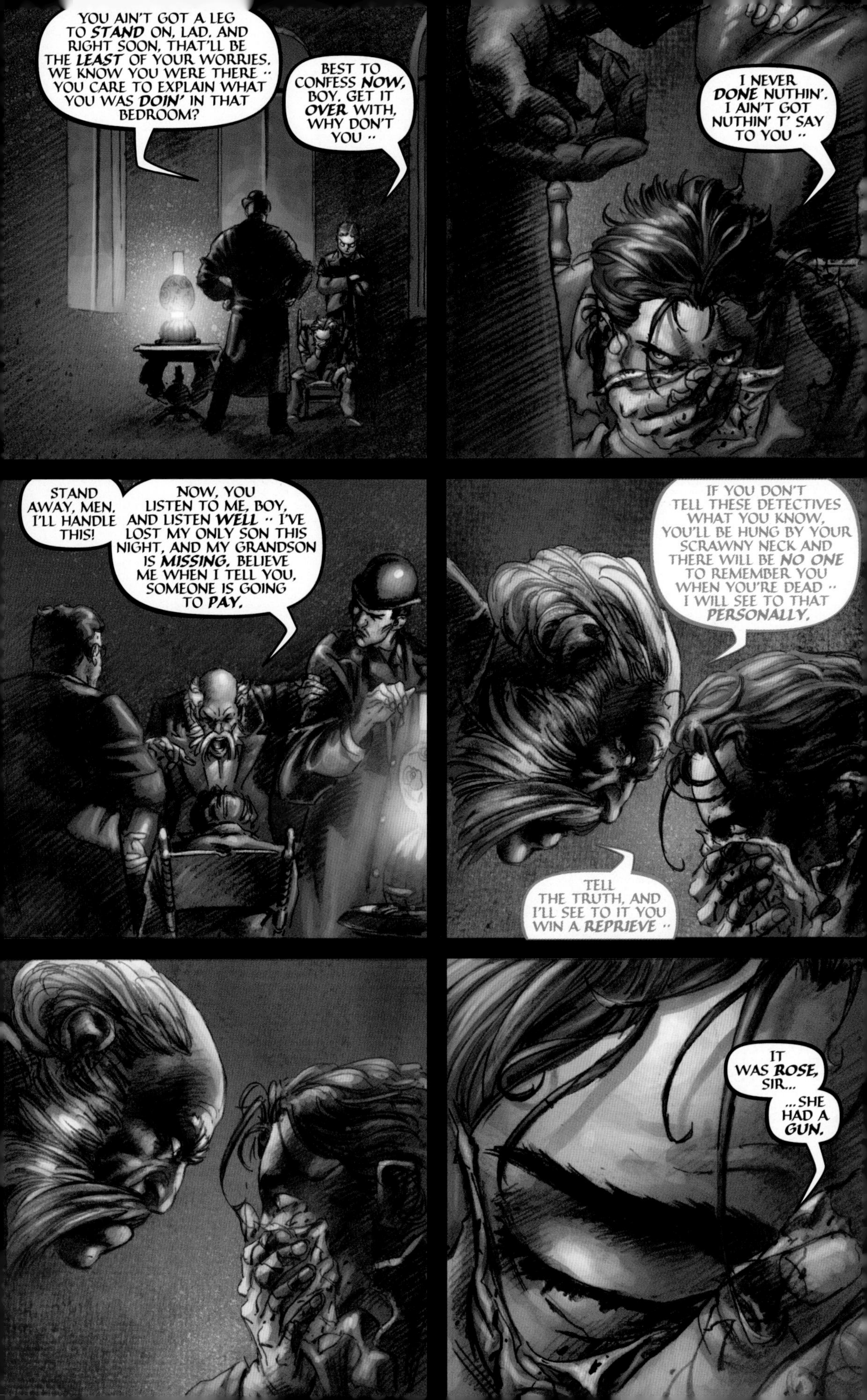
YOU AIN'T GOT A LEG TO STAND ON, LAD. AND RIGHT SOON, THAT'LL BE THE LEAST OF YOUR WORRIES. WE KNOW YOU WERE THERE .. YOU CARE TO EXPLAIN WHAT YOU WAS DOIN' IN THAT BEDROOM?
BEST TO CONFESS NOW, BOY. GET IT OVER WITH, WHY DON'T YOU ..
I NEVER DONE NUTHIN'. I AIN'T GOT NUTHIN' T' SAY TO YOU ..
STAND AWAY, MEN. I'LL HANDLE THIS!
NOW, YOU LISTEN TO ME, BOY, AND LISTEN WELL .. I'VE LOST MY ONLY SON THIS NIGHT, AND MY GRANDSON IS MISSING. BELIEVE ME WHEN I TELL YOU, SOMEONE IS GOING TO PAY.
IF YOU DON'T TELL THESE DETECTIVES WHAT YOU KNOW, YOU'LL BE HUNG BY YOUR SCRAWNY NECK AND THERE WILL BE NO ONE TO REMEMBER YOU WHEN YOU'RE DEAD .. I WILL SEE TO THAT PERSONALLY.
TELL THE TRUTH, AND I'LL SEE TO IT YOU WIN A REPRIEVE ..
IT WAS ROSE, SIR...
...SHE HAD A GUN.

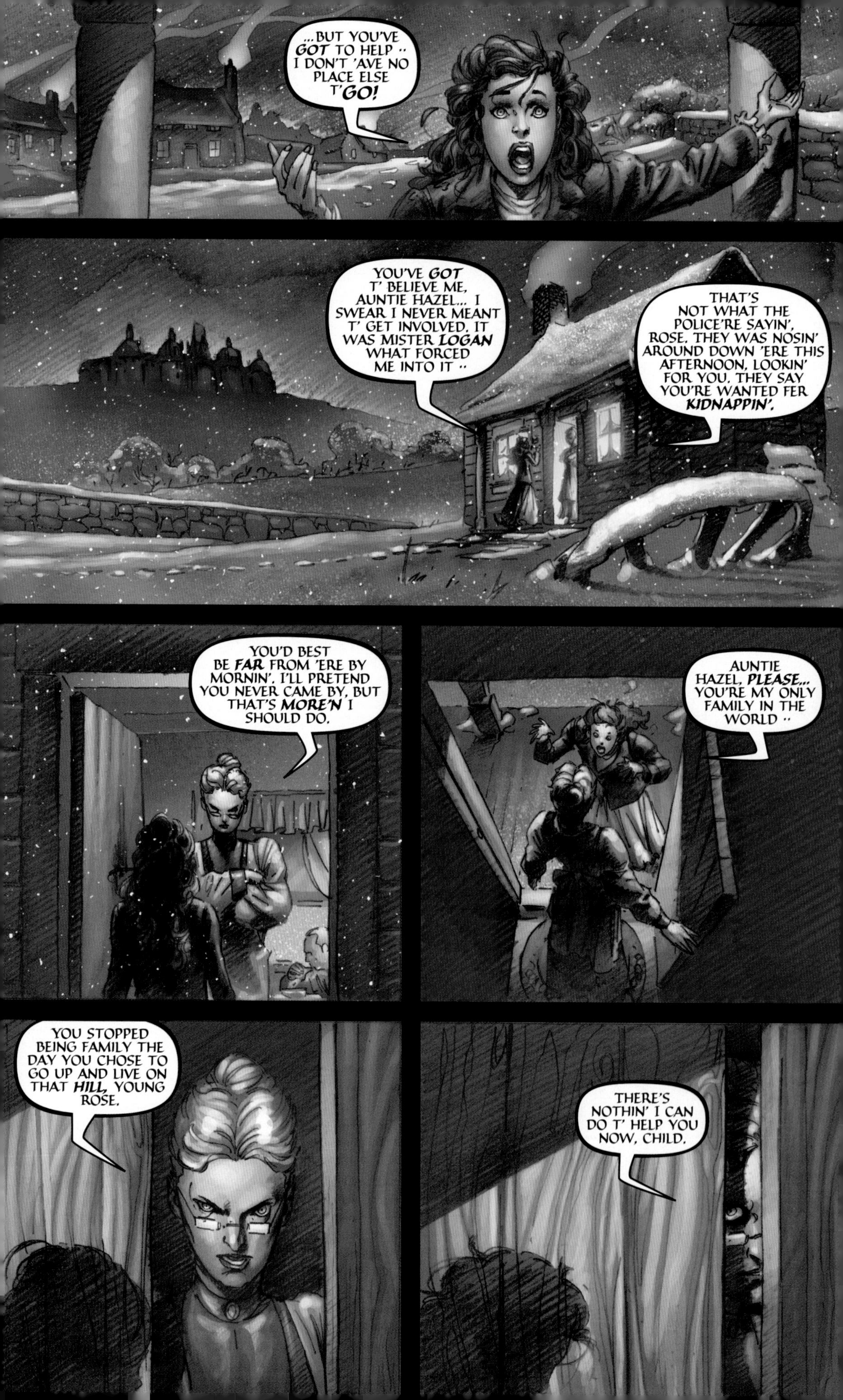
...BUT YOU'VE GOT TO HELP .. I DON'T 'AVE NO PLACE ELSE T'GO!
YOU'VE GOT T' BELIEVE ME, AUNTIE HAZEL... I SWEAR I NEVER MEANT T' GET INVOLVED. IT WAS MISTER LOGAN WHAT FORCED ME INTO IT ..
THAT'S NOT WHAT THE POLICE'RE SAYIN', ROSE. THEY WAS NOSIN' AROUND DOWN 'ERE THIS AFTERNOON, LOOKIN' FOR YOU. THEY SAY YOU'RE WANTED FER KIDNAPPIN'.
YOU'D BEST BE FAR FROM 'ERE BY MORNIN'. I'LL PRETEND YOU NEVER CAME BY, BUT THAT'S MORE'N I SHOULD DO.
AUNTIE HAZEL, PLEASE... YOU'RE MY ONLY FAMILY IN THE WORLD ..
YOU STOPPED BEING FAMILY THE DAY YOU CHOSE TO GO UP AND LIVE ON THAT HILL, YOUNG ROSE.
THERE'S NOTHIN' I CAN DO T' HELP YOU NOW, CHILD.

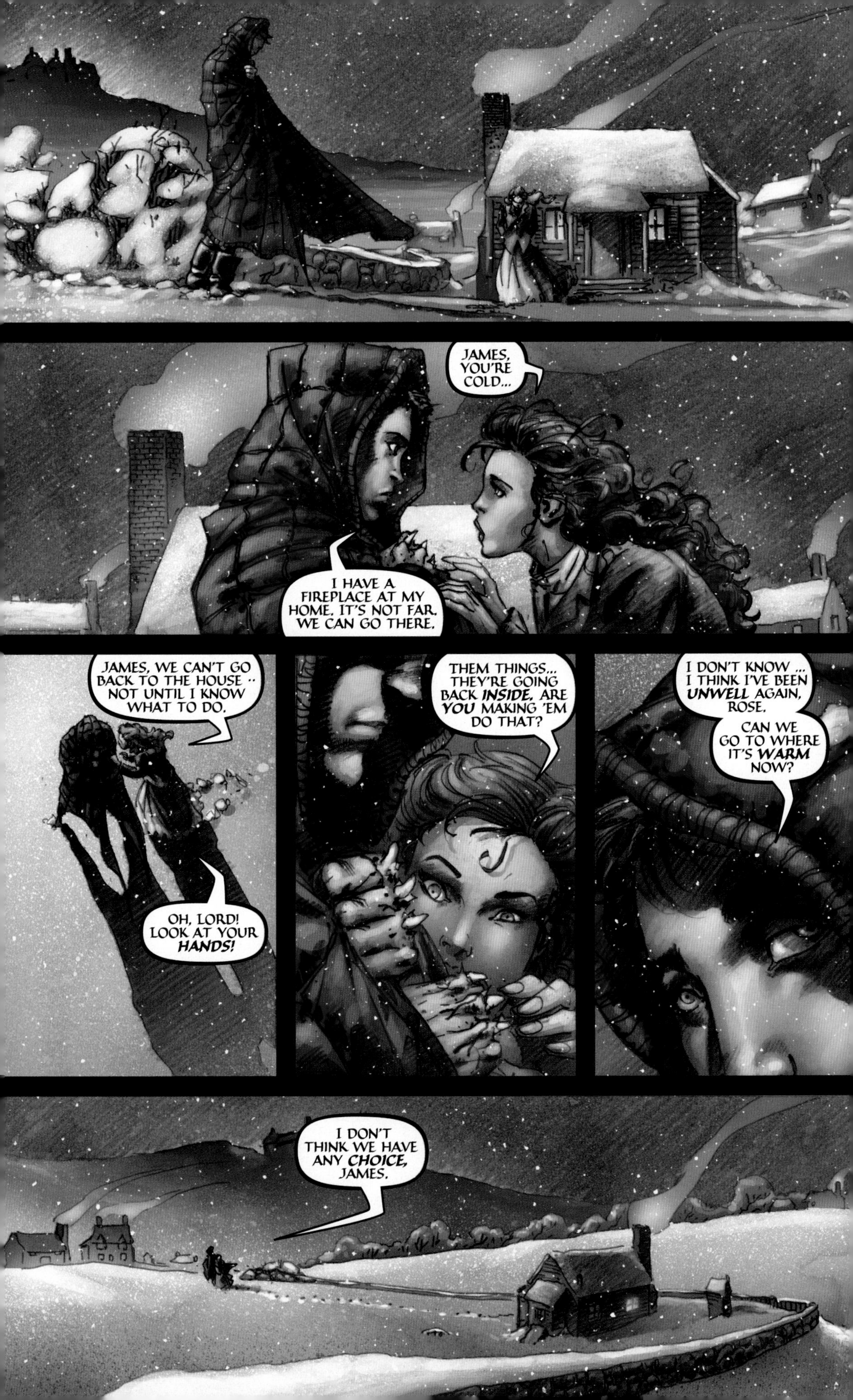
JAMES, YOU'RE COLD...
I HAVE A FIREPLACE AT MY HOME. IT'S NOT FAR. WE CAN GO THERE.
JAMES, WE CAN'T GO BACK TO THE HOUSE -- NOT UNTIL I KNOW WHAT TO DO.
OH, LORD! LOOK AT YOUR *HANDS!*
THEM THINGS... THEY'RE GOING BACK *INSIDE.* ARE *YOU* MAKING 'EM DO THAT?
I DON'T KNOW ... I THINK I'VE BEEN *UNWELL* AGAIN, ROSE.
CAN WE GO TO WHERE IT'S *WARM* NOW?
I DON'T THINK WE HAVE ANY *CHOICE,* JAMES.

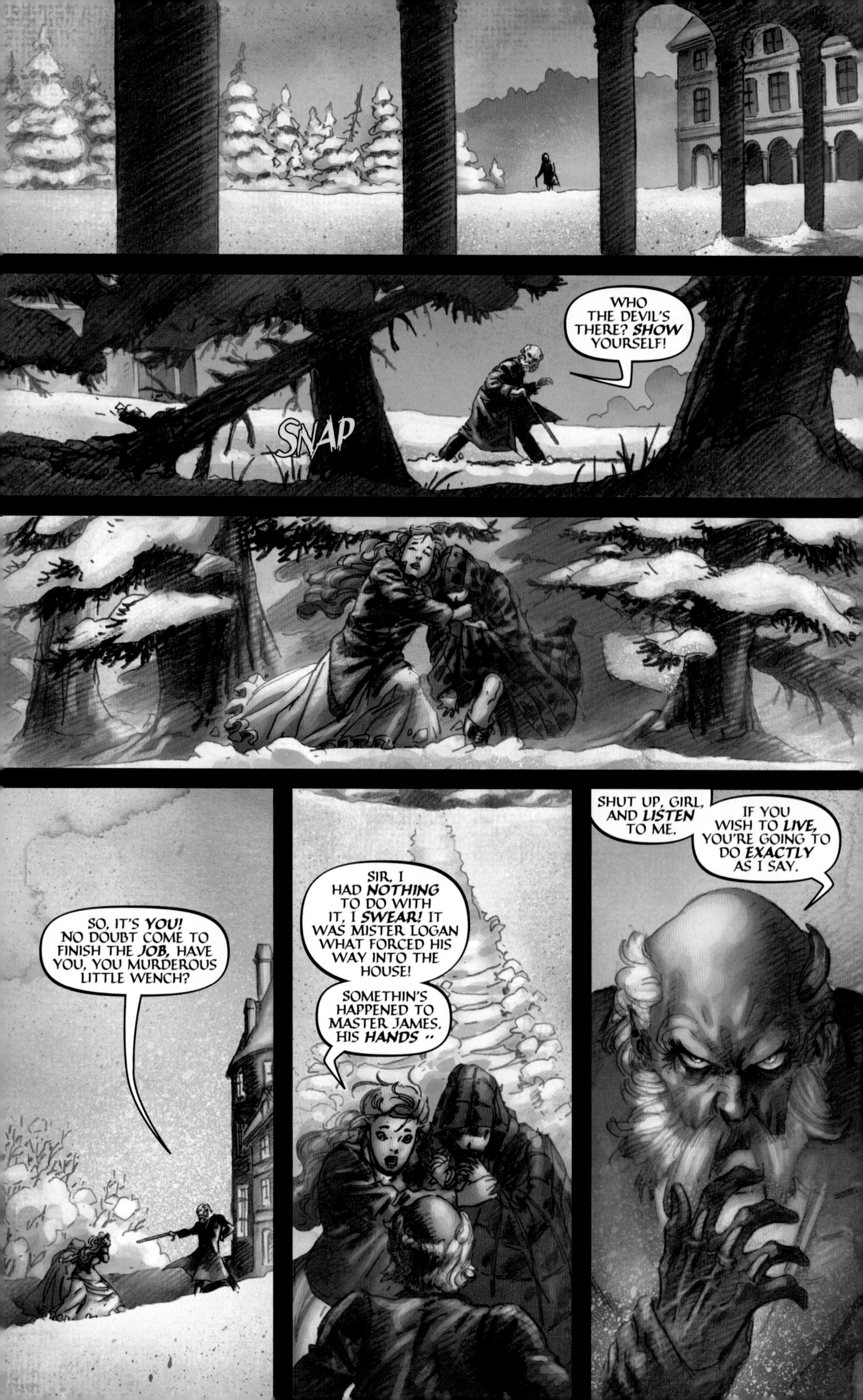
WHO THE DEVIL'S THERE? SHOW YOURSELF!
SNAP
SO, IT'S YOU! NO DOUBT COME TO FINISH THE JOB, HAVE YOU, YOU MURDEROUS LITTLE WENCH?
SIR, I HAD NOTHING TO DO WITH IT, I SWEAR! IT WAS MISTER LOGAN WHAT FORCED HIS WAY INTO THE HOUSE!
SOMETHIN'S HAPPENED TO MASTER JAMES, HIS HANDS ..
SHUT UP, GIRL, AND LISTEN TO ME.
IF YOU WISH TO LIVE, YOU'RE GOING TO DO EXACTLY AS I SAY.

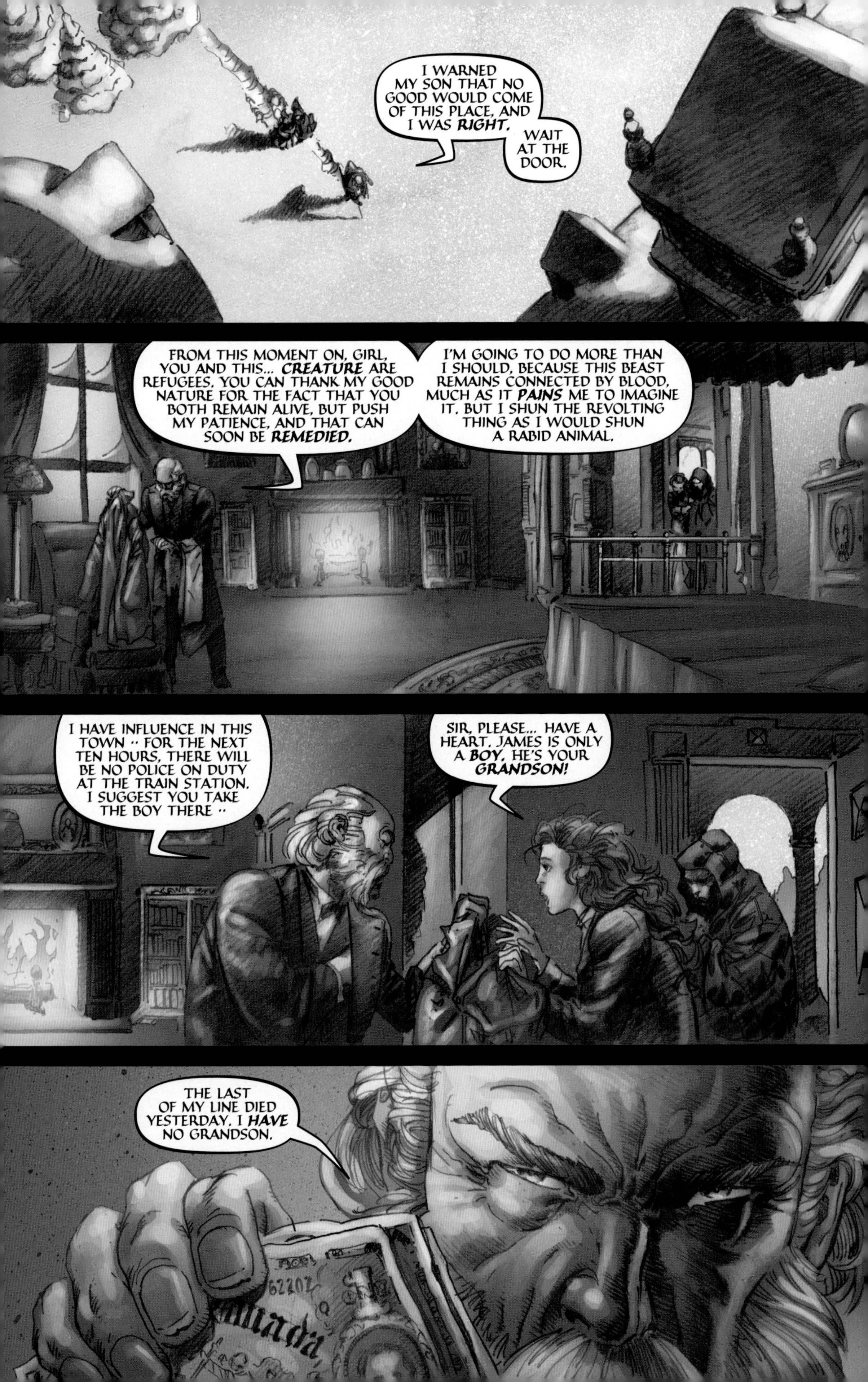
I WARNED MY SON THAT NO GOOD WOULD COME OF THIS PLACE, AND I WAS RIGHT.
WAIT AT THE DOOR.
FROM THIS MOMENT ON, GIRL, YOU AND THIS... CREATURE ARE REFUGEES. YOU CAN THANK MY GOOD NATURE FOR THE FACT THAT YOU BOTH REMAIN ALIVE, BUT PUSH MY PATIENCE, AND THAT CAN SOON BE REMEDIED.
I'M GOING TO DO MORE THAN I SHOULD, BECAUSE THIS BEAST REMAINS CONNECTED BY BLOOD, MUCH AS IT PAINS ME TO IMAGINE IT. BUT I SHUN THE REVOLTING THING AS I WOULD SHUN A RABID ANIMAL.
I HAVE INFLUENCE IN THIS TOWN -- FOR THE NEXT TEN HOURS, THERE WILL BE NO POLICE ON DUTY AT THE TRAIN STATION. I SUGGEST YOU TAKE THE BOY THERE --
SIR, PLEASE... HAVE A HEART. JAMES IS ONLY A BOY. HE'S YOUR GRANDSON!
THE LAST OF MY LINE DIED YESTERDAY. I HAVE NO GRANDSON.

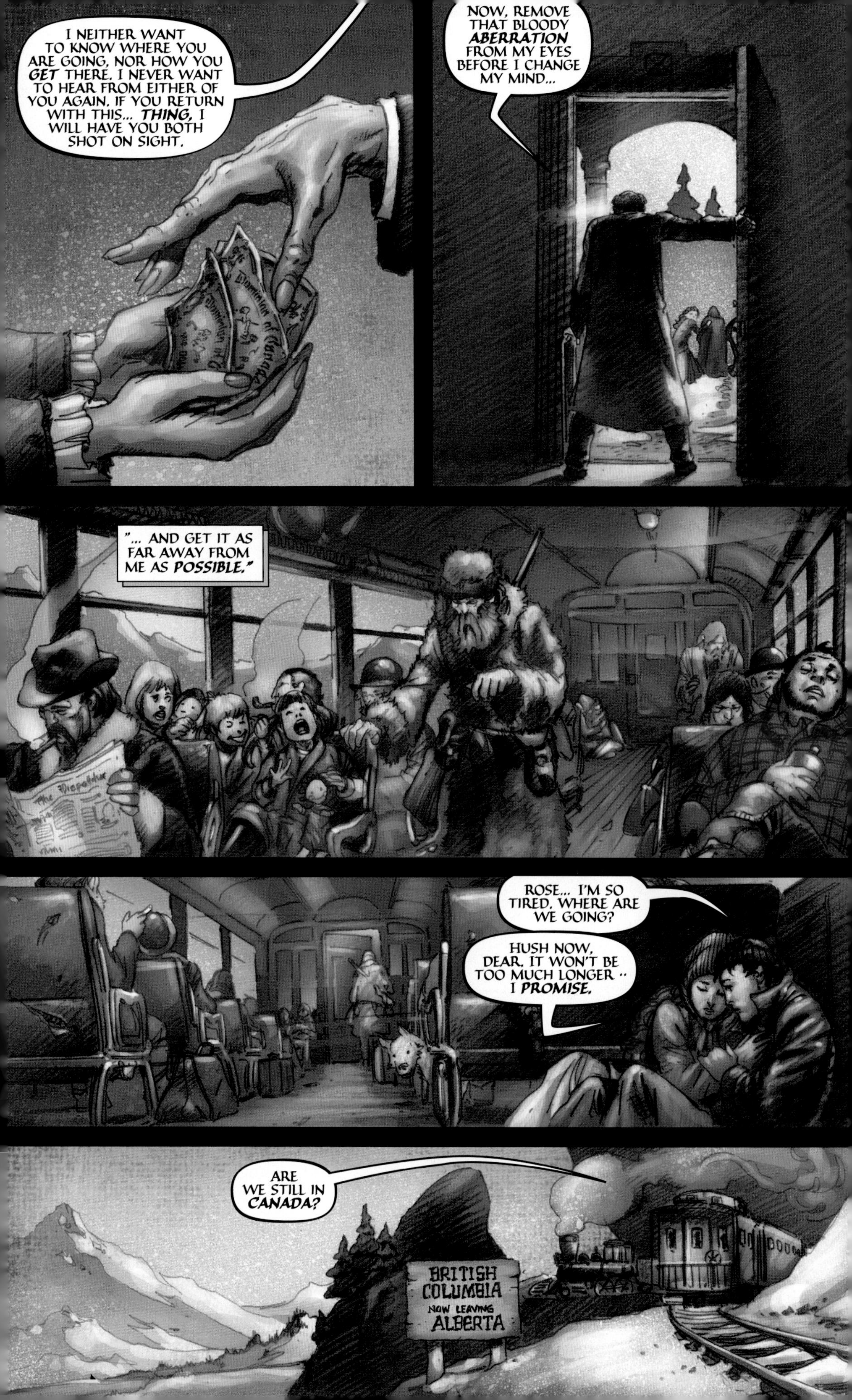
I NEITHER WANT TO KNOW WHERE YOU ARE GOING, NOR HOW YOU GET THERE. I NEVER WANT TO HEAR FROM EITHER OF YOU AGAIN. IF YOU RETURN WITH THIS... THING, I WILL HAVE YOU BOTH SHOT ON SIGHT.
NOW, REMOVE THAT BLOODY ABERRATION FROM MY EYES BEFORE I CHANGE MY MIND...
"... AND GET IT AS FAR AWAY FROM ME AS POSSIBLE."
ROSE... I'M SO TIRED. WHERE ARE WE GOING?
HUSH NOW, DEAR. IT WON'T BE TOO MUCH LONGER .. I PROMISE.
ARE WE STILL IN CANADA?
BRITISH COLUMBIA
NOW LEAVING
ALBERTA

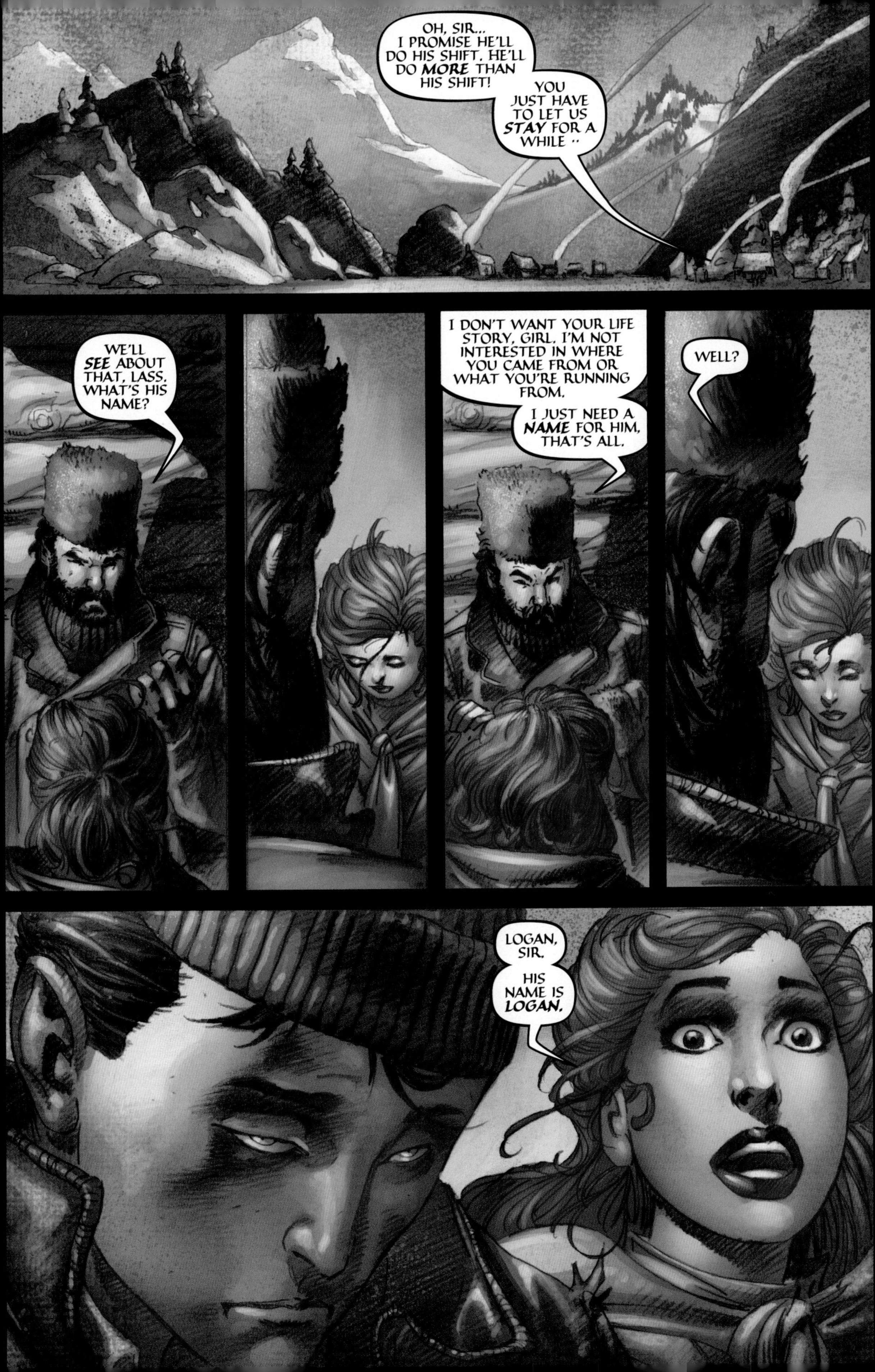
OH, SIR... I PROMISE HE'LL DO HIS SHIFT. HE'LL DO MORE THAN HIS SHIFT!
YOU JUST HAVE TO LET US STAY FOR A WHILE ..
WE'LL SEE ABOUT THAT, LASS. WHAT'S HIS NAME?
I DON'T WANT YOUR LIFE STORY, GIRL. I'M NOT INTERESTED IN WHERE YOU CAME FROM OR WHAT YOU'RE RUNNING FROM.
I JUST NEED A NAME FOR HIM, THAT'S ALL.
WELL?
LOGAN, SIR.
HIS NAME IS LOGAN.

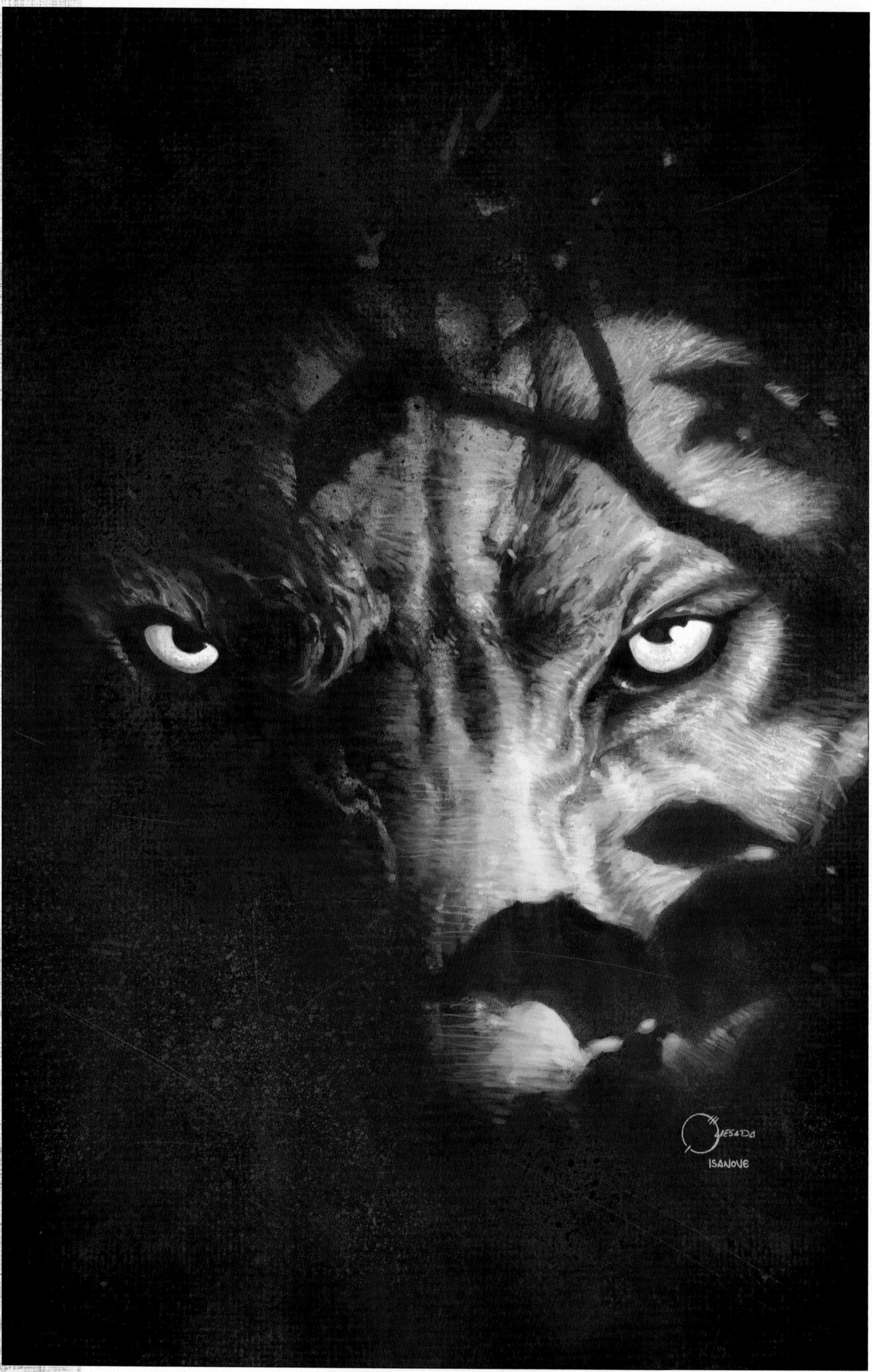
ISANOVE

PART IV – **HEAVEN AND HELL**

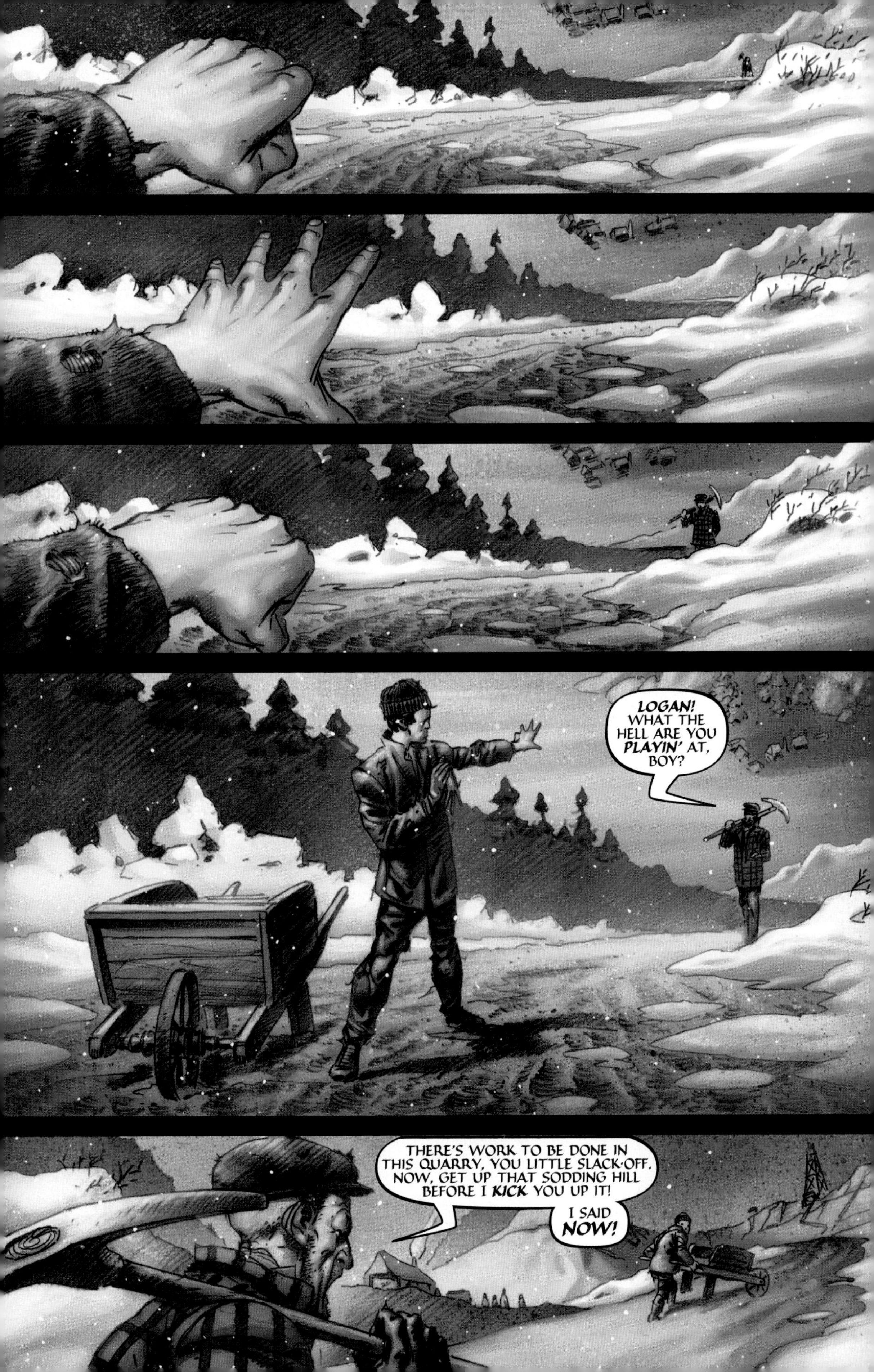
LOGAN! WHAT THE HELL ARE YOU PLAYIN' AT, BOY?
THERE'S WORK TO BE DONE IN THIS QUARRY, YOU LITTLE SLACK-OFF. NOW, GET UP THAT SODDING HILL BEFORE I KICK YOU UP IT!
I SAID NOW!

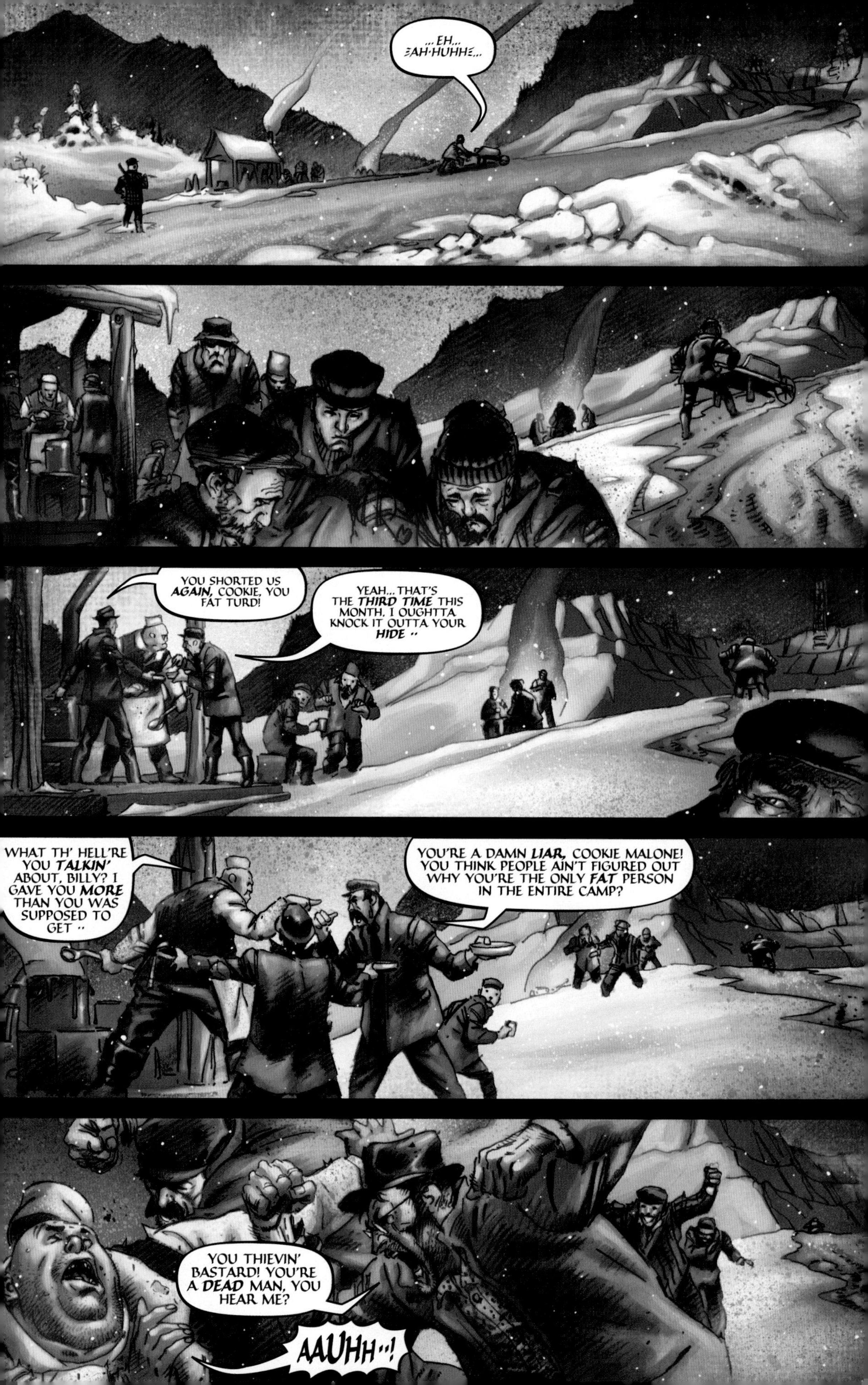

...EH... ƎAH·HUHHƎ...
YOU SHORTED US AGAIN, COOKIE, YOU FAT TURD!
YEAH... THAT'S THE THIRD TIME THIS MONTH. I OUGHTTA KNOCK IT OUTTA YOUR HIDE --
WHAT TH' HELL'RE YOU TALKIN' ABOUT, BILLY? I GAVE YOU MORE THAN YOU WAS SUPPOSED TO GET --
YOU'RE A DAMN LIAR, COOKIE MALONE! YOU THINK PEOPLE AIN'T FIGURED OUT WHY YOU'RE THE ONLY FAT PERSON IN THE ENTIRE CAMP?
YOU THIEVIN' BASTARD! YOU'RE A DEAD MAN, YOU HEAR ME?
AAUHH--!

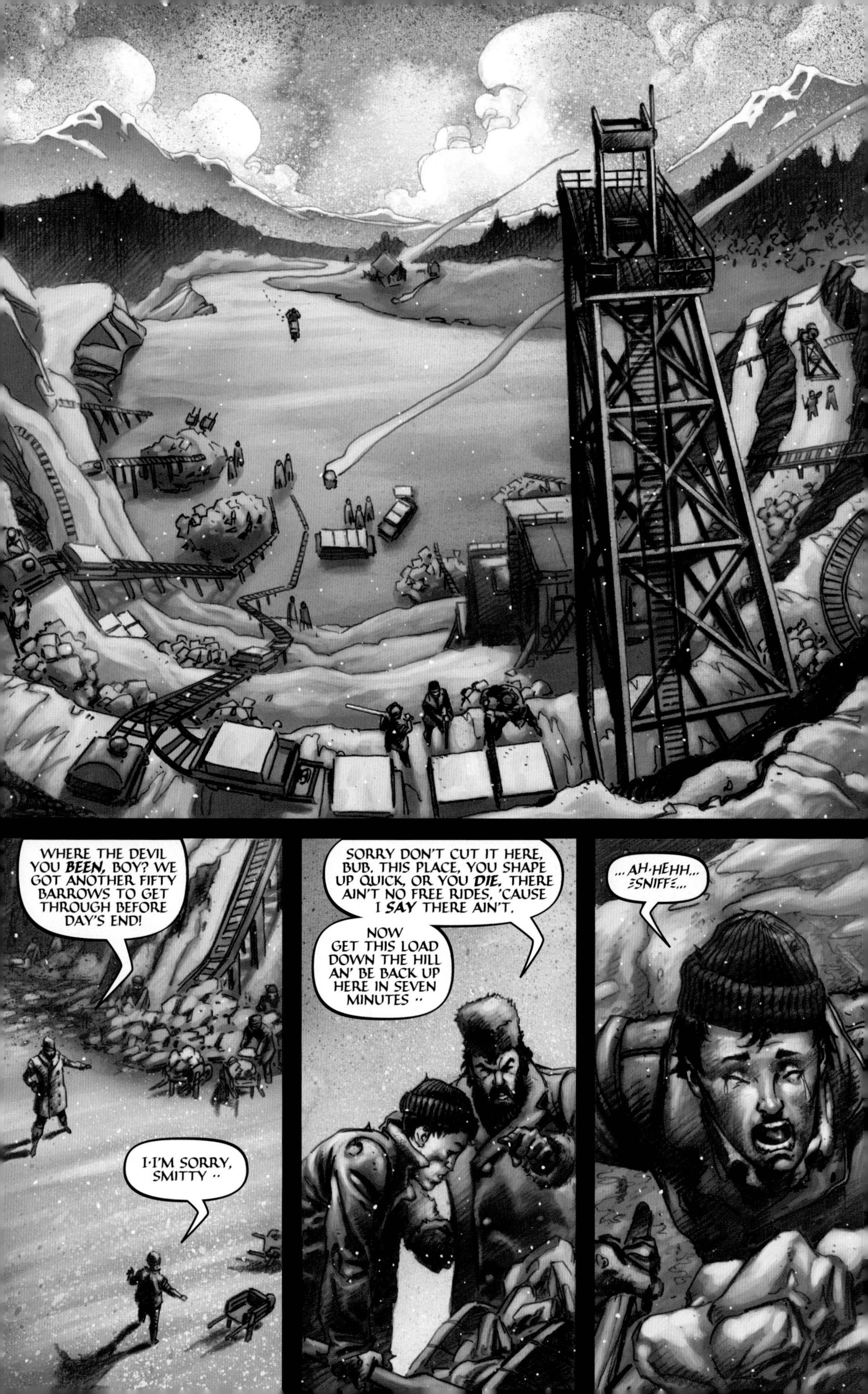
WHERE THE DEVIL YOU ***BEEN,*** BOY? WE GOT ANOTHER FIFTY BARROWS TO GET THROUGH BEFORE DAY'S END!
I-I'M SORRY, SMITTY ..
SORRY DON'T CUT IT HERE, BUB. THIS PLACE, YOU SHAPE UP QUICK, OR YOU ***DIE.*** THERE AIN'T NO FREE RIDES, 'CAUSE I ***SAY*** THERE AIN'T.
NOW GET THIS LOAD DOWN THE HILL AN' BE BACK UP HERE IN SEVEN MINUTES ..
... AH-HEHH... ≈SNIFF≈...

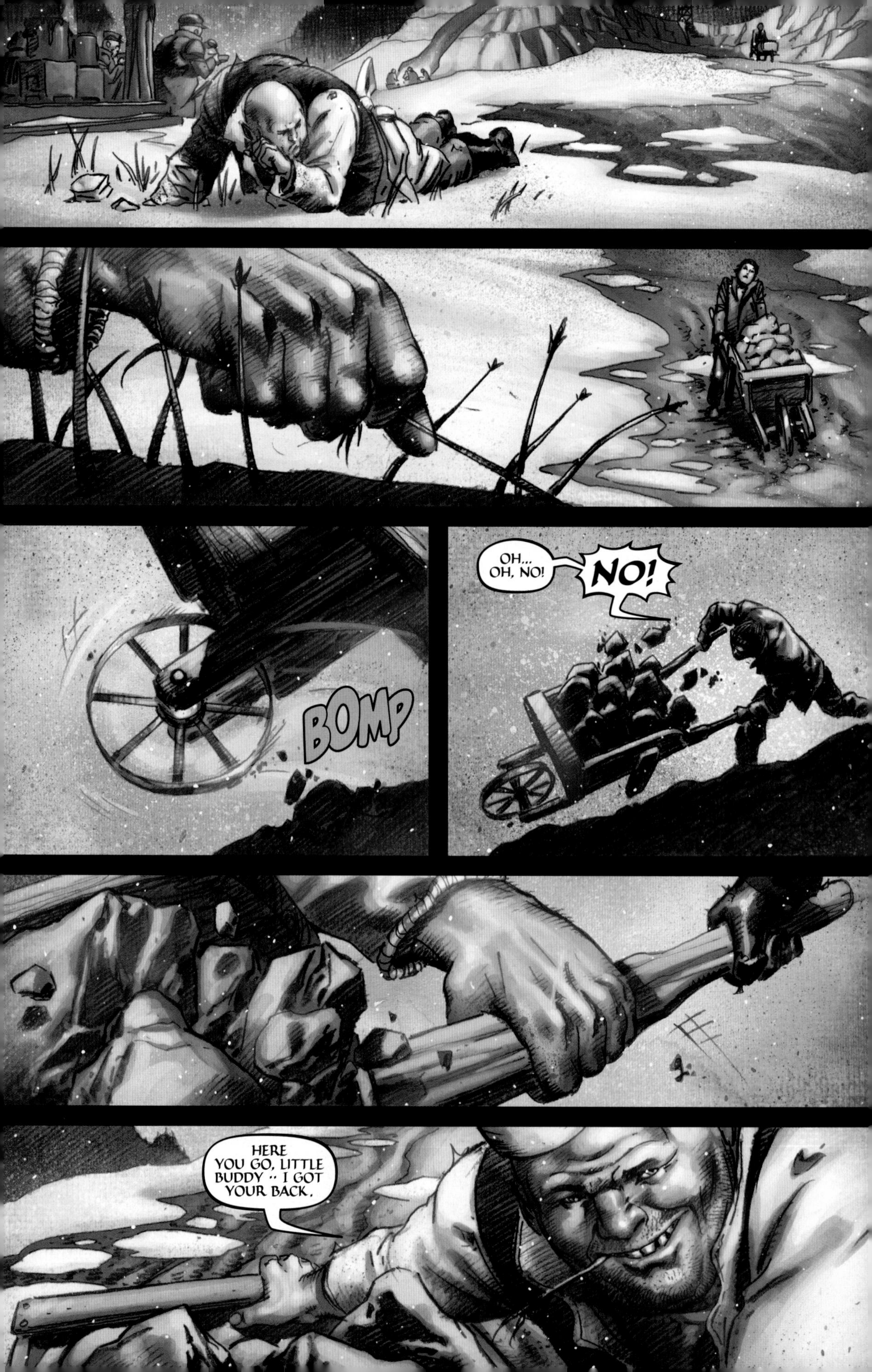
BOMP
OH... OH, NO!
NO!
HERE YOU GO, LITTLE BUDDY .. I GOT YOUR BACK.

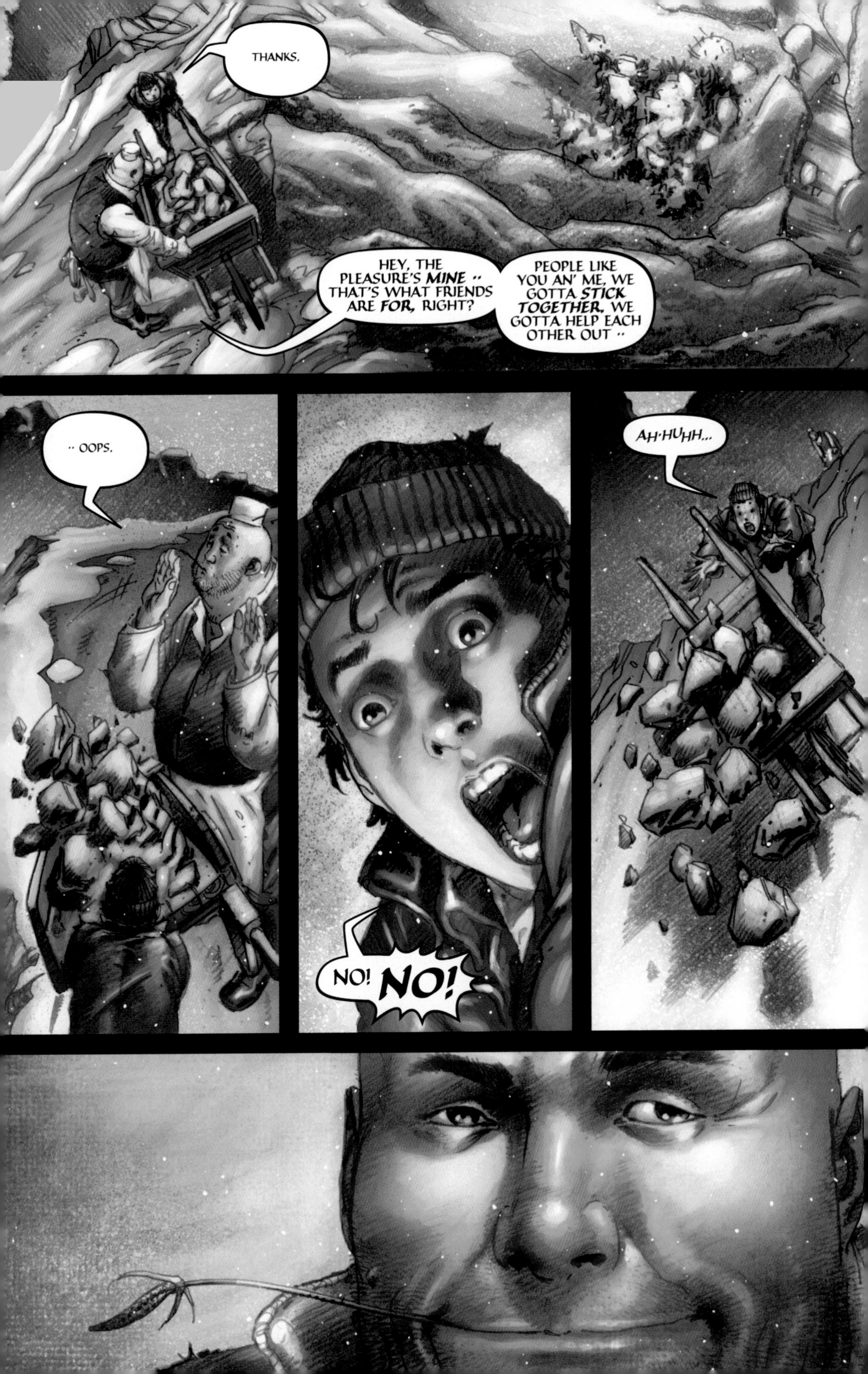
THANKS.
HEY, THE PLEASURE'S MINE .. THAT'S WHAT FRIENDS ARE FOR, RIGHT?
PEOPLE LIKE YOU AN' ME, WE GOTTA STICK TOGETHER, WE GOTTA HELP EACH OTHER OUT ..
.. OOPS.
NO! NO!
AH-HUHH...

SLAM

JAMES ··?

JAMES, ARE YOU ALL RIGHT? WHAT'S HAPPENED?

NOTHING.

Oh, JAMES... I'M SO SORRY FOR BRINGING YOU HERE ·· I JUST DIDN'T KNOW WHERE ELSE TO GO.

BUT WE HAVE TO BE *CAREFUL* FOR A WHILE, OKAY? WE HAVE TO MAKE SURE NO ONE KNOWS WHO WE ARE... WE CAN'T GET INVOLVED.

YOU CAN TELL ME WHAT IT IS, JAMES ·· I *PROMISE.*

IS THERE SOMETHING YOU WANT TO SAY?

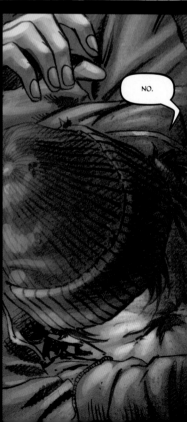

NO.

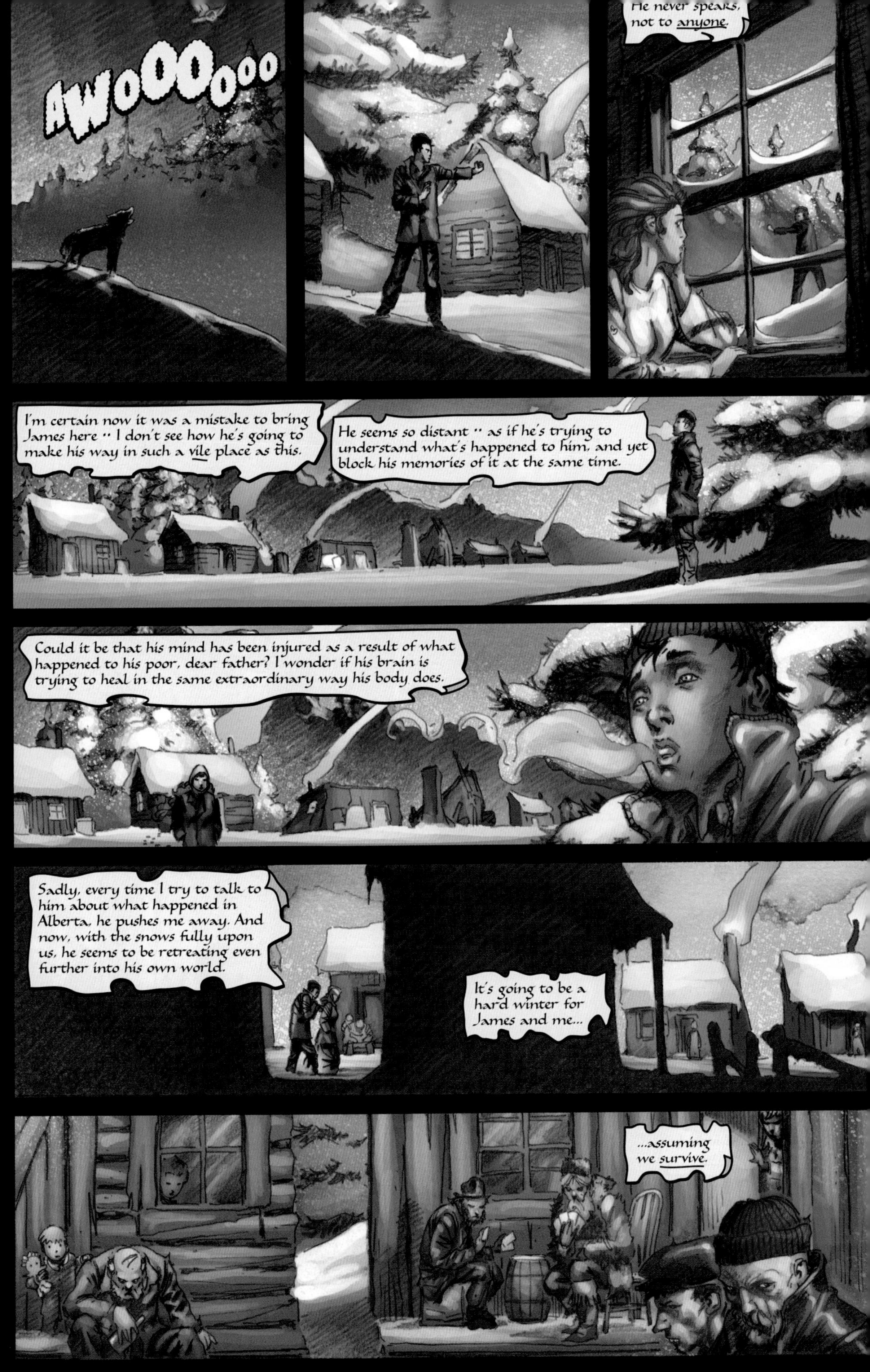
AWOOOooo
He never speaks, not to anyone.
I'm certain now it was a mistake to bring James here -- I don't see how he's going to make his way in such a vile place as this.
He seems so distant -- as if he's trying to understand what's happened to him, and yet block his memories of it at the same time.
Could it be that his mind has been injured as a result of what happened to his poor, dear father? I wonder if his brain is trying to heal in the same extraordinary way his body does.
Sadly, every time I try to talk to him about what happened in Alberta, he pushes me away. And now, with the snows fully upon us, he seems to be retreating even further into his own world.
It's going to be a hard winter for James and me...
...assuming we survive.

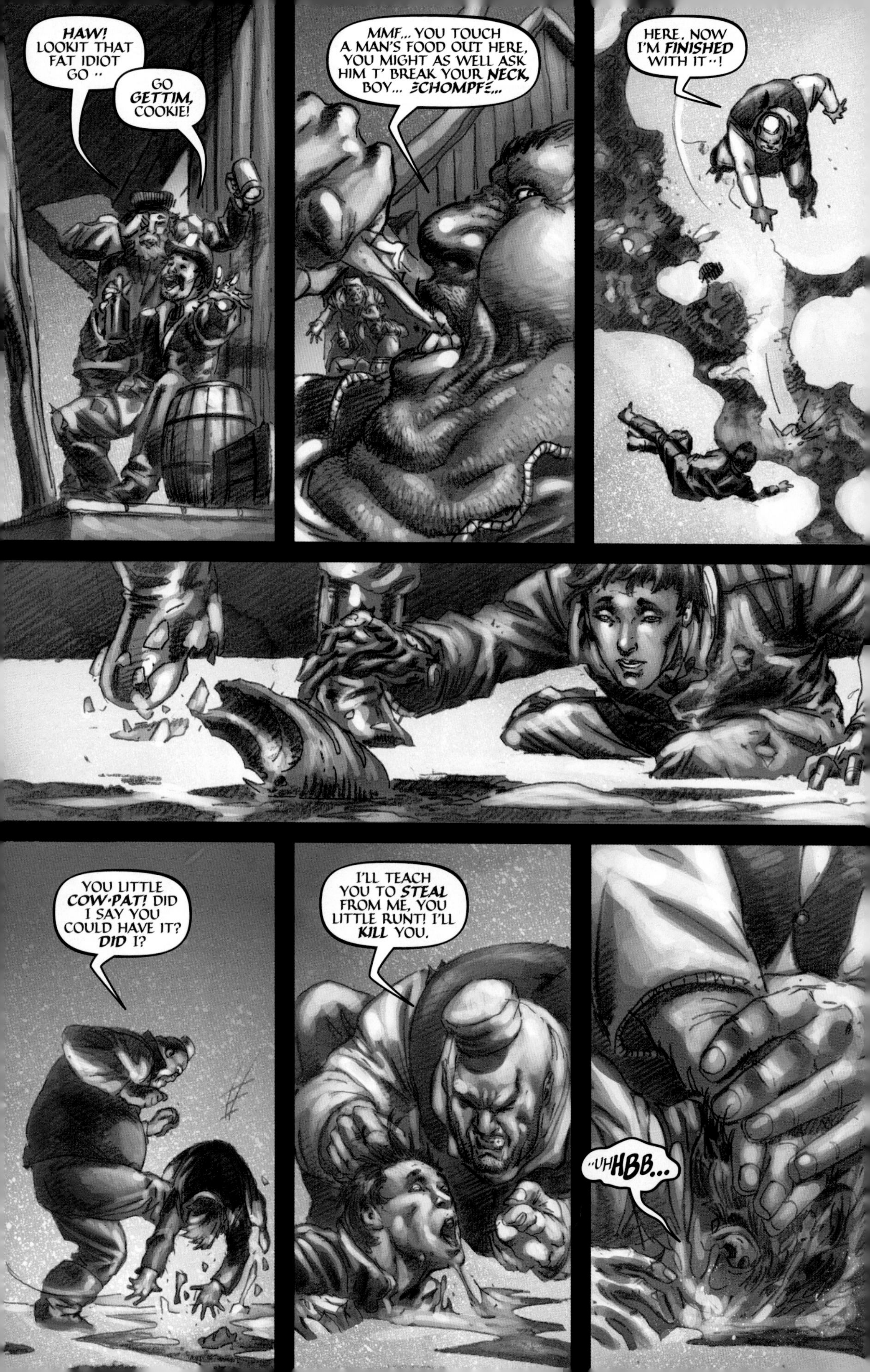
HAW! LOOKIT THAT FAT IDIOT GO ..
GO GETTIM, COOKIE!
MMF... YOU TOUCH A MAN'S FOOD OUT HERE, YOU MIGHT AS WELL ASK HIM T' BREAK YOUR NECK, BOY... CHOMPF...
HERE. NOW I'M FINISHED WITH IT ..!
YOU LITTLE COW-PAT! DID I SAY YOU COULD HAVE IT? DID I?
I'LL TEACH YOU TO STEAL FROM ME, YOU LITTLE RUNT! I'LL KILL YOU.
..UHHBB...

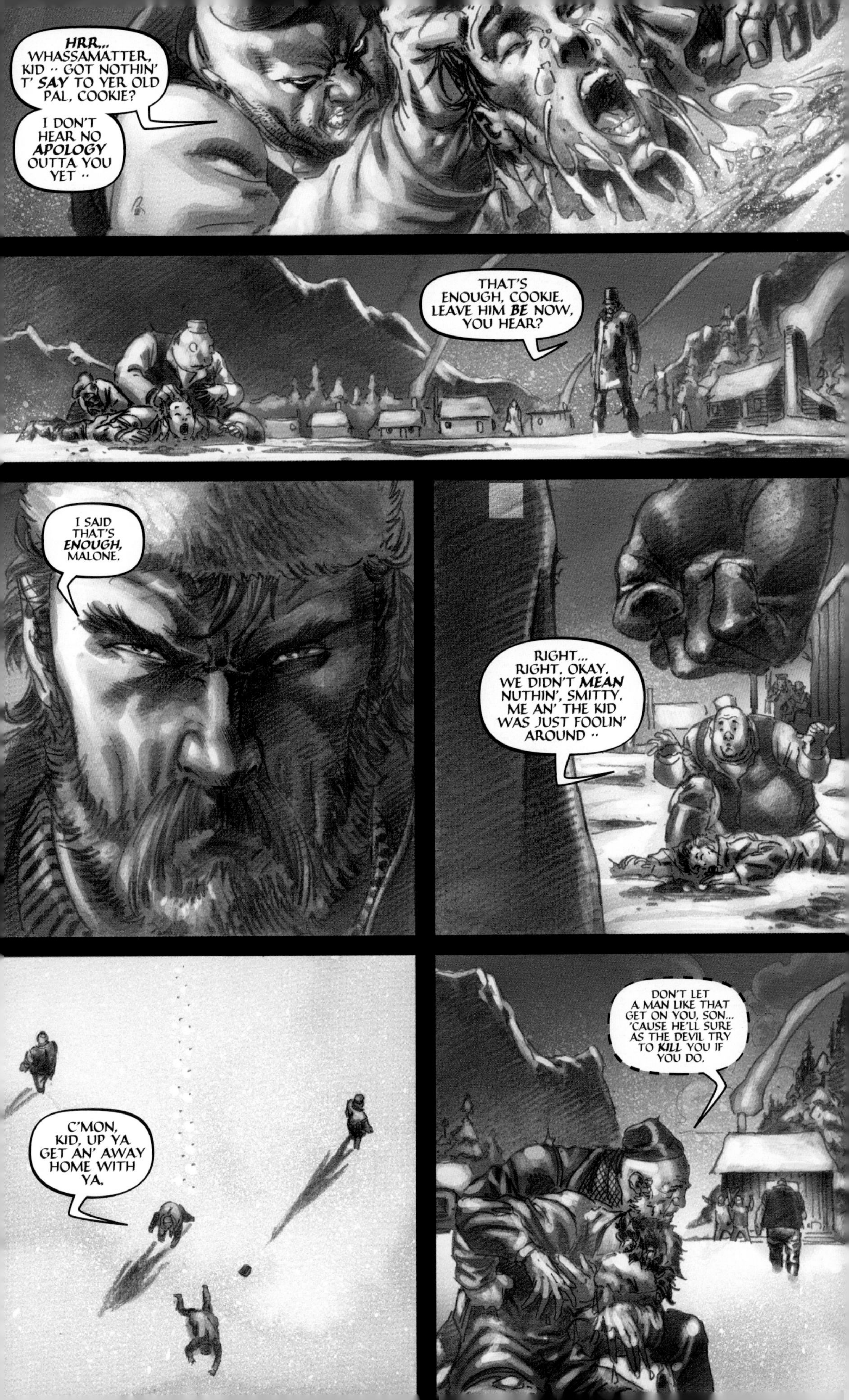
HRR... WHASSAMATTER, KID .. GOT NOTHIN' T' SAY TO YER OLD PAL, COOKIE?
I DON'T HEAR NO APOLOGY OUTTA YOU YET ..
THAT'S ENOUGH, COOKIE. LEAVE HIM BE NOW, YOU HEAR?
I SAID THAT'S ENOUGH, MALONE.
RIGHT... RIGHT. OKAY. WE DIDN'T MEAN NUTHIN', SMITTY. ME AN' THE KID WAS JUST FOOLIN' AROUND ..
C'MON, KID, UP YA GET AN' AWAY HOME WITH YA.
DON'T LET A MAN LIKE THAT GET ON YOU, SON... 'CAUSE HE'LL SURE AS THE DEVIL TRY TO KILL YOU IF YOU DO.

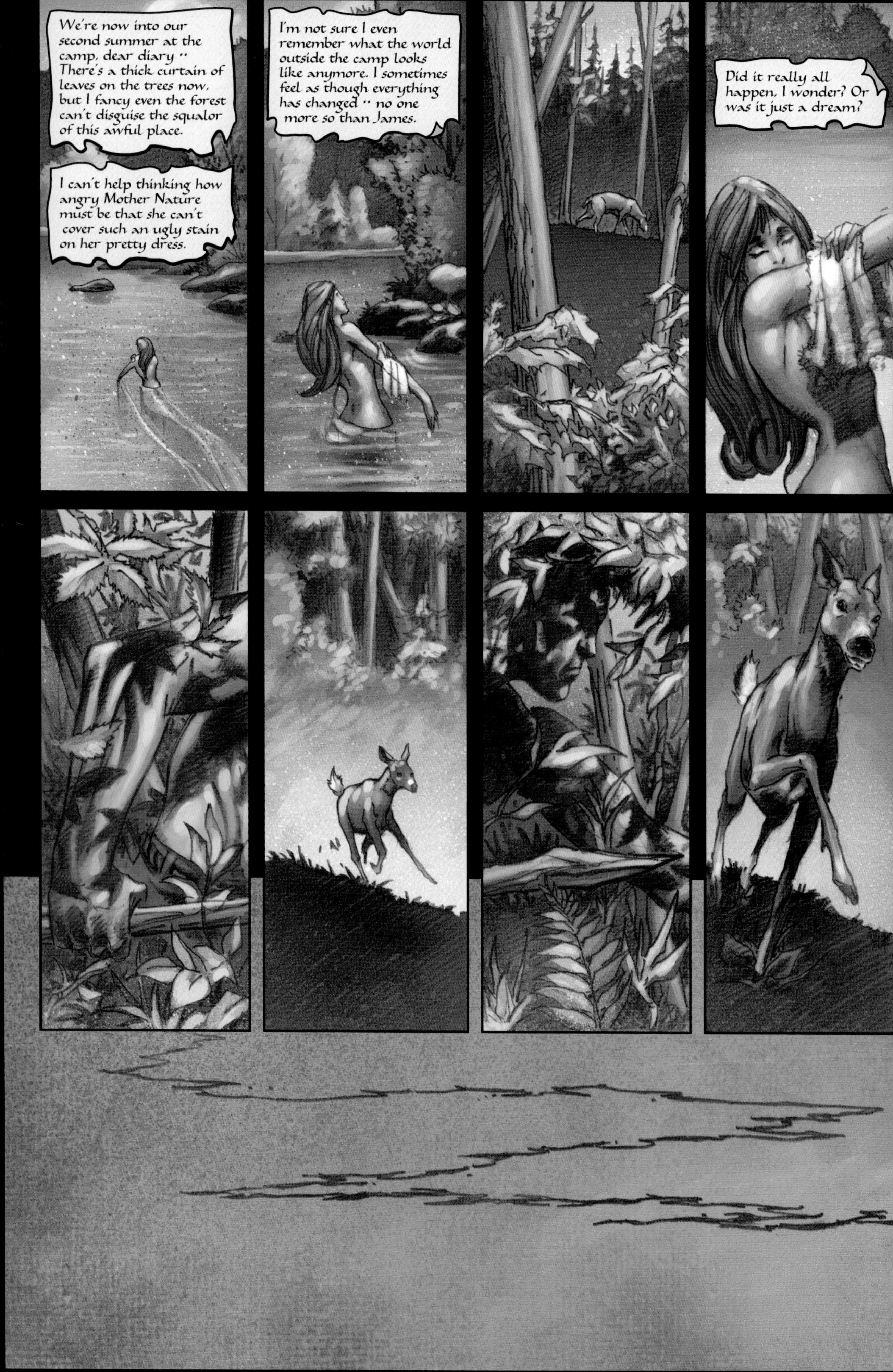
We're now into our second summer at the camp, dear diary -- There's a thick curtain of leaves on the trees now, but I fancy even the forest can't disguise the squalor of this awful place.
I can't help thinking how angry Mother Nature must be that she can't cover such an ugly stain on her pretty dress.
I'm not sure I even remember what the world outside the camp looks like anymore. I sometimes feel as though everything has changed -- no one more so than James.
Did it really all happen, I wonder? Or was it just a dream?

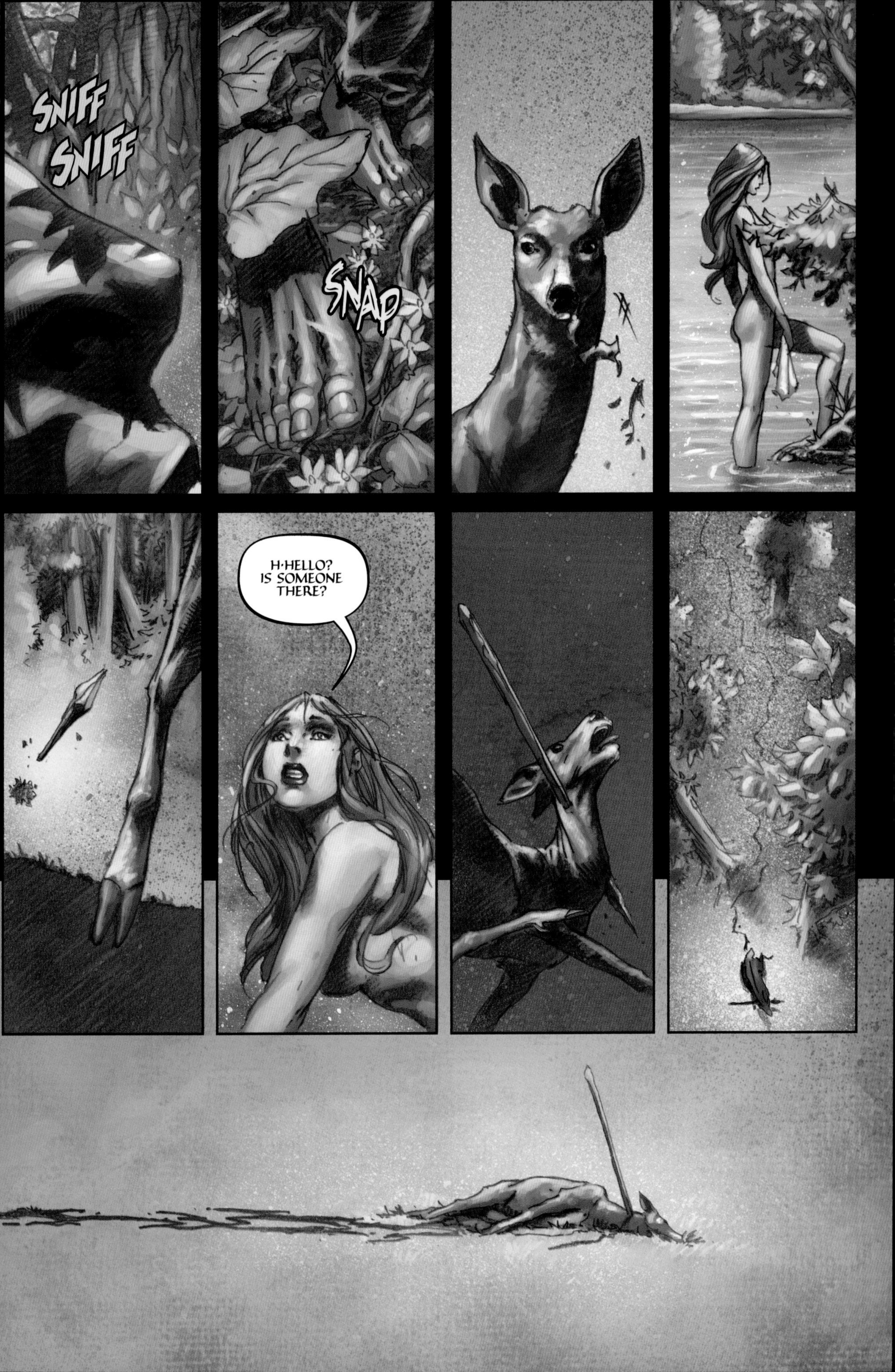
SNIFF
SNIFF
SNAP
H-HELLO? IS SOMEONE THERE?

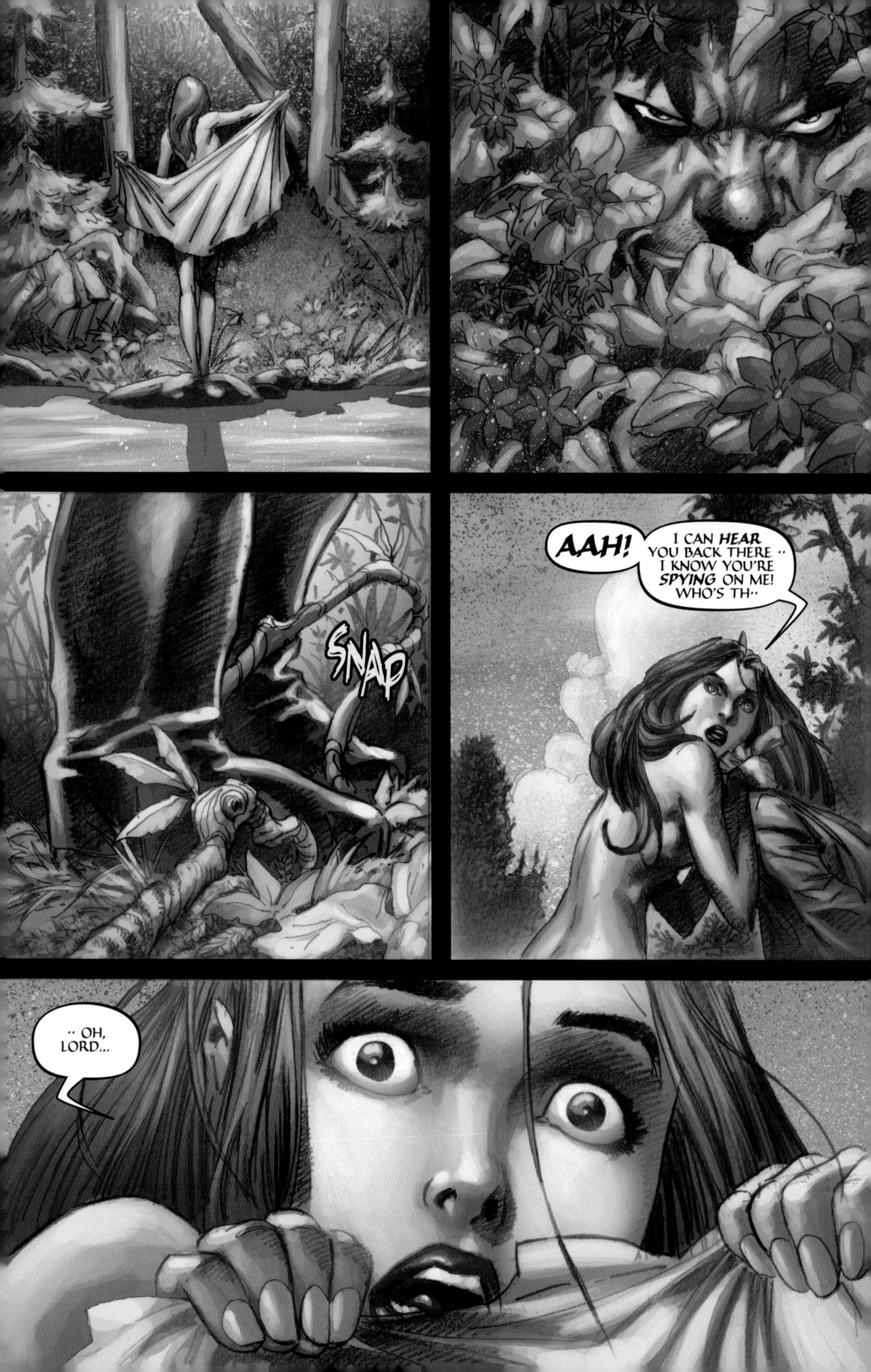
SNAP
AAH!
I CAN HEAR YOU BACK THERE .. I KNOW YOU'RE SPYING ON ME! WHO'S TH..
.. OH, LORD...

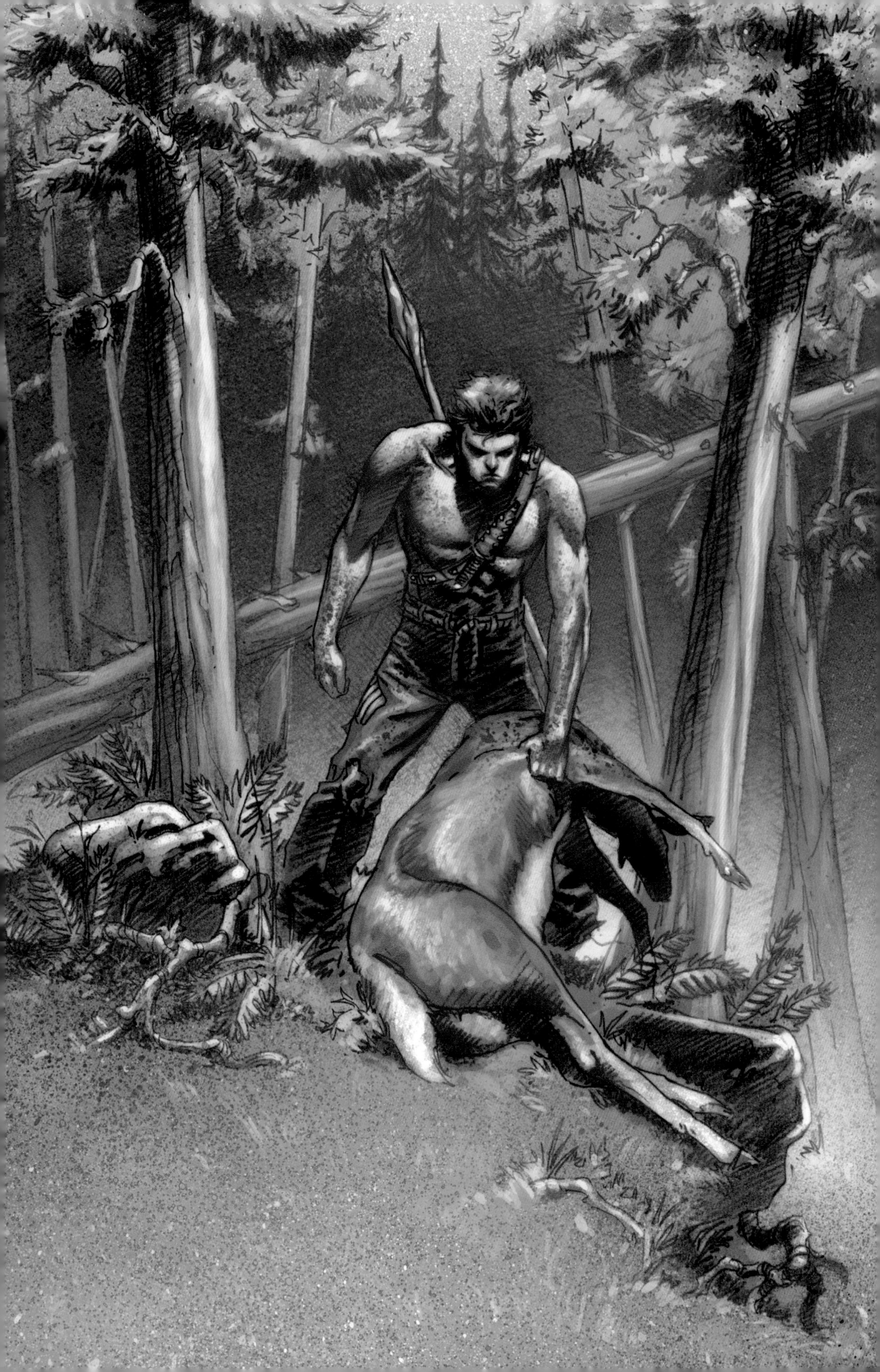

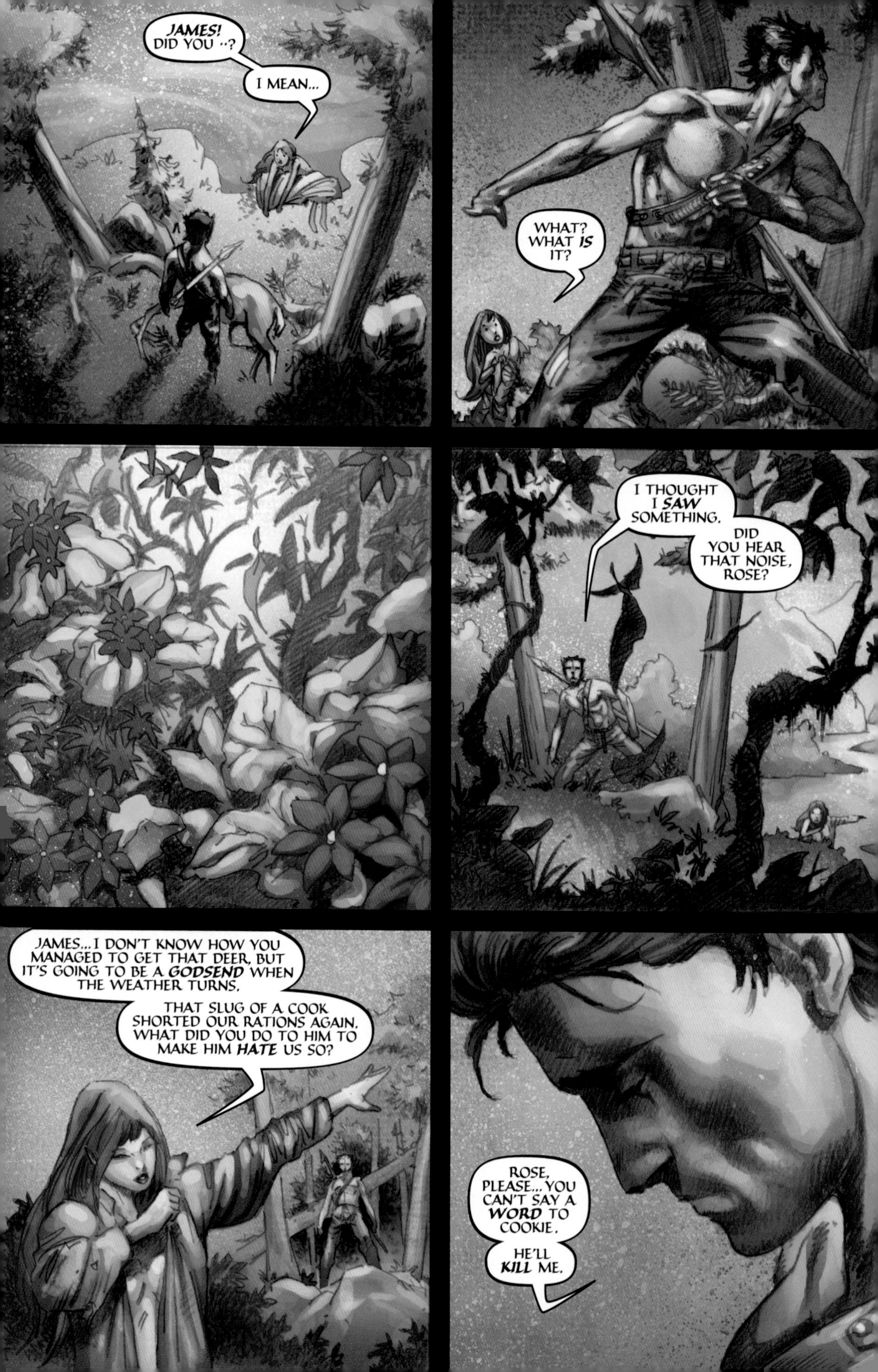
JAMES! DID YOU ··?
I MEAN...
WHAT? WHAT IS IT?
I THOUGHT I SAW SOMETHING.
DID YOU HEAR THAT NOISE, ROSE?
JAMES... I DON'T KNOW HOW YOU MANAGED TO GET THAT DEER, BUT IT'S GOING TO BE A GODSEND WHEN THE WEATHER TURNS.
THAT SLUG OF A COOK SHORTED OUR RATIONS AGAIN. WHAT DID YOU DO TO HIM TO MAKE HIM HATE US SO?
ROSE, PLEASE... YOU CAN'T SAY A WORD TO COOKIE.
HE'LL KILL ME.

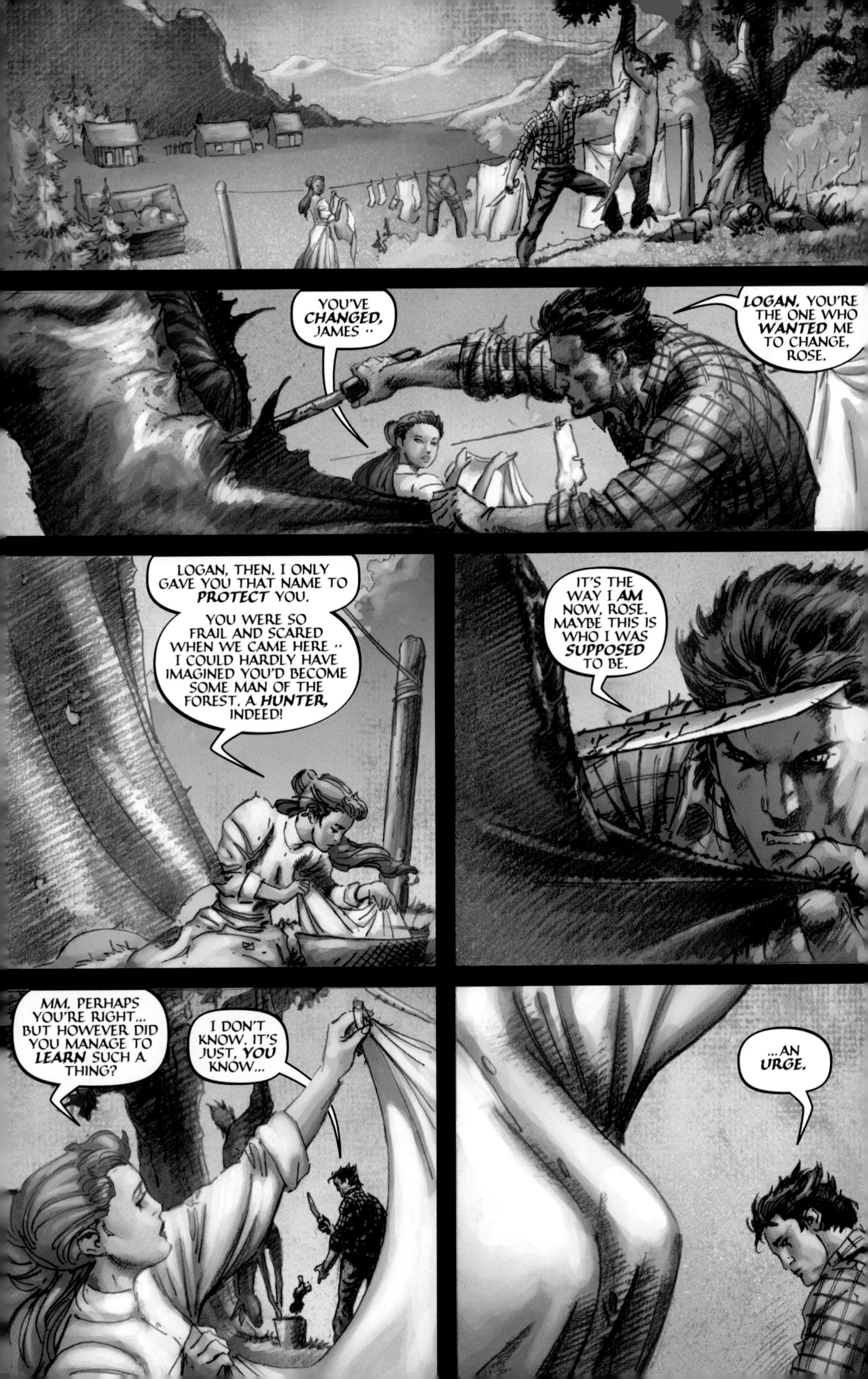

YOU'VE CHANGED, JAMES ..
LOGAN, YOU'RE THE ONE WHO WANTED ME TO CHANGE, ROSE.
LOGAN, THEN. I ONLY GAVE YOU THAT NAME TO PROTECT YOU.
YOU WERE SO FRAIL AND SCARED WHEN WE CAME HERE .. I COULD HARDLY HAVE IMAGINED YOU'D BECOME SOME MAN OF THE FOREST. A HUNTER, INDEED!
IT'S THE WAY I AM NOW, ROSE. MAYBE THIS IS WHO I WAS SUPPOSED TO BE.
MM. PERHAPS YOU'RE RIGHT... BUT HOWEVER DID YOU MANAGE TO LEARN SUCH A THING?
I DON'T KNOW. IT'S JUST, YOU KNOW...
...AN URGE.

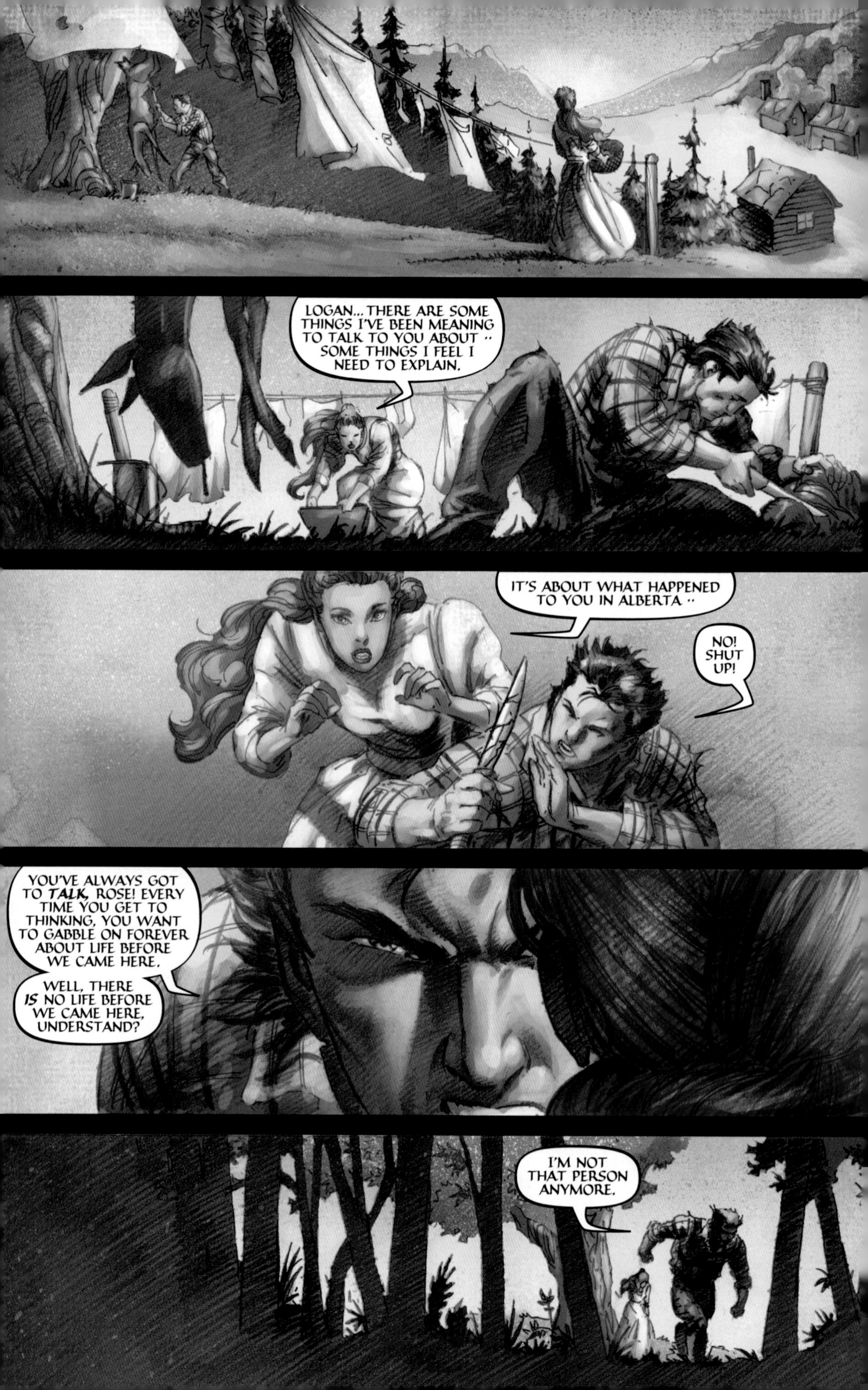
LOGAN... THERE ARE SOME THINGS I'VE BEEN MEANING TO TALK TO YOU ABOUT .. SOME THINGS I FEEL I NEED TO EXPLAIN.
IT'S ABOUT WHAT HAPPENED TO YOU IN ALBERTA ..
NO! SHUT UP!
YOU'VE ALWAYS GOT TO TALK, ROSE! EVERY TIME YOU GET TO THINKING, YOU WANT TO GABBLE ON FOREVER ABOUT LIFE BEFORE WE CAME HERE.
WELL, THERE IS NO LIFE BEFORE WE CAME HERE, UNDERSTAND?
I'M NOT THAT PERSON ANYMORE.

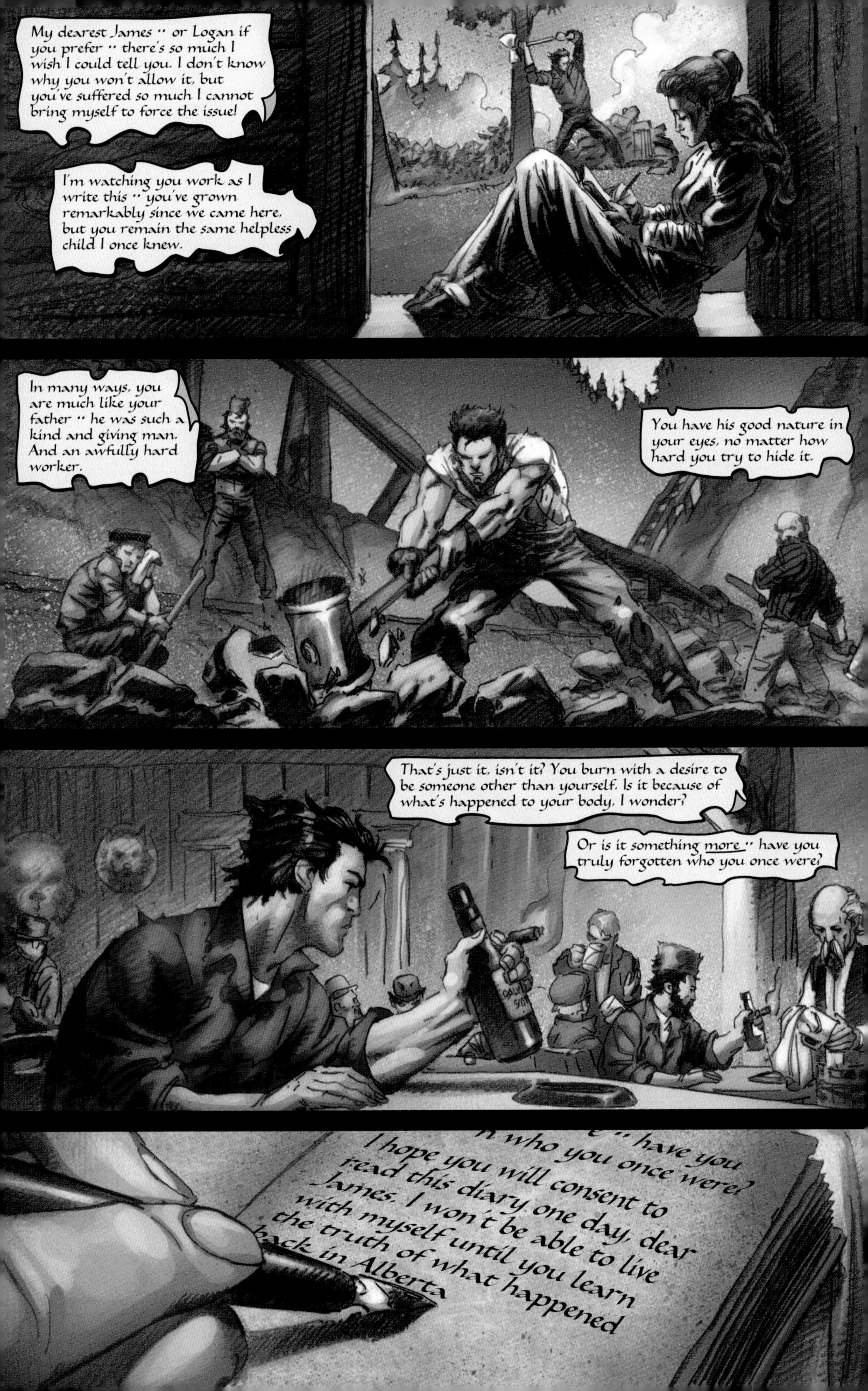
My dearest James -- or Logan if you prefer -- there's so much I wish I could tell you. I don't know why you won't allow it, but you've suffered so much I cannot bring myself to force the issue!
I'm watching you work as I write this -- you've grown remarkably since we came here, but you remain the same helpless child I once knew.
In many ways, you are much like your father -- he was such a kind and giving man. And an awfully hard worker.
You have his good nature in your eyes, no matter how hard you try to hide it.
That's just it, isn't it? You burn with a desire to be someone other than yourself. Is it because of what's happened to your body, I wonder?
Or is it something more -- have you truly forgotten who you once were?
have you
who you once were?
I hope you will consent to
read this diary one day, dear
James. I won't be able to live
with myself until you learn
the truth of what happened
back in Alberta

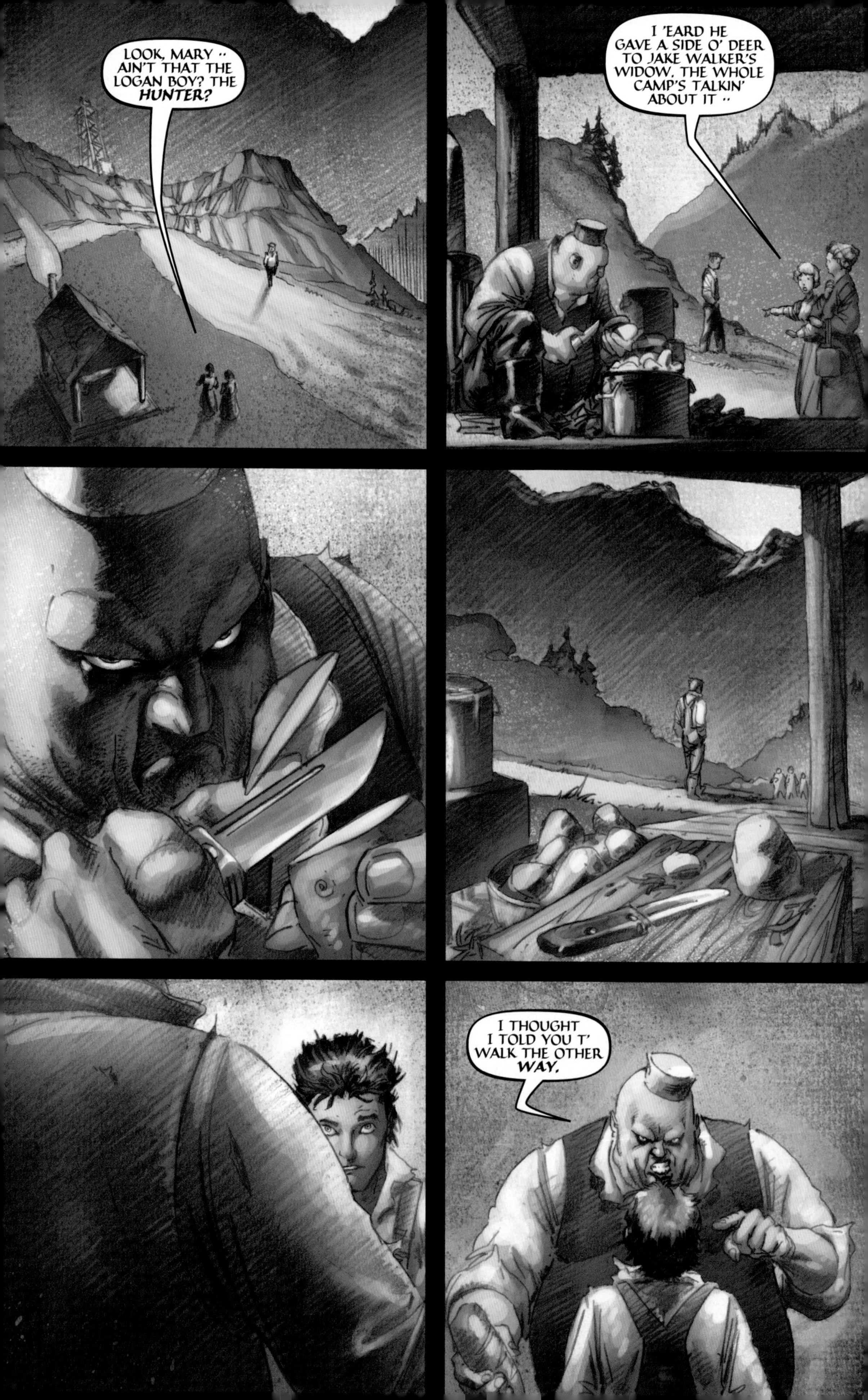
LOOK, MARY .. AIN'T THAT THE LOGAN BOY? THE *HUNTER?*
I 'EARD HE GAVE A SIDE O' DEER TO JAKE WALKER'S WIDOW. THE WHOLE CAMP'S TALKIN' ABOUT IT ..
I THOUGHT I TOLD YOU T' WALK THE OTHER *WAY.*

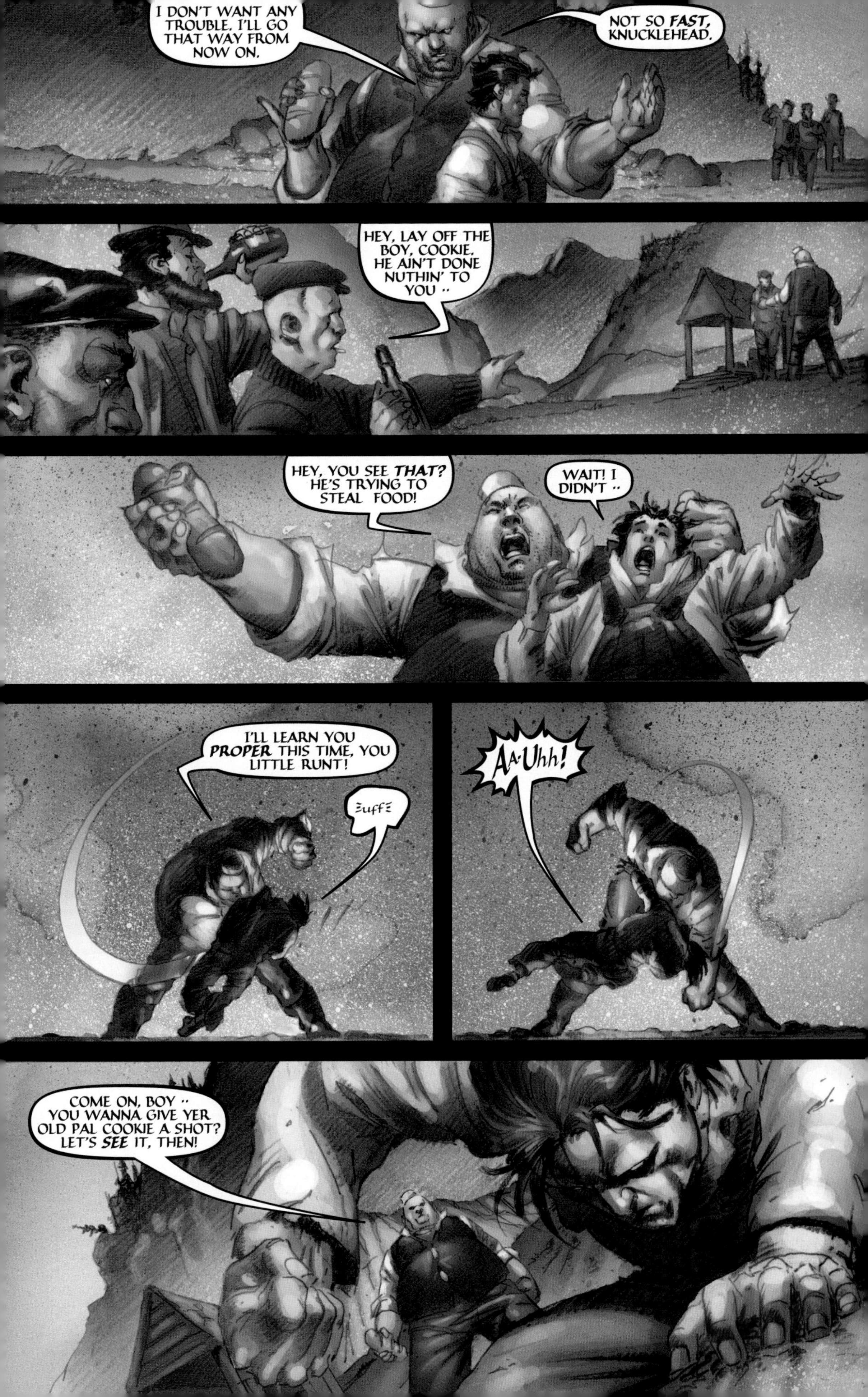
I DON'T WANT ANY TROUBLE. I'LL GO THAT WAY FROM NOW ON.
NOT SO FAST, KNUCKLEHEAD.
HEY, LAY OFF THE BOY, COOKIE. HE AIN'T DONE NUTHIN' TO YOU ..
HEY, YOU SEE THAT? HE'S TRYING TO STEAL FOOD!
WAIT! I DIDN'T ..
I'LL LEARN YOU PROPER THIS TIME, YOU LITTLE RUNT!
UFF
AA-UHH!
COME ON, BOY .. YOU WANNA GIVE YER OLD PAL COOKIE A SHOT? LET'S SEE IT, THEN!

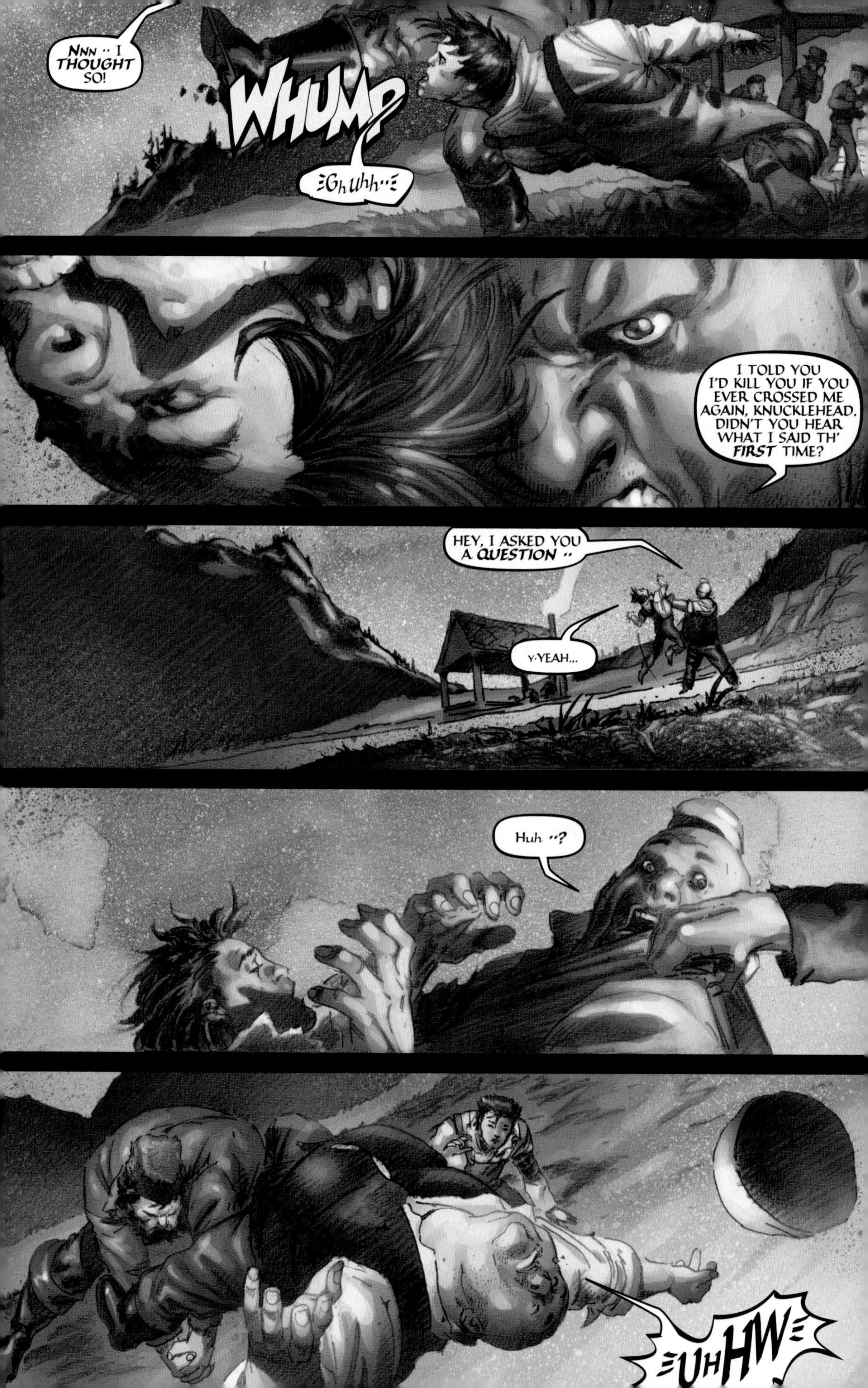
NNN .. I THOUGHT SO!
WHUMP
GHUHH..
I TOLD YOU I'D KILL YOU IF YOU EVER CROSSED ME AGAIN, KNUCKLEHEAD. DIDN'T YOU HEAR WHAT I SAID TH' FIRST TIME?
HEY, I ASKED YOU A QUESTION ..
Y-YEAH...
Huh ..?
UHHW

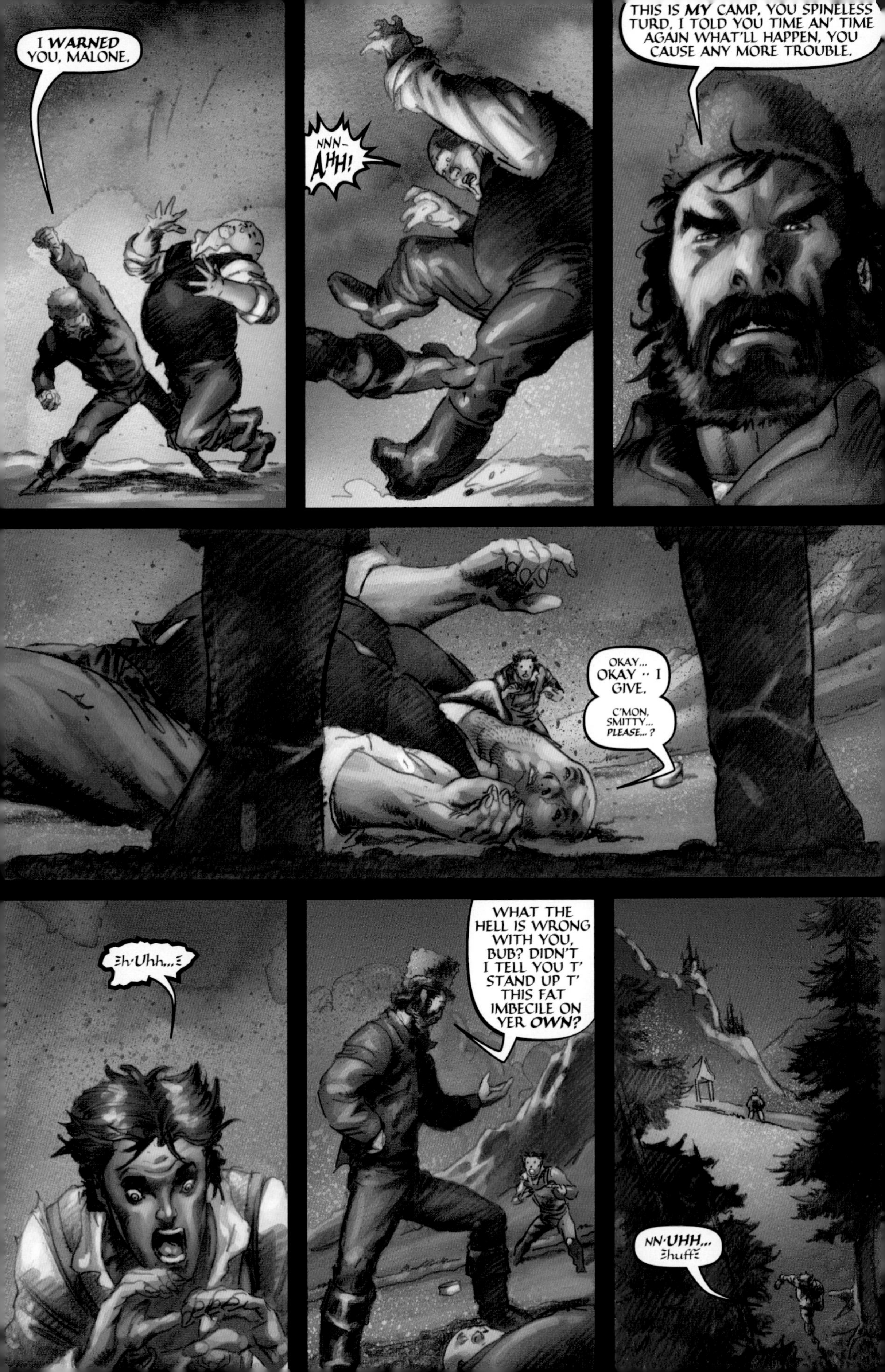
I WARNED YOU, MALONE.
NNN-AHH!
THIS IS MY CAMP, YOU SPINELESS TURD. I TOLD YOU TIME AN' TIME AGAIN WHAT'LL HAPPEN, YOU CAUSE ANY MORE TROUBLE.
OKAY... OKAY -- I GIVE.
C'MON, SMITTY... PLEASE...?
Uhh...
WHAT THE HELL IS WRONG WITH YOU, BUB? DIDN'T I TELL YOU T' STAND UP T' THIS FAT IMBECILE ON YER OWN?
NN-UHH...
huff

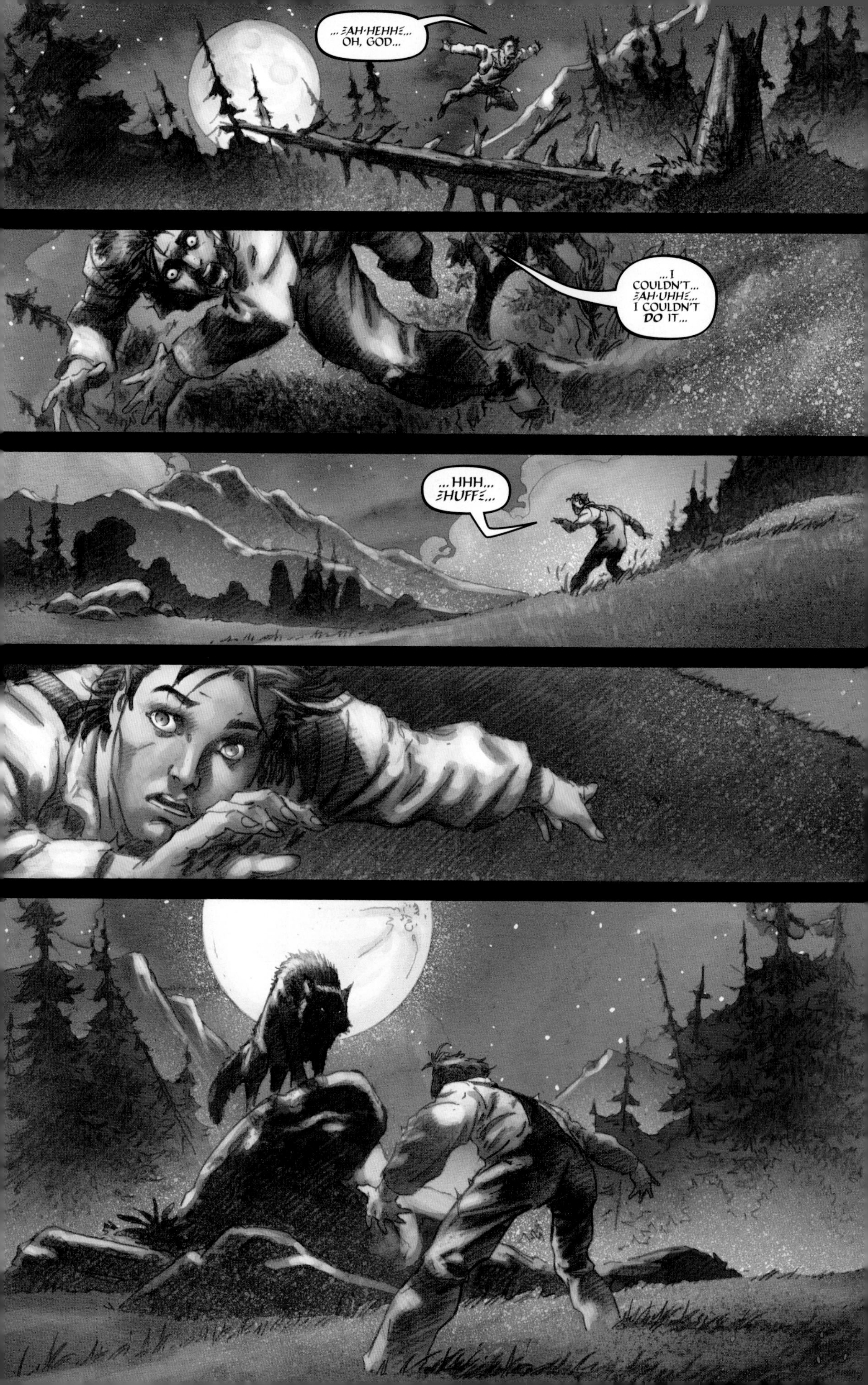
...ƎAH·HEHHƎ... OH, GOD...
...I COULDN'T... ƎAH·UHHƎ... I COULDN'T DO IT...
...HHH... ƎHUFFƎ...

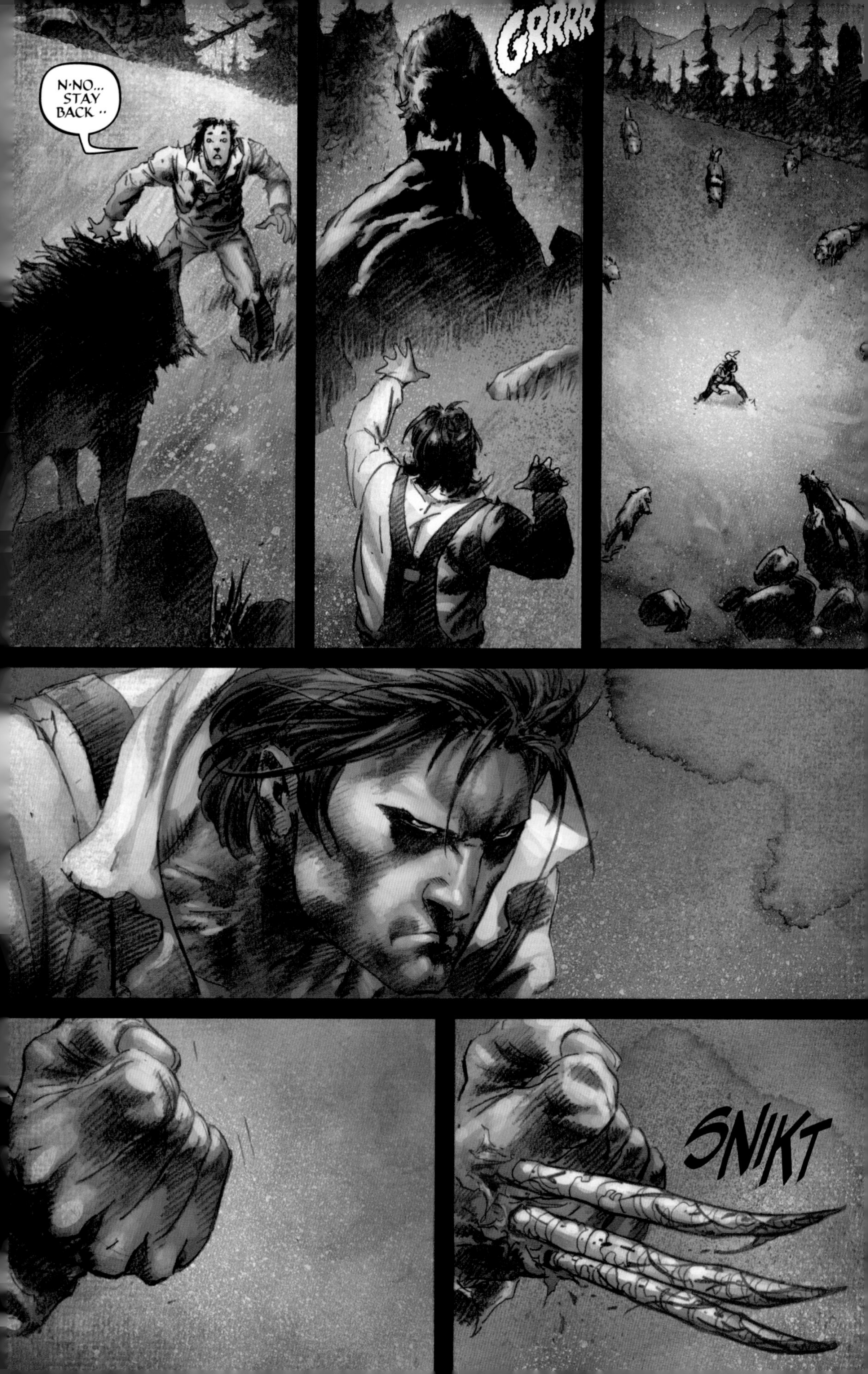
N-NO... STAY BACK ..
GRRRR
SNIKT

GRRR

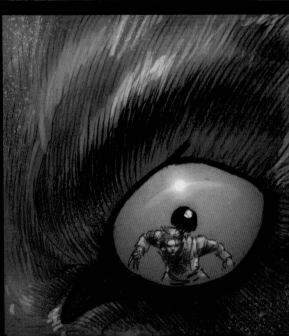

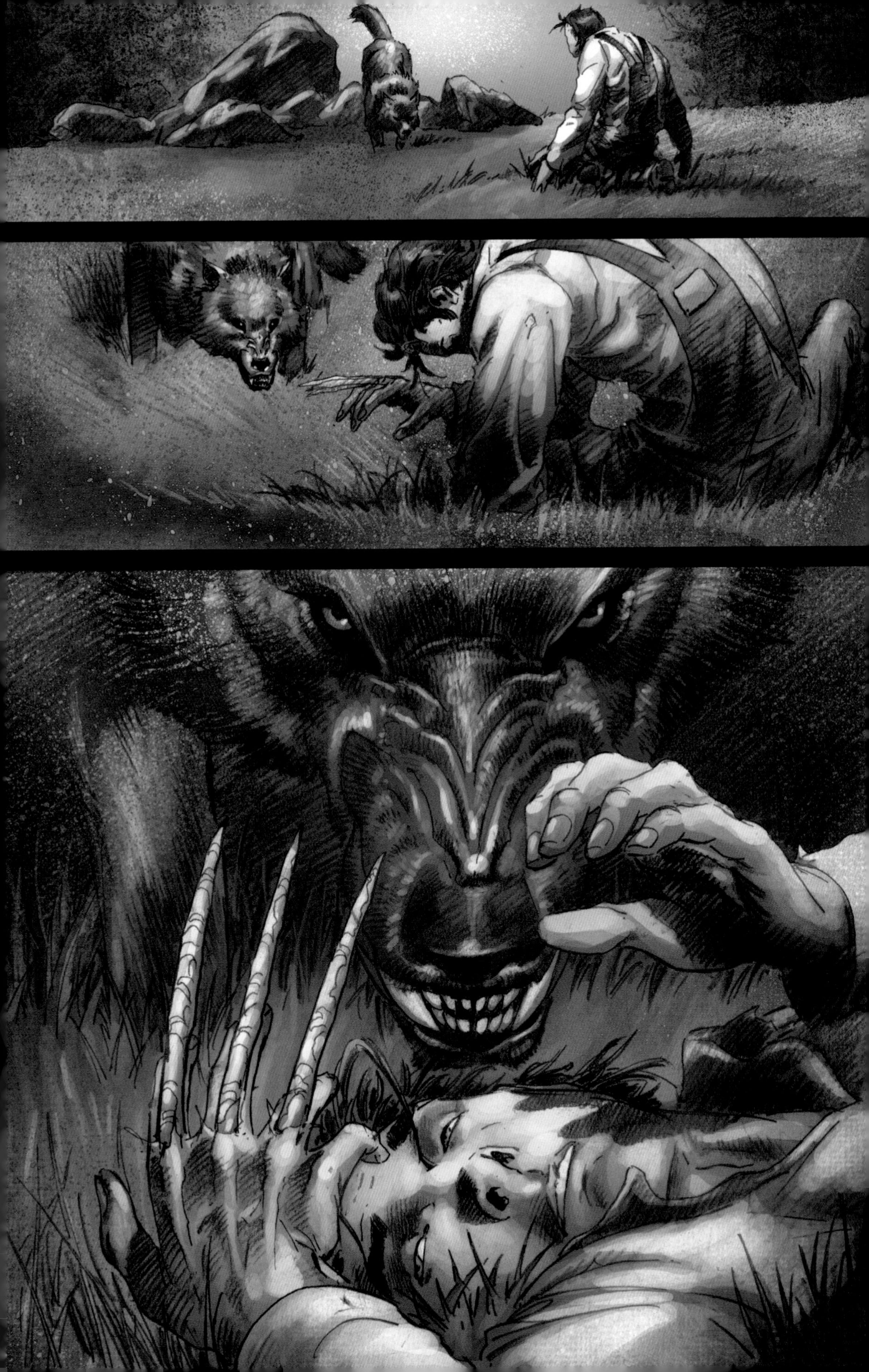

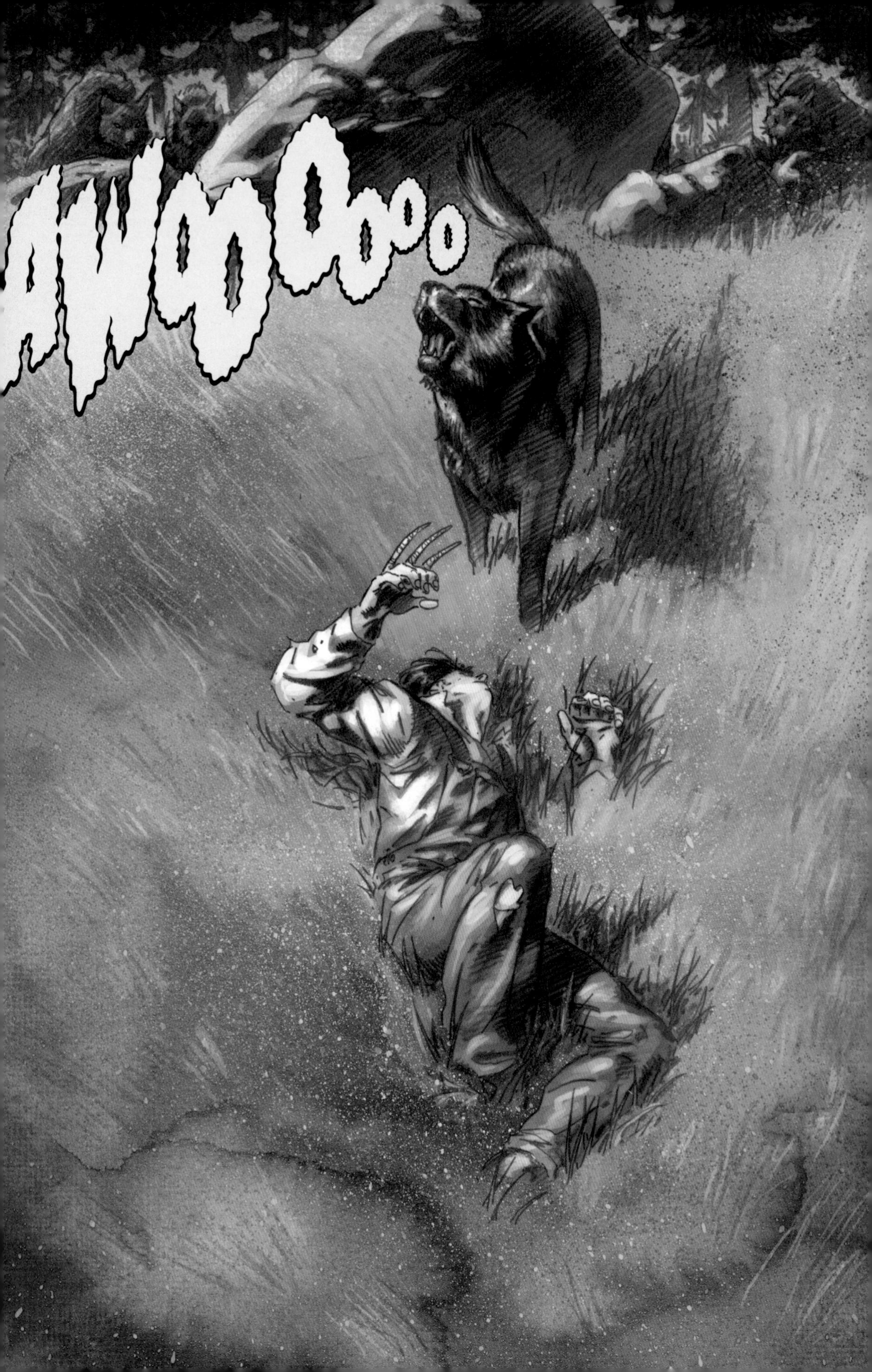
AWOOOooo

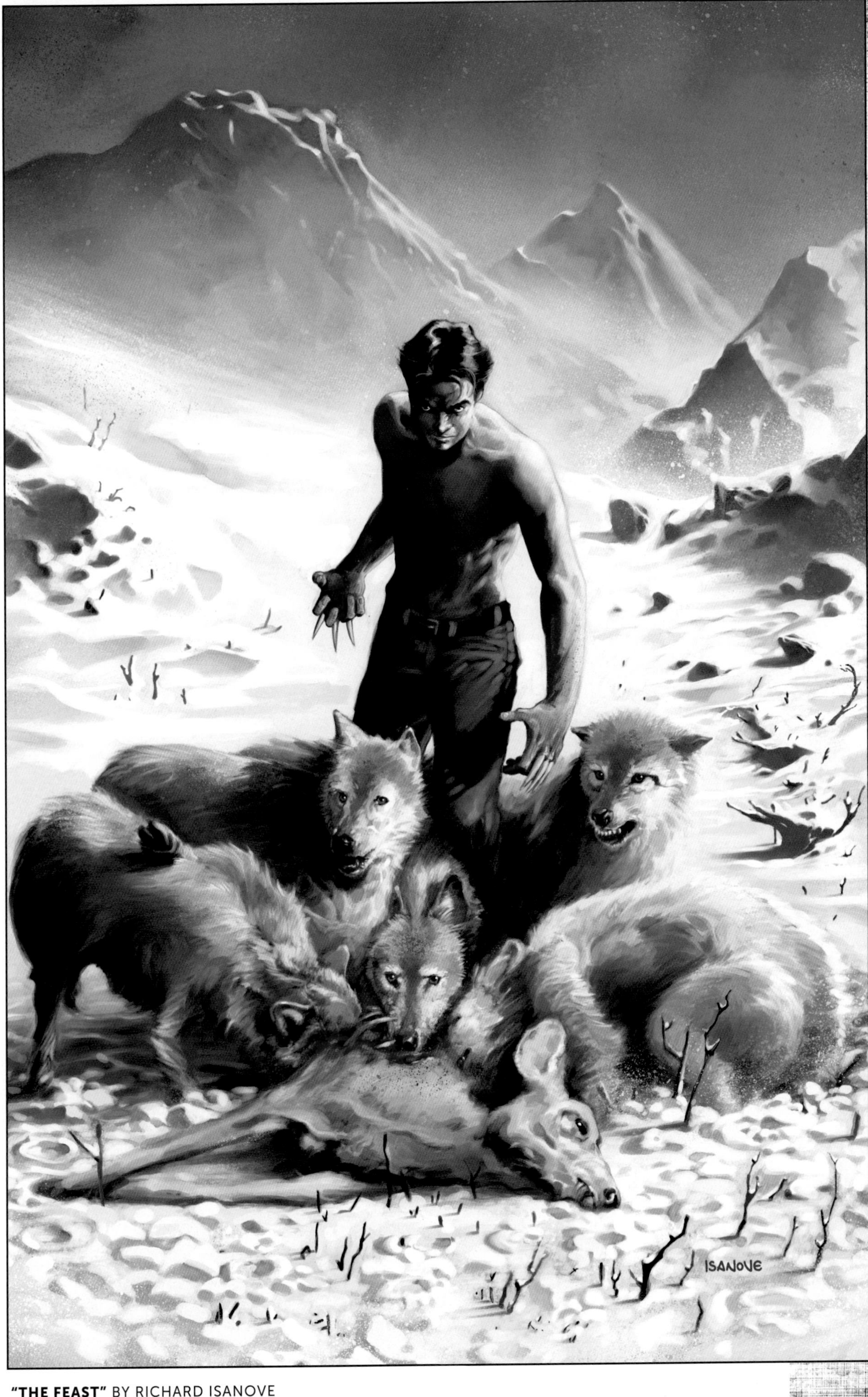
ISANOVE

**"THE FEAST"** BY RICHARD ISANOVE

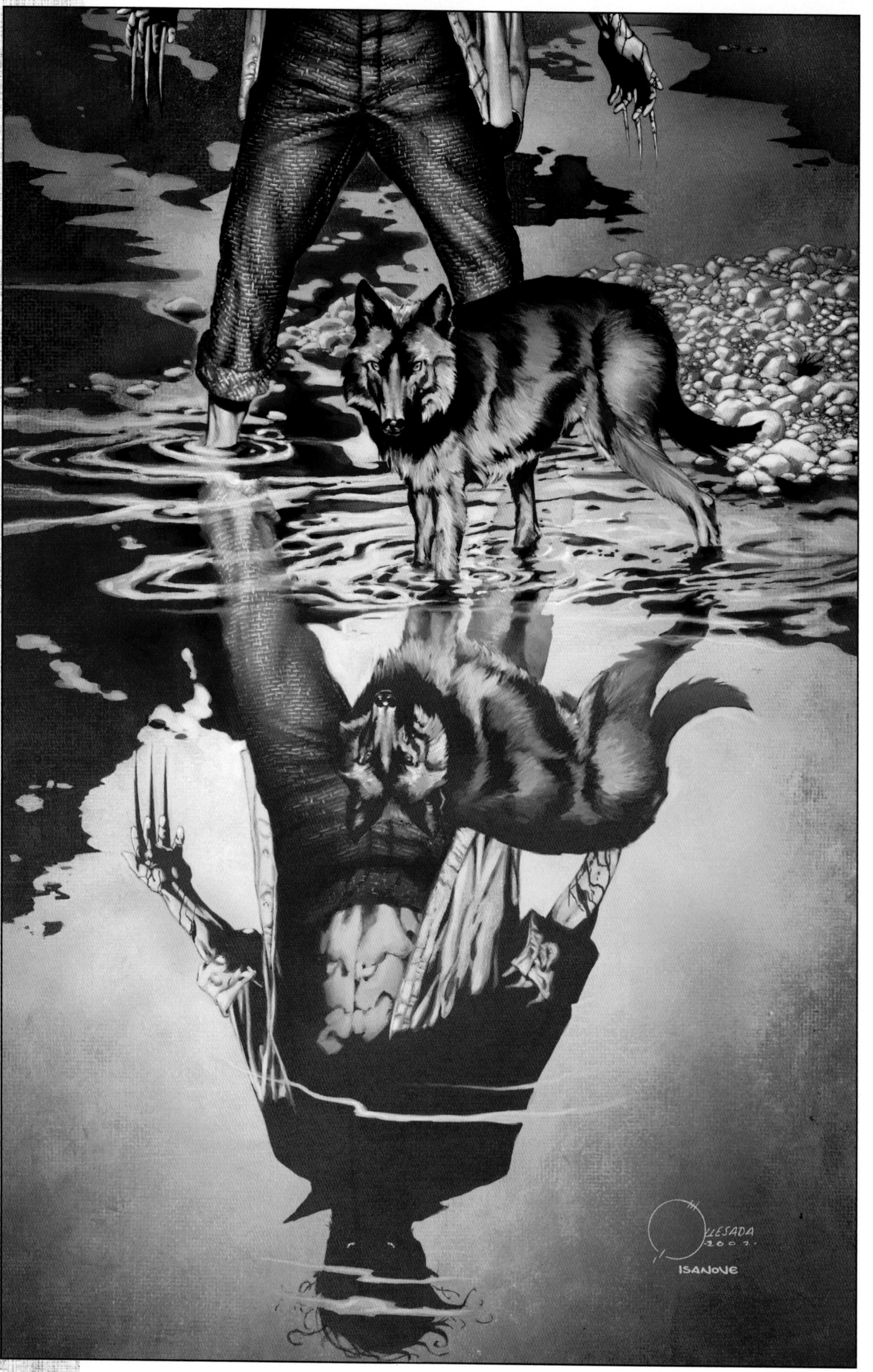
QUESADA
2002
ISANOVE

# PART V – **REVELATION**

"TYGER! TYGER! BURNING BRIGHT IN THE FORESTS OF THE NIGHT, WHAT IMMORTAL HAND OR EYE COULD FRAME THY FEARFUL SYMMETRY?"

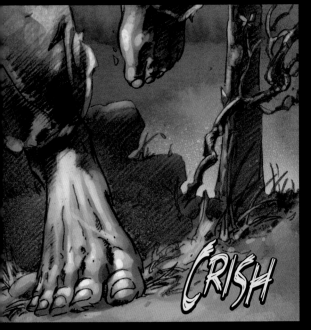

CRISH

"IN WHAT DISTANT DEEPS OR SKIES BURNT THE FIRE OF THINE EYES?"

"ON WHAT WINGS DARE HE ASPIRE? WHAT THE HAND DARE SEIZE THE FIRE?"

CROOSH

KRIK

"AND WHAT SHOULDER, AND WHAT ART, COULD TWIST THE SINEWS OF THY HEART, AND WHEN THY HEART BEGAN TO BEAT..."

"...WHAT DREAD HAND? AND WHAT DREAD FEET?"

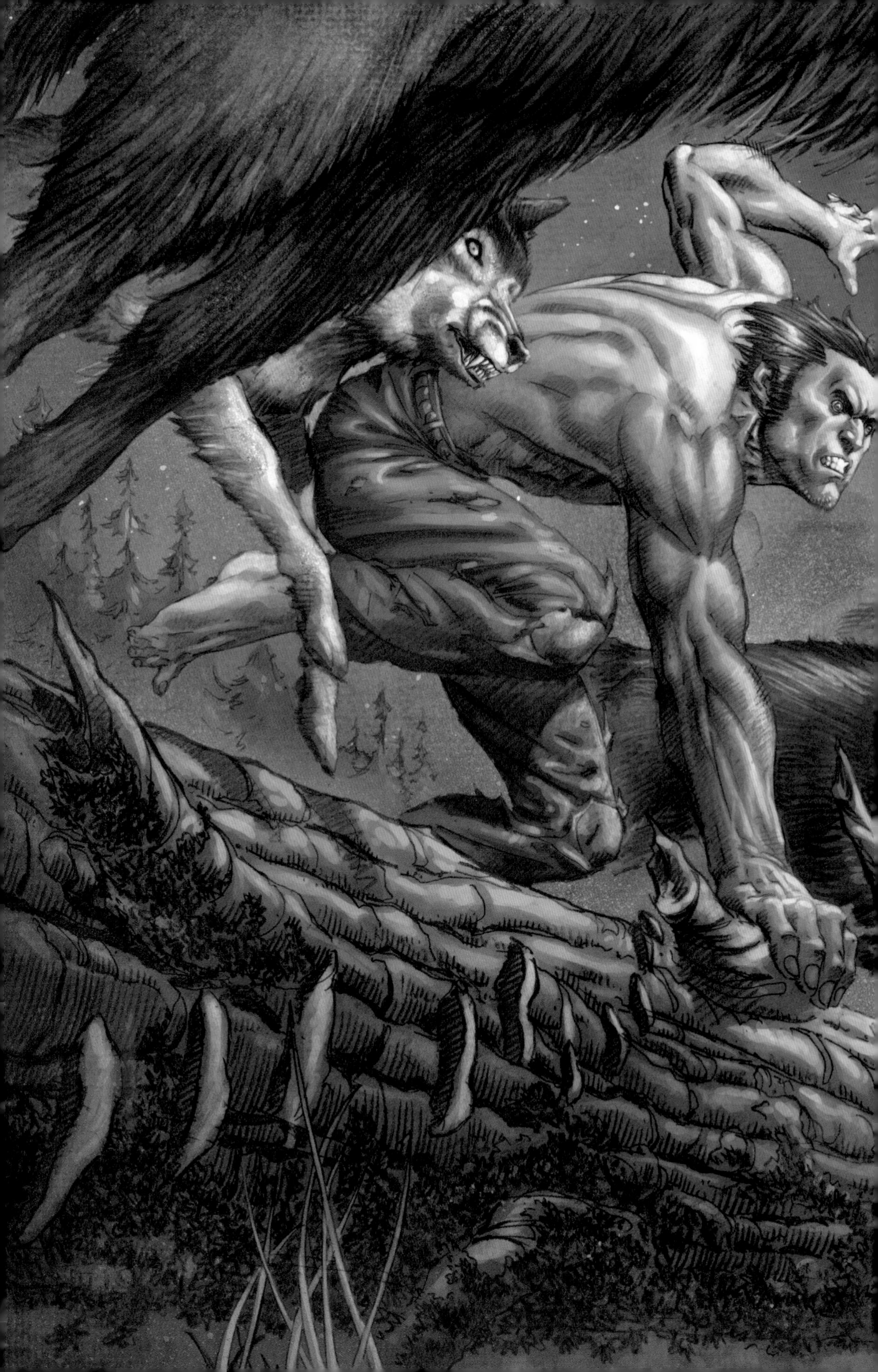

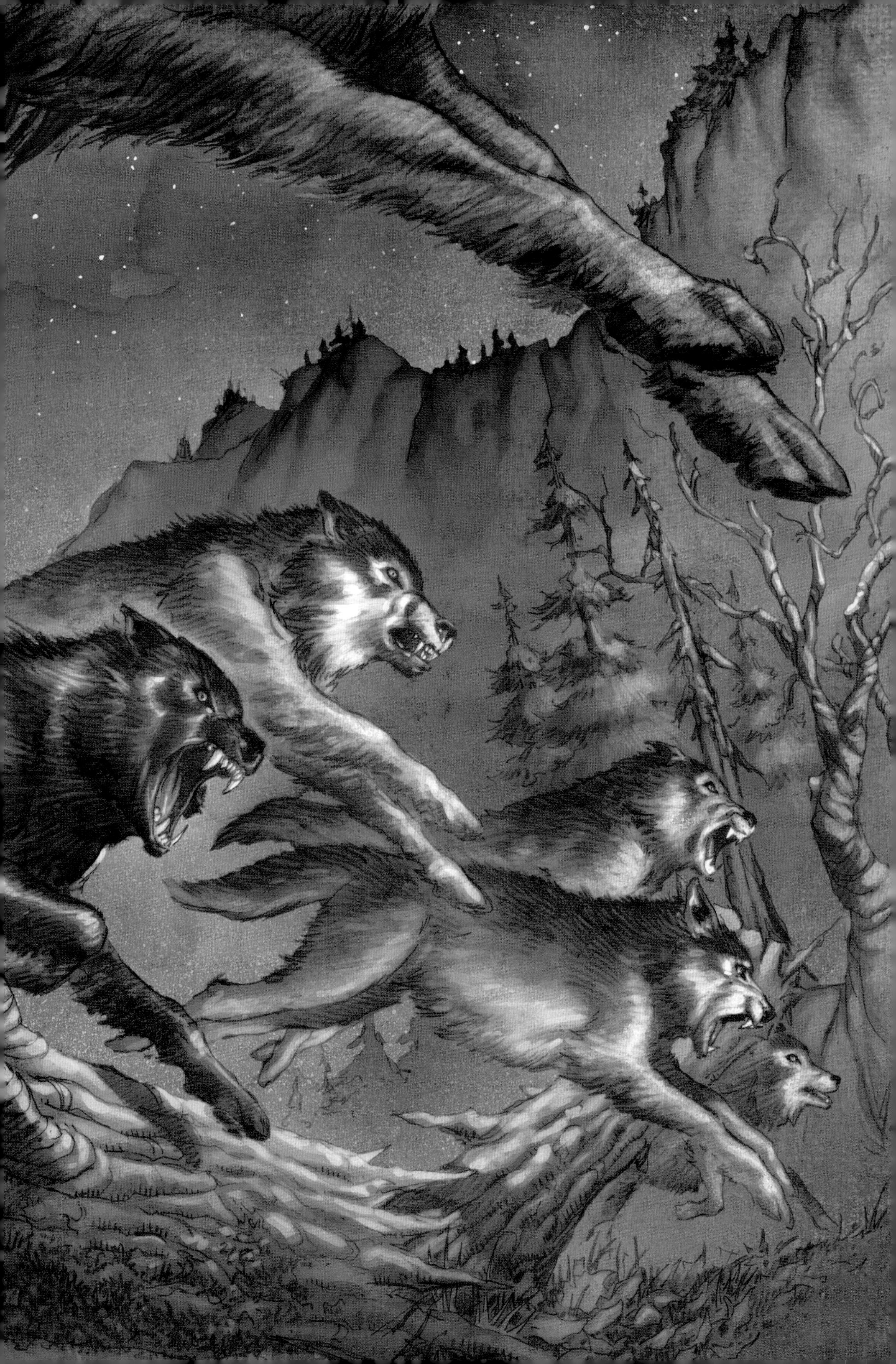

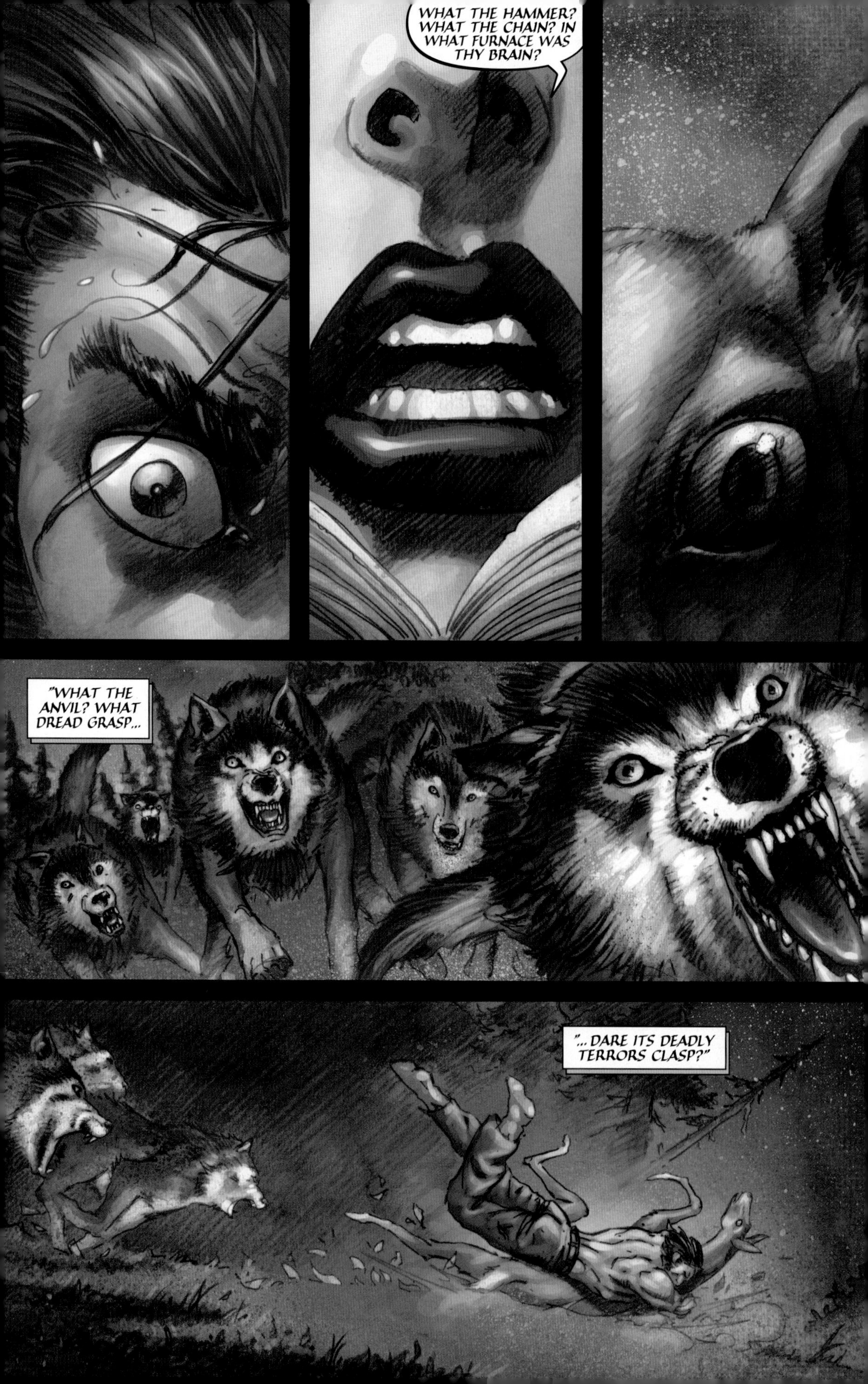
WHAT THE HAMMER? WHAT THE CHAIN? IN WHAT FURNACE WAS THY BRAIN?
"WHAT THE ANVIL? WHAT DREAD GRASP...
"... DARE ITS DEADLY TERRORS CLASP?"

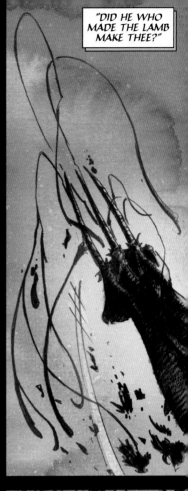

"DID HE WHO MADE THE LAMB MAKE THEE?"

WHEN THE STARS THREW DOWN THEIR SPEARS, AND WATER'D HEAVEN WITH THEIR TEARS, DID HE SMILE HIS WORK TO SEE?

TYGER! TYGER! BURNING BRIGHT, IN THE FORESTS OF THE NIGHT, WHAT IMMORTAL HAND OR EYE...

"... DARE FRAME THY FEARFUL SYMMETRY?"

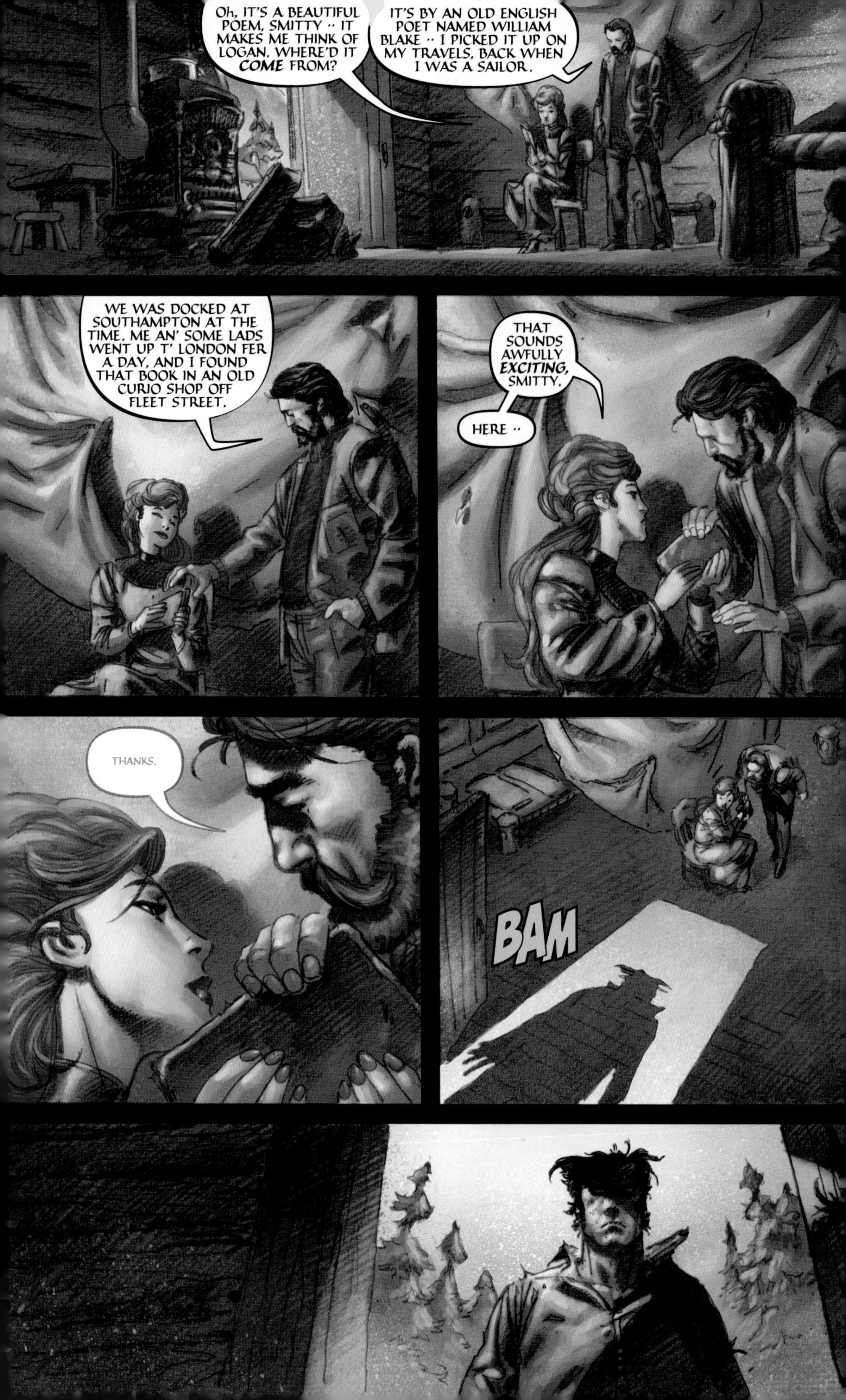
Oh, IT'S A BEAUTIFUL POEM, SMITTY -- IT MAKES ME THINK OF LOGAN. WHERE'D IT COME FROM?
IT'S BY AN OLD ENGLISH POET NAMED WILLIAM BLAKE -- I PICKED IT UP ON MY TRAVELS, BACK WHEN I WAS A SAILOR.
WE WAS DOCKED AT SOUTHAMPTON AT THE TIME. ME AN' SOME LADS WENT UP T' LONDON FER A DAY, AND I FOUND THAT BOOK IN AN OLD CURIO SHOP OFF FLEET STREET.
THAT SOUNDS AWFULLY EXCITING, SMITTY.
HERE --
THANKS.
BAM

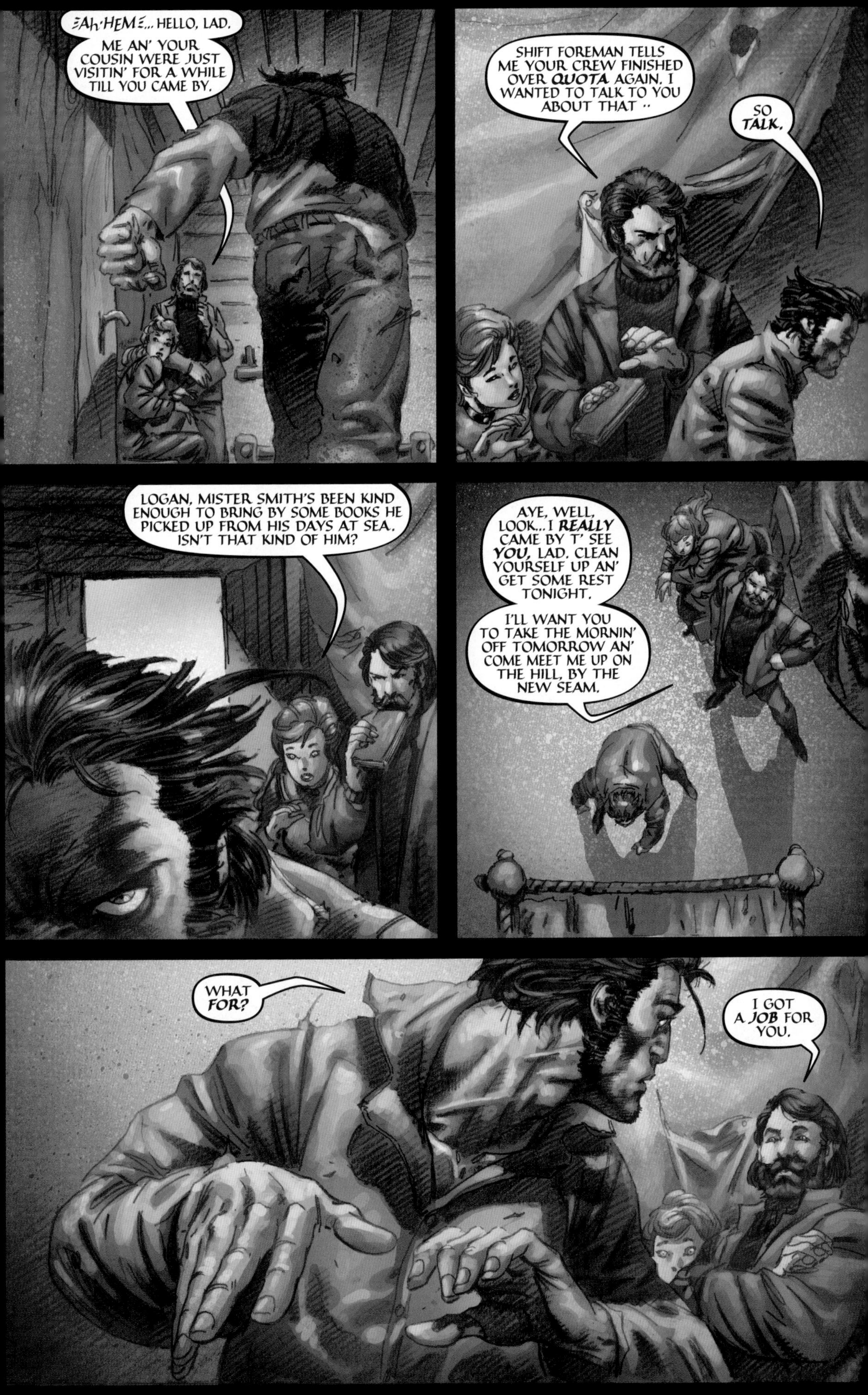

AH-HEM... HELLO, LAD.
ME AN' YOUR COUSIN WERE JUST VISITIN' FOR A WHILE TILL YOU CAME BY.
SHIFT FOREMAN TELLS ME YOUR CREW FINISHED OVER QUOTA AGAIN. I WANTED TO TALK TO YOU ABOUT THAT ..
SO TALK.
LOGAN, MISTER SMITH'S BEEN KIND ENOUGH TO BRING BY SOME BOOKS HE PICKED UP FROM HIS DAYS AT SEA. ISN'T THAT KIND OF HIM?
AYE, WELL, LOOK...I REALLY CAME BY T' SEE YOU, LAD. CLEAN YOURSELF UP AN' GET SOME REST TONIGHT.
I'LL WANT YOU TO TAKE THE MORNIN' OFF TOMORROW AN' COME MEET ME UP ON THE HILL, BY THE NEW SEAM.
WHAT FOR?
I GOT A JOB FOR YOU.

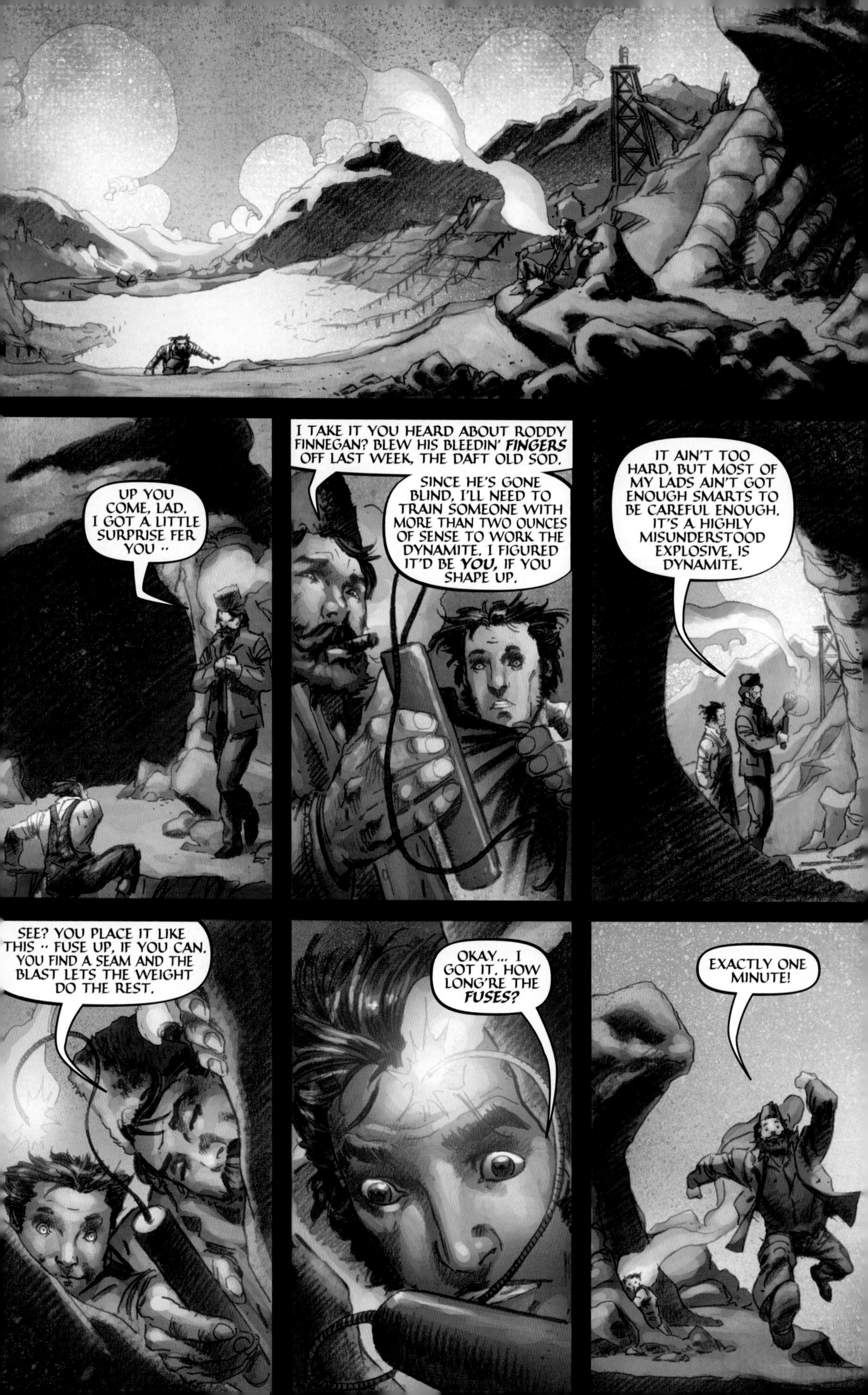
UP YOU COME, LAD. I GOT A LITTLE SURPRISE FER YOU ..
I TAKE IT YOU HEARD ABOUT RODDY FINNEGAN? BLEW HIS BLEEDIN' FINGERS OFF LAST WEEK, THE DAFT OLD SOD.
SINCE HE'S GONE BLIND, I'LL NEED TO TRAIN SOMEONE WITH MORE THAN TWO OUNCES OF SENSE TO WORK THE DYNAMITE. I FIGURED IT'D BE YOU, IF YOU SHAPE UP.
IT AIN'T TOO HARD, BUT MOST OF MY LADS AIN'T GOT ENOUGH SMARTS TO BE CAREFUL ENOUGH. IT'S A HIGHLY MISUNDERSTOOD EXPLOSIVE, IS DYNAMITE.
SEE? YOU PLACE IT LIKE THIS .. FUSE UP, IF YOU CAN. YOU FIND A SEAM AND THE BLAST LETS THE WEIGHT DO THE REST.
OKAY... I GOT IT. HOW LONG'RE THE FUSES?
EXACTLY ONE MINUTE!

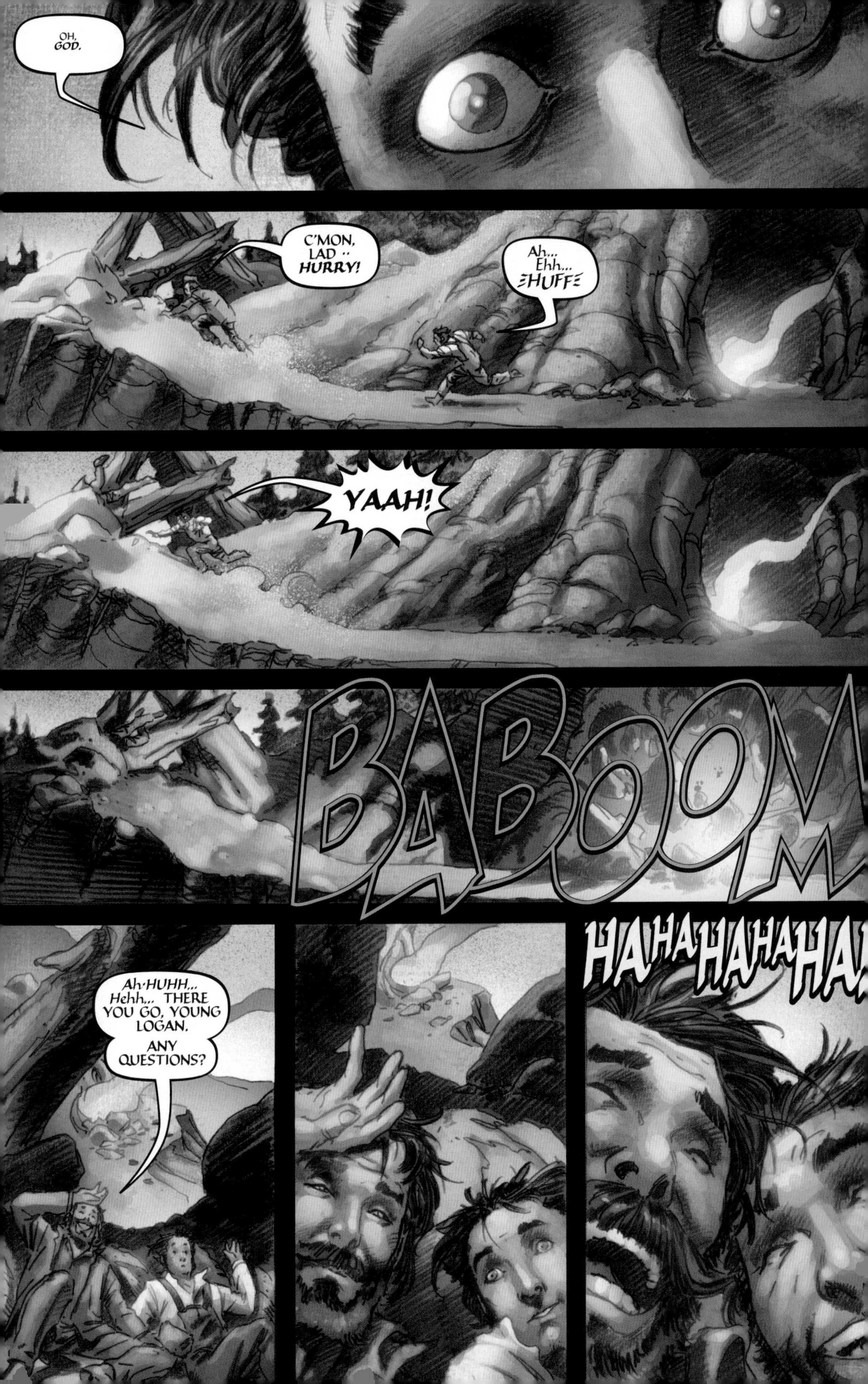
OH, GOD.
C'MON, LAD .. HURRY!
Ah... Ehh... HUFF
YAAH!
BABOOM
Ah-HUHH... Hehh... THERE YOU GO, YOUNG LOGAN. ANY QUESTIONS?
HAHAHAHAHAHA!

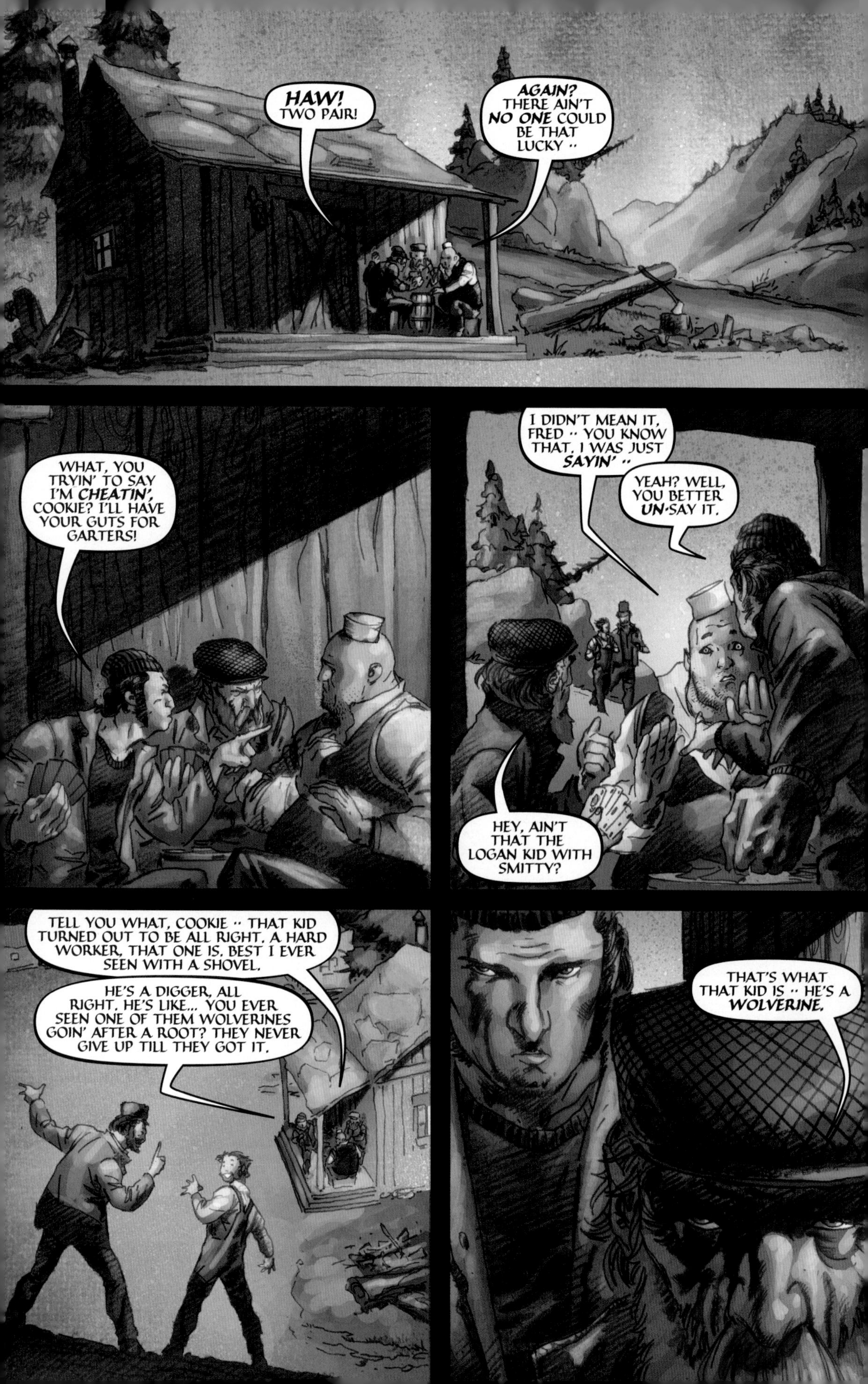
HAW! TWO PAIR!
AGAIN? THERE AIN'T NO ONE COULD BE THAT LUCKY ..
WHAT, YOU TRYIN' TO SAY I'M CHEATIN', COOKIE? I'LL HAVE YOUR GUTS FOR GARTERS!
I DIDN'T MEAN IT, FRED .. YOU KNOW THAT. I WAS JUST SAYIN' ..
YEAH? WELL, YOU BETTER UN-SAY IT.
HEY, AIN'T THAT THE LOGAN KID WITH SMITTY?
TELL YOU WHAT, COOKIE .. THAT KID TURNED OUT TO BE ALL RIGHT. A HARD WORKER, THAT ONE IS. BEST I EVER SEEN WITH A SHOVEL.
HE'S A DIGGER, ALL RIGHT. HE'S LIKE... YOU EVER SEEN ONE OF THEM WOLVERINES GOIN' AFTER A ROOT? THEY NEVER GIVE UP TILL THEY GOT IT.
THAT'S WHAT THAT KID IS .. HE'S A WOLVERINE.

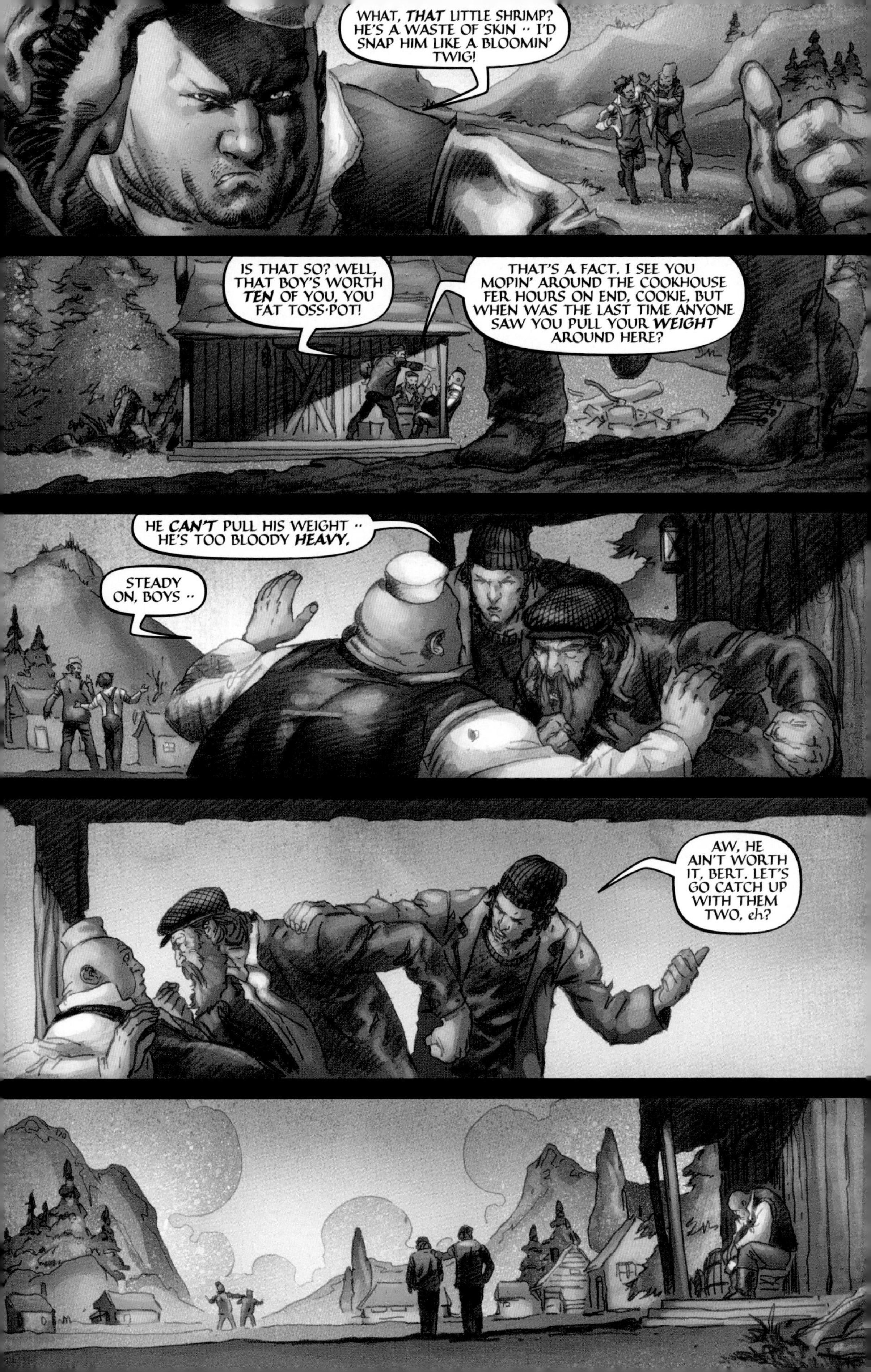
WHAT, THAT LITTLE SHRIMP? HE'S A WASTE OF SKIN .. I'D SNAP HIM LIKE A BLOOMIN' TWIG!
IS THAT SO? WELL, THAT BOY'S WORTH TEN OF YOU, YOU FAT TOSS-POT!
THAT'S A FACT. I SEE YOU MOPIN' AROUND THE COOKHOUSE FER HOURS ON END, COOKIE, BUT WHEN WAS THE LAST TIME ANYONE SAW YOU PULL YOUR WEIGHT AROUND HERE?
HE CAN'T PULL HIS WEIGHT .. HE'S TOO BLOODY HEAVY.
STEADY ON, BOYS ..
AW, HE AIN'T WORTH IT, BERT. LET'S GO CATCH UP WITH THEM TWO, eh?

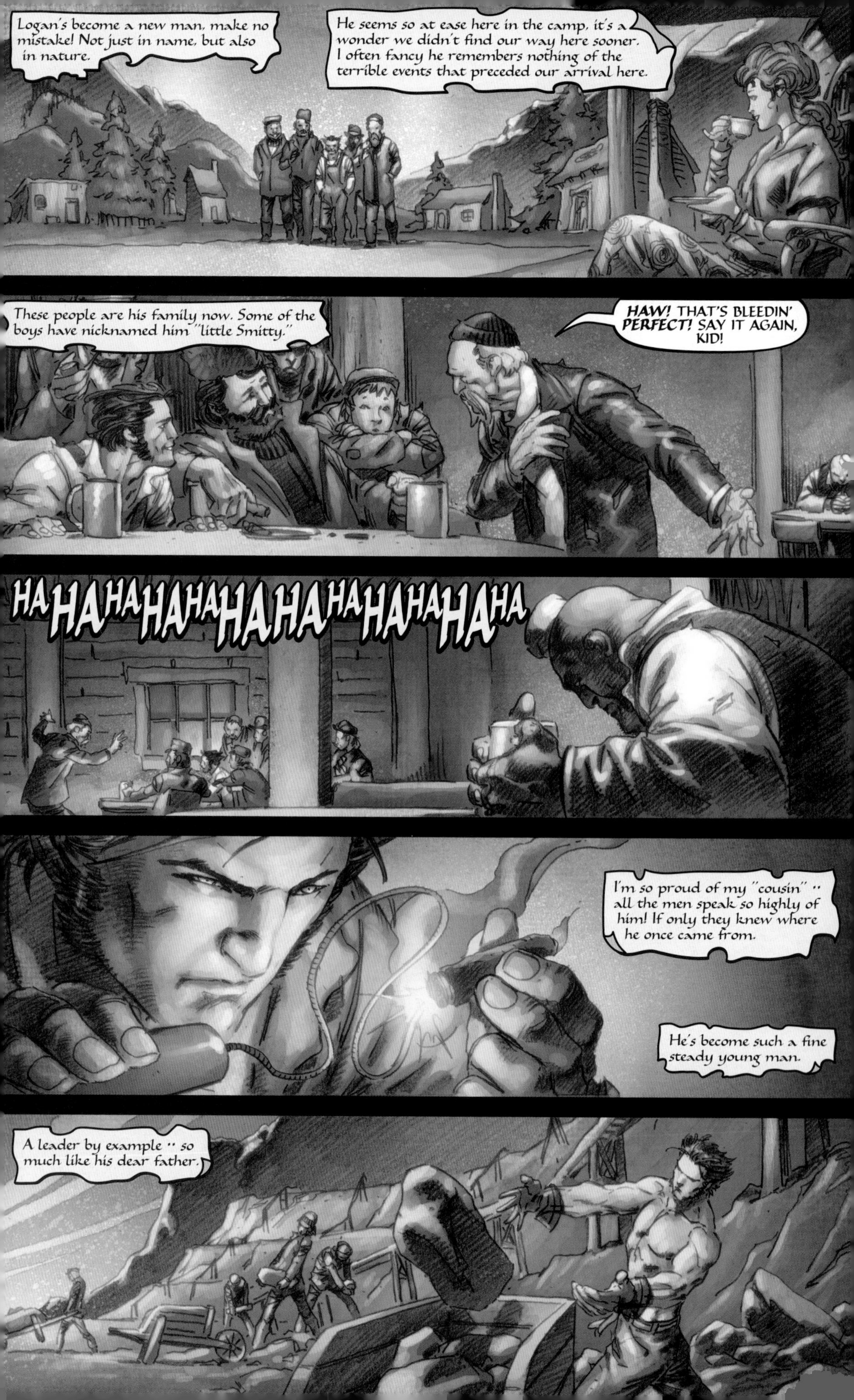
Logan's become a new man, make no mistake! Not just in name, but also in nature.
He seems so at ease here in the camp, it's a wonder we didn't find our way here sooner. I often fancy he remembers nothing of the terrible events that preceded our arrival here.
These people are his family now. Some of the boys have nicknamed him "little Smitty."
HAW! THAT'S BLEEDIN' PERFECT! SAY IT AGAIN, KID!
HAHAHAHAHAHAHAHAHAHAHAHAHA
I'm so proud of my "cousin" .. all the men speak so highly of him! If only they knew where he once came from.
He's become such a fine steady young man.
A leader by example .. so much like his dear father.

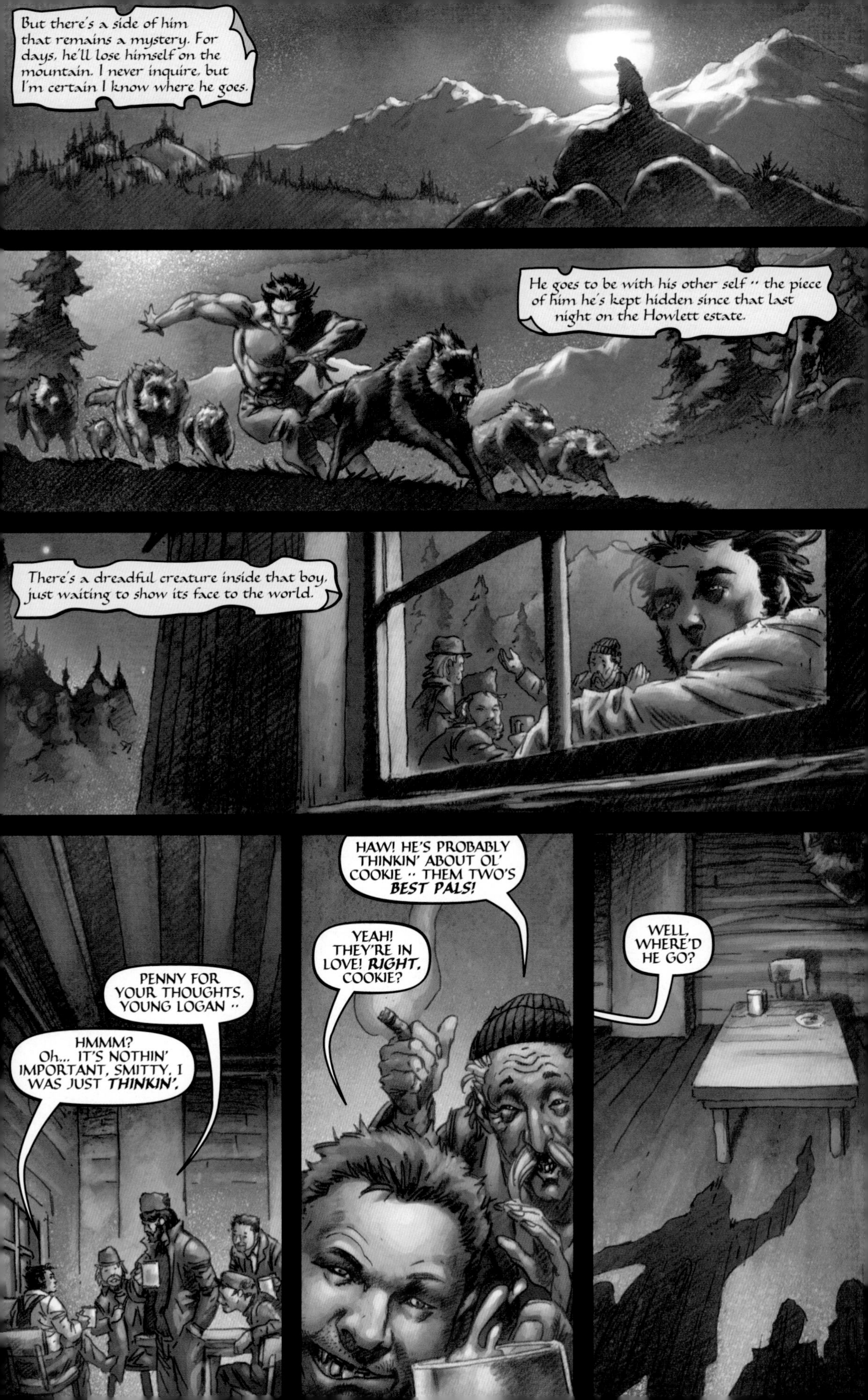
But there's a side of him that remains a mystery. For days, he'll lose himself on the mountain. I never inquire, but I'm certain I know where he goes.
He goes to be with his other self -- the piece of him he's kept hidden since that last night on the Howlett estate.
There's a dreadful creature inside that boy, just waiting to show its face to the world.
PENNY FOR YOUR THOUGHTS, YOUNG LOGAN --
HMMM? Oh... IT'S NOTHIN' IMPORTANT, SMITTY. I WAS JUST THINKIN'.
HAW! HE'S PROBABLY THINKIN' ABOUT OL' COOKIE -- THEM TWO'S BEST PALS!
YEAH! THEY'RE IN LOVE! RIGHT, COOKIE?
WELL, WHERE'D HE GO?

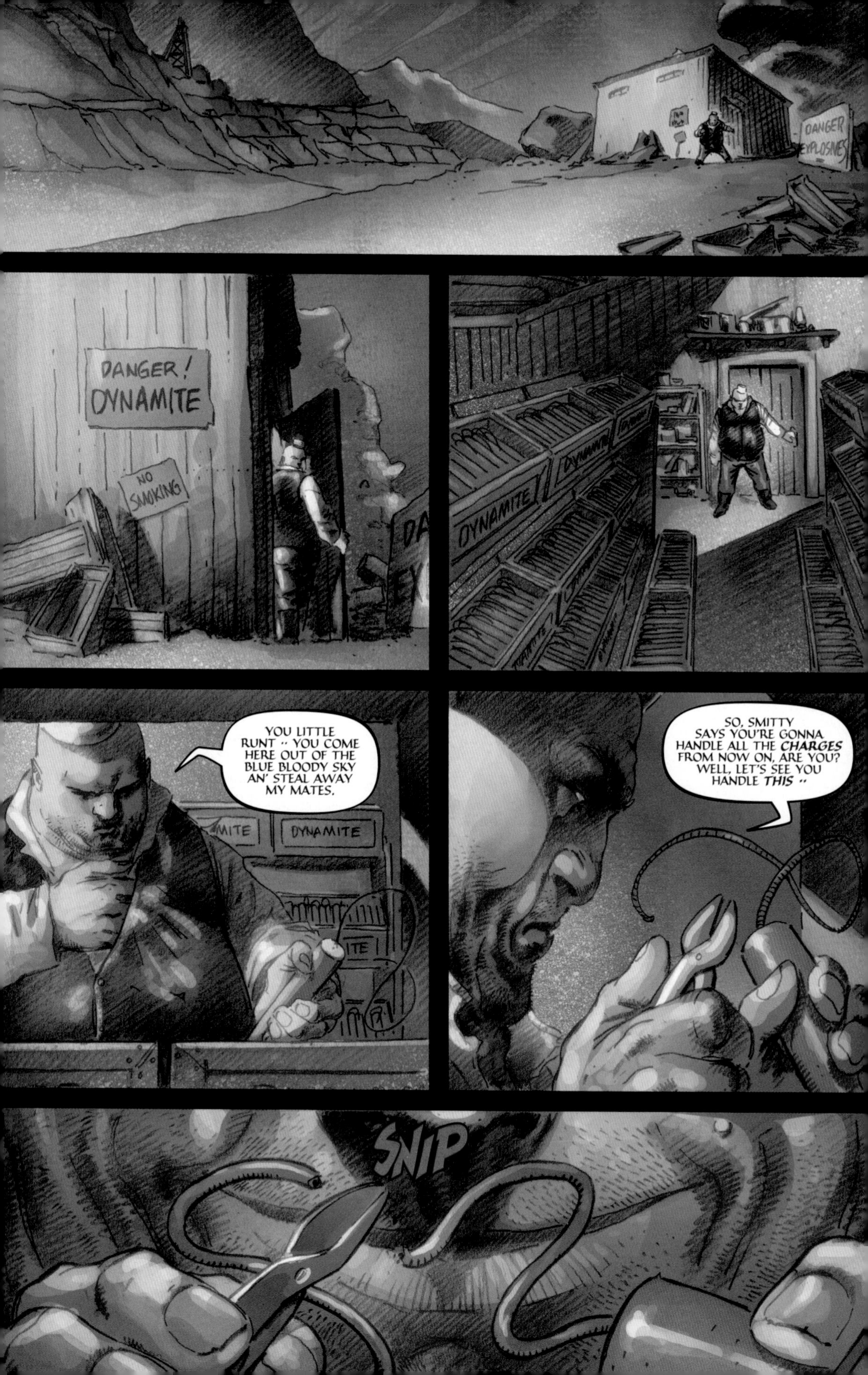
DANGER EXPLOSIVES
DANGER! DYNAMITE
NO SMOKING
DYNAMITE
YOU LITTLE RUNT -- YOU COME HERE OUT OF THE BLUE BLOODY SKY AN' STEAL AWAY MY MATES.
DYNAMITE
SO, SMITTY SAYS YOU'RE GONNA HANDLE ALL THE CHARGES FROM NOW ON, ARE YOU? WELL, LET'S SEE YOU HANDLE THIS --
SNIP

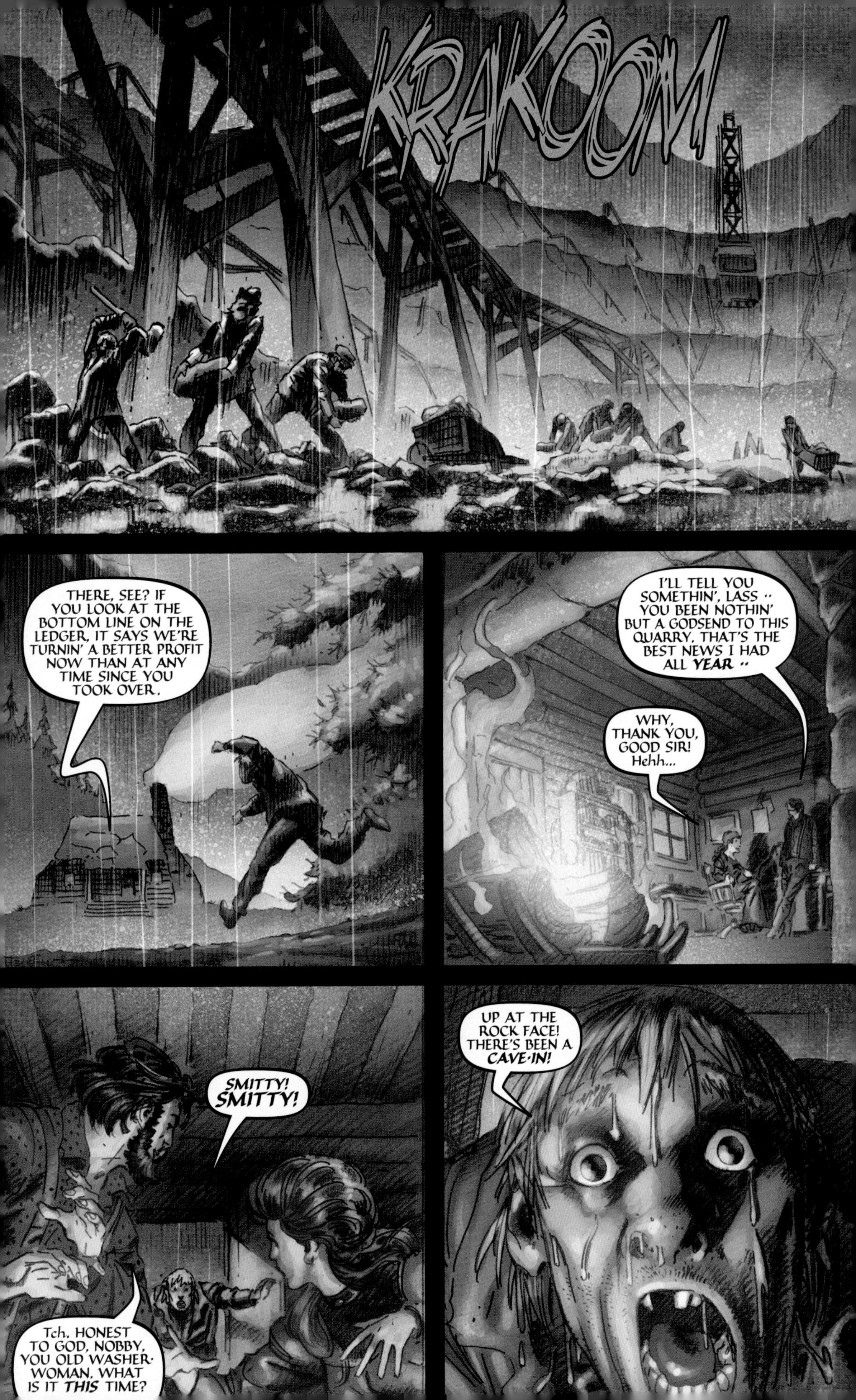
KRAKOOM
THERE, SEE? IF YOU LOOK AT THE BOTTOM LINE ON THE LEDGER, IT SAYS WE'RE TURNIN' A BETTER PROFIT NOW THAN AT ANY TIME SINCE YOU TOOK OVER.
I'LL TELL YOU SOMETHIN', LASS .. YOU BEEN NOTHIN' BUT A GODSEND TO THIS QUARRY. THAT'S THE BEST NEWS I HAD ALL YEAR ..
WHY, THANK YOU, GOOD SIR! Hehh...
SMITTY! SMITTY!
Tch. HONEST TO GOD, NOBBY, YOU OLD WASHER-WOMAN. WHAT IS IT THIS TIME?
UP AT THE ROCK FACE! THERE'S BEEN A CAVE-IN!

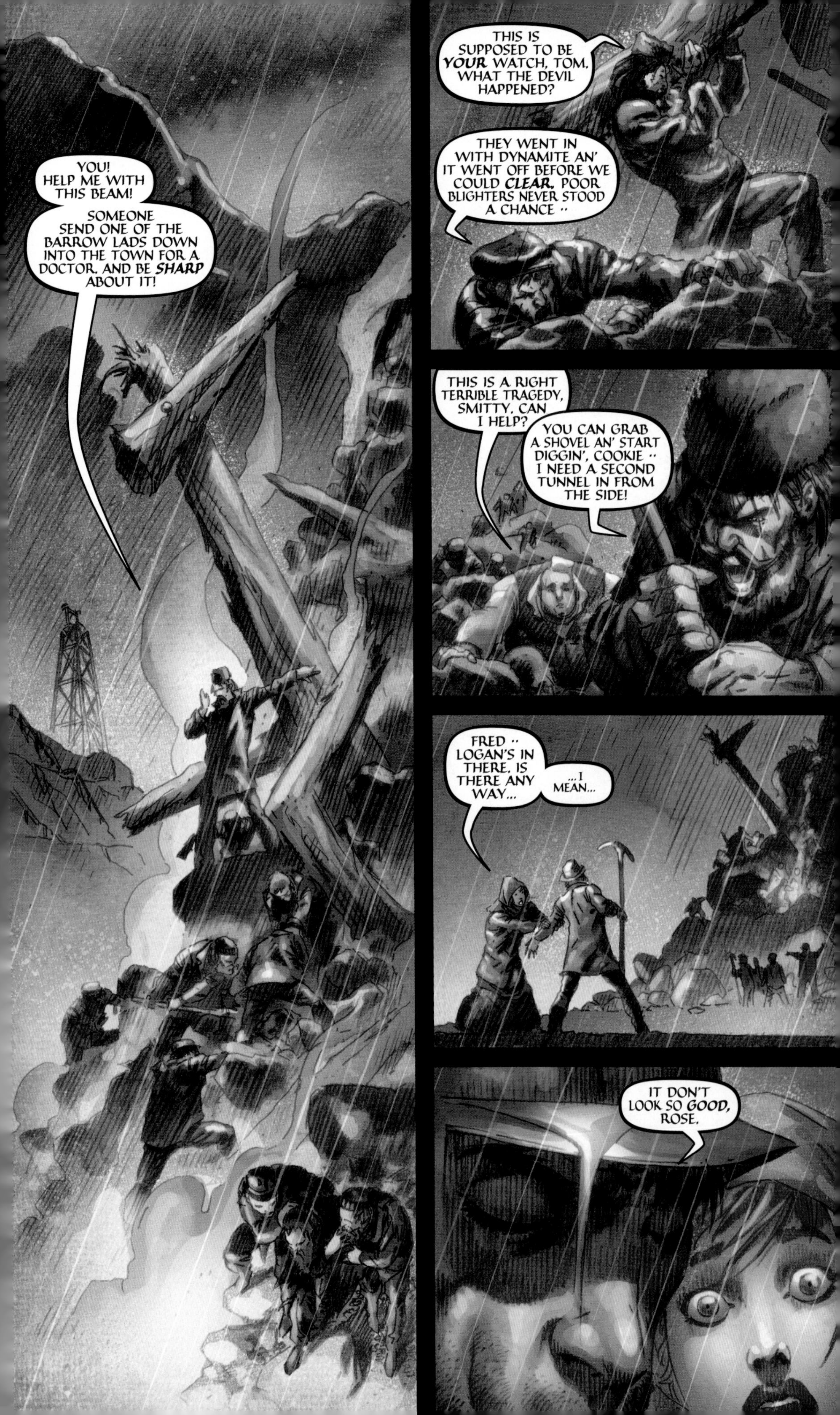
YOU! HELP ME WITH THIS BEAM!
SOMEONE SEND ONE OF THE BARROW LADS DOWN INTO THE TOWN FOR A DOCTOR, AND BE *SHARP* ABOUT IT!
THIS IS SUPPOSED TO BE *YOUR* WATCH, TOM. WHAT THE DEVIL HAPPENED?
THEY WENT IN WITH DYNAMITE AN' IT WENT OFF BEFORE WE COULD *CLEAR*. POOR BLIGHTERS NEVER STOOD A CHANCE ..
THIS IS A RIGHT TERRIBLE TRAGEDY, SMITTY. CAN I HELP?
YOU CAN GRAB A SHOVEL AN' START DIGGIN', COOKIE .. I NEED A SECOND TUNNEL IN FROM THE SIDE!
FRED .. LOGAN'S IN THERE. IS THERE ANY WAY...
...I MEAN...
IT DON'T LOOK SO *GOOD*, ROSE.

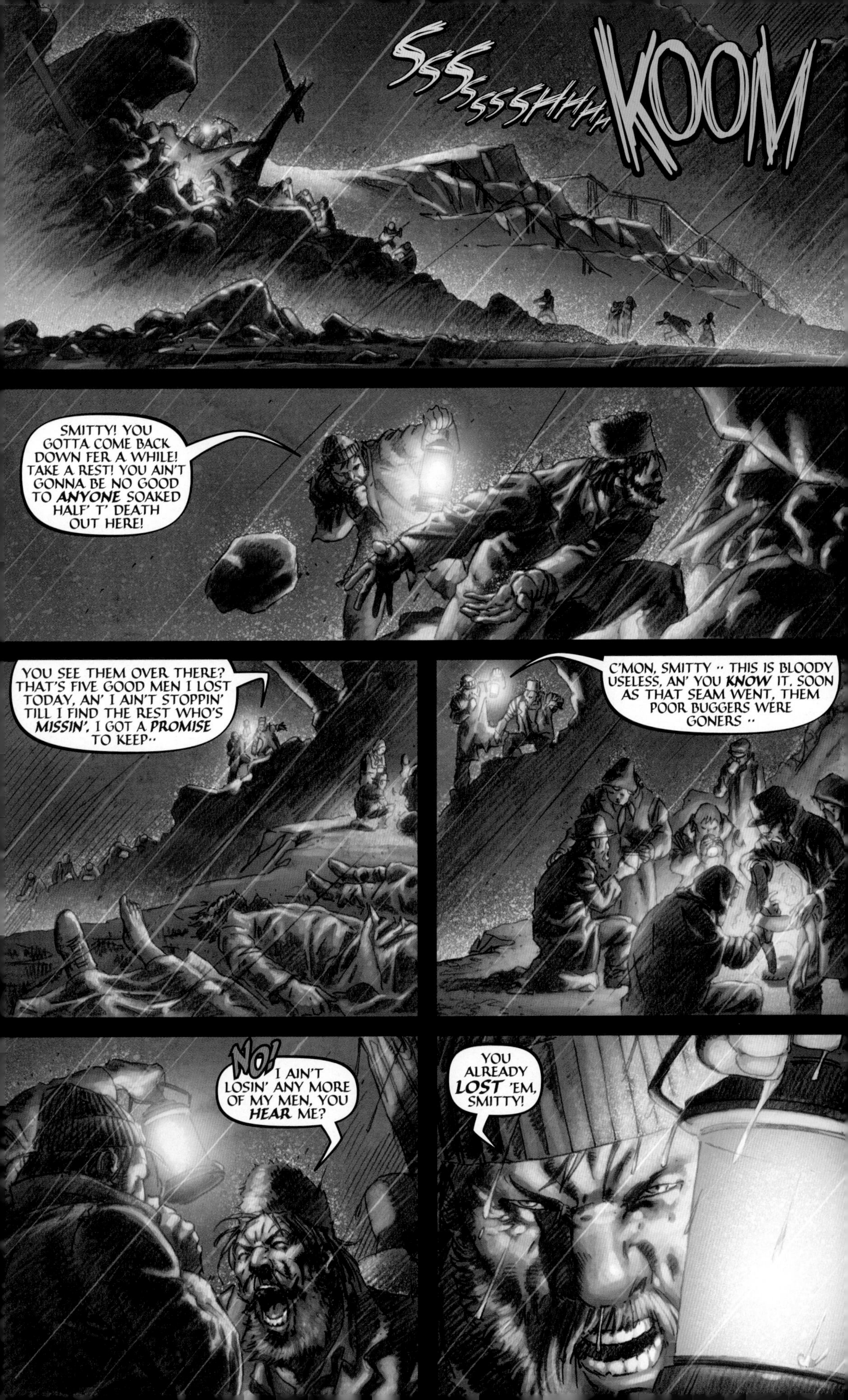
SSSSSSSSHHHHH KOOM
SMITTY! YOU GOTTA COME BACK DOWN FER A WHILE! TAKE A REST! YOU AIN'T GONNA BE NO GOOD TO ANYONE SOAKED HALF' T' DEATH OUT HERE!
YOU SEE THEM OVER THERE? THAT'S FIVE GOOD MEN I LOST TODAY, AN' I AIN'T STOPPIN' TILL I FIND THE REST WHO'S MISSIN'. I GOT A PROMISE TO KEEP..
C'MON, SMITTY .. THIS IS BLOODY USELESS, AN' YOU KNOW IT. SOON AS THAT SEAM WENT, THEM POOR BUGGERS WERE GONERS ..
NO! I AIN'T LOSIN' ANY MORE OF MY MEN, YOU HEAR ME?
YOU ALREADY LOST 'EM, SMITTY!

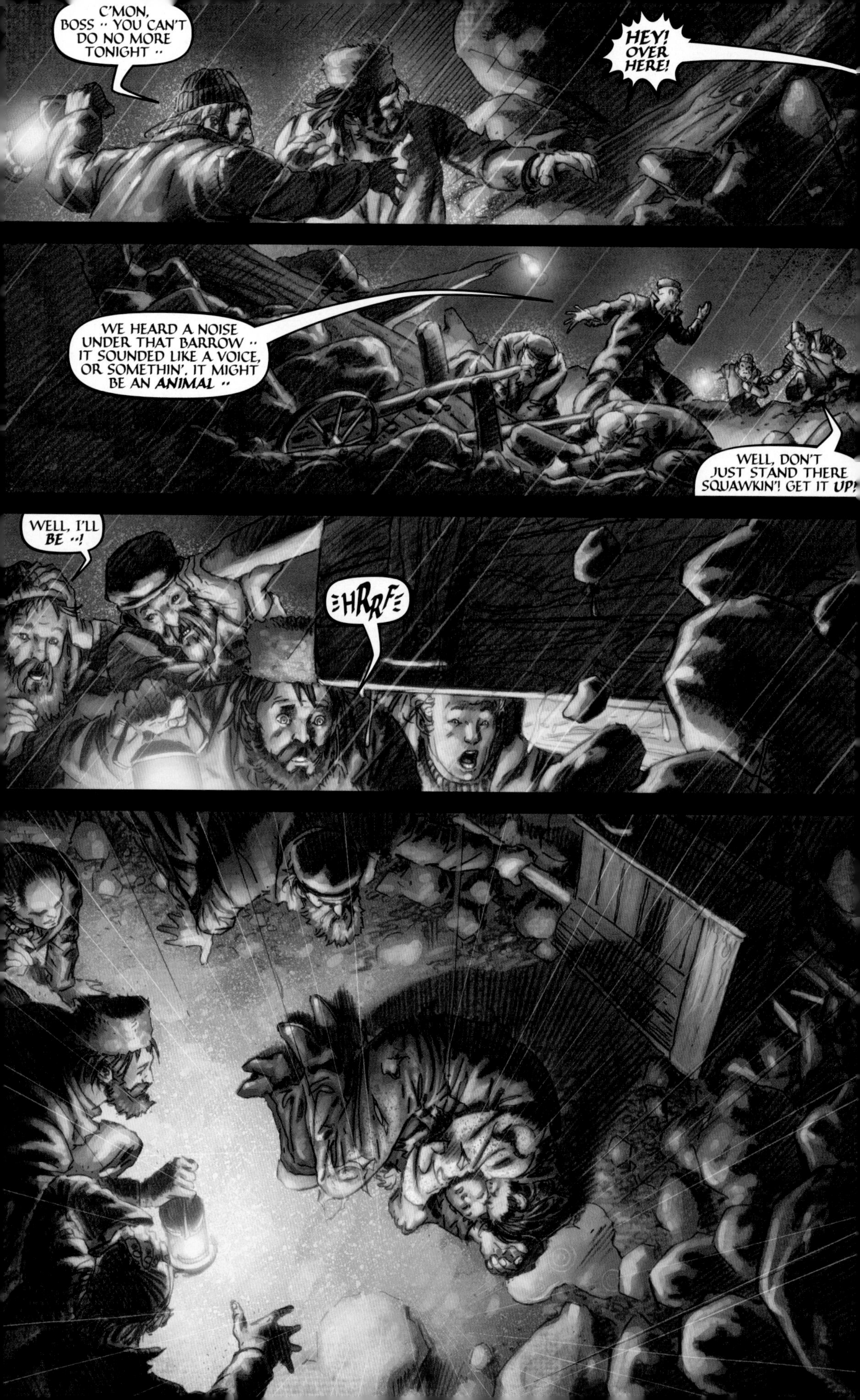
C'MON, BOSS -- YOU CAN'T DO NO MORE TONIGHT --
HEY! OVER HERE!
WE HEARD A NOISE UNDER THAT BARROW -- IT SOUNDED LIKE A VOICE, OR SOMETHIN', IT MIGHT BE AN ANIMAL --
WELL, DON'T JUST STAND THERE SQUAWKIN'! GET IT UP!
WELL, I'LL BE --!
HRRF

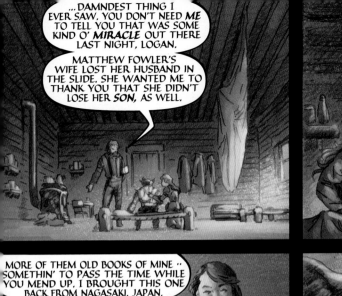

...DAMNDEST THING I EVER SAW. YOU DON'T NEED *ME* TO TELL YOU THAT WAS SOME KIND O' *MIRACLE* OUT THERE LAST NIGHT, LOGAN.

MATTHEW FOWLER'S WIFE LOST HER HUSBAND IN THE SLIDE. SHE WANTED ME TO THANK YOU THAT SHE DIDN'T LOSE HER *SON*, AS WELL.

HERE YOU GO, LAD... THIS IS FOR YOU··

WHAT IS IT?

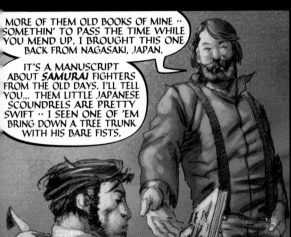

MORE OF THEM OLD BOOKS OF MINE·· SOMETHIN' TO PASS THE TIME WHILE YOU MEND UP. I BROUGHT THIS ONE BACK FROM NAGASAKI, JAPAN.

IT'S A MANUSCRIPT ABOUT *SAMURAI* FIGHTERS FROM THE OLD DAYS. I'LL TELL YOU... THEM LITTLE JAPANESE SCOUNDRELS ARE PRETTY SWIFT·· I SEEN ONE OF 'EM BRING DOWN A TREE TRUNK WITH HIS BARE FISTS.

MATTER OF FACT, I LEARNED A LOT FROM THEM... ABOUT THE WORLD AN' ABOUT LIFE. IT'S A STRONG PERSON WHO FOLLOWS HIS OWN PATH, THEY SAY. I SEE THAT STRENGTH IN *YOU*, LOGAN.

YOU SHOULD HAVE *DIED* LAST NIGHT. I DON'T KNOW HOW YOU SAVED THAT BOY, AN' I AIN'T GONNA *PRY*, BUT WHATEVER IT *IS* ABOUT YOU, SON, YOU NEED T' KNOW IT DON'T MAKE NO DIFFERENCE TO ME ONE WAY OR THE OTHER, UNDERSTAND?

ANYWAY, I GOTTA GET BACK T' THE QUARRY.

MISS ROSE·· CAN I ASK YOU TO WALK WITH ME FOR A FEW MINUTES?

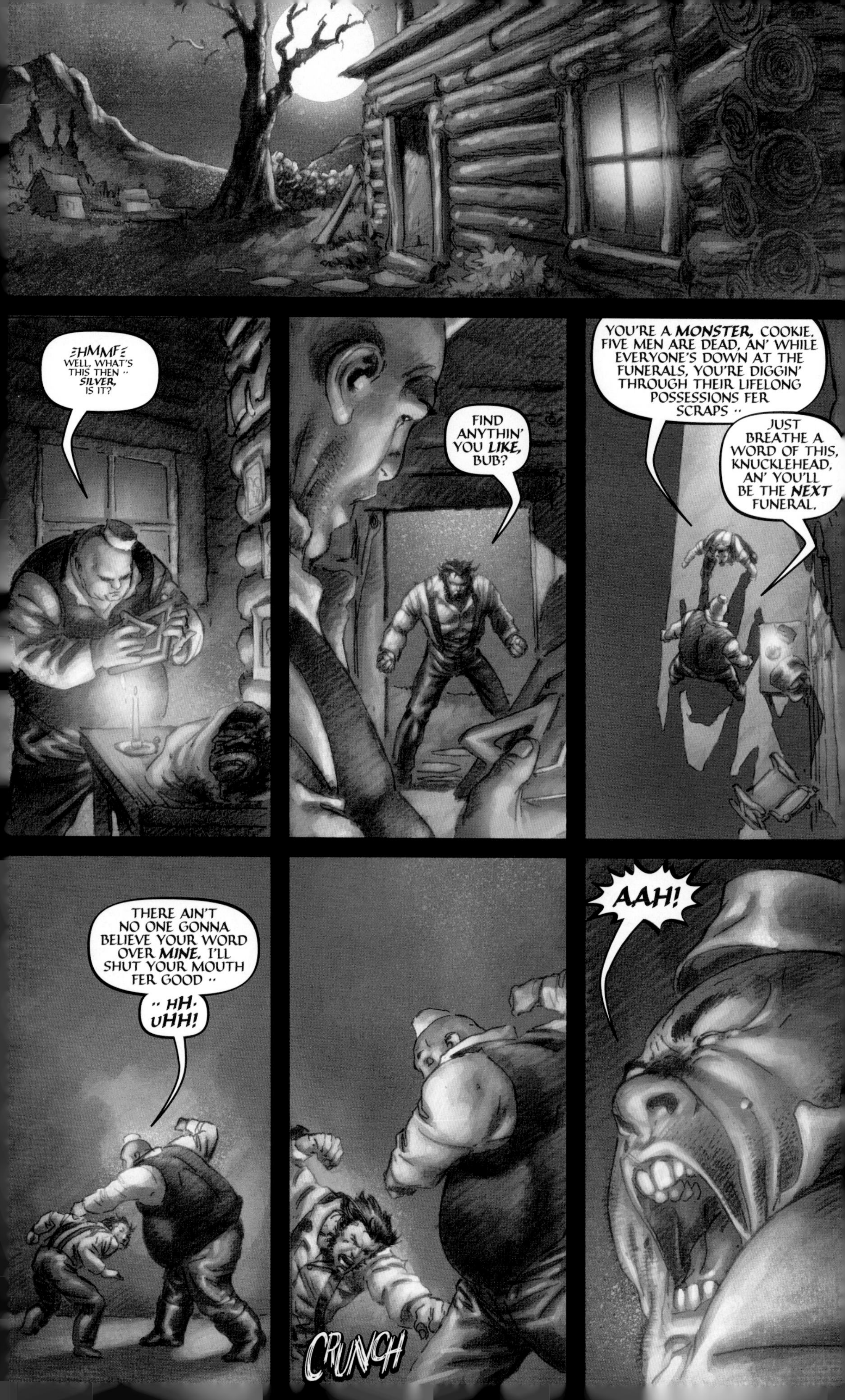
HMMF
WELL, WHAT'S THIS THEN .. SILVER, IS IT?
FIND ANYTHIN' YOU LIKE, BUB?
YOU'RE A MONSTER, COOKIE. FIVE MEN ARE DEAD, AN' WHILE EVERYONE'S DOWN AT THE FUNERALS, YOU'RE DIGGIN' THROUGH THEIR LIFELONG POSSESSIONS FER SCRAPS ..
JUST BREATHE A WORD OF THIS, KNUCKLEHEAD, AN' YOU'LL BE THE NEXT FUNERAL.
THERE AIN'T NO ONE GONNA BELIEVE YOUR WORD OVER MINE. I'LL SHUT YOUR MOUTH FER GOOD ..
.. HH. UHH!
CRUNCH
AAH!

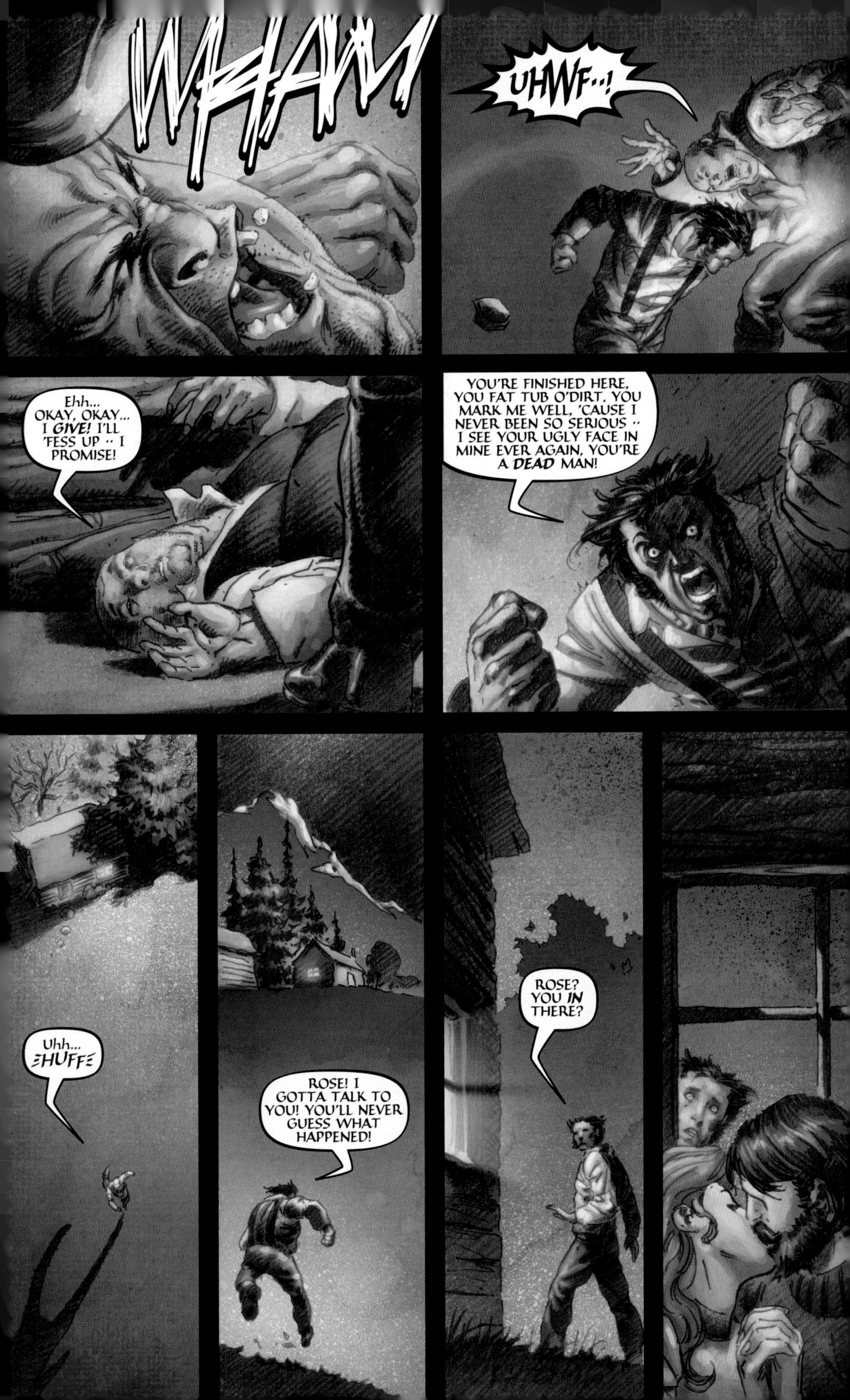
WHAM
UHWF..!
Ehh... OKAY, OKAY... I GIVE! I'LL 'FESS UP .. I PROMISE!
YOU'RE FINISHED HERE, YOU FAT TUB O'DIRT. YOU MARK ME WELL, 'CAUSE I NEVER BEEN SO SERIOUS .. I SEE YOUR UGLY FACE IN MINE EVER AGAIN, YOU'RE A DEAD MAN!
Uhh... HUFF
ROSE! I GOTTA TALK TO YOU! YOU'LL NEVER GUESS WHAT HAPPENED!
ROSE? YOU IN THERE?

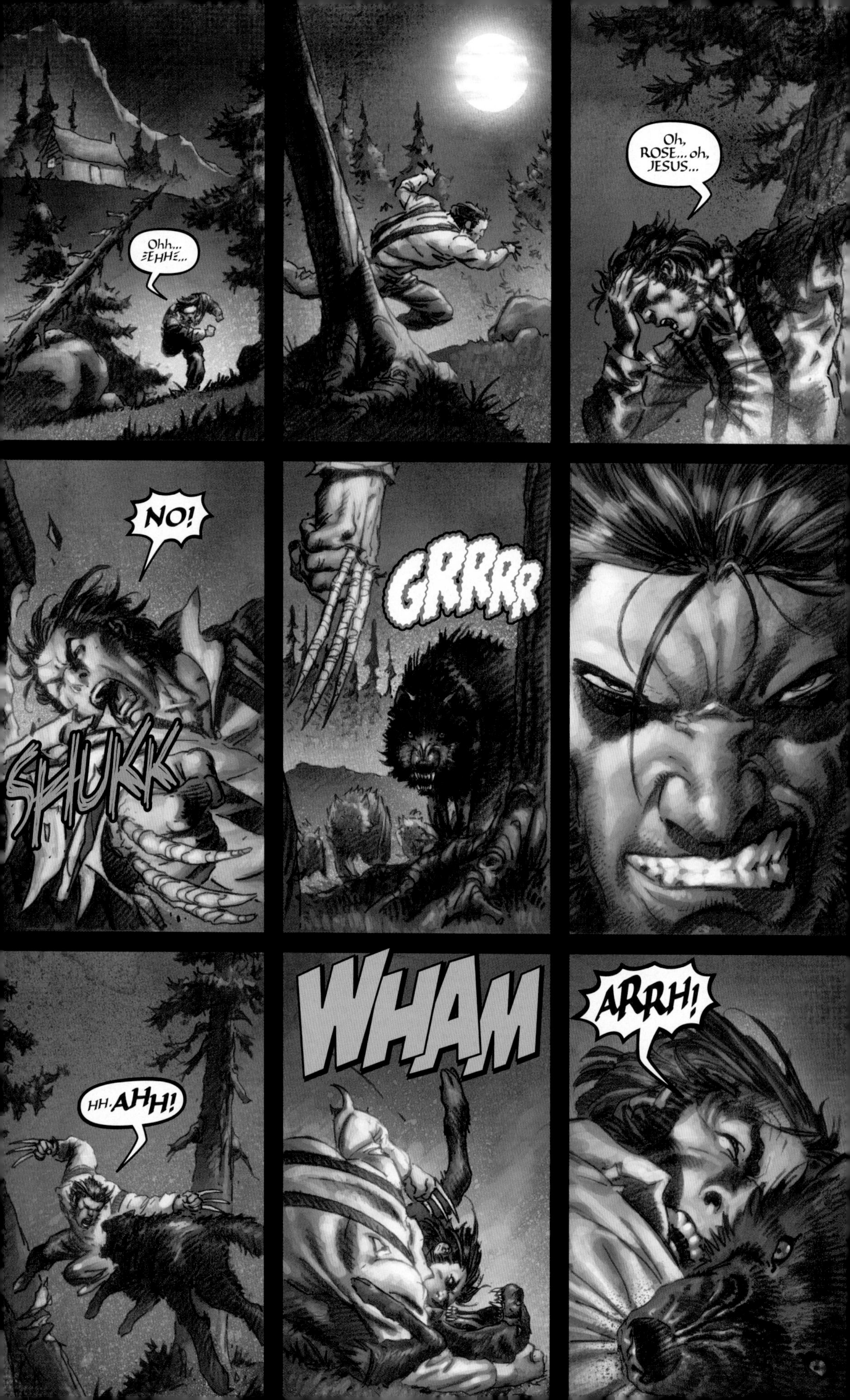
Ohh... ΞEHHΞ...
Oh, ROSE... oh, JESUS...
NO!
SHUKK
GRRRR
HH.AHH!
WHAM
ARRH!

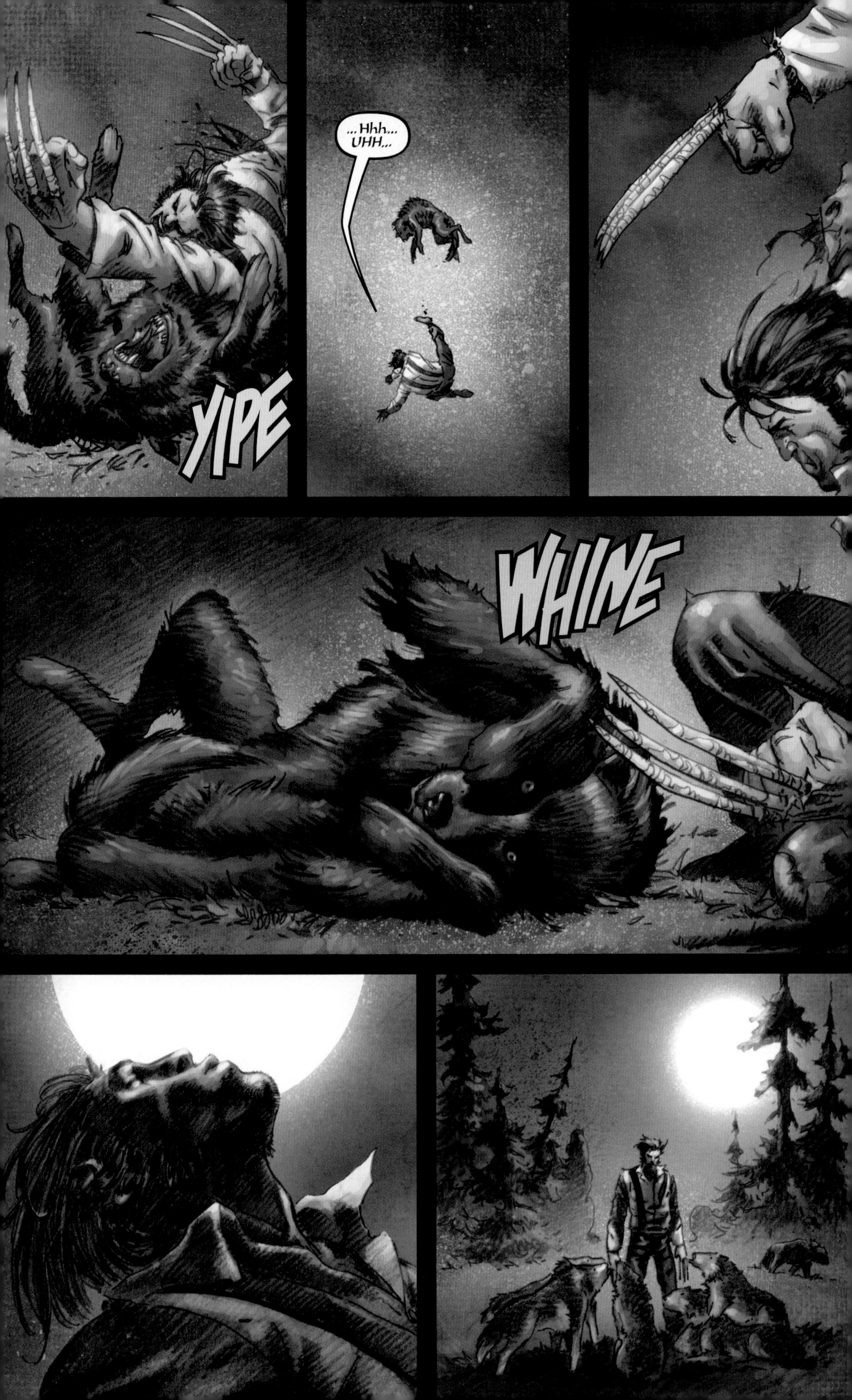
YIPE
...Hhh...
UHH...
WHINE

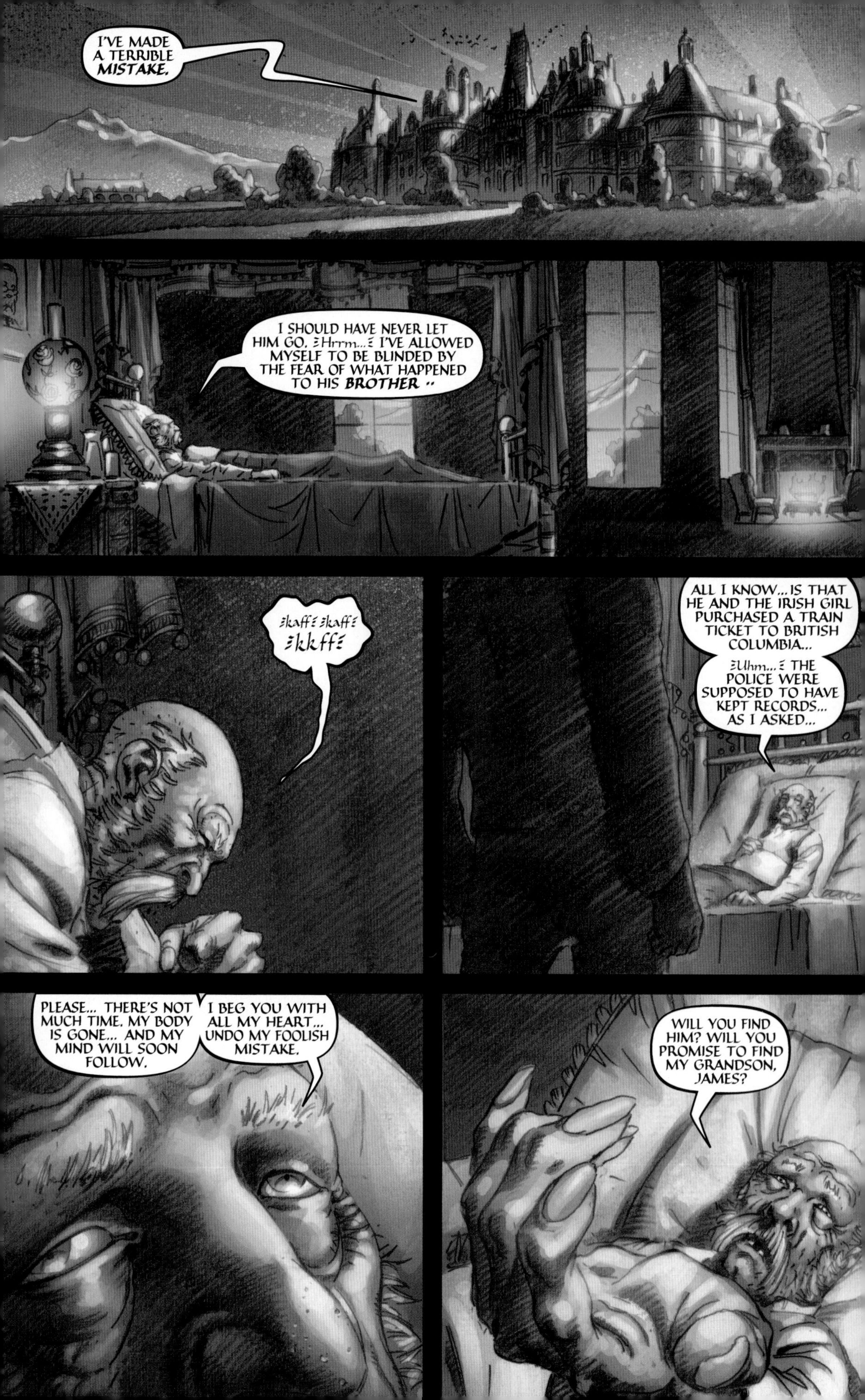
I'VE MADE A TERRIBLE MISTAKE.
I SHOULD HAVE NEVER LET HIM GO. Hrrm... I'VE ALLOWED MYSELF TO BE BLINDED BY THE FEAR OF WHAT HAPPENED TO HIS BROTHER ..
kaff kaff kkff
ALL I KNOW... IS THAT HE AND THE IRISH GIRL PURCHASED A TRAIN TICKET TO BRITISH COLUMBIA...
Uhm... THE POLICE WERE SUPPOSED TO HAVE KEPT RECORDS... AS I ASKED...
PLEASE... THERE'S NOT MUCH TIME. MY BODY IS GONE... AND MY MIND WILL SOON FOLLOW.
I BEG YOU WITH ALL MY HEART... UNDO MY FOOLISH MISTAKE.
WILL YOU FIND HIM? WILL YOU PROMISE TO FIND MY GRANDSON, JAMES?

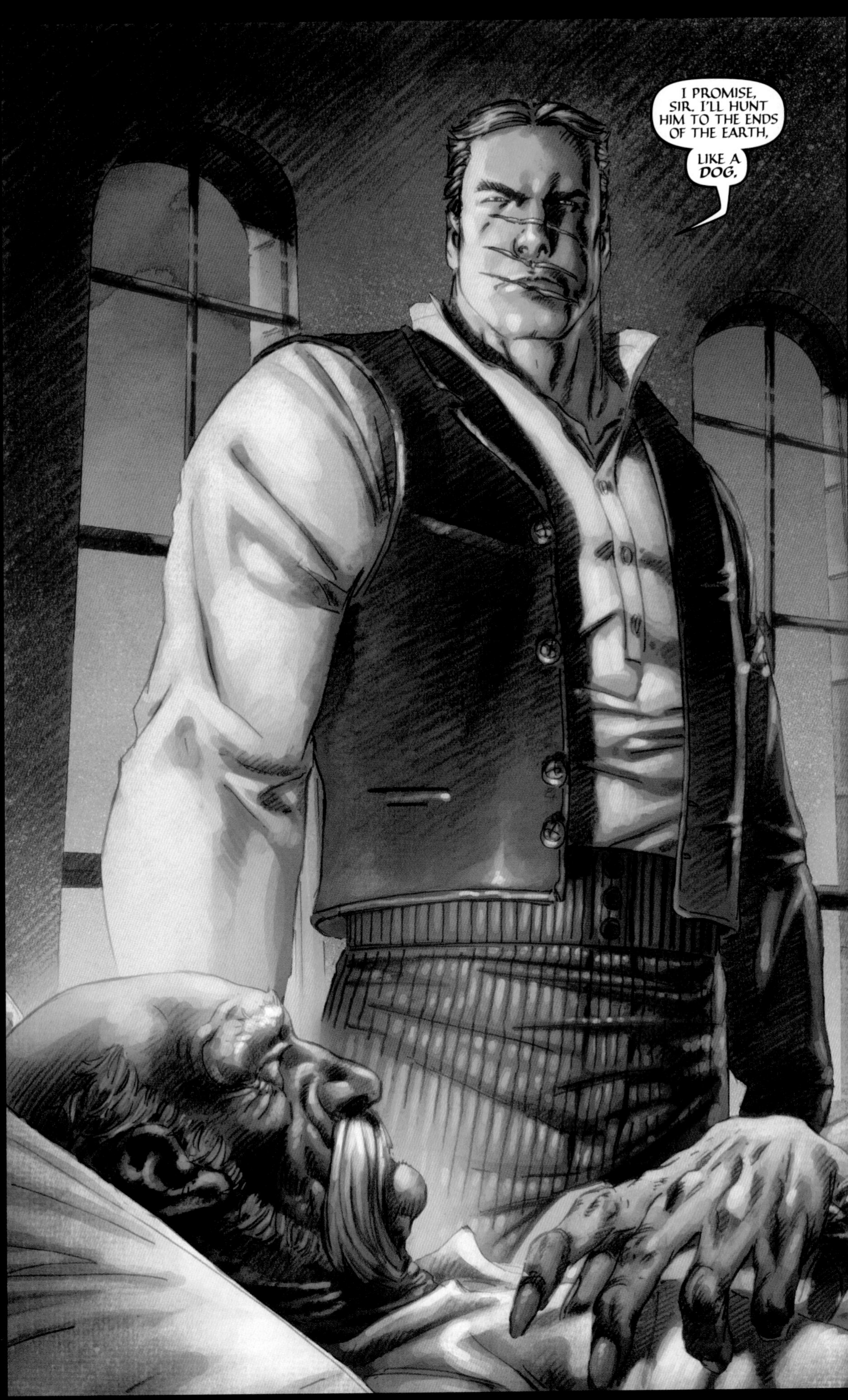
I PROMISE, SIR. I'LL HUNT HIM TO THE ENDS OF THE EARTH,
LIKE A DOG.

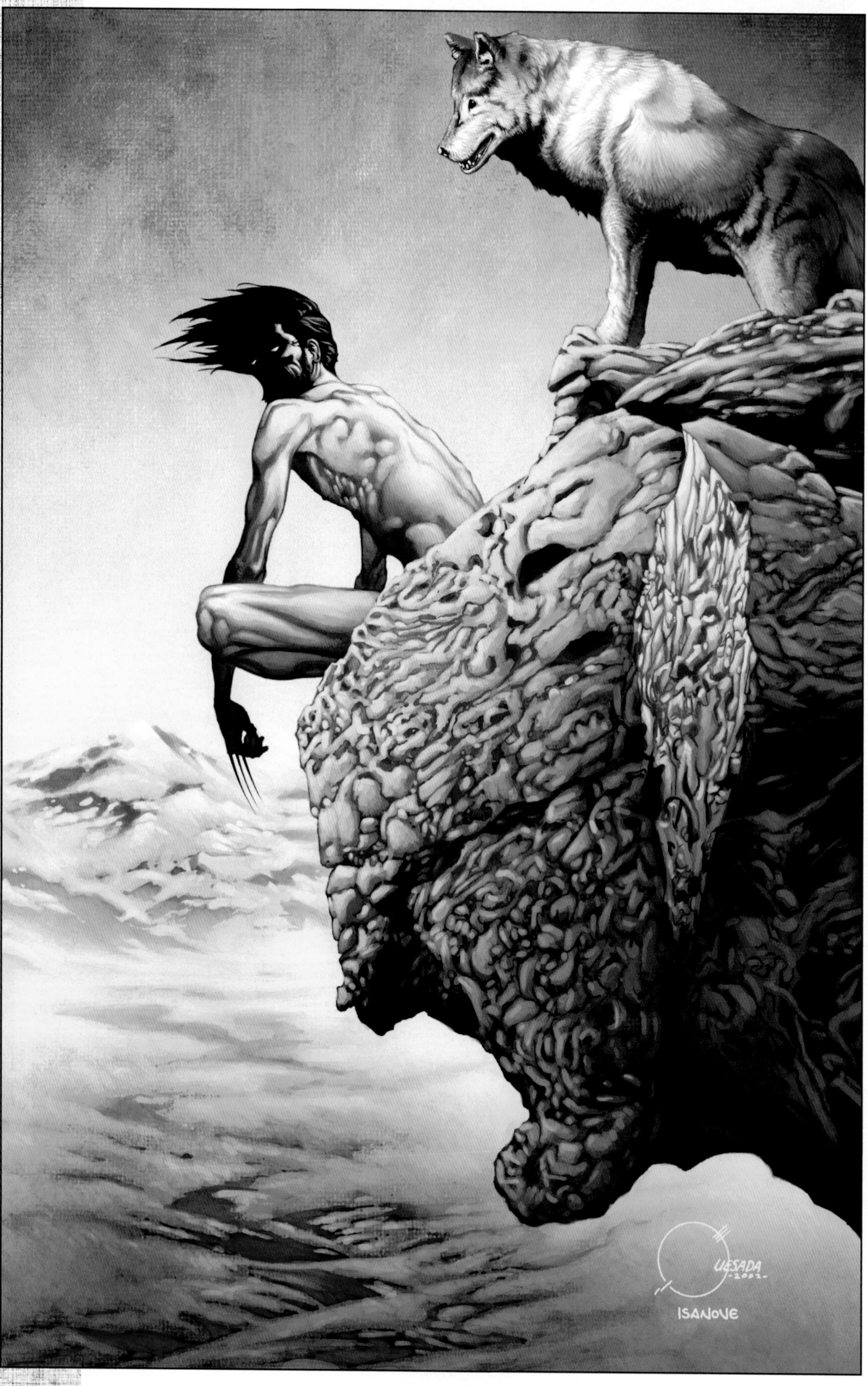
UESADA
-2002-
ISANOVE

PART VI – **DUST TO DUST**

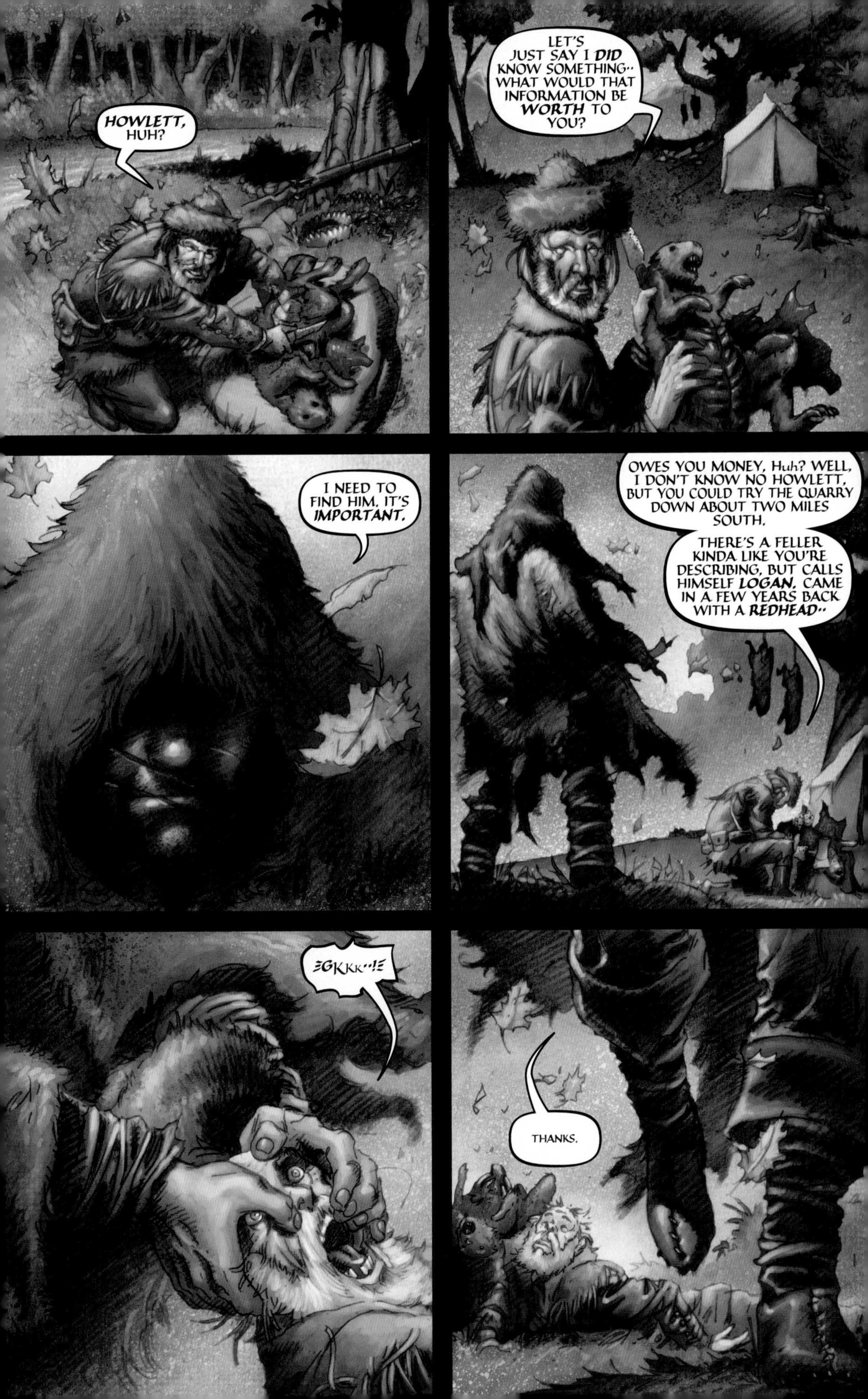
HOWLETT, HUH?
LET'S JUST SAY I DID KNOW SOMETHING.. WHAT WOULD THAT INFORMATION BE WORTH TO YOU?
I NEED TO FIND HIM. IT'S IMPORTANT.
OWES YOU MONEY, Huh? WELL, I DON'T KNOW NO HOWLETT, BUT YOU COULD TRY THE QUARRY DOWN ABOUT TWO MILES SOUTH.
THERE'S A FELLER KINDA LIKE YOU'RE DESCRIBING, BUT CALLS HIMSELF LOGAN. CAME IN A FEW YEARS BACK WITH A REDHEAD..
GKKK..!
THANKS.

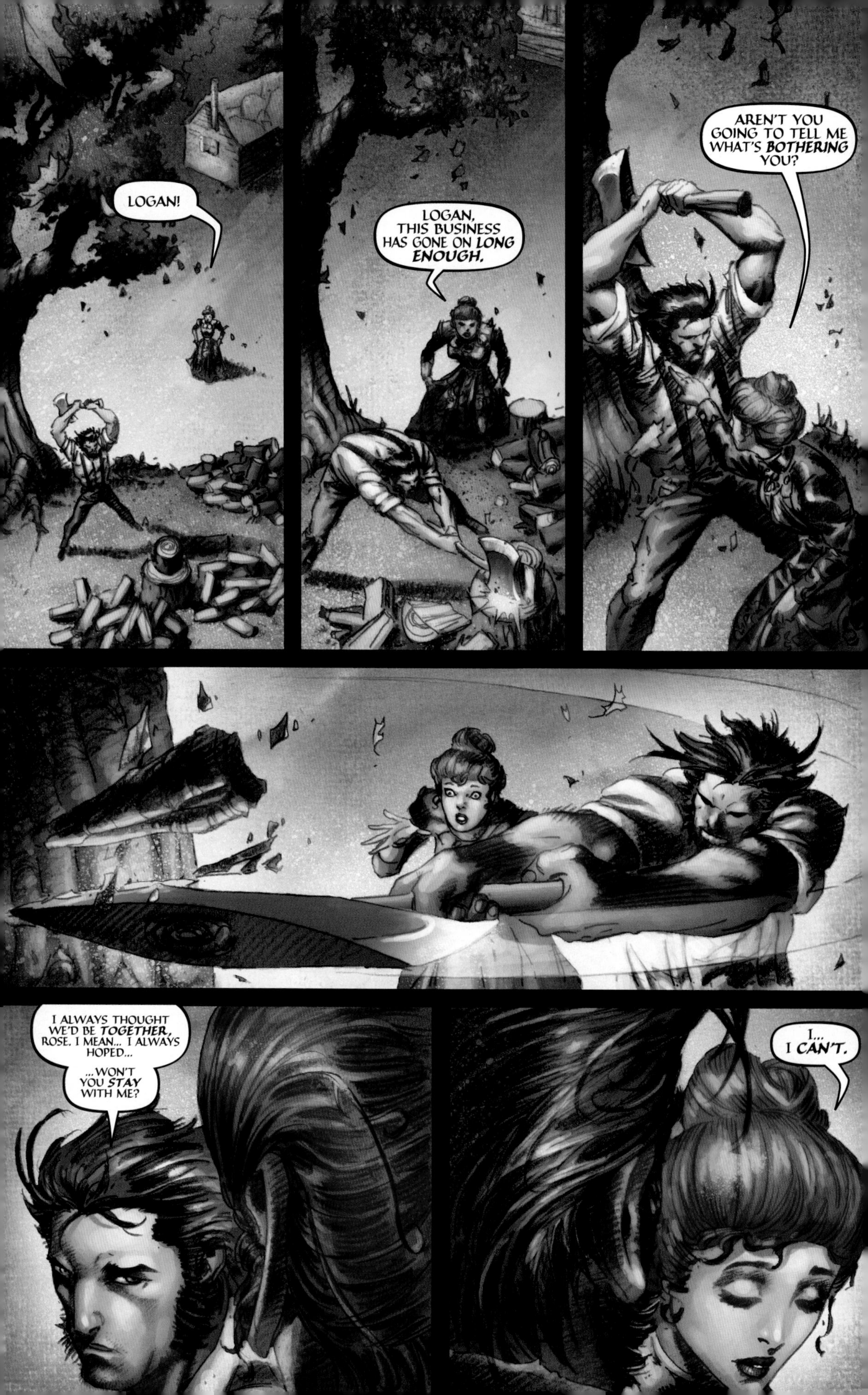
LOGAN!
LOGAN, THIS BUSINESS HAS GONE ON LONG ENOUGH.
AREN'T YOU GOING TO TELL ME WHAT'S BOTHERING YOU?
I ALWAYS THOUGHT WE'D BE TOGETHER, ROSE. I MEAN... I ALWAYS HOPED...
...WON'T YOU STAY WITH ME?
I... I CAN'T.

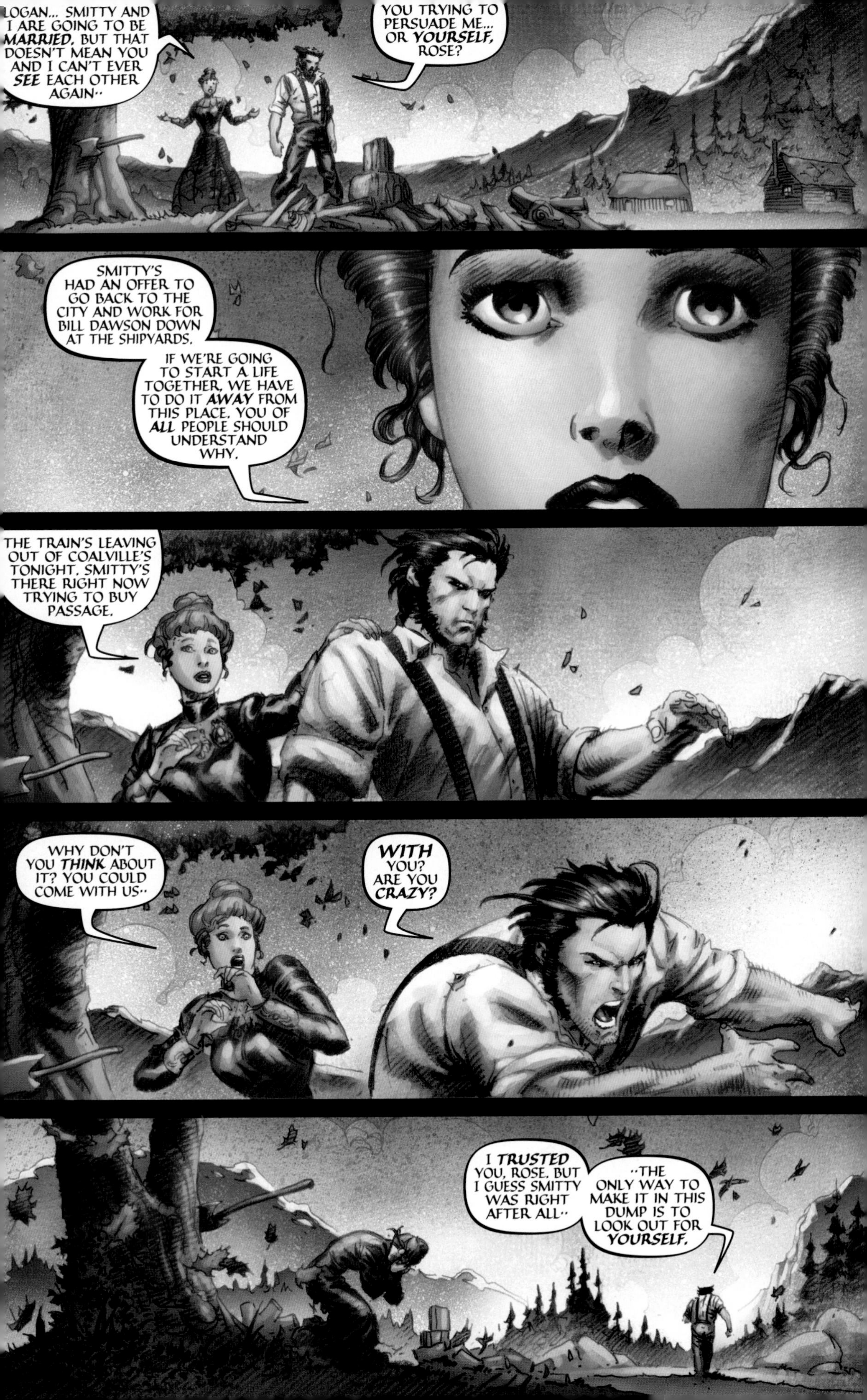
LOGAN... SMITTY AND I ARE GOING TO BE MARRIED, BUT THAT DOESN'T MEAN YOU AND I CAN'T EVER SEE EACH OTHER AGAIN..
YOU TRYING TO PERSUADE ME... OR YOURSELF, ROSE?
SMITTY'S HAD AN OFFER TO GO BACK TO THE CITY AND WORK FOR BILL DAWSON DOWN AT THE SHIPYARDS.
IF WE'RE GOING TO START A LIFE TOGETHER, WE HAVE TO DO IT AWAY FROM THIS PLACE. YOU OF ALL PEOPLE SHOULD UNDERSTAND WHY.
THE TRAIN'S LEAVING OUT OF COALVILLE'S TONIGHT. SMITTY'S THERE RIGHT NOW TRYING TO BUY PASSAGE.
WHY DON'T YOU THINK ABOUT IT? YOU COULD COME WITH US..
WITH YOU? ARE YOU CRAZY?
I TRUSTED YOU, ROSE. BUT I GUESS SMITTY WAS RIGHT AFTER ALL..
..THE ONLY WAY TO MAKE IT IN THIS DUMP IS TO LOOK OUT FOR YOURSELF.

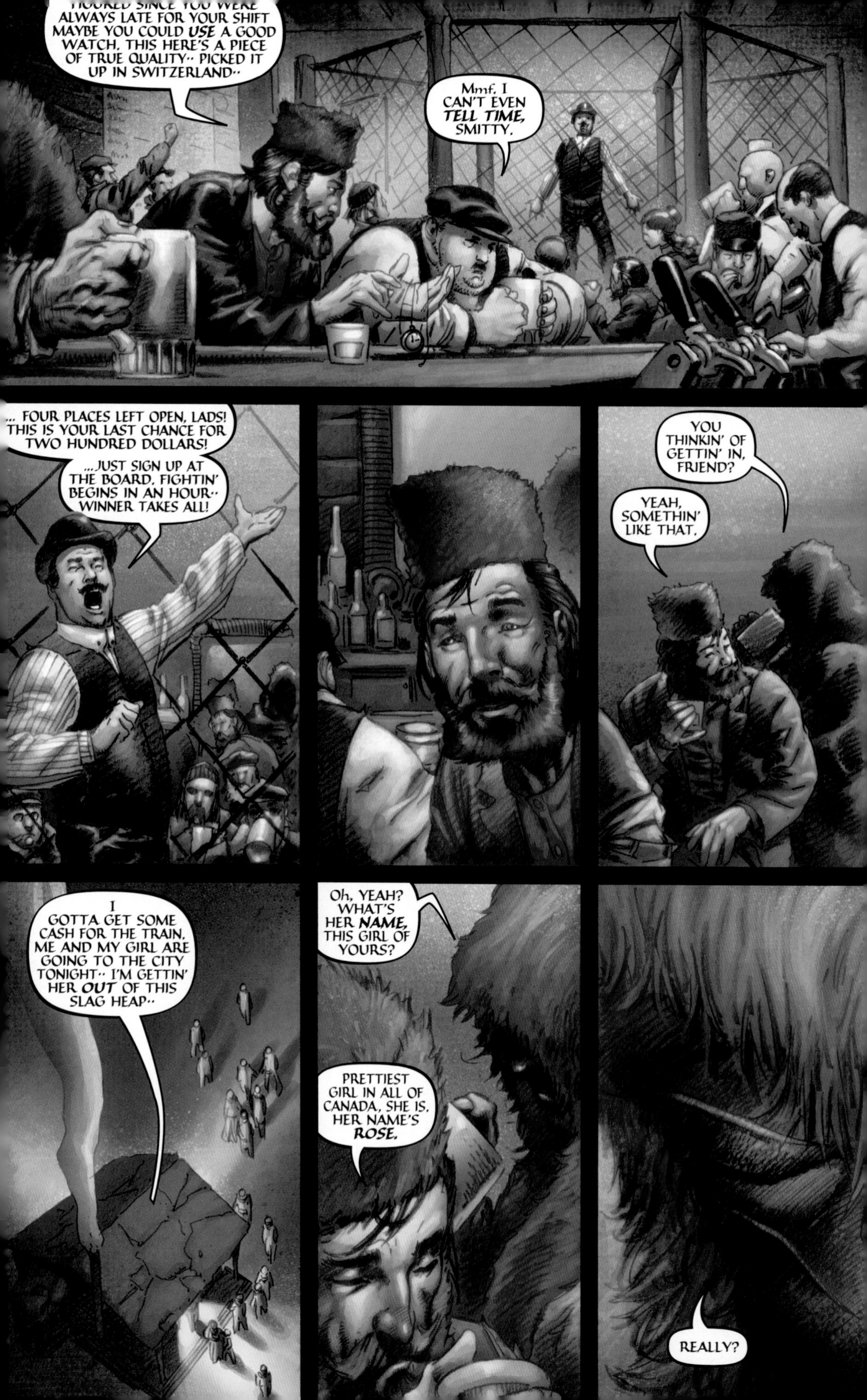
ALWAYS LATE FOR YOUR SHIFT MAYBE YOU COULD USE A GOOD WATCH. THIS HERE'S A PIECE OF TRUE QUALITY.. PICKED IT UP IN SWITZERLAND..
Mmf. I CAN'T EVEN TELL TIME, SMITTY.
... FOUR PLACES LEFT OPEN, LADS! THIS IS YOUR LAST CHANCE FOR TWO HUNDRED DOLLARS!
...JUST SIGN UP AT THE BOARD. FIGHTIN' BEGINS IN AN HOUR.. WINNER TAKES ALL!
YOU THINKIN' OF GETTIN' IN, FRIEND?
YEAH, SOMETHIN' LIKE THAT.
I GOTTA GET SOME CASH FOR THE TRAIN. ME AND MY GIRL ARE GOING TO THE CITY TONIGHT.. I'M GETTIN' HER OUT OF THIS SLAG HEAP..
Oh, YEAH? WHAT'S HER NAME, THIS GIRL OF YOURS?
PRETTIEST GIRL IN ALL OF CANADA, SHE IS. HER NAME'S ROSE.
REALLY?

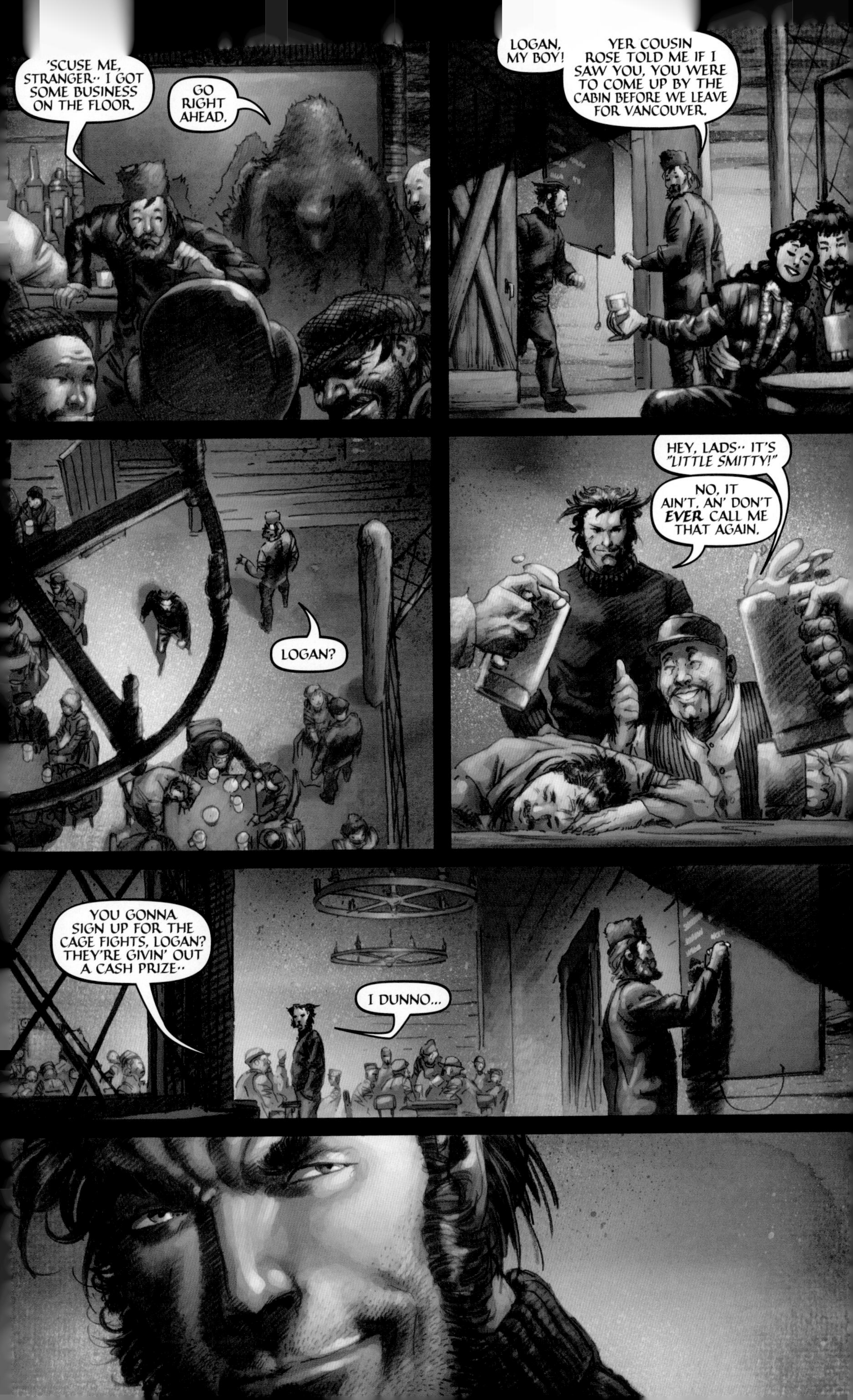
'SCUSE ME, STRANGER·· I GOT SOME BUSINESS ON THE FLOOR.
GO RIGHT AHEAD.
LOGAN, MY BOY!
YER COUSIN ROSE TOLD ME IF I SAW YOU, YOU WERE TO COME UP BY THE CABIN BEFORE WE LEAVE FOR VANCOUVER.
LOGAN?
HEY, LADS·· IT'S "LITTLE SMITTY!"
NO, IT AIN'T. AN' DON'T **EVER** CALL ME THAT AGAIN.
YOU GONNA SIGN UP FOR THE CAGE FIGHTS, LOGAN? THEY'RE GIVIN' OUT A CASH PRIZE··
I DUNNO...

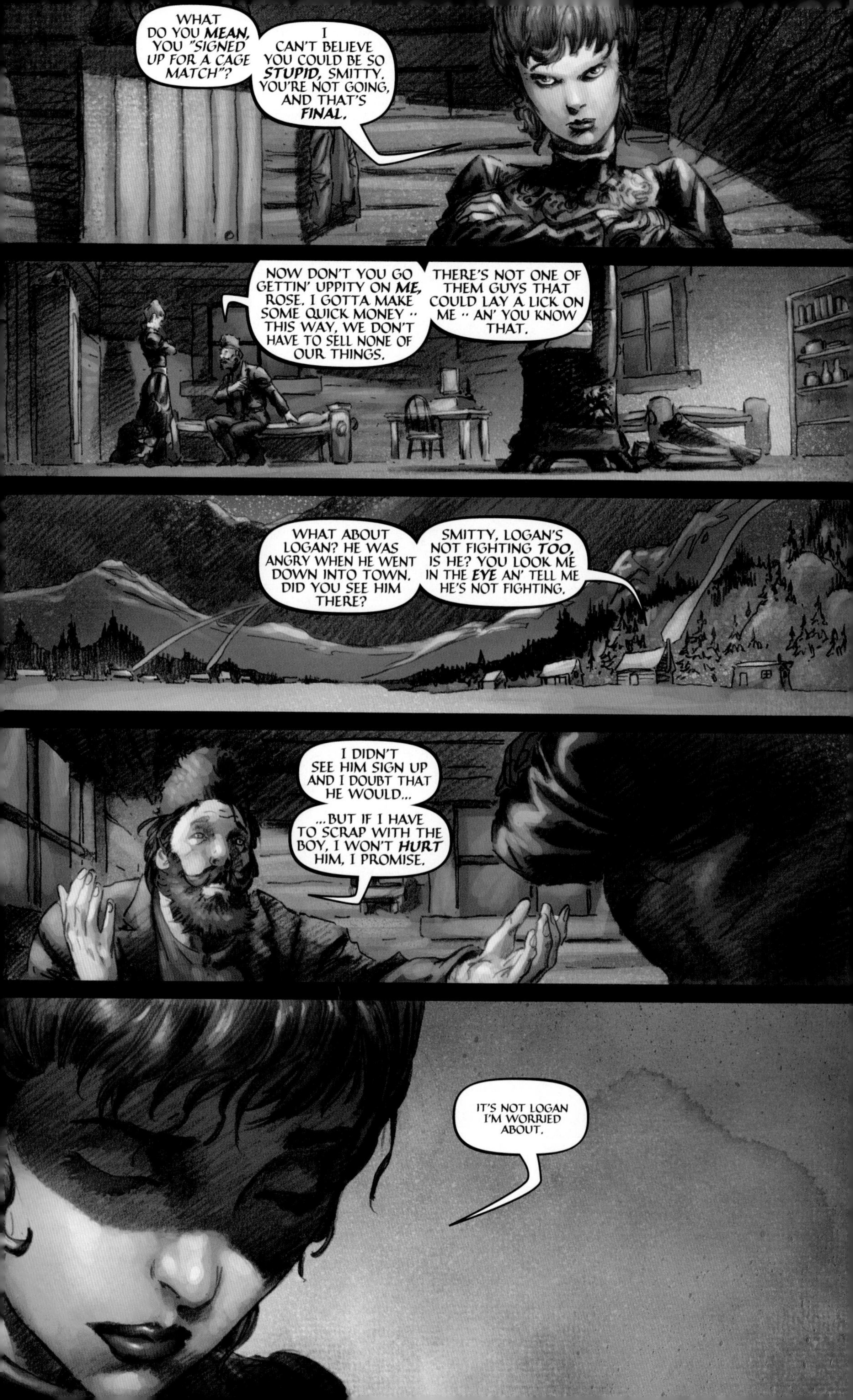

WHAT DO YOU MEAN, YOU "SIGNED UP FOR A CAGE MATCH"?
I CAN'T BELIEVE YOU COULD BE SO STUPID, SMITTY. YOU'RE NOT GOING, AND THAT'S FINAL.
NOW DON'T YOU GO GETTIN' UPPITY ON ME, ROSE. I GOTTA MAKE SOME QUICK MONEY -- THIS WAY, WE DON'T HAVE TO SELL NONE OF OUR THINGS.
THERE'S NOT ONE OF THEM GUYS THAT COULD LAY A LICK ON ME -- AN' YOU KNOW THAT.
WHAT ABOUT LOGAN? HE WAS ANGRY WHEN HE WENT DOWN INTO TOWN. DID YOU SEE HIM THERE?
SMITTY, LOGAN'S NOT FIGHTING TOO, IS HE? YOU LOOK ME IN THE EYE AN' TELL ME HE'S NOT FIGHTING.
I DIDN'T SEE HIM SIGN UP AND I DOUBT THAT HE WOULD...
...BUT IF I HAVE TO SCRAP WITH THE BOY, I WON'T HURT HIM, I PROMISE.
IT'S NOT LOGAN I'M WORRIED ABOUT.

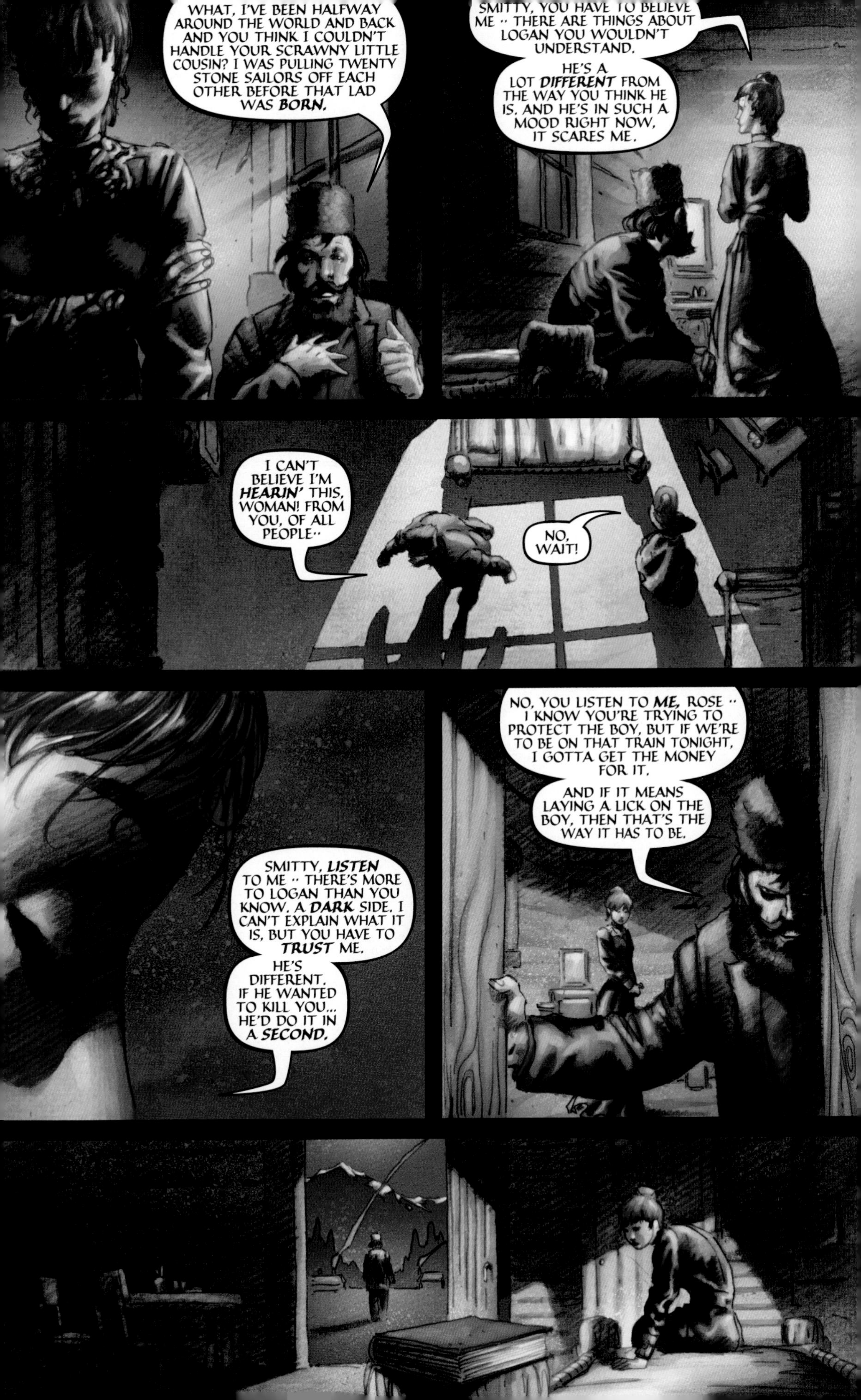

WHAT, I'VE BEEN HALFWAY AROUND THE WORLD AND BACK AND YOU THINK I COULDN'T HANDLE YOUR SCRAWNY LITTLE COUSIN? I WAS PULLING TWENTY STONE SAILORS OFF EACH OTHER BEFORE THAT LAD WAS BORN.
SMITTY, YOU HAVE TO BELIEVE ME -- THERE ARE THINGS ABOUT LOGAN YOU WOULDN'T UNDERSTAND.
HE'S A LOT DIFFERENT FROM THE WAY YOU THINK HE IS, AND HE'S IN SUCH A MOOD RIGHT NOW, IT SCARES ME.
I CAN'T BELIEVE I'M HEARIN' THIS, WOMAN! FROM YOU, OF ALL PEOPLE--
NO, WAIT!
SMITTY, LISTEN TO ME -- THERE'S MORE TO LOGAN THAN YOU KNOW. A DARK SIDE. I CAN'T EXPLAIN WHAT IT IS, BUT YOU HAVE TO TRUST ME.
HE'S DIFFERENT. IF HE WANTED TO KILL YOU... HE'D DO IT IN A SECOND.
NO, YOU LISTEN TO ME, ROSE -- I KNOW YOU'RE TRYING TO PROTECT THE BOY, BUT IF WE'RE TO BE ON THAT TRAIN TONIGHT, I GOTTA GET THE MONEY FOR IT.
AND IF IT MEANS LAYING A LICK ON THE BOY, THEN THAT'S THE WAY IT HAS TO BE.

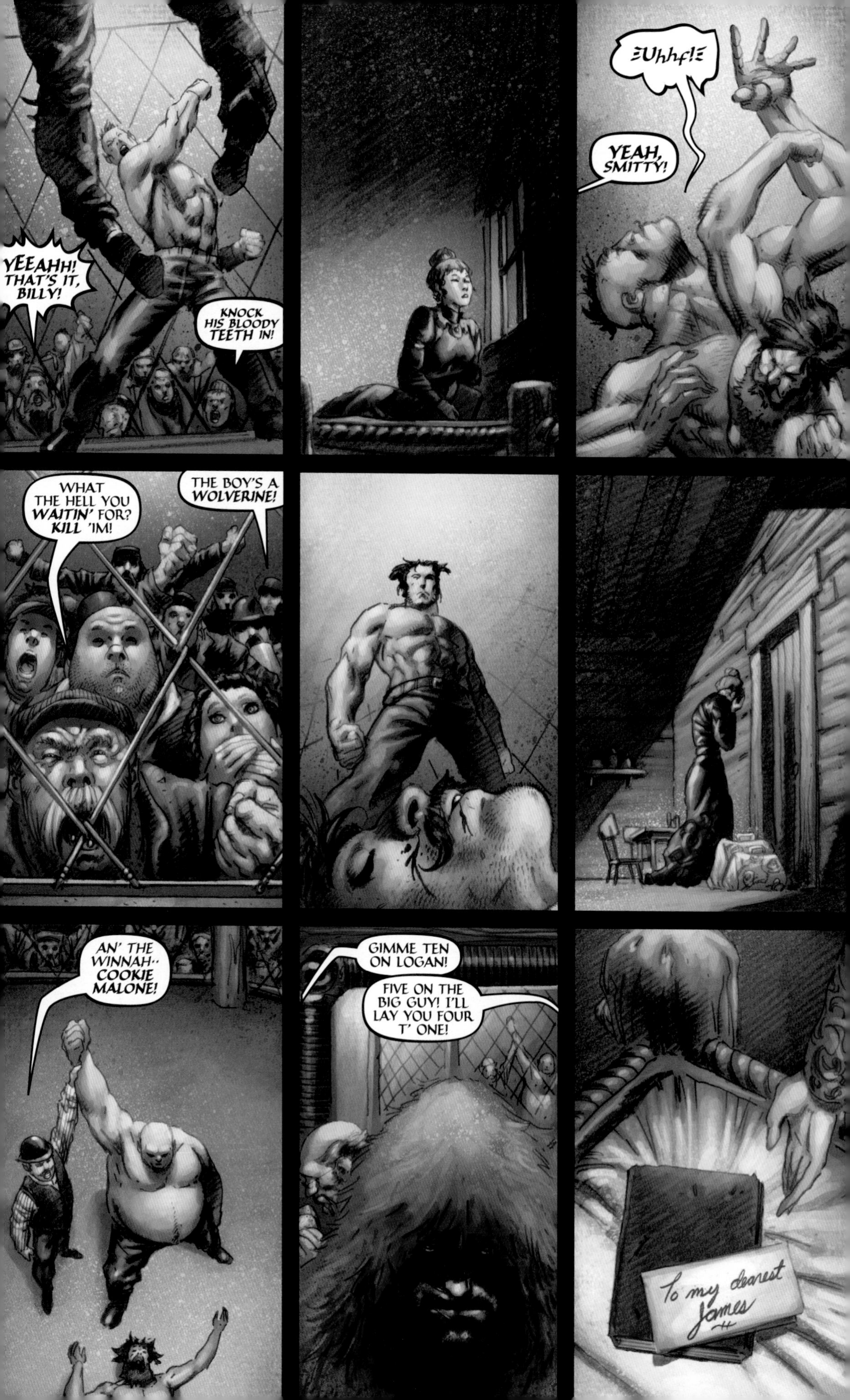
YEEAHH! THAT'S IT, BILLY!
KNOCK HIS BLOODY TEETH IN!
UHHF!
YEAH, SMITTY!
WHAT THE HELL YOU WAITIN' FOR? KILL 'IM!
THE BOY'S A WOLVERINE!
AN' THE WINNAH.. COOKIE MALONE!
GIMME TEN ON LOGAN!
FIVE ON THE BIG GUY! I'LL LAY YOU FOUR T' ONE!
To my dearest James

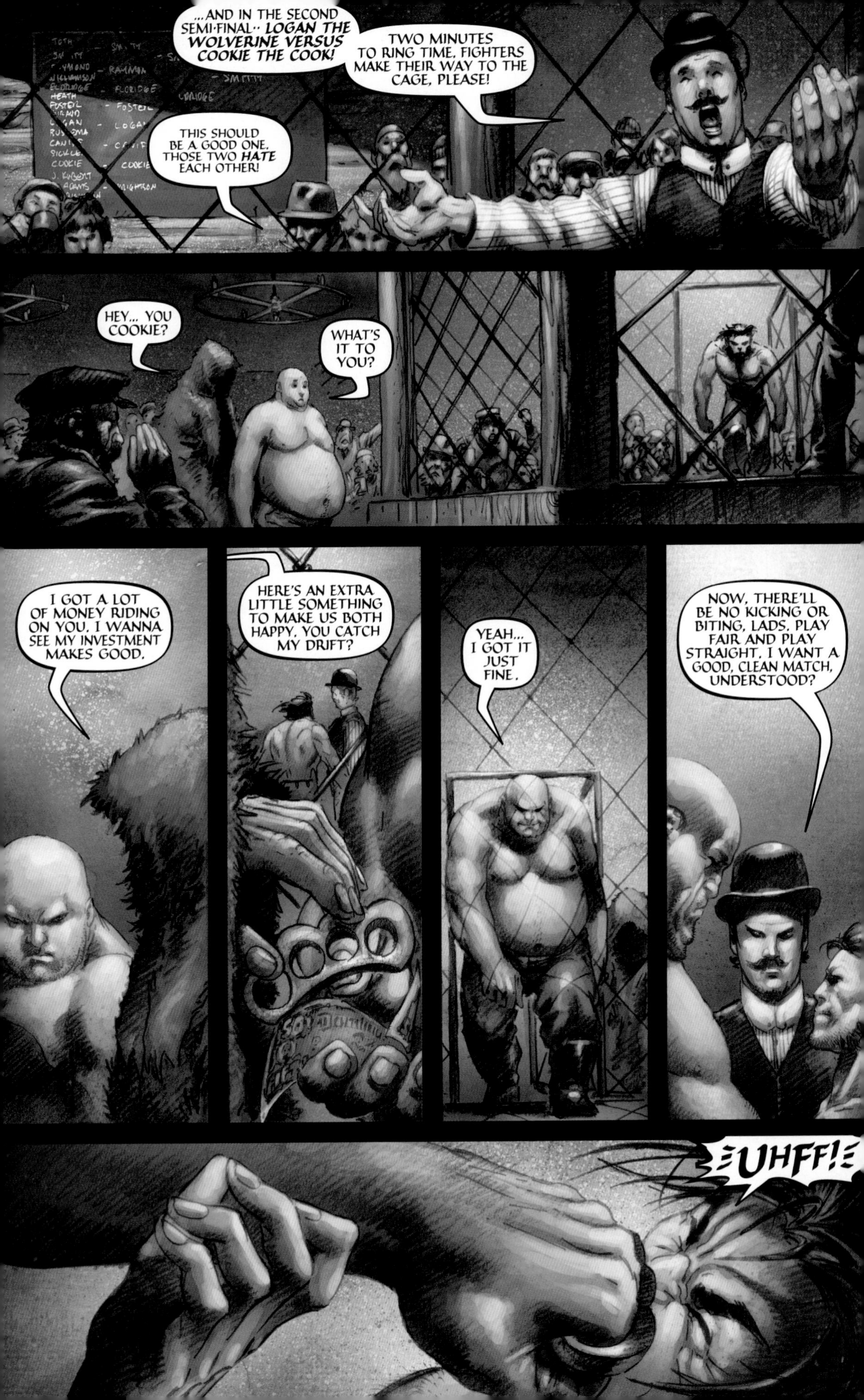
...AND IN THE SECOND SEMI-FINAL.. LOGAN THE WOLVERINE VERSUS COOKIE THE COOK!
TWO MINUTES TO RING TIME, FIGHTERS MAKE THEIR WAY TO THE CAGE, PLEASE!
THIS SHOULD BE A GOOD ONE. THOSE TWO HATE EACH OTHER!
HEY... YOU COOKIE?
WHAT'S IT TO YOU?
I GOT A LOT OF MONEY RIDING ON YOU. I WANNA SEE MY INVESTMENT MAKES GOOD.
HERE'S AN EXTRA LITTLE SOMETHING TO MAKE US BOTH HAPPY. YOU CATCH MY DRIFT?
YEAH... I GOT IT JUST FINE.
NOW, THERE'LL BE NO KICKING OR BITING, LADS. PLAY FAIR AND PLAY STRAIGHT. I WANT A GOOD, CLEAN MATCH, UNDERSTOOD?
UHFF!

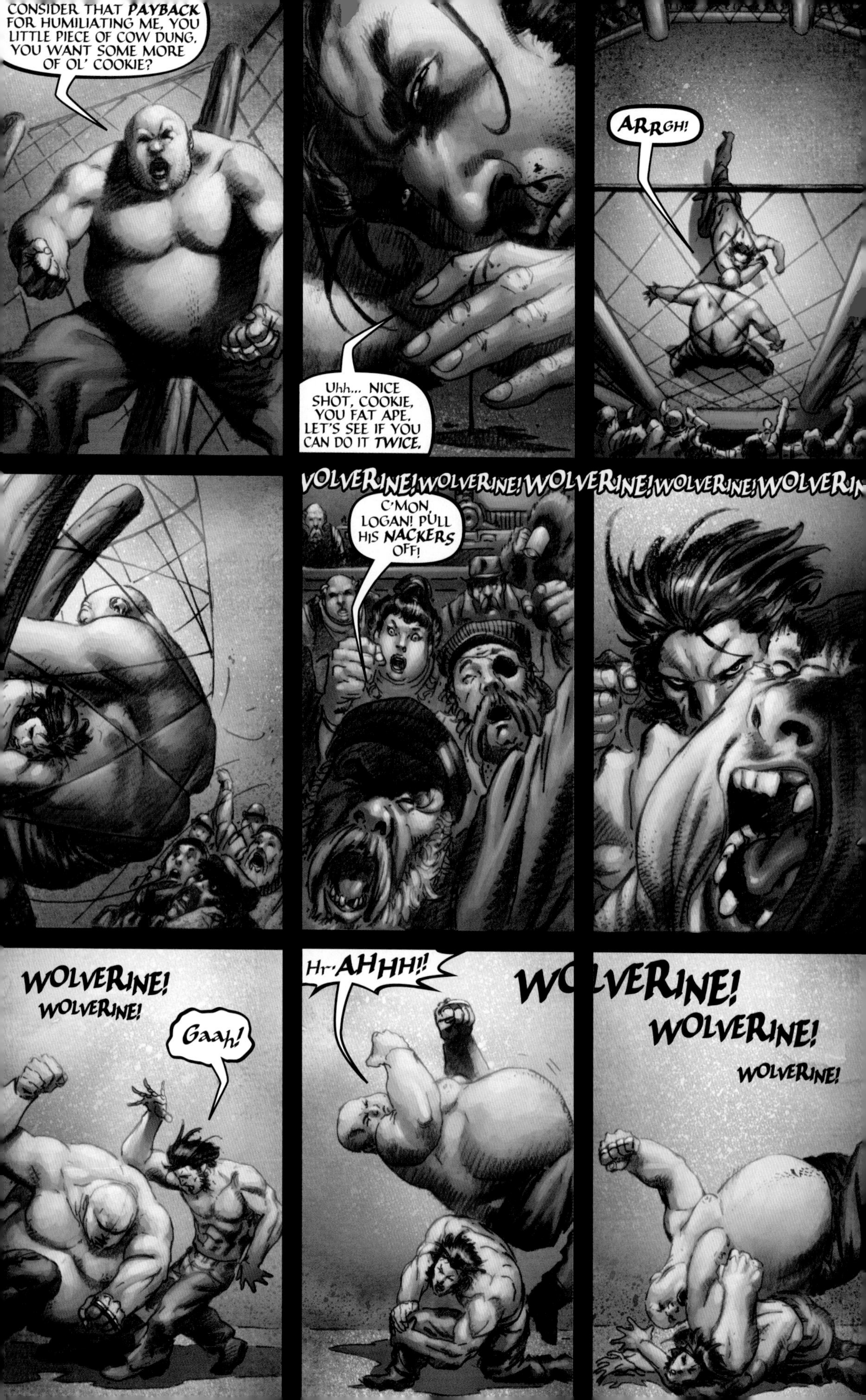
CONSIDER THAT PAYBACK FOR HUMILIATING ME, YOU LITTLE PIECE OF COW DUNG. YOU WANT SOME MORE OF OL' COOKIE?
Uhh... NICE SHOT, COOKIE, YOU FAT APE. LET'S SEE IF YOU CAN DO IT TWICE.
ARRGH!
WOLVERINE! WOLVERINE! WOLVERINE! WOLVERINE! WOLVERINE!
C'MON, LOGAN! PULL HIS NACKERS OFF!
WOLVERINE!
WOLVERINE!
Gaah!
Hr-AHHH!!
WOLVERINE!
WOLVERINE!
WOLVERINE!

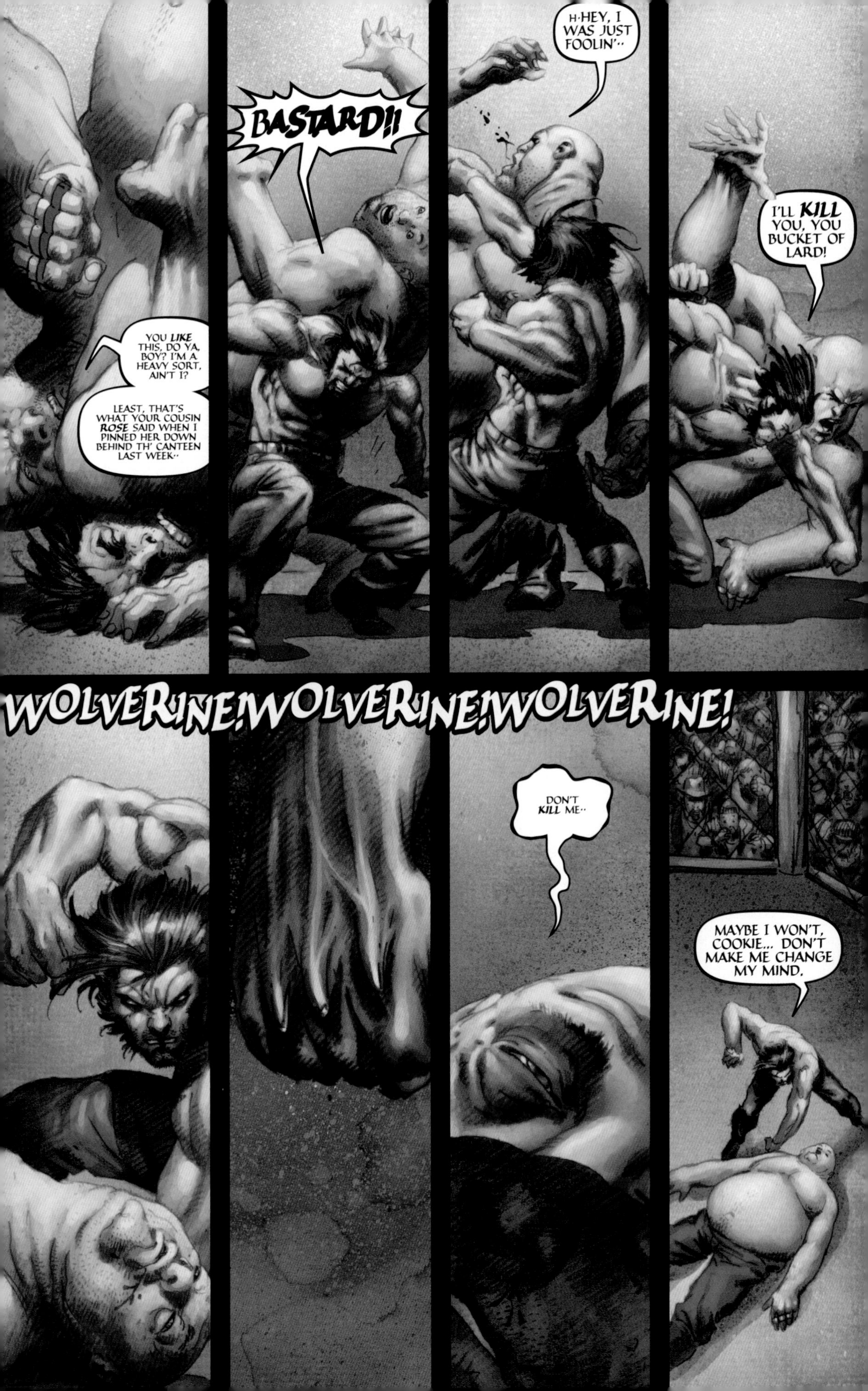
YOU LIKE THIS, DO YA, BOY? I'M A HEAVY SORT, AIN'T I?
LEAST, THAT'S WHAT YOUR COUSIN ROSE SAID WHEN I PINNED HER DOWN BEHIND TH' CANTEEN LAST WEEK..
BASTARD!!
H-HEY, I WAS JUST FOOLIN'..
I'LL KILL YOU, YOU BUCKET OF LARD!
WOLVERINE! WOLVERINE! WOLVERINE!
DON'T KILL ME..
MAYBE I WON'T, COOKIE... DON'T MAKE ME CHANGE MY MIND.

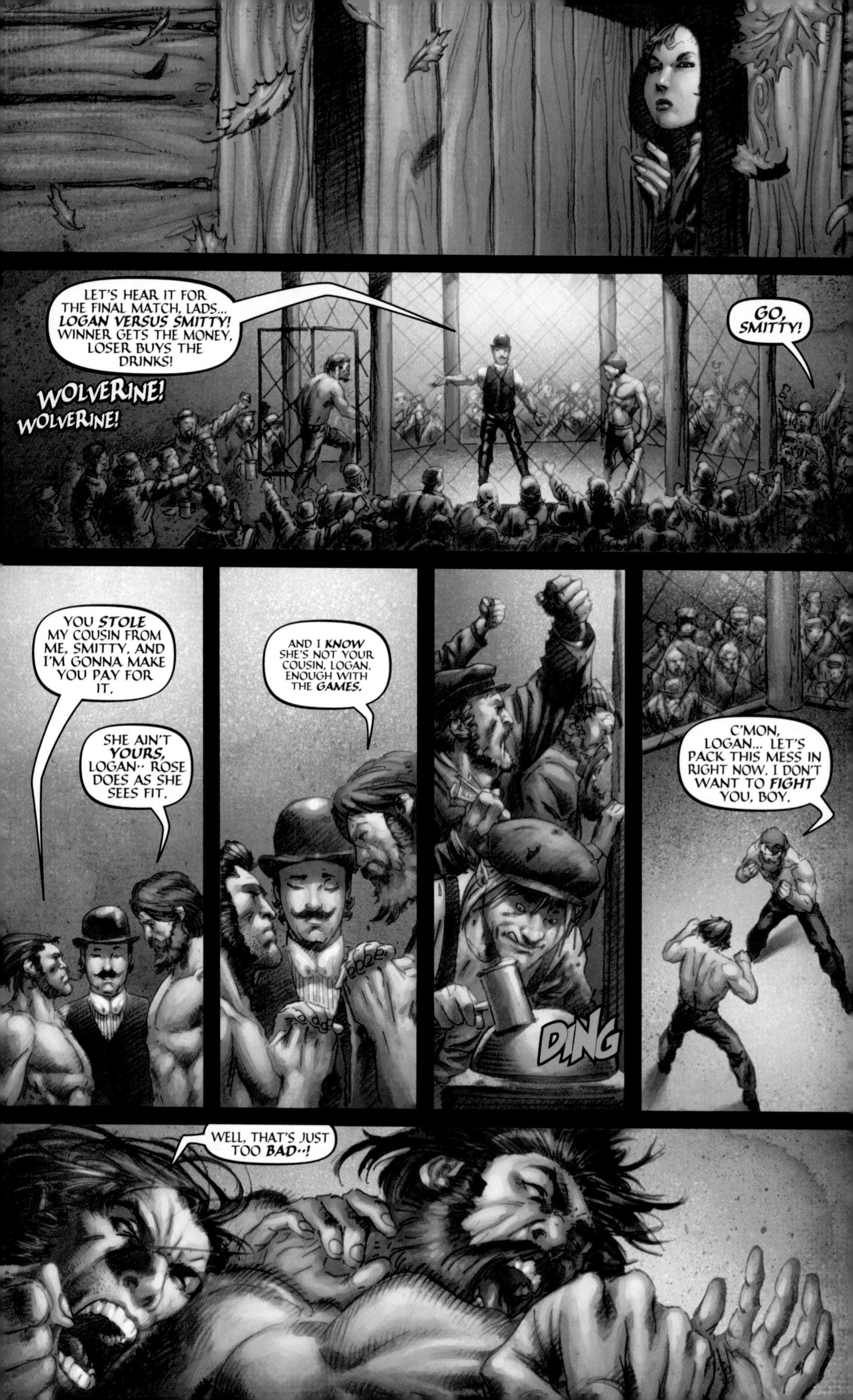
LET'S HEAR IT FOR THE FINAL MATCH, LADS... LOGAN VERSUS SMITTY! WINNER GETS THE MONEY, LOSER BUYS THE DRINKS!
GO, SMITTY!
WOLVERINE! WOLVERINE!
YOU STOLE MY COUSIN FROM ME, SMITTY. AND I'M GONNA MAKE YOU PAY FOR IT.
SHE AIN'T YOURS, LOGAN.. ROSE DOES AS SHE SEES FIT.
AND I KNOW SHE'S NOT YOUR COUSIN, LOGAN. ENOUGH WITH THE GAMES.
DING
C'MON, LOGAN... LET'S PACK THIS MESS IN RIGHT NOW. I DON'T WANT TO FIGHT YOU, BOY.
WELL, THAT'S JUST TOO BAD..!

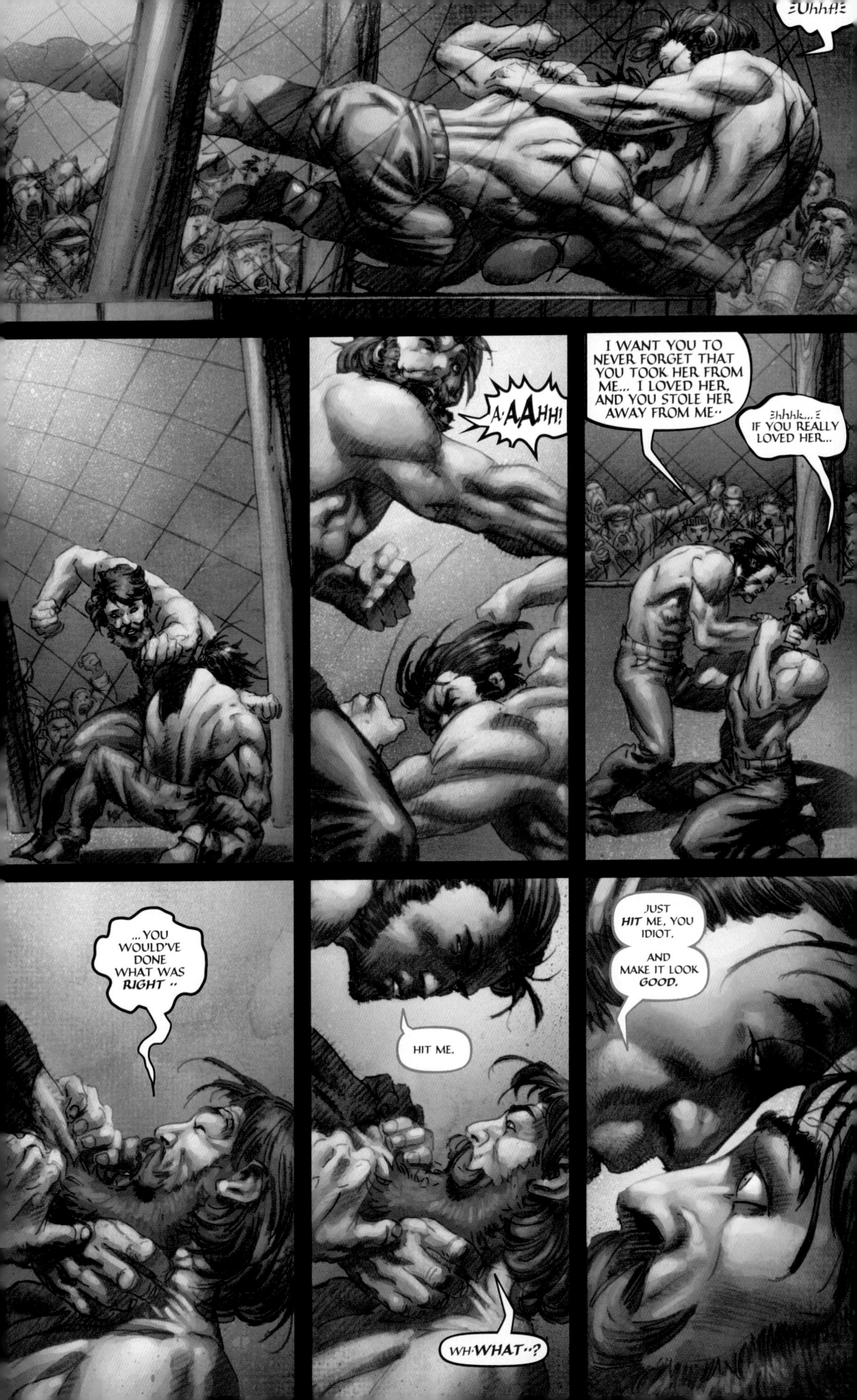
ƎUhhf!Ǝ
A-AAHH!
I WANT YOU TO NEVER FORGET THAT YOU TOOK HER FROM ME... I LOVED HER, AND YOU STOLE HER AWAY FROM ME..
ƎhhhK...Ǝ IF YOU REALLY LOVED HER...
...YOU WOULD'VE DONE WHAT WAS RIGHT..
HIT ME.
WH-WHAT..?
JUST HIT ME, YOU IDIOT.
AND MAKE IT LOOK GOOD.

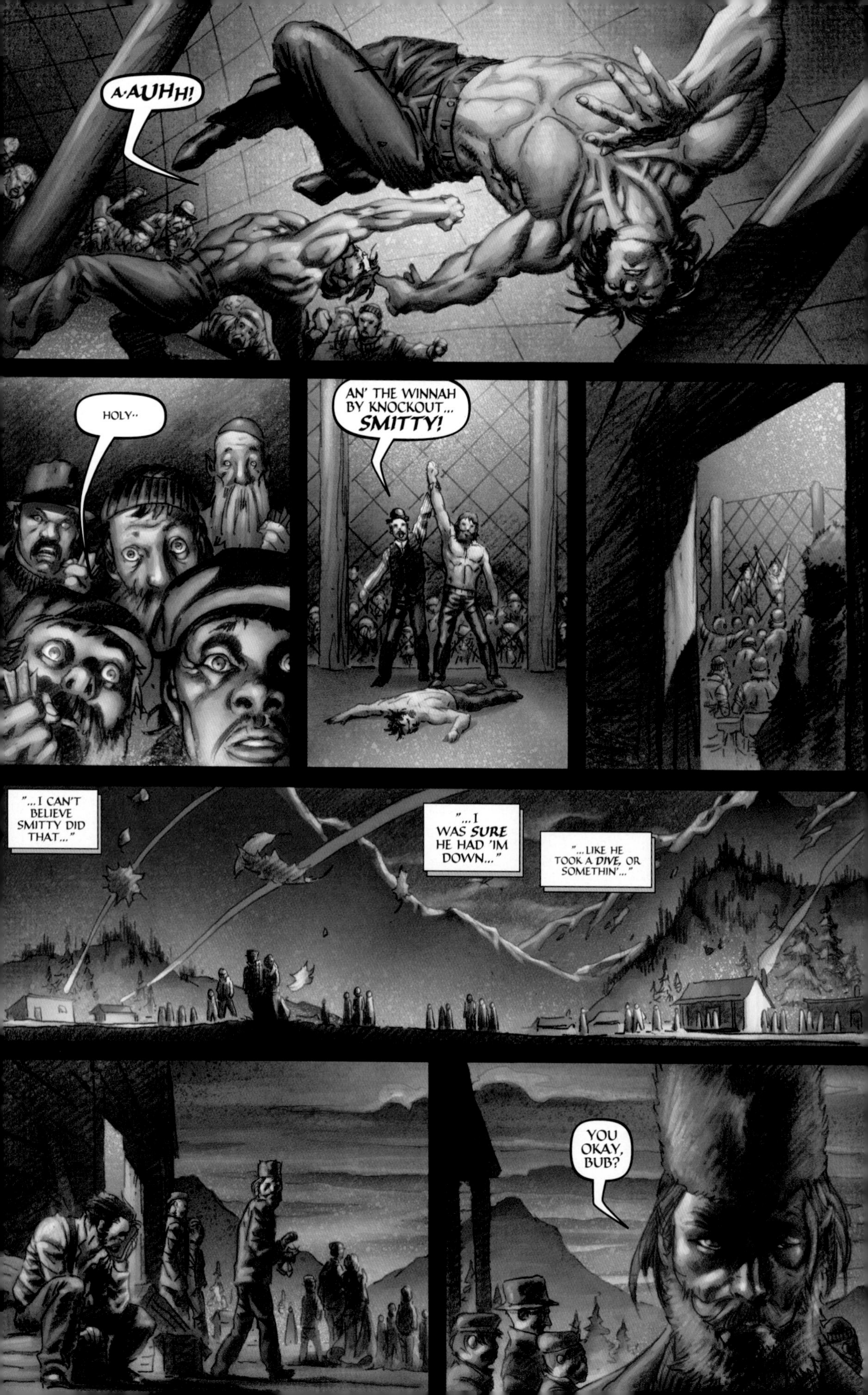
A-AUHH!
HOLY..
AN' THE WINNAH BY KNOCKOUT... SMITTY!
"...I CAN'T BELIEVE SMITTY DID THAT..."
"...I WAS SURE HE HAD 'IM DOWN..."
"...LIKE HE TOOK A DIVE, OR SOMETHIN'..."
YOU OKAY, BUB?

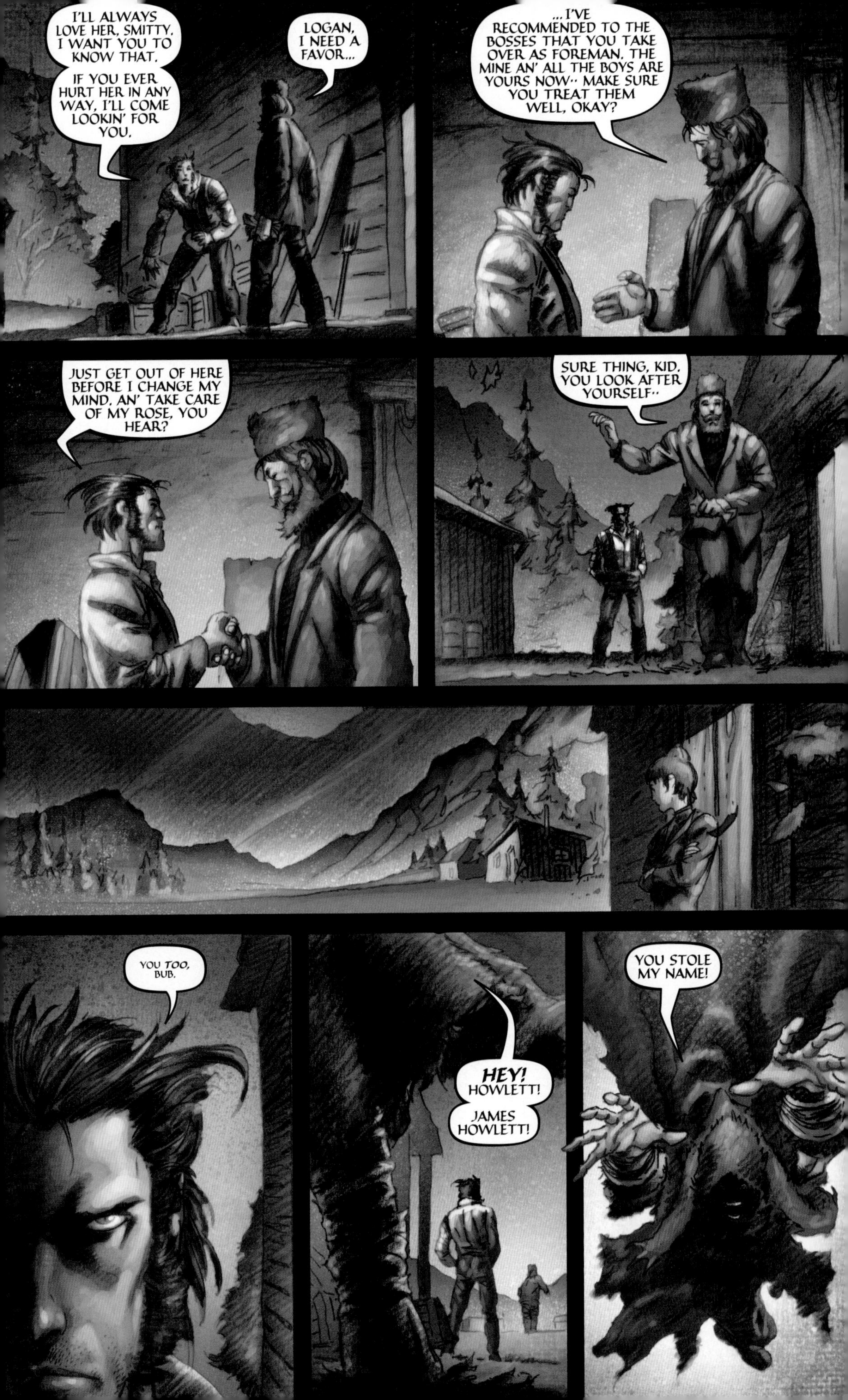
I'LL ALWAYS LOVE HER, SMITTY. I WANT YOU TO KNOW THAT.
IF YOU EVER HURT HER IN ANY WAY, I'LL COME LOOKIN' FOR YOU.
LOGAN, I NEED A FAVOR...
...I'VE RECOMMENDED TO THE BOSSES THAT YOU TAKE OVER AS FOREMAN. THE MINE AN' ALL THE BOYS ARE YOURS NOW.. MAKE SURE YOU TREAT THEM WELL, OKAY?
JUST GET OUT OF HERE BEFORE I CHANGE MY MIND. AN' TAKE CARE OF MY ROSE, YOU HEAR?
SURE THING, KID. YOU LOOK AFTER YOURSELF..
YOU TOO, BUB.
HEY! HOWLETT!
JAMES HOWLETT!
YOU STOLE MY NAME!

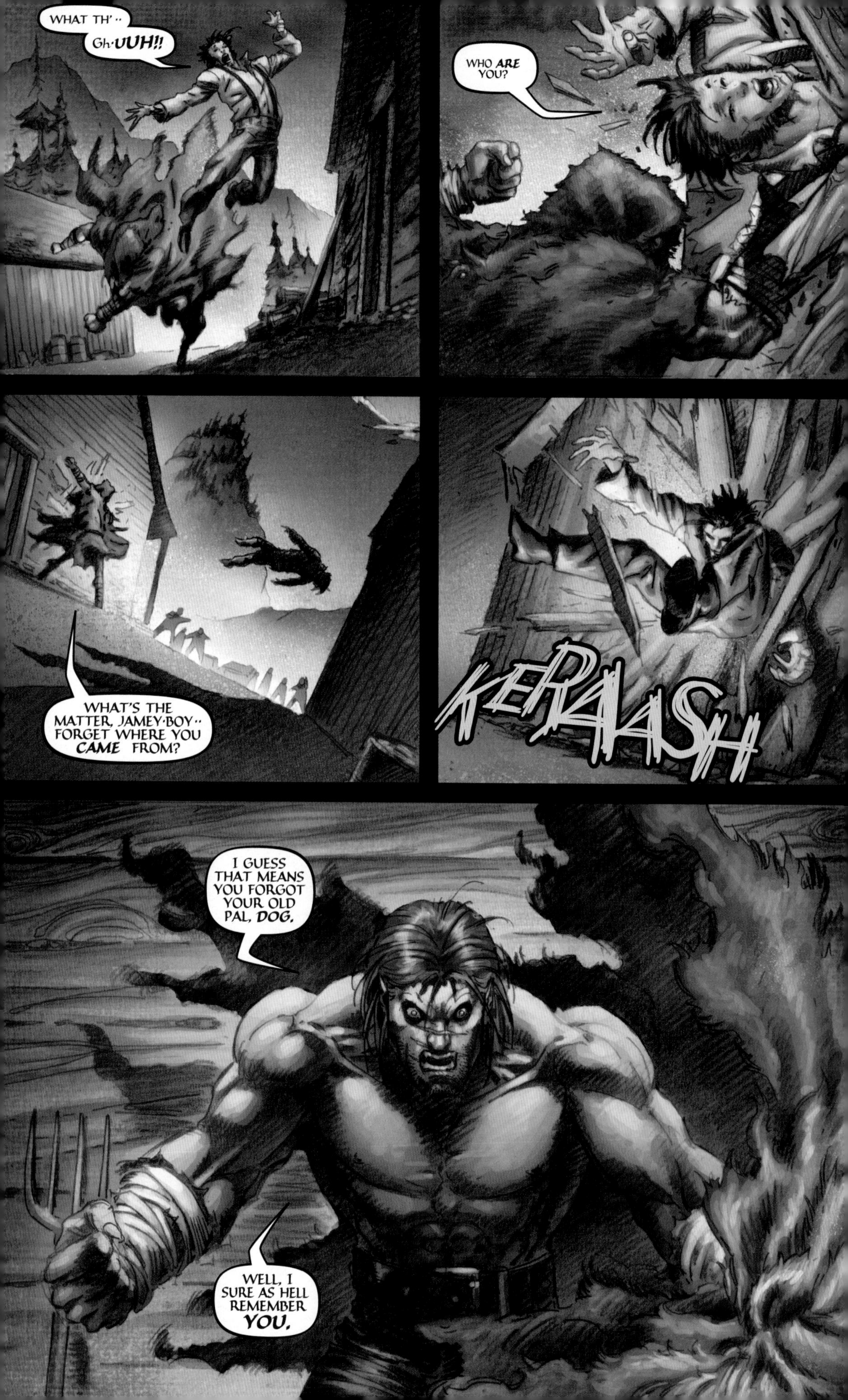
WHAT TH'..
Gh·UUH!!
WHO ARE YOU?
WHAT'S THE MATTER, JAMEY·BOY.. FORGET WHERE YOU CAME FROM?
KERRAASH
I GUESS THAT MEANS YOU FORGOT YOUR OLD PAL, DOG.
WELL, I SURE AS HELL REMEMBER YOU.

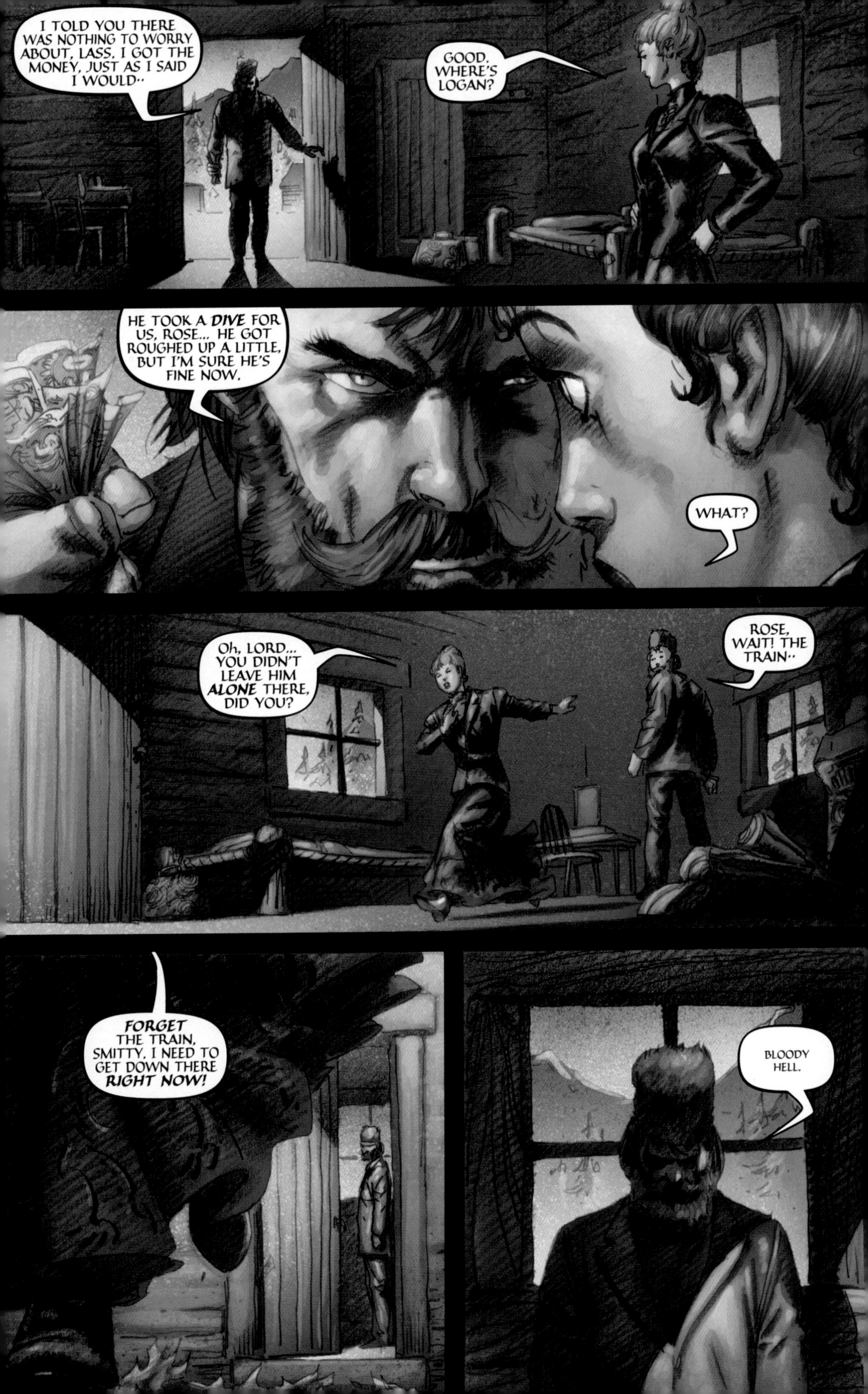
I TOLD YOU THERE WAS NOTHING TO WORRY ABOUT, LASS. I GOT THE MONEY, JUST AS I SAID I WOULD..
GOOD. WHERE'S LOGAN?
HE TOOK A DIVE FOR US, ROSE... HE GOT ROUGHED UP A LITTLE, BUT I'M SURE HE'S FINE NOW.
WHAT?
Oh, LORD... YOU DIDN'T LEAVE HIM ALONE THERE, DID YOU?
ROSE, WAIT! THE TRAIN..
FORGET THE TRAIN, SMITTY. I NEED TO GET DOWN THERE RIGHT NOW!
BLOODY HELL.

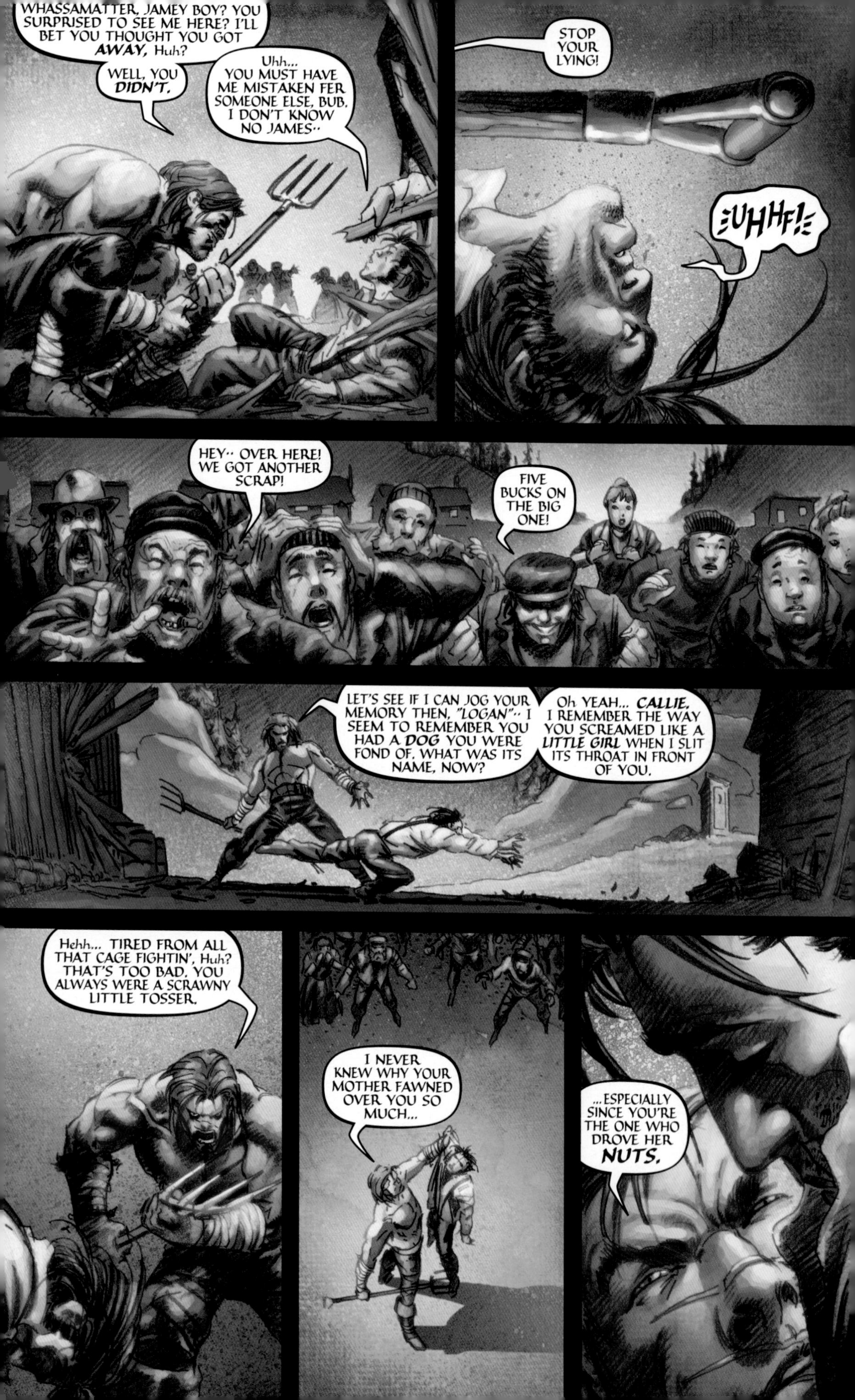
WHASSAMATTER, JAMEY BOY? YOU SURPRISED TO SEE ME HERE? I'LL BET YOU THOUGHT YOU GOT AWAY, Huh?
WELL, YOU DIDN'T.
Uhh... YOU MUST HAVE ME MISTAKEN FER SOMEONE ELSE, BUB. I DON'T KNOW NO JAMES..
STOP YOUR LYING!
UHHF!
HEY.. OVER HERE! WE GOT ANOTHER SCRAP!
FIVE BUCKS ON THE BIG ONE!
LET'S SEE IF I CAN JOG YOUR MEMORY THEN, "LOGAN".. I SEEM TO REMEMBER YOU HAD A DOG YOU WERE FOND OF. WHAT WAS ITS NAME, NOW?
Oh YEAH... CALLIE. I REMEMBER THE WAY YOU SCREAMED LIKE A LITTLE GIRL WHEN I SLIT ITS THROAT IN FRONT OF YOU.
Hehh... TIRED FROM ALL THAT CAGE FIGHTIN', Huh? THAT'S TOO BAD. YOU ALWAYS WERE A SCRAWNY LITTLE TOSSER.
I NEVER KNEW WHY YOUR MOTHER FAWNED OVER YOU SO MUCH...
...ESPECIALLY SINCE YOU'RE THE ONE WHO DROVE HER NUTS.

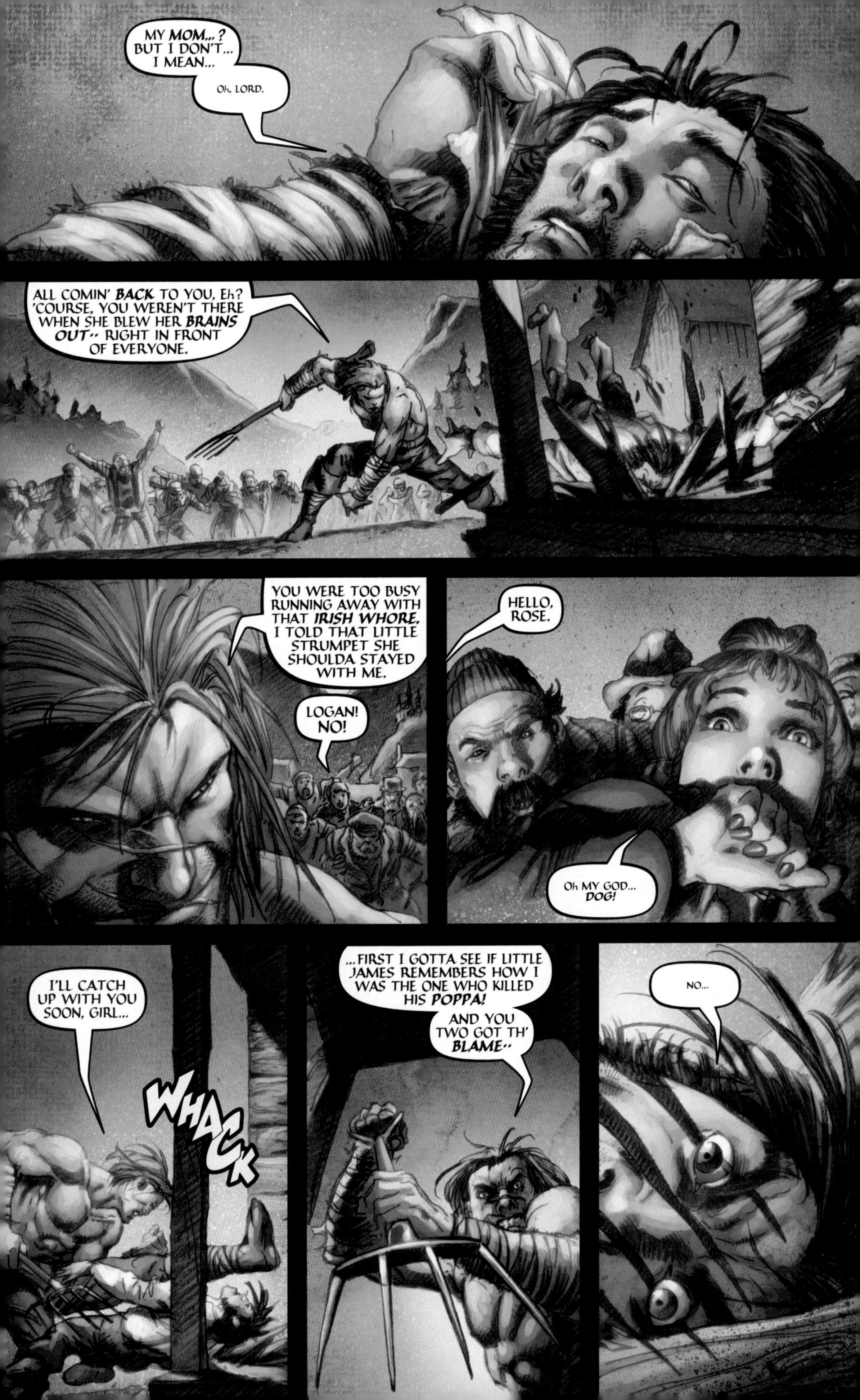
MY MOM...? BUT I DON'T... I MEAN...
Oh, LORD.
ALL COMIN' BACK TO YOU, Eh? 'COURSE, YOU WEREN'T THERE WHEN SHE BLEW HER BRAINS OUT-- RIGHT IN FRONT OF EVERYONE.
YOU WERE TOO BUSY RUNNING AWAY WITH THAT IRISH WHORE. I TOLD THAT LITTLE STRUMPET SHE SHOULDA STAYED WITH ME.
LOGAN! NO!
HELLO, ROSE.
Oh MY GOD... DOG!
I'LL CATCH UP WITH YOU SOON, GIRL...
WHACK
...FIRST I GOTTA SEE IF LITTLE JAMES REMEMBERS HOW I WAS THE ONE WHO KILLED HIS POPPA!
AND YOU TWO GOT TH' BLAME--
NO...

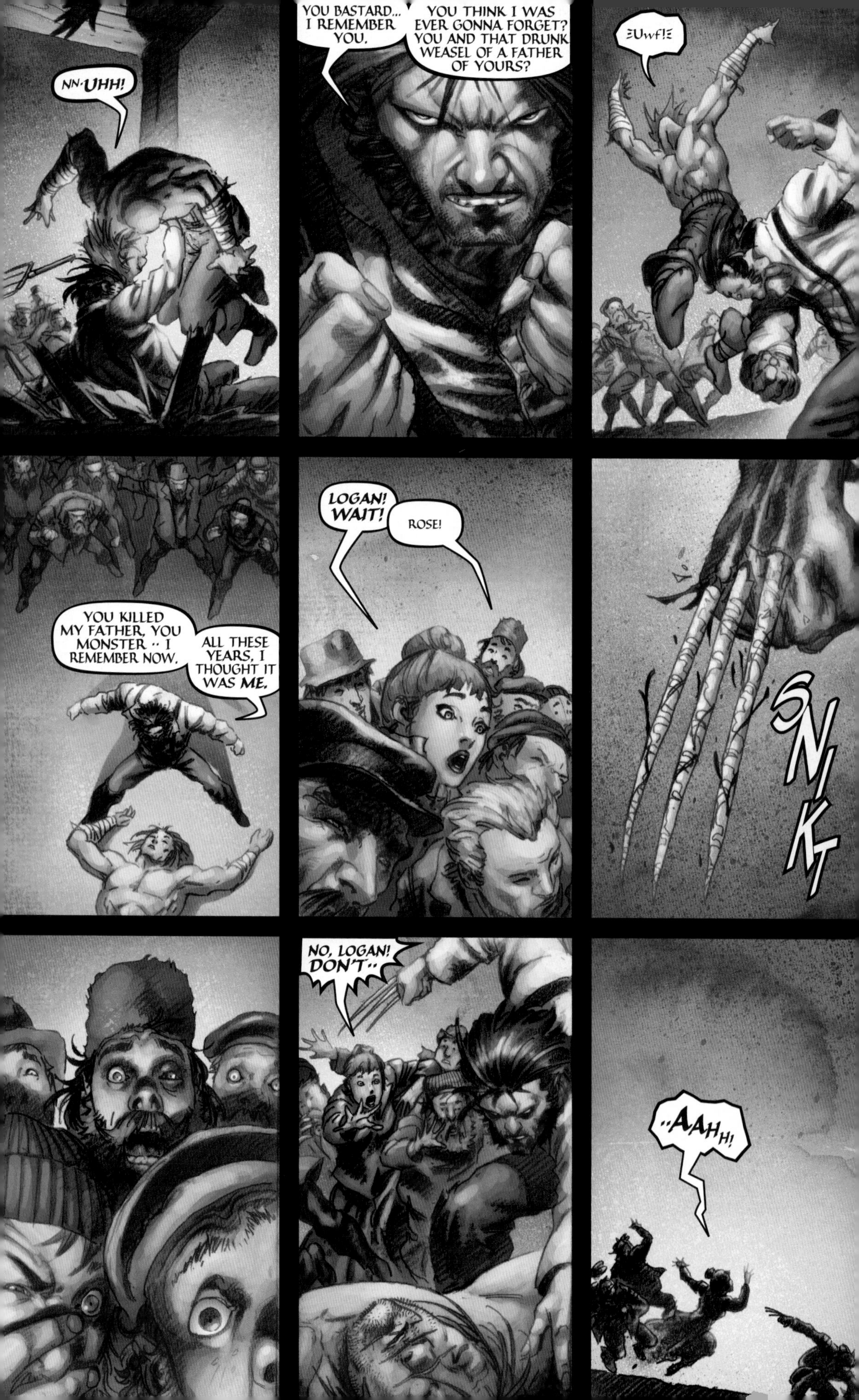
NN-UHH!
YOU BASTARD... I REMEMBER YOU.
YOU THINK I WAS EVER GONNA FORGET? YOU AND THAT DRUNK WEASEL OF A FATHER OF YOURS?
UWF!
YOU KILLED MY FATHER, YOU MONSTER -- I REMEMBER NOW.
ALL THESE YEARS, I THOUGHT IT WAS ME.
LOGAN! WAIT!
ROSE!
SNIKT
NO, LOGAN! DON'T--
--AAHH!

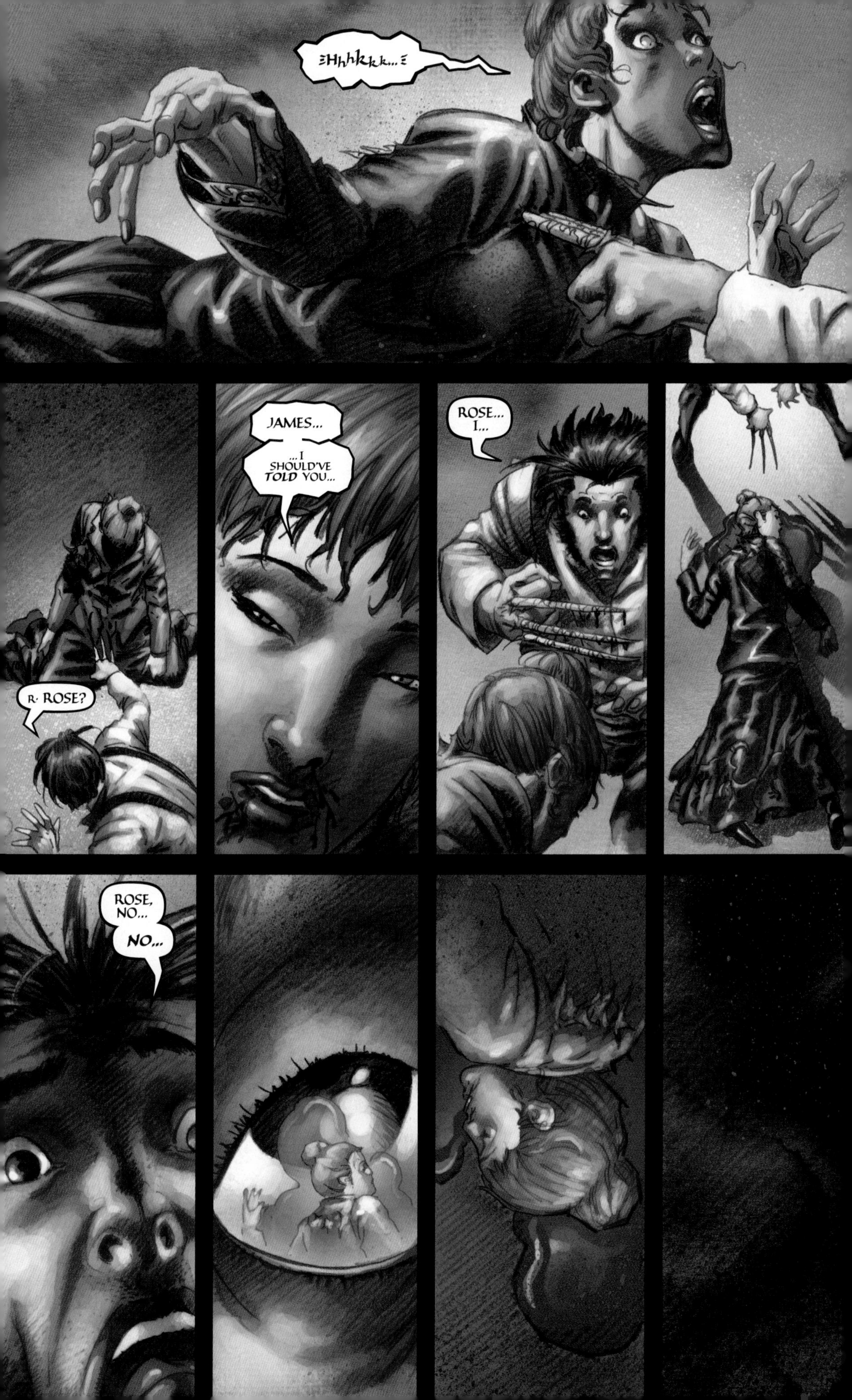
Hhhkkk...
JAMES...
...I SHOULD'VE TOLD YOU...
R- ROSE?
ROSE... I...
ROSE, NO...
NO...

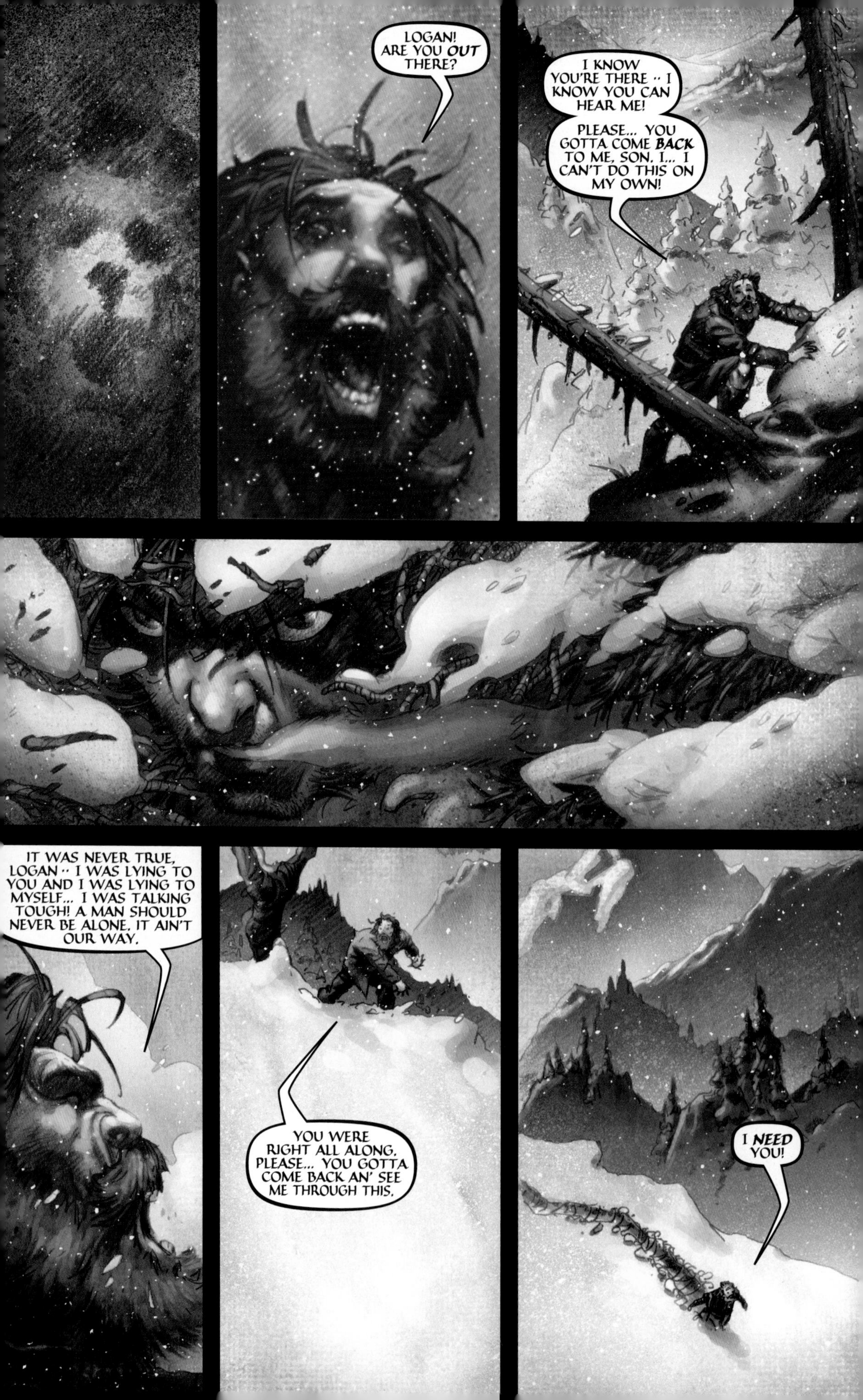
LOGAN! ARE YOU OUT THERE?
I KNOW YOU'RE THERE -- I KNOW YOU CAN HEAR ME!
PLEASE... YOU GOTTA COME BACK TO ME, SON. I... I CAN'T DO THIS ON MY OWN!
IT WAS NEVER TRUE, LOGAN -- I WAS LYING TO YOU AND I WAS LYING TO MYSELF... I WAS TALKING TOUGH! A MAN SHOULD NEVER BE ALONE. IT AIN'T OUR WAY.
YOU WERE RIGHT ALL ALONG. PLEASE... YOU GOTTA COME BACK AN' SEE ME THROUGH THIS.
I NEED YOU!

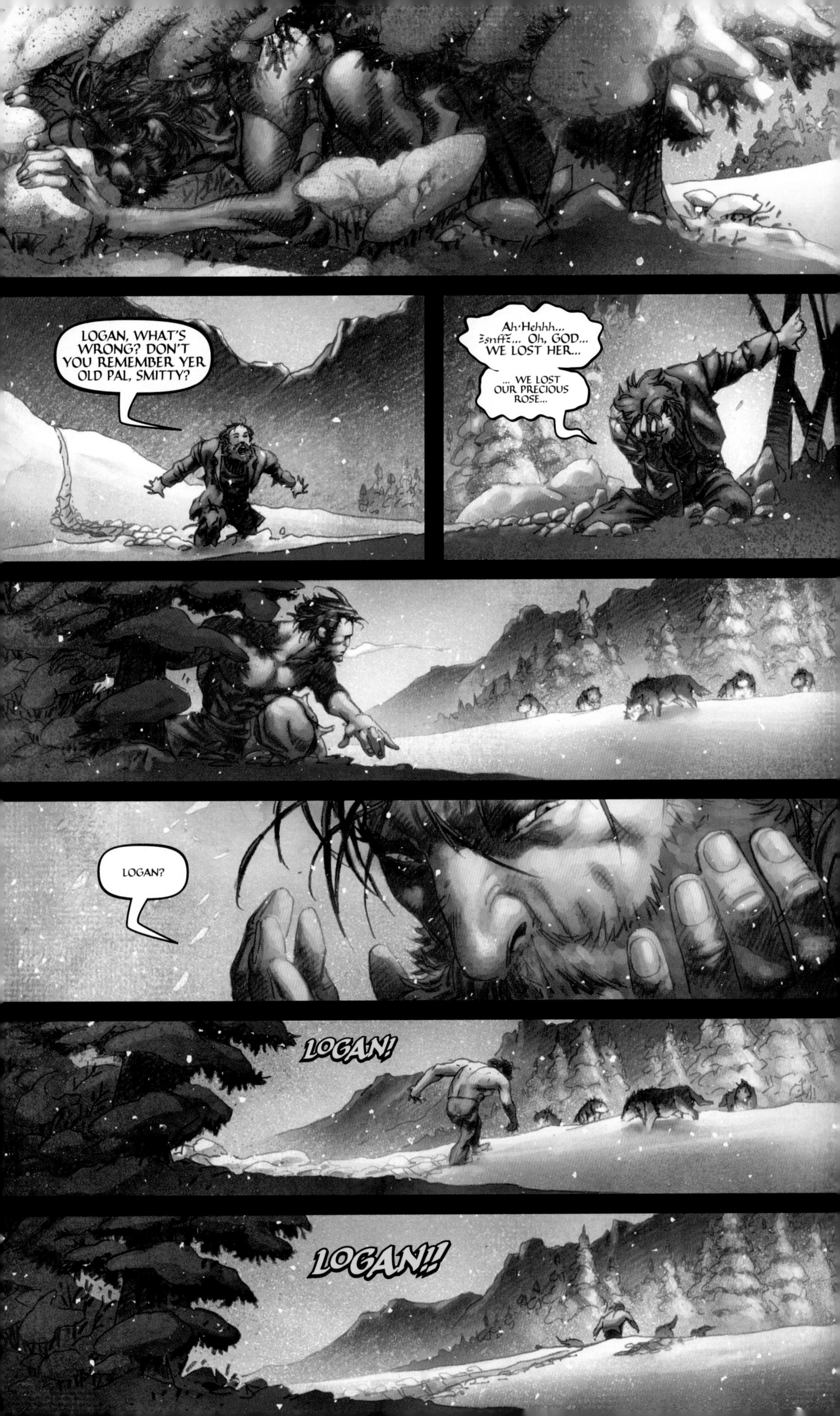
LOGAN, WHAT'S WRONG? DON'T YOU REMEMBER YER OLD PAL, SMITTY?
Ah-Hehhh... snff... Oh, GOD... WE LOST HER...
... WE LOST OUR PRECIOUS ROSE...
LOGAN?
LOGAN!
LOGAN!!

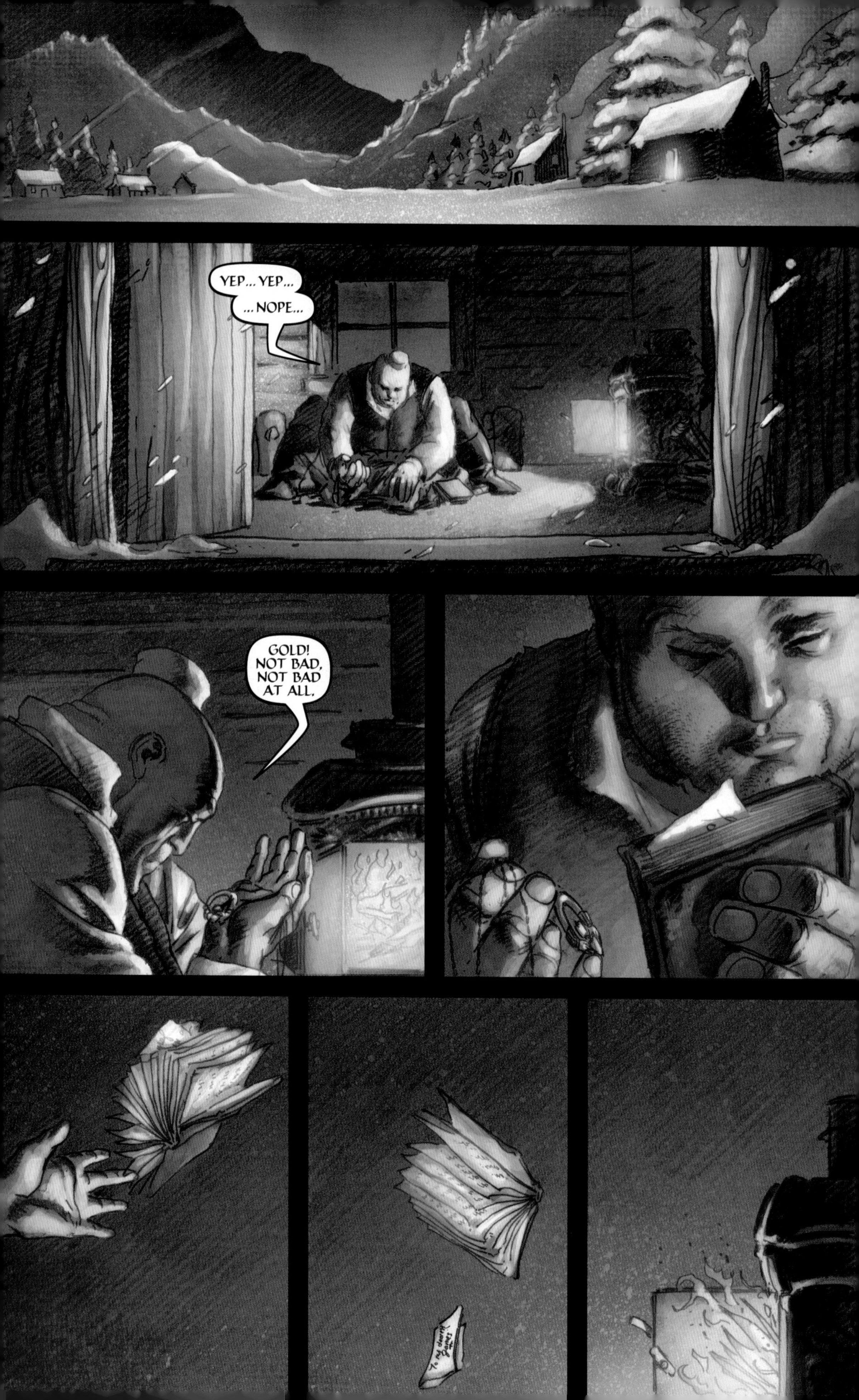
YEP... YEP...
...NOPE...
GOLD! NOT BAD, NOT BAD AT ALL.

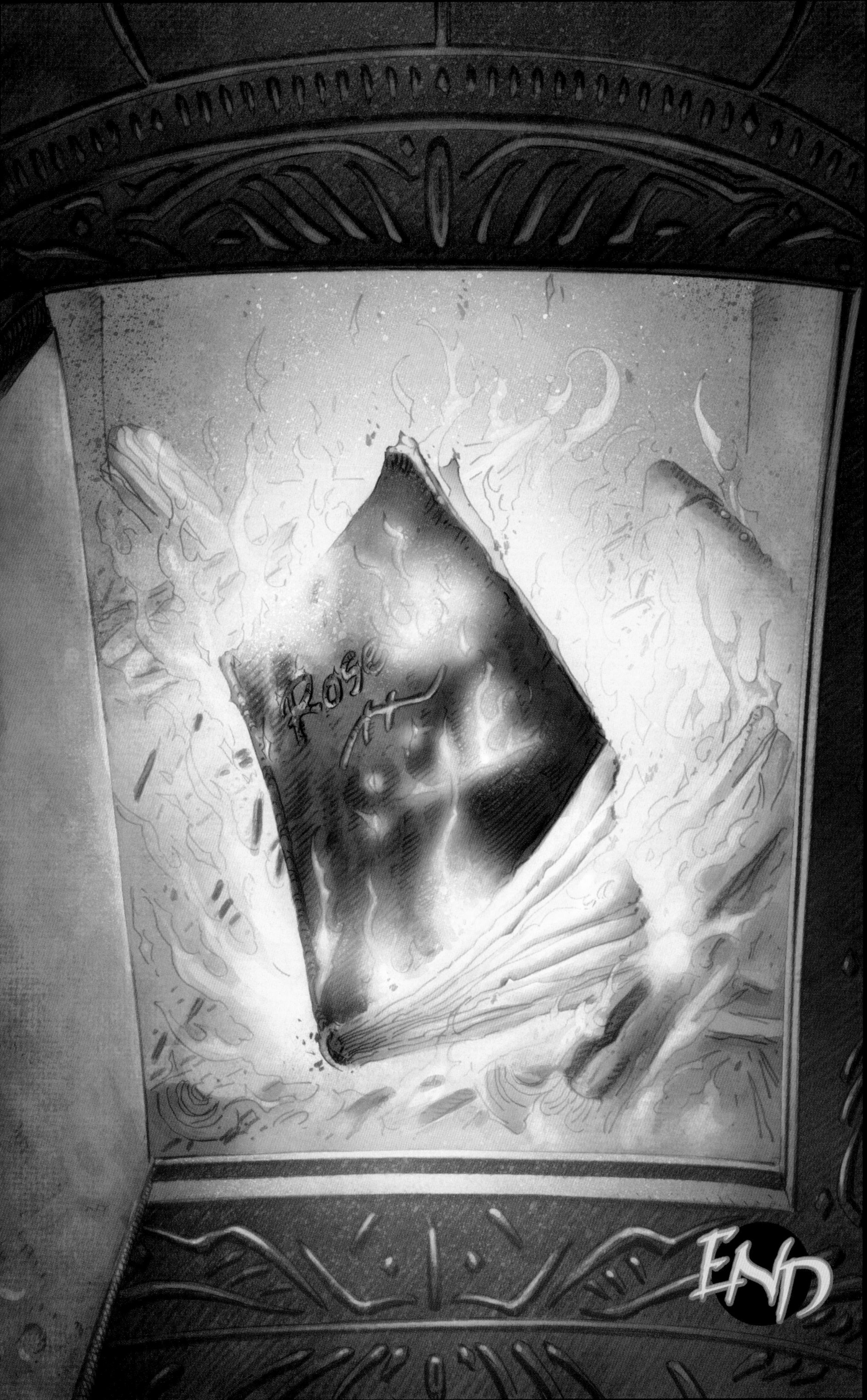
Rose
END

# THE BEGINNING

BY BILL JEMAS

THIS ALL STARTED IN THE BASEMENT OF JOE QUESADA'S HOUSE IN NEW JERSEY.

Joe had just taken on the chief job and invited his editors to an all-day creative session. Paul Jenkins had flown up from Atlanta to help out. (Paul and Joe had done some great work together in recent years, including THE INHUMANS and THE SENTRY.)

I showed up in the middle of the morning with the meeting already in progress. Joe was standing in front of his new staff with a clipboard and markers, and he was dying up there. Nobody had any ideas for their new boss.

This group of editors was, and is, the best in the business. These were the same men and women who would turn Marvel (and the comics industry) around during the next 18 months. But that morning, they were a quiet bunch. To be fair, and to make a long story short, this team had stuck with Marvel through thick and thin. The thin was the bankruptcy, when Marvel employees had to survive the deepest depression in the history of the comics market and the tender mercies of Carl Icahn. Conditions like that make you learn to keep your head low, so when Joe asked for hot new ideas, he got a lot of cold blank stares and SECRET WARS III, and INFINITY GAUNTLET IV. This was a very uncomfortable scene and way, way too embarrassing to watch.

So I sat in the corner with Paul, eating donuts, when it hit me. . . I turned to Paul, "What is the greatest story Marvel never told?" He didn't miss a beat: "The origin of Wolverine." Of course, we're sure we're geniuses, and we're about to spring this on everybody when Joe calls for the lunch break.

Paul and I were so full of sugar and oil that we couldn't eat lunch. We tracked down Joe, who was sitting with an editor munching on a burger. Paul asked Joe, "What is the greatest story Marvel never told?" Joe didn't miss a beat. "The origin of Wolverine," but then he blurted out "But we could never tell it." The editor patiently explained to Paul and me that our brilliant and original idea had come up (and had been shot down) in every brainstorm session since Wolverine made his spectacular and mysterious first appearance in INCREDIBLE HULK #181. Joe added that revealing the origin of Wolverine would ruin the character.

Now it's time for fun with Joey. We can't print exactly what I said to Joe, but the gist was "When we named you editor in chief, we thought we were passing the torch that lights the House of Ideas. I didn't think I was handing you a big chicken suit." Anyway, Joe got jolted back to being Joe, and got excited enough to blast out forty great marketing ideas in the following four minutes.

Joe started the afternoon session with a challenge to his team, "Bill Jemas wants us to tell the origin of Wolverine. Bill says this will be the best-selling book in the entire industry in 2001. What should we tell him?"

As a group, the editors politely, but firmly, told me, "no way." Over the next hour, they explained that the essence of Logan is the search for his past; take that away and you destroy the Wolverine character. Destroy Wolverine, the most important X-Men character, and you destroy the X-Men. Destroy the X-Men, the most important Marvel family, and you destroy Marvel.

The bottom line was that Marvel was afraid. We were afraid to tell the story of the most courageous character in our Universe.

Then something interesting happened; the senior editors, Tom Brevoort, Ralph Macchio and Mark Powers started thinking and talking like senior editors. I believe it was Tom who stood up and said, "If we can tell a great story, we should go ahead and tell it. That's what we do."

That whole afternoon, I had the ideas that you are about to read in the following outline swirling around in my brain. I thought that the policy discussion was much more important than a bull session on my little springboard. More importantly, we had to do this right. Some of the best creators in the world work for Marvel and on the X-Men; those people deserved the first shot at writing Origin.

Let's fast-forward over the next several months. Joe kept asking for Origin pitches from the top talent in the industry, and kept getting turned down. He was offering the keys to the Jag, and nobody wanted to drive. Finally, Joe went back to Paul. Paul turned in a pretty fair pitch, but we all (Paul, too) agreed that it wasn't the right way to go.

Now it's March 2001, and we really needed to get this thing started. I went home and sat with my two sons – they were six and nine at the time – and we talked about what Logan would have been like as a kid. What kind of childhood could make a kid grow up as tough as Wolverine on the outside and give him a heart of gold on the inside?

This kind...

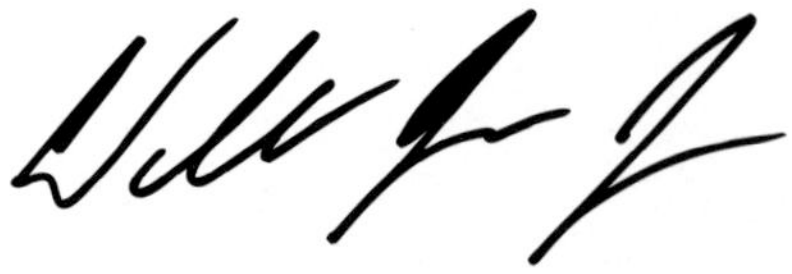

BILL JEMAS
FORMER PRESIDENT & COO PUBLISHING,
CONSUMER PRODUCTS AND NEW MEDIA
2002

# ORIGIN TREATMENT

BY BILL JEMAS

## PART ONE — TEXAS — SET IN DALLAS SUBURB

### TEXAS CHARACTERS

**Dawg:** Middle-school bully — nasty brutish and short.
- Wolverine junior, but this kid is all beast and no heart. Terrorizes the soft suburban kids.

**Mac:** Dawg's dad — the bad guy
- Physically he's a picture of the Claremont/Miller Wolverine, cowboy hat, sideburns, and boots. But he's tall and lean.
- Manages a team of illegals for a mid-sized landscaping business.

**Rosa:** the heroine
- Poor, beautiful, illegal immigrant, red-head, Latina High School Freshman.
- She's the nanny for Dawg's main victim — James. Dawg has a huge crush on her; she's too old for him, but plays Dawg to save James from beatings.

**James:** Dawg's favorite victim/ exact opposite of Dawg.
- Tallish, flabby, wealthy, bookish.
- James's parents are materialistic suburban yuppies. They have as little involvement as possible with their son.

### BOOK I — SUBURBAN COWBOY
### MIDDLE SCHOOL

**Dawg:** terrorizes the schoolyard, he's fourteen and boss of the 8th grade — extorts lunch money. Roughs up the kids and calls them "bub" and "darlin."

**Rosa:** high school junior. Very good in math, but struggles in English language classes — refuses to move to a bilingual class.

**Class out:** Rosa works for James's family. Her job is to take care of James, their 7th grade son, and of course, to do a ton of housework. Rosa saves James from a full-frontal pounding by Dawg, and walks him home from school.

### ROSA'S JOB

James does his homework and eats a ton of junk food while Rosa does all the housework.

James gets a playdate — after homework — that's just more junk food and TV with an equally fat friend. Rosa does more work with the Jamaican nanny from next door watching her and telling her to work slower. In this world, the parents have nothing to do with the kids.

Rosa serves dinner to James's family.

She serves and cleans up (eats in the kitchen).

James complains about getting beat up at school and then leaves the table.

Father tells mom to sign the kid up for karate and to call the school . . . then remembers that Dawg's last name is the same as the guy who does their landscaping, Mac — Father will see if Mac's son is the bully.

### DAWG'S DINNER — MEET MAC

Dawg cleans the tools and pickup for his dad's landscaping crew. Mac (phone in hand) calls Dawg in and smacks him in the head. Mac drinks hard and beats Dawg even harder.

### SCHOOL IS HELL

Dawg stalks James through the day.

Other kids find this funny.

James tells teacher — she ignores it.

Fight, fight, fight.

Big circle of kids, Dawg pounding James in the middle.

Rosa sweeps in — collars Dawg — he swings — she gets a fat lip, and he stalks away. Kids disperse.

James crying; Rosa comforts him — don't worry little Logan, I'll always be there for you. (In this original treatment, the reveal at the end of this first chapter was that James's last name was Logan. It was later decided the name switch would occur a little differently. In the final version the name switch was done to conceal James's identity from anyone looking for him in ORIGIN #3.)

### BOOK II — LIVING IN THE MATERIAL WORLD — TEXAS

James comes home from school all beat up.

Mr. Logan is more concerned that his hired help defied him than with the bumps and bruises on his son and Rosa.

Mr. Logan fires Mac, and gets a couple of neighbors to do the same.

Mac goes away with an apology and a smile. Even tears up the last bill.

James takes a karate class, but he's a wet noodle.

Instructor screams, James cries, that's it for karate.

But James does like Japanese culture and starts reading books on Japan.

Mac gives Dawg another beating and Dawg goes even harder after James.

Nobody talks to James at school. He seems to embrace the loner role.

Mac plans to kidnap James.

Blackmails Rosa — visits her at her shack. Threatens to turn in her whole family. Promises that nobody gets hurt and she gets $1,000.

Sets up simple snatch where Rosa will lead James into Mac's hands.

More Logan Family home life — getting and spending.

Lot of action going on around James — but he is essentially alone.

Rosa goes through with it. Mac snatches James.

Mac to Rosa: for your own good, we have to make it look real. Smacks her hard on the head and knocks her out. Puts the ransom note down her shirt.

### BOOK III — OUTTA HERE — TEXAS

Rosa staggers into the Logan's house and hands over the ransom note.

Parents have 24 hours to raise $250,000. Any police, the kid is dead and you are next.

Mr. and Mrs. Logan — We don't have $250,000. We are in debt. House is worth less than we paid. All our money is in the business. We have $5,000 in cash. Rosa hears them.

Mr. Logan puts $5,000 in a briefcase and a gun in his pocket. Will negotiate when the time comes.

Drop off disaster — both Parents killed.

Rosa comes to save James. Confesses to James. Both your parents are dead. I'm getting you out of here.

Mac shows up. Ties up Rosa — upside down. Goes after James.

James pops his first claw — it's a self-defense mechanism that triggers when his life is at stake — kills Mac.

Rosa and Logan have a motorcycle and $5,000. Let's get up to Canada. The further north the better.

## PART TWO — CANADA — LUMBER MILL IN THE DEEP WOODS

### CANADIAN CHARACTERS

**Cookie:** The camp cook is James's main tormentor. "I'm sharpening my knife for you."

**The Foreman:** Young, powerful leader of the camp. No formal schooling, but very smart. Puts James under his brutish protection. (This character will become the basis for Smitty in the final version.)

**Victor Creed:** Traveling fighter — kicks through small towns and lumber camps, fighting all newcomers for prize money.

**The Promoter:** Secretly recruiting the Canadian backwoods for Weapon X fighters.

### BOOK IV — CALL OF THE WILD — CANADA

The end of the line: Rosa and James run out of luck and money in Canada. Stumble into a riverside sawmill.

The Foreman gives them a chance and some low-paying jobs.

James's workday — splinters and burns.

Kitchen work at breakfast, lunch and dinner.

Hurling scrap wood and bark pulper.

Cookie and the Foreman.

Cookie had been the camp whipping boy, but now he has his own. James tries to keep a low profile, but Cookie constantly torments him.

Foreman won't let Cookie go too far. Likes to talk to James. Wants to see him toughen up. Rosa does office work and odd jobs.

James toughens up.

Works hard, the guys accept him.

He's getting buff and strong, and Rosa begins to notice.

Mini-love triangle — Foreman — Rosa — James.

### CALL OF THE WILD

James goes hunting to supplement their meager income.

He's a natural hunter. He is also starting to mutate and wants to keep it a secret.

Up against a wolfpack — pops the claw.

Cookie kicks butt. Cookie sees James messed up/tired & hurt — now's the time to attack.

Wolvie will not pop the claws in front of everybody. Cookie cuts James — Foreman breaks it up, but James is badly hurt.

### BOOK V — BROKEN HEART — CANADA

James works the heavy machinery in the mill. Lives the lumberman's life. Hard work, hard play.

James becomes a big-time hunter. Brings home rare pelts. Captures wild mink, Rosa starts to raise them.

Rosa and Foreman start to fall in love.

James — out of jealousy/frustration becomes a fighter.

Beats up Cookie — kicks him out of camp.

Gets into bar room brawls and gets a bit of a reputation.

Rosa moves in with Foreman. James moves into the bunks with the guys. Heartbreaker for him, but he takes it like a man.

### BOOK VI — CAPTURED — CANADA

Victor Creed finishing off an opponent. Packing up the cage with the promoter. Reveal that the promoter and Creed work for a covert branch of the Canadian Army — Weapon X. They are searching for mutants for the super-soldier program.

The sawmill is in trouble — this part of the wilderness is all but bare. Foreman has to move the mill, but doesn't have the money.

James spends more time in the woods and less at work. Still goes to the bar with the boys. Promoter for a touring cage fight comes to the bar. Introduces "Big Cat" with tall tales and bar talk. $10,000 to any man who can beat him.

Rosa and Foreman — sunny day with James. They have to close the mill and move to the city. They can't afford to move the mill. James is invited, but that's not for him.

Foreman hears about the cage fight — wants a shot at the money. James watches — he has no plans to fight — until he sees what Victor does to people. Cold cocks Foreman and goes into the ring with the champ.

Wolverine fights Sabretooth — wins the $10,000, but has to pop the claw to do it.

James turns money over to Rosa. They will go further north together. But James is captured by Weapon X.

# CONFESSIONS of an EIC

BY JOE QUESADA

As I'm sure you've noticed by now this compilation of ORIGIN is filled with so much extra stuff that I'm feeling a bit useless at this point. To be quite honest, I'm at a lack for what to write because so much has already been said and said so much better than I could in these few short paragraphs. I mean, I could regale you with funny tales that went even behind-the-scenes of the behind-the-scenes stuff, but then this book would venture off quickly into something more akin to our MAX mature readers imprint than something suitable for the likes of ol' Wolverine.

## HURRAYS!

Of course I could use this space to shine a spotlight on the real stars of this book. I mean what can be said about Paul Jenkins, Andy Kubert, Richard Isanove and Comicraft that hasn't already been lavished upon them? Along with Editors Mike Marts and Mike Raicht, they've created not only a new technique in sequential art, but the standard by which all new projects of this era will be measured. What they have created is the first great project of the new comics millennium!

## STONES

So, this leads me to a place where I need to either really get to the essence of what this series is all about or stop typing and say, "Thanks, True Believer, for purchasing this book... I hope you enjoyed it!" What did it take to tell this tale? What is really at the core of all this verbiage, ink and paper? It's funny, the one thing that it took for us at Marvel to even consider attempting to write Wolverine's origin is the one ingredient that ol' Wolvie and all our heroes have in spades...

...fearlessness!

It's something that we were really lacking at Marvel at the time, yet it was fearlessness that was the cornerstone upon which Stan Lee, Jack Kirby, Steve Ditko and so many others built the Marvel Universe. As a matter of fact, it had seemed as if every major publisher had become complacent with playing things safe and doing things just because "that's the way they've always been done," even in the face of many a brave creator trying to individually stay the tide of erosion that was eating away at the comics industry. That is until the day Bill Jemas strolled through the door of Marvel.

In my year and a half as Marvel's EIC, I've been continually surprised by Bill's ability to shift gears on the fly, and more importantly, his talent to do so many things. From brilliant business initiatives that have all but saved the comics industry, kept our competition guessing and more importantly, in our rear-view mirror, to being the impetus for stories like the one you've just read.

## DISCOVERING THE SECRET

I think the day that everything became perfectly clear to me about Bill was sometime long after the famous meeting in my basement that spawned the idea of Wolverine's origin. I remember Bill walking in with this Marvel strategy card game called "ReCharge." It was just in the process of being designed. All the art looked amazing (as Marvel art always does), so I asked Bill about the game's designers, who they were and how he had found them. Bill's response was as simple as it was shocking, "You're looking at them," he said. That's when the lightbulb went on and all the pieces started to fall into place. All this time I'd been in awe of this tall, lanky, geeky guy who, if not for the bit of salt and pepper around his temples, could pass for an overzealous, hormone-enraged teenager, anxiously awaiting his dateless prom night. How could he be one of the shrewdest businesspeople I've ever met and one of the brightest creators I've ever been around, and also have a talent for designing strategy games? How can he be so proficient at all these things? That's when I discovered Bill's secret. You see, Bill just doesn't know the meaning of the word can't! It's not in the way his brain is wired. Where most of us would sit there and say, "Well, I've never designed a game before, so I really can't do this," Bill just studies a few games and goes about creating one. So, what is it that keeps him from stopping himself before he starts? What's his X-Factor, his mutant ability? Simple, much like our wonderful, hairy, two-dimensional Canucklehead, Bill is the three-dimensional embodiment of his most vaunted trait. He's fearless!

## LIKE A BLUNT HAMMER TO MY HEAD

Now that was one very important lesson for me. You see, it brought back all these memories of being a kid and having that fearless nature, that thing inside you that says, "Hey, I can be an astronaut if I want!" That thing that life tends to beat out of us as we get on with it. It's a lesson that I learned to apply to everything I do now at Marvel because I realized I wasn't learning it for the first time. I was just reminded that, much like Wolverine, we all have this trait deep inside of our forgotten past. We all have a "Rose" in our personal ORIGIN that perhaps we've forgotten with the passage of time. For me, my "Rose" came back to me in a flash by Bill's simple ability to not see defeat as an option or even a roadblock.

## DEADLINE

Now, as the caption above looms larger and larger with each passing minute, I realize that I better bring this thing to a close and wrap it up with some snappy encapsulation of my overall point! So what are we really talking about here? After you've read all the inside stuff, the behind-the-scenes history, the sketches and the lost plot points, keep in mind that's not really what this project was all about for us. Sure it makes for interesting reading, but the lesson for me, for all of us at Marvel, was not in the pages, but in the doing. We slowly began believing that this project had to be done and then soon enough we realized that we couldn't not do this project. Why? Because we simply didn't know that we couldn't any longer and that is a belief that we have carried with us ever since. It's the trademark of this new Marvel, which you will see, smell, and taste in every new project and idea we come up with. Will we always succeed? Of course not, but as long as we have the incredible support of the world's greatest fans, it will always be and remain "The Marvel Age" of comics!

"Thanks, True Believer, for purchasing this book ... I hope you enjoyed it!"

See ya in the funnybooks,

JQ
EEK!
2002

# A FEW WORDS

BY PAUL JENKINS

Ever seen one of those daytime soap operas? You remember the part where Chase tells Daphne he's been impregnated with Troy's alien love-baby? I've seen that in real life.

It happened a couple of years ago, back when Joe Quesada had just become the new editor in chief of Marvel Comics. Joe and I had shared some success working together with Marvel Knights and as a result we'd become quite good friends. (Understand, this was in the days before Joe went Hollywood and would actually return his mates' phone calls, but I digress.)

Anyway, Joe asked if I'd be willing to come up to his secret island retreat to participate in his first conference with all of the Marvel editors — he thought it would be helpful to bring along a comic book writer for everyone to laugh at when discussing creative issues. Actually, Joe was under the mistaken impression I'd had some kind of previous editorial experience. If he'd checked closer, he would have learned that every company I ever did editorial work for has either folded, exploded, or slid into the sea.

Joe's first editorial meeting was very different from those of the previous few years: For a start, no one was fired. Instead of being told what they could not do — a favorite pastime of Marvel executives in years past—the assembled editors were now being encouraged to come up with bold and interesting new ideas. Enter Marvel President Bill Jemas (who, for those of you who don't know, is the biggest punk in the comic industry). "Is there any reason," asked Bill with a completely straight face, "why we can't do the origin of Wolverine?"

And it is at that moment when thirty-five people looked as though they'd just been informed they were the father of Bill's alien love-baby.

Actually, it's a pretty neat idea when you think about it: a character's mysterious origin can only be shrouded in secrecy for so long before said character begins to look like a twerp. Thirty-five years seemed to be about right for our man Logan. Now that these small pieces of his past have been revealed, I believe it will help reenergize the character in a small way. You may disagree, but this is my section and it's the only chance I get to spout off about character development and to thank the few worthy people below.

First of all, I want to set the record straight: for those people who have speculated on the storytelling involvement of Bill Jemas and Joe Quesada, this story is as much theirs as mine. In fact, Bill and Joe contributed more to the original concept than I did, and this should be recognized. If Marvel Entertainment is a driving force in the comics industry, I'd say we're lucky to have such cool and creative people at the wheel.

I don't have to say much about working with Andy Kubert or Richard Isanove — all you have to do is turn to page one, where you'll find their truly amazing artwork speaks for them.

On a personal note, I will add that Andy's not only an extremely talented chap and a pleasure to work with, but he's also polite enough to listen to me jabbering away for an hour about character motivation without putting the phone down. As you can see,

Andy's a brilliant storyteller and I hope he gets all the recognition he deserves for this wonderful piece of work.

Richard Isanove is really a lovely bloke even though he's French. When we embarked on this mission, the idea was to enhance Andy's pencils with painterly techniques that had never been tried, let alone perfected. Richard has managed to do both, and he only attempted formal surrender twice in the entire time he worked on the book.

It is a little known fact that Mike Marts — the editor for this ambitious project — is a nice guy. I say that with the utmost respect in the hopes that he'll finally come clean and admit this to the world. His long-suffering assistant, Mike Raicht, is a good lad, grade one, in my opinion. Thanks, lads, for your patience and steady hand.

Finally, some long-overdue thanks to some people who've been very important in my life and career.

To Rick Veitch: thanks for your sage advice and for loaning me your storytelling instincts back in the day. I really appreciate it.

To Kevin Eastman: thanks for giving me my start, helping me along and generally being a great friend. You deserve for your generosity to be returned to you a hundred times over.

To Lou Stathis: I miss you every day, mate. You taught me how to write not just for you but for every editor I'll ever work with.

To Melinda (soon to be Mrs. Jenkins): thanks for putting up with me. You are the most beautiful person in the world.

In fact, the same goes to all of you: Thanks for putting up with me.

PAUL JENKINS
ATLANTA, 2002

# CLIMBING THE HILL

BY JOE QUESADA

Some of this stuff is gathered together from my conversations with Bill Jemas, Paul Jenkins and some of my own thoughts and ideas about where the story should go. The bulk of my thoughts at the moment focus primarily on the early half of the story and stop somewhere around the time Logan hits the Canadian outback. I feel that the six issues should be split in two. Three for the early Vanderhurst years and three for the Canadian years. *(Vanderhurst was the new name for the Logan family from Bill J's Texas springboard. Eventually the family name would change to Howlett and the name Logan would come into play a different way.)* Also, please keep in mind that the names I'm using are only for the purpose of getting these bullet points down and done.

The basic action in young Logan's early years takes place in a beautiful estate that I'll call Strathmore for now. *(Eventually to follow suit and become the Howlett Estate.)* The Strathmore Estate and House are built on a mount in the beautiful hills of Asheville, North Carolina. *(This, of course, would later change to Canada.)* The family that built the mansion is the Vanderhursts. The gardener's family name is McMorris but the townsfolk call him Mac for short. *(Mac, in this version, would eventually become the elder gardener Logan, the father of Dawg.)* Mac's son is called Dawg; maybe his real name is Dawson, but because of his weird animal-like appearance, everyone's naturally shortened his name. It is very important that Mac and Dawg's appearance and attitude be very similar to how we see Wolvie today. We want the fans to make that instant connection.

The Vanderhurst family made its fortune in ironworks. Old Man Vanderhurst was a tyrant but a completely self-made man with little to no patience for slackers in his life.

Old Man Vanderhurst had several children; the youngest, John, was obviously a child of privilege. John was a kindhearted boy who, though born with a silver spoon in his mouth, always tried to be as generous to those in need as possible. This pissed off the old man to no end.

John became engaged to the lovely Maria Elizabeth Harnegie, another child of means from what seemed to be the ever growing American royalty. *(The name Maria would eventually be dropped and James's mother would be known simply as Elizabeth.)*

The two called upon the greatest architects and designers of the times to build a house from scratch that would rival the castles of ancient Europe. They chose a spot in Asheville, NC to erect their home. *(Early on, the writers and editors were not sure whether or not we were going to make Wolverine a true Canadian or a transplanted one. Eventually, it was agreed that his back-story should stay consistent and that he should be in Canada. It was leaked that he would possibly be American, however, in order to get the fans talking about the book and to stir up some possible controversy.)*

At the bottom of the hill lay a small shantytown made up of Southern ex-slaves and Scot-Irish emigrants, most of whom struggled to make what little they could from working in the nearby coal mines.

John, being the kind of man he was, offered the townspeople a form of on the job training. He would teach them the trades of furniture building, horsemanship, wine making and gardening since these were all trades that would be needed in order to keep Strathmore House running. They were also trades that they then could carry with them wherever they chose to go. This also created less of a rift between the impoverished townfolk and the mega-rich Vanderhurst.

Mac was so adept at learning the art of gardening and horticulture that he eventually became the head groundsman for the estate. His wife died at a young age and left him and his son Dawg behind. Dawg assisted his father on a daily basis. Although Mac was appreciative of the training the Vanderhursts gave him, there was something troubling him, burning at the very pit of his being, and it would always come to a head when he would see the lady of the house.

Old Man Vanderhurst never approved of this mixing of the classes.

After the house's construction Maria gave birth to her and John's first son, Scott, and shortly after, Maria became pregnant with their second son Tiberious. *(The name Tiberious would eventually be switched to James.)*

John took a liking to Dawg, who was by far the youngest worker in his stable. He was surprised that Dawg didn't attend the private school he had created for the townsfolk. Dawg said that his father felt it better he learn a trade.

John imports from England and hires Rose, a beautiful redheaded nanny who bears a striking resemblance to a redhead we all know and love. *(She would eventually come from the town close to the estate.)*

Rose begins her tutoring of Scott; little Ty plays in the same room, too young to care. *(Scott would never actually appear in the book and would only be mentioned as the son who died through the book's first two chapters.)* John occasionally spies Dawg peeking in on Rose and Scott as they run through their studies. John interprets this as maybe the boy has a desire to learn. Dawg, in reality, has the hots for Rose.

Dawg is brought into the house to be tutored along with Scott. John's wife Maria grows attached to Dawg, seeing him as almost another son. Still, at the end of the day, Dawg has to pack up his stuff and travel down the hill.

He tells his father of the lessons he learns and his father decides to teach him one of his own. He beats the boy badly, telling him that no matter how much the people at the top of the hill may pretend to care, he's just a charity case, just like this whole town.

**End issue 1. Dawg beaten to a pulp by his old man, his feral blood racing.** *(Issue one would eventually start with the arrival of Rose and we would never get to meet the mysterious brother, Scott. We would also only see glimpses of the construction of the Howlett Estate.)*

The tutoring continues for quite some time. Dawg's only dose of reality comes when the family throws its great Gatsby-like parties that he always has to view from outside the neatly cut shrubs.

Mac's hatred for the family increases. It seems especially directed to John with an always-warm spot for Maria. Sometimes the very sight of her makes him cower and melt.

One day the worst happens. Scott dies of a fever. He is taken from his family at the height of his youth. Maria is inconsolable. From this point on she begins wearing dresses that cover her up to the top of her neck.

Funeral for Scott, with an elaborate casket.

Weeks after the tragedy, Dawg comes to the house to receive his schooling. Maria turns him away. Dawg is a constant reminder of the child she just lost. Mac sees this and his whole demeanor around Maria changes.

Ty is now old enough to begin to study, so he continues with Rose. He too has a schoolboy crush on the young tutor. Dawg, now back to tending the grounds, watches Ty from a distance, jealousy burning in his heart.

Ty misses his brother and gets a dog as a present from his father, who thinks that this will help the boy forget.

Dawg becomes a sort of torturing bully. Whenever little Ty would be playing in the yard, Dawg would scare him by threatening that one day he would cut his heart out.

We see several instances when Dawg corners Ty and scares him until he wets himself. Ty is the epitome of the little rich Lord Fauntleroy. He's meek and weak and will amount to nothing great in the end. Dawg seems to derive tremendous pleasure from watching Ty wet himself.

Ty sees his father get smacked around and berated by Old Man Vanderhurst. He sees his dad get the "You'll never amount to anything" speech. This only makes Ty feel worse about himself. Watching your father get whacked around and take it can do that to a person.

Ty comes to his father's side one day after one of the Old Man's outbursts. They have their first and only man to man talk. They discuss Dawg's bullying. Dad gives advice and a family trinket. This trinket is so important to our story later that it can be changed to fit what we need. I don't care what he gives him as long as it has significance.

Next day, Dawg comes to torture little Ty. Ty won't have any more of it and weakly punches Dawg in the nose. The punch doesn't do a thing but Dawg is so astounded by the affront that he goes ballistic. He grabs Ty's dog and slices its throat!

**End of issue 2. Now I want fans thinking what a jerk little Wolvie was.**

Ty cries to his daddy and John fires Mac for what his son did. Maria asks John if that wasn't too harsh a punishment, almost taking Mac's side. John gives her a knowing stare, the only time, in fact, that we've ever seen anything resembling strength of conviction in his eyes in this whole story. Something silent and deep is exchanged between the two.

Later that night Ty tries to comfort his mother. They talk about his brother and all she can keep repeating through her tears is how he was taken from them too soon. Ty leaves the room but just before closing the door behind him he looks back to see his mother unsnapping her long necked dress. He's frozen in the moment not sure whether to turn away in shame or not. The dress slips down slowly to reveal her back and the horrible claw marks she's been hiding. They're obviously not human but made by something far more loathsome.

Mac and Dawg begin to conspire about kidnapping a family member for money. Mac insists it should be Maria; Dawg wants the runt. Mac wins the argument.

The kidnapping is botched. In the melee, John is murdered by Dawg as Mac holds Maria, Rose and Ty at gunpoint. In a childish rage Ty screams "No!" and tries to bull over Mac to get to his dying father. Mac is caught by such surprise and at such a low angle that he never gets to fire the gun properly. It goes off hitting Dawg, who goes flying out of a window out of sight. Ty is buried in Mac's abdomen area, feverishly trying to punch his way through to his father. A surprised look comes across Mac as he collapses to the ground. We see that he's in a puddle of blood and in the distance we see young Ty crying over his father's body with his bloody fists exposing tiny bony claws. This is the moment our readers go "Oh my God!"

As surprised as he is to see these strange things coming out of his hands, nothing is stranger than the sight of his mother cradling Mac's lifeless head in her arms. Sobbing uncontrollably, Maria tells Rose to take Ty away. Run; get out of this miserable place. Run as fast and as far as you can. *(In the final version Wolverine's mother would actually take her own life and would not have a significant role in the rest of the story.)*

**End of issue 3**

This is what leads us to our adventure in the North Canadian Forest. A couple of random thoughts that were assembled for this sequence. First see some of Bill's notes.

The name Logan comes from the Blackfoot Indians. Much the same way that we have Sasquatch, they have the legend of this Were-Man that they call "The Logan."

Rose takes care of Ty while he learns to be a man in the Canadian outback. She falls in love with a young man who remarkably resembles Scott Summers. It isn't of course, but it establishes Logan's future addiction for love triangles involving redheads.

Bill had a great idea. Since Wolvie has a healing factor it would only make sense that his brain had a similar ability. We've explained in the past how Weapon X made Wolvie forget all kinds of stuff. Why don't we establish that Wolvie was just as responsible for his own memory loss? For example, if he suffers a trauma that's deep enough, then his brain's healing factor would try to fix that. What's the best way to quickly relieve trauma? Forget that it ever happened!

What I propose is that while Wolvie is becoming Wolvie in Canada; his mother survives and goes to work for a hat factory in NYC. She turns her back on the fortune but always thinks of her poor son, Ty, and where he must be.

The Weapon X program or Team X, whatever they were called, finds out Wolvie's history and for whatever reason that we can think of, needs him to suffer a serious trauma. We'll have to come up with a convincing reason.

They reach out to Maria and tell her that her son has gone AWOL in the Canadian woods. He's become this thing called a Logan. They need her help to reach him.

They tell Wolvie that Dawg is still alive and is coming to finish the job.

We set both pieces in motion. Wolvie attacks in his feral rage and guts the person who he thinks is Dawg.

It's really his mother and Wolvie's brain just fries completely. How do you forget someone who's been with you most of your life? Well, if you had a healing factor you would just forget most of your life.

His mother's last words to him were "He was taken from us."

What I see as the conclusion to our story is flashing forward to today. We see a shadowy figure sniffing around the North Carolina woods. We see an old mansion that has been completely taken over by nature. Vines and decay cover the exterior and the grounds are all but gone.

Of course, it is Wolvie. He holds up the trinket that we set up earlier as something to help bring him to this spot.

He sniffs and sniffs. The claws come out and he begins digging and digging. We see a casket marked "Scott Vanderhurst." Wolvie opens it up and finds it empty. Is his brother dead? What really happened to Scott?

We close the story with Wolvie clawing his way through the vines and growth and entering the mansion. We know that all the answers he seeks will be inside ...

... as will a whole host of new questions.

**Things left unanswered**
Was Mac, Ty and Scott's father?
What happened to Scott? Is he still out there?
What happened to Dawg? Is he dead?

MORE THOUGHTS

Somewhere in issue one or two we have to establish that Maria keeps a journal with all the family happenings. It should be kept in a well-secured place.

In issue two we need to establish that John found the journal. The implication is that Maria had an affair with Mac and maybe the kids are not John's true sons. This should probably happen during the sequence that Old Man Vanderhurst is cursing and hitting John. Maybe John came to him asking for advice after finding the journal. The Old Man slaps him around for being less of a man.

**ORIGIN #1** COVER PENCILS BY JOE QUESADA

# THE EDITORS SPEAK
BY MIKE MARTS & MIKE RAICHT

THE JOB SEEMED AN EASY ONE.

When Editor in Chief Joe Quesada walked down the hall to ask us if we'd accept ORIGIN into our office, "yes" blurted out of our mouths before Joe could even finish his sentence. I mean, what else could we say? It was a no-brainer. The schedule had already been set, the freelancers were all chosen and most of the story had already been hammered out. The pieces were all in place. Wolverine's ORIGIN was surely the easiest book an editor could hope for.

At least, that's what we thought at first.

But as the epic storyline contained within this volume proves (not to mention the heaps upon mounds upon loads of supplemental material), ORIGIN was anything but easy. But you won't hear us complaining. Nope. Not when you take a step back and realize just what type of a project ORIGIN really is.

Forget for a minute all the sales hoopla, all the advanced promotion and all the months of preparation. Forget the fact that Marvel's best selling book in over five years topped the charts at #1 for several months in a row. Forget all the hype... and think about what we've got here. The story readers have been waiting years for. The true history of everybody's favorite X-Man. The *origin* of Wolverine!

So who cared if this book was a challenge? It was a welcome challenge.

By the time we got our hands dirty working on the title, Andy Kubert had already finished a dozen character sketches and Paul Jenkins, Bill Jemas and Joe had constructed an extremely tight outline for the first three issues, which explored Logan's early formative years.

What hadn't been resolved yet was what the next three issues would be about. We knew that Logan would experience horrible tragedy at home. We knew that he and his companion Rose would be forced into exile and escape into the Canadian wilderness. But what would happen then? Joe had a few ideas. Paul had a few others. And not to be outdone, Bill had a few of his own, as well.

The trick was throwing everyone's ideas into the proverbial blender and making sure the end result was a concoction everyone would be happy with—Joe, Bill, Paul, Andy, us, and most importantly, the readers. Not an easy trick, mind you, but one we accepted with vigor and enthusiasm. To perform this trick, however, would require hours upon hours of plot meetings, brainstorm sessions, conference calls and emails. Many, many emails.

We saved a few of those email exchanges and we're presenting them here, just to give you a small indication of how big a project Origin became, and how determined we all were to create an extraordinary, one-of-a-kind story for the ages ... like the one you now hold in your hands.

Sit back and enjoy.

MIKE MARTS
EDITOR

MIKE RAICHT
ASSISTANT EDITOR
2002

# THE E-MAIL CHAIN

**From:** Quesada, Joe
**Sent:** Monday, July 30, 2001 9:31 AM
**To:** Marts, Michael; Jemas, Bill; Raicht, Michael
**Subject:** Origin #4 Plot

So basically, Logan has some dreams, gets food splattered on him by Cookie, saves some guys in the quarry, dreams some more, desires Rose, dreams some more, sees Rose with Smitty.

This is not exciting enough. Here's how I can validate that statement — I can't think of a cover image that's good enough.

First of all, it should be Cookie that Logan gets his mannerisms from. Cookie says Bub and smokes cigars.

There is little story here and Paul misses a very good moment. He touches on the fact that Logan ages slowly and everyone around him is growing older. We need a scene cut where we see poor Logan mewling about Rose and how much he loves her. We don't realize that time has passed, but from off panel we hear Rose's voice. When we turn the page we get a full page shot of Rose, she's a gorgeous woman and Logan still looks 13.

---

**From:** Marts, Michael
**Sent:** Monday, July 30, 2001 10:51 AM
**To:** Jemas, Bill; Raicht, Michael; Quesada, Joe
**Subject:** RE: Origin #4 Plot

I agree with Joe that there seems to be something missing from this story. This issue will end up being a "coming of age" story more than any of the other issues, but I never get a sense that Logan is really becoming a man, at least not in any concrete, physical way.

Maybe this could be improved by making the conflict between Rose/Cookie/Logan even greater. Cookie could be some real slob who lusts after Rose, really laying it on thick with the advances. He taunts the small Logan throughout most of the story and Logan plays the victim. But Logan eventually comes of age and confronts Cookie at a time when Rose is really in danger from the slobbering bastard, and eventually wins, playing the hero. Logan is thrilled at finally standing up to someone and "becoming a man" and figures he's proven himself to the woman he loves ... only to be betrayed by her in Paul's final scene.

JQ: This is very good and a great idea to make significant in the story! I still feel like we need something else.

Also, cut back on the number of dream sequences to one, and probably not start off with it. Maybe it would be better to start off the issue after a couple of years have passed, pick up halfway through Paul's outline and fill in the necessary pieces as we go along.

As for cover image, Joe, what about playing with wolf imagery. Maybe Logan and a wolf on a hill top?

JQ: I'm looking for Wolf reference as we speak!

---

**From:** Quesada, Joe
**Sent:** Monday, July 30, 2001 12:47 PM
**To:** Jemas, Bill; Marts, Michael; Raicht, Michael

**Subject:** RE: Origin #4 Plot

Here are a few more ideas. This can make it a better more rounded story.

If we open with a dream sequence it should just be a panel with a close up of 2 burning eyes (wolf eyes but we don't know it yet), just evil and scary! The eyes speak to him in ways only a poofy British writer can figure out ;-). No running with the wolves, just the eyes. When he runs with the Wolves for the first time it should happen for real, not in a dream. Logan wakes up in a cold sweat, scared but also slightly aroused at what's happening to him (remember it's puberty) We make reference to the fact that he's been having these dreams for a while. We'll come back to this.

Cookie tortures poor baby Logan and has the hots for his "sister" Rose.

There is a collapse at the Quarry, 20 men buried alive. It takes them days to dig everyone out and the only survivor is Logan—no one of course can figure it out. Must be the Lord's will. While Logan is buried, Cookie is working on Rose and Smitty is her rescuer but let's not tip our hand to the obvious romance that is happening behind closed doors.

The first time his healing factor is seen by the world is during the fight with Cookie! Remember, Cookie smokes cigars and says "Bub" all the time, Smitty is the Scott Summers metaphor. Logan finds Cookie on the verge of raping Rose and they get into a brawl. Cookie slices a big bloody X on Logan's chest and he sees it heal before his very eyes. This Logan guy wasn't saved by God in the Quarry, he's the Devil's spawn!

Once Logan rescues Rose, Cookie begins his attempt at character defamation, calling Logan a freak and getting everyone in the camp scared. Logan is rejected by everyone he turns to.

He goes to see Smitty or Rose (pick one) to help him and ease his suffering and finds them embracing!

Betrayed he runs into the snowy woods and keeps running losing track of time. He tears at his clothes for no good reason except that it looks cool until he's buck-naked. During this running rage his claws (I like this bit) extract and contract involuntarily, causing all sorts of pain and making for some very cool visuals!

Logan collapses in a circular clearing, on his knees his body steaming from the sweat. He hears a noise and looks around 360 degrees at the woods that surround him. He sees hundreds of the eyes he was seeing in his dreams. Now you can end the issue there or....

He finds a small patch of woods with no glowing eyes and makes a bee-line for it expecting it to be his only clearing and path to safety. He runs desperately but the wolves are following close behind. Soon they catch up and that's when it becomes apparent to the frightened young Logan that they aren't chasing him but following. He is the Alpha Male. This scene ends with a young Logan dissolving into a splash page of an older teenage Logan jumping over snow covered hills followed by his pack. Maybe a deer in the foreground as if they're hunting it. This is all probably better for issue #5 as an opening but I offer it just in case.

So we close issue #4 with the eyes glowing in the woods. Make it only one set.

Issue #5 opens with the eyes coming out of the shadow and it's the biggest wolf you've ever seen! As it comes out of the woods a million other pair appear in the shadows! The Alpha Male does battle with Logan and he kills it. Next thing we see is the pack come out of the shadows and they lick his wounds clean.

Jump cut to him running in the snowy woods by himself, suddenly one wolf is running by him and then more and more and then wee see that they are on the hunt and he's the new king of the jungle!

What do you guys think. Does this work better as a story?

If we agree that there's something here then I'll forward these notes to Paul.

JQ

---

From:Jemas, Bill
Sent: Tuesday, July 31, 2001 9:02 AM
To:Marts, Michael; Jenkins, Paul; Quesada, Joe
Re:RE: Origin #4 Plot

There really isn't much new in these notes or in the attached outline. I understand Paul's concern with dumping everything but the kitchen sink into these books — so I thought it would be a good idea to lay out the four main priorities that we have been discussing for the past several months.

In that spirit, the attached outline doesn't add much new stuff — but it does re-jigger most of the current scenes into three books with well-defined plots.

**Wolverine earned his claws.**

THE QUARRY: Logan is a soft kid who has to get tough or die. Based on his abilities and hard work he rises to the top of the heap among the workers — but is constantly undone by treachery.

THE WILD AND THE WOLF PACK: Logan works his way up to leader of the pack — vroom vroom.

**Rose carries the guilt in her heart and the story in her diary.**

LOGAN'S PAST: she shields him for his own good — and maybe for hers, too.

LOGAN'S LOVE: she treats it like a crush.

TOM is Rose's lover and Logan's father figure — but Logan had to earn Tom's respect. I'm not locked on Mac or Tom, but please not Tad or Todd. (Tom's name is changed to Smitty in the final version of the script.)

**Treachery and Enemies**

COOKIE wants Logan to replace him on the bottom rung. When Logan gets tough — he can take on Cookie head-on — but Cookie always finds the back door.

DAWG WANTS IT ALL:
Kill Logan to avenge the death of his father.
Take Rose as his wife.
Inherit the Howlett family fortune.
Cookie is nothing compared to this enemy.

**Show it — don't say it. This is a big bold graphic action movie.**

We are avoiding the basic comic book pratfalls of flashbacks and cryptic references to be revealed later.

The Diary is a great tool for explaining the meaning behind the action — but should not be a substitute for action.

Each comic will have a beginning, middle and end and be readable by someone who hasn't read anything except that comic.

## Book Four — Opening Scene

Scrawny, short kid struggles up dirt path carved out of the side of the rock slope.

Knees and elbows scraping — two steps forward, one step back — works his way past a group of diggers with pickaxes and shovels.

Diggers are making fun of Cookie (he's ugly, fat, lazy, etc.).

They take the foreground — and turn up the heat on Cookie — we see the kid in background dump the barrow and turn back down toward the diggers.

Kid slips and barrow rolls out of control with the little dork running after.

Cookie stops the cart — has everybody's attention — including ours because this is now like the Logan/Dawg scene in the first book of the first arc.

Cookie rolls the barrow down the steep side of the hill and sends Logan tumbling down after. The diggers fall over laughing — as we get a close-up of Cookie's smiling, pockmarked face and his yellow rot-toothed grin.

Logan is out in the real world and Cookie makes Dawg look like a ten-year-old bully.

Now we can get to Rose — either in the office with Tom or writing in the diary.

## BOOK 4 — SMACKED ALL THE WAY DOWN
**Beginning — hitting bottom socially**
Logan and Rose — work for room & board
Logan stumbling through manual labor
Rose menial labor in camp office

Cookie — puts Logan at bottom of the pecking order
Cookie at the bottom of the camp food chain
Cookie abuses/degrades Logan — workers love it

Tom: Rose & Logan are too low to see Tom does not help Logan when Cookie attacks
"Kid, you have to fight your own battles"
Tom barely knows Rose is alive

### Hitting bottom physically

**Winter hardship — near starvation at Quarry**
Cookie steals some of their food ration

Logan to Rose — don't complain — he'll kill me

Turning the corner

Logan — the hunter provides food for the camp
Starts with a couple of rabbits — for Rose
Hunts — kills deer — feeds the entire camp
Logan — first encounter with the Wolfpack
He sees Wolves — his claws pop on their own
He runs back to Rose — heals along the way

Logan returns to Rose with a hundred questions
Logan to Rose: I don't remember anything
Rose will not tell Logan the truth — he goes to sleep
Rose writes a note to Logan on inside cover of her
Diary: she will give the book to him someday he will
know all about his past

End — Logan finds his place in the wild
Cookie and Logan II
Cookie uses dirty trick to humiliate and beat up Logan

Tom stops Cookie from killing Logan

Logan and the Wolves I
Pops claws — retracts
Belly up — accepted

## BOOK 5 — RISING ALL THE WAY UP

Beginning — Setting up the bad guys

Grandfather dying and repenting
Grandfather talking to mysterious Servant
Wants to give his fortune to James — please find him
James Howlet has fallen off the face of the Earth

Logan — Cookie and the Miners
Logan is boss of the camp — digs like a Wolverine
Cookie madder than ever — secret dirty tricks

Tom — Rose — Logan — love triangle starts
Tom hangs out at their cabin
Tom shows Logan how to use dynamite

Great Times — Logan hits his stride
Logan becomes Tom's right hand man

Logan's nights
Drinks and plays with the workers
Then runs wild with the wolf pack — #2 dog

Rose and Tom start to get romantic at night

Great Treachery

At the mansion — Grandfather's Servant
Finds Rose's letters to housekeeper -letters recap
the Dawg thing — still don't know it's him
Now Servant knows where Rose and Wolvie are

At the Camp — huge cave in
Cookie sabotage — Logan escapes
Logan and Tom — daring rescue — save all but one
worker
Logan's arm gets ripped to shreds
Rose bandages fully-healed arm

End — Wolverine: "I am the top dog"

Cookie and Logan III
Cookie is going through dead guy's stuff
Logan blows away Cookie

Rose and Tom tell Logan they are in love
Logan swallows his pride — and goes to the woods

Logan and the Wolves II
Wolverine takes over the pack — "lead dog"

Grandfather to Servant — "Can you find my
grandson?"
Servant:"Yes I will Sir, I will be like a hound dawg"
Reveal — Dawg's scarred face mirrors the cover of
issue #4

## BOOK 6 — DEFEAT — ESCAPE

Beginning — Enter the bad guy
Dawg kills a trapper
They meet outside of the quarry. You're Logan —
what a coincidence — there's a Logan in camp
Dawg kills the trapper to keep his secret

Dawg befriends Tom at the canteen
Bumps into Logan — doesn't remember Dawg
They see cage getting set up for prize-fights
Rose and Tom — getting married and getting out

Logan will take over the camp
Tom — needs money and he knows how to get it

Murder #1 — fails

Dawg traps Tom in his cabin
I'm killing you and Howlett — and taking Rose
Tom lights dynamite fuse — drops it between cabin
planks
Dawg dives out the front — leaves Tom for dead
Tom dives out the back — knocked out cold

Rose knows
Rose rushes to the cabin — Tom out cold for hours
Tom finally wakes up and he tells her about Dawg
Rose goes to warn Logan

Cage at the canteen
Logan winning big time
Everyone fights hard but fair
Logan exhausted — enter Dawg

Dawg gives Cookie brass knuckles and $50
Logan wins — but is battered and tired

End: Dawg ambushes Logan
Rose tries to break up the fight
Logan accidentally kills her

Dawg "saw it all" — Logan is a monster/killer
Logan runs for the woods

Logan and the Wolves III
Wolverine runs wild in the woods

Cookie burns the diary

## CHARACTER DESIGNS BY ANDY KUBERT

Being asked to work on one of the most exciting comic projects in recent memory was enough of a jolt to me. I was floored when I got the call. I remember that time so vividly.

So you can imagine the angst that I felt when I read the first script, and talked with Paul at length as to how to interpret his (along with Joe and Bill's) ideas of what these characters should look and act like. Paul and I had a few long, in-depth conversations that helped to put me at ease. Paul is an excellent storyteller; like when you're in grade school and the teacher is reading a book to you, showing the pictures at the same time. Except I saw the pictures in my mind as he was talking. I saw exactly how these characters should look and act.

After the initial conversation about the characters, I immediately set out to get all the reference for the costumes and clothing for that time period at my library. I had also found a few books at a bookstore. I spent a great deal of time sifting through all the reference that I had acquired, trying to piece together the characters that I had envisioned with the costumes. I love going through reference, thumbing through the old books and reading about the items and time period that I am referencing. Reading about the things that I will be drawing really helps me to reach the right frame of mind for when I set out to do the storytelling.

These are the thoughts that we had as we were putting together the characters. And a few ideas that I had thrown in there myself...

Andy Kubert

ANDY KUBERT
2002

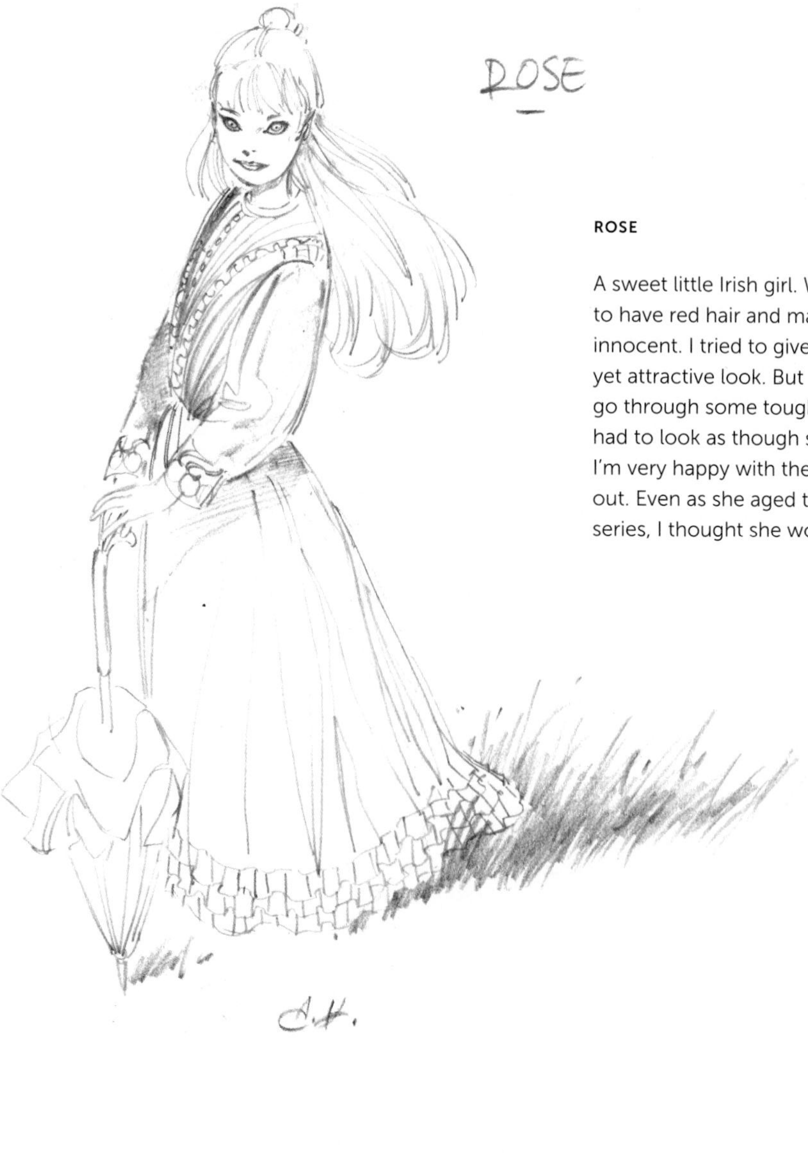
ROSE
A.K.

**ROSE**

A sweet little Irish girl. We wanted her to have red hair and make her very innocent. I tried to give her a refined, yet attractive look. But she was going to go through some tough times, and she had to look as though she could take it. I'm very happy with the way she turned out. Even as she aged throughout the series, I thought she worked well.

#### LITTLE JAMES

James was to be thin, sickly looking. He wasn't supposed to look anything like Logan looks today which I thought was a great idea. He was also supposed to be a spoiled little rich kid. I thought of Alfalfa from "The Little Rascals" when I envisioned his look. And the dress costume, which was actually worn by wealthy boys from that time period, really helped get his soft demeanor across.

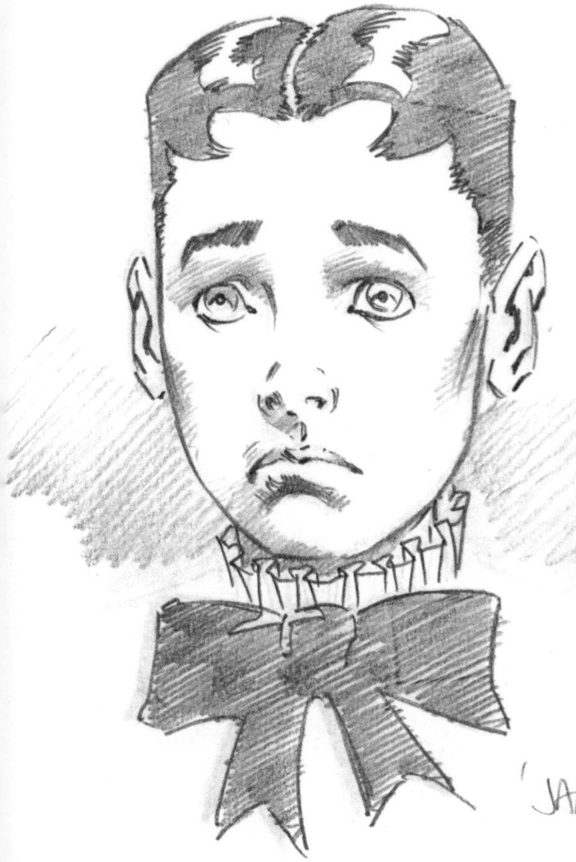
'JAMES'

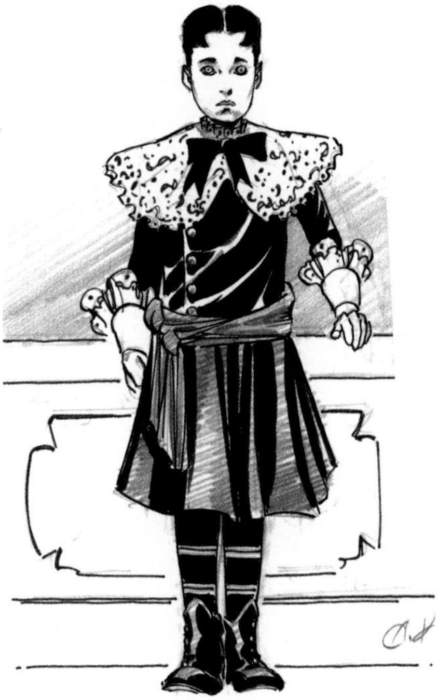

#### DAWG

Dawg was a snot-nosed little punk with ripped clothes and hair that was never combed. He was a total bully. A troublemaker. There were a few kids around my neighborhood when I was a kid that always picked on the skinny, weaker kids. They all kind of gelled into one look, having the same kind of turned up nose and squinty eyes, like they were looking for a fight. And for me, that look turned into Dawg.

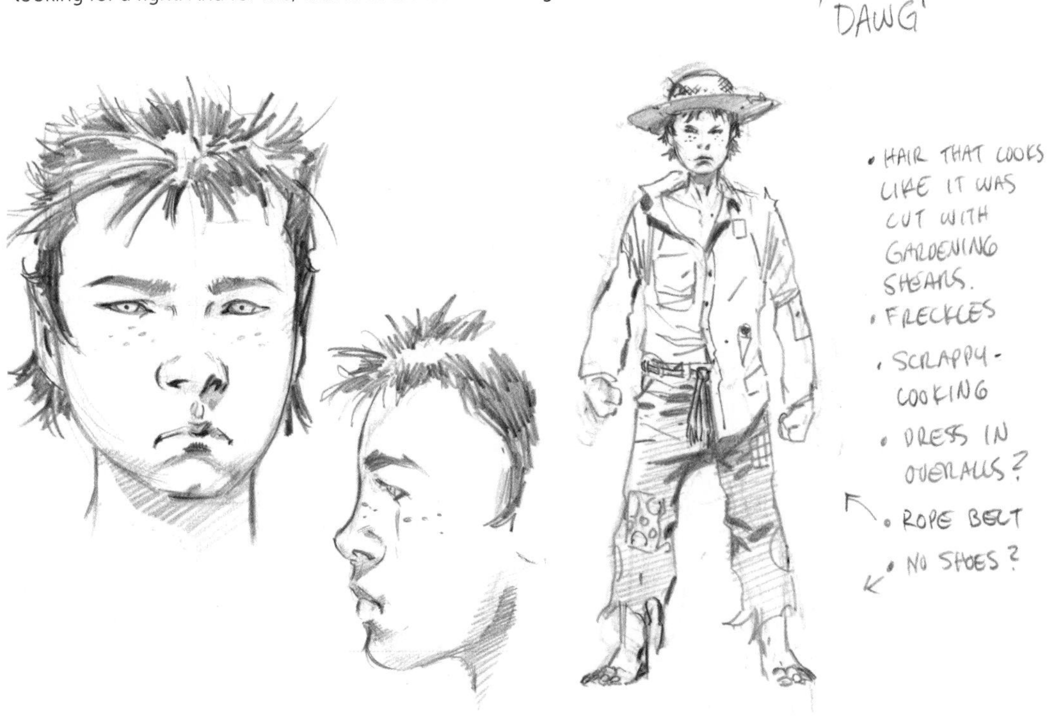
'DAWG'
• HAIR THAT LOOKS LIKE IT WAS CUT WITH GARDENING SHEARS.
• FRECKLES
• SCRAPPY-LOOKING
• DRESS IN OVERALLS?
• ROPE BELT
• NO SHOES?

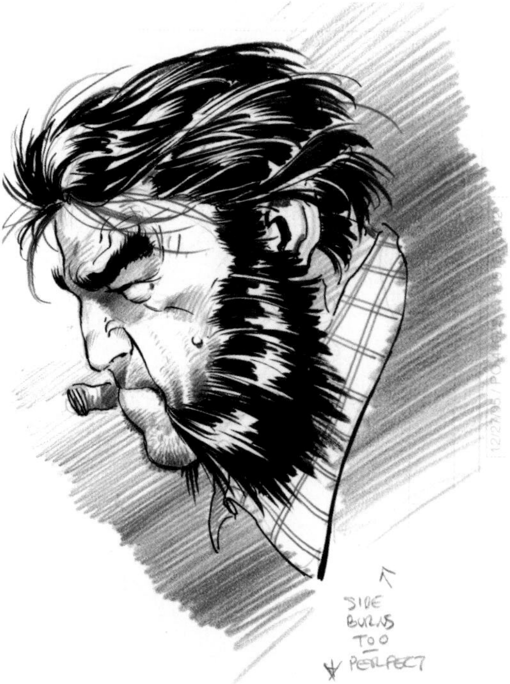
SIDE BURNS TOO PERFECT

THOMAS LOGAN

He was easy. Thomas was to look like a crusty Wolverine. I picked the clothing from a book I had bought which had old pictures of miners and poor people in it. The beard style was also perfect for this time period. I enjoyed drawing Thomas. Too bad he didn't make it past the second issue.

JOHN HOWLETT

John was to have a kind, gentle demeanor about him. But when he got mad, you knew he meant business. Clean-shaven, always impeccably dressed. I pictured him as a young Jimmy Stewart. Again, the costume and hairstyle were taken from old reference book photographs.

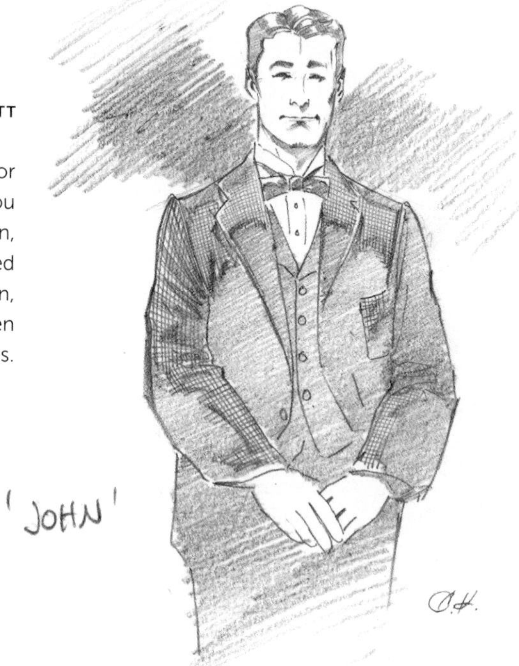
'JOHN'

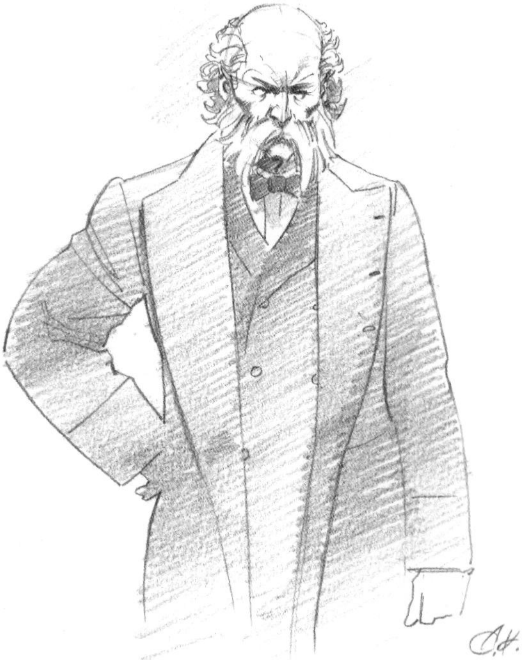

OLD MAN HOWLETT

This guy was to be one of the surly types; old, yet feisty. I thought a bit of Ebeneezer Scrooge when I was drawing him, even with his costuming. I love the beard and moustaches that were in style back then. He was another of my favorites to draw.

**ELIZABETH HOWLETT**

This woman needed to have the look of a woman with a lot of skeletons in her closet. I thought she should be pale and very sickly looking, usually dressed in black. To me, this sketch makes her look a bit like an alien. I kinda liked that.

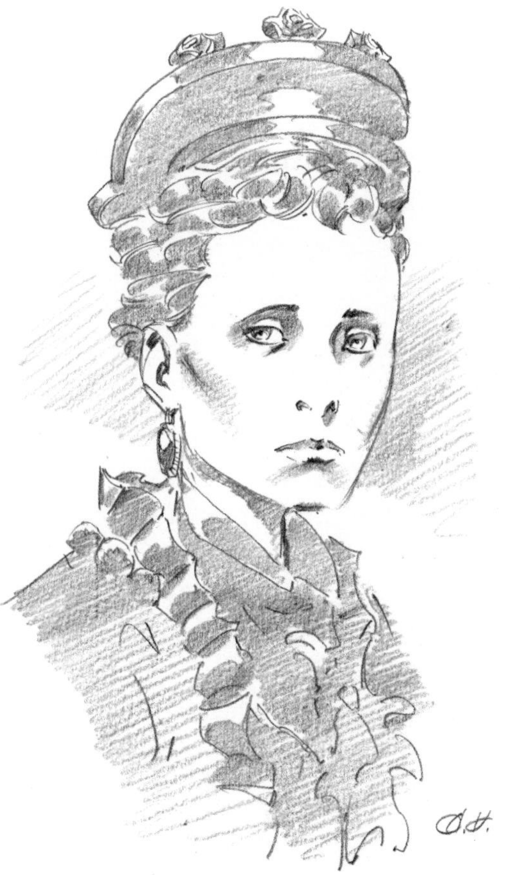
'ELIZABETH'

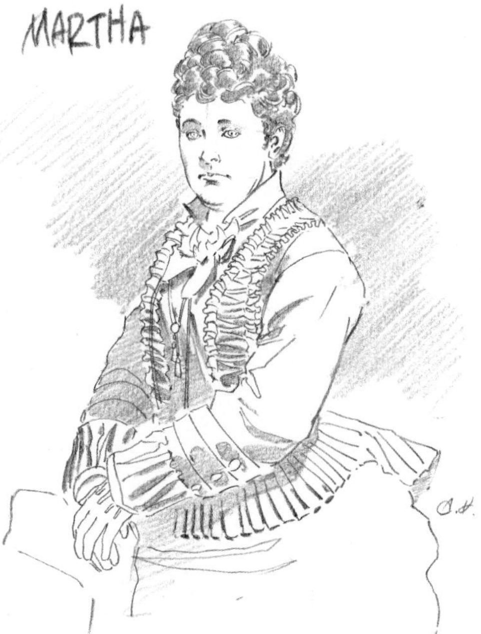
MARTHA

**MARTHA**

Martha was the housekeeper. I guess I watch too much TV, but I was thinking of a typical television housekeeper as I put this together. I thought she should be a bit pudgy, with hair piled high. She was to be very faithful, and I think this came across in her look.

**KENNETH**

Kenneth was the stable-master, and I saw him as John's right-hand man for any job that came up. I saw him as a big, burly type of guy; one you would like to pal around with, or go out to the pub and have a few pints with.

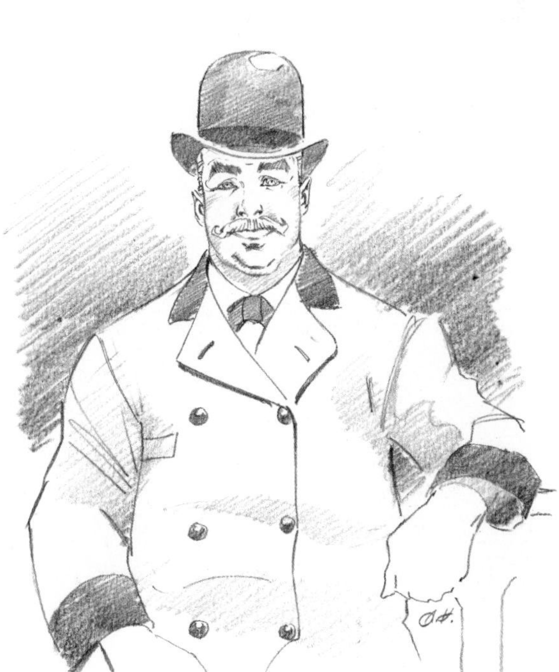
Kenneth

## THE PAINTED PROCESS

BY RICHARD ISANOVE

STEP 1: THE LINE ART

After scanning a quickly painted canvas, apply the drawing onto it.

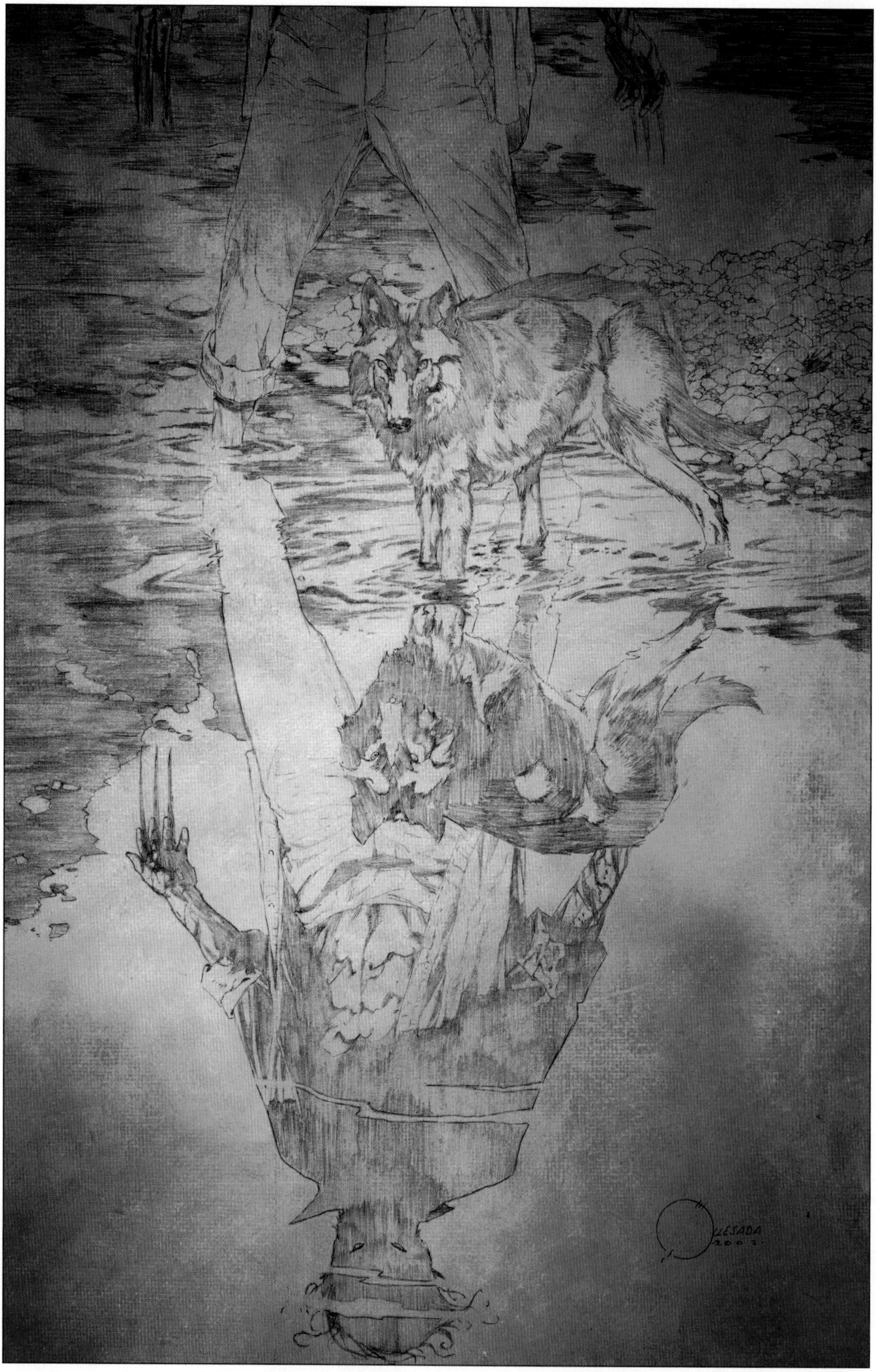

STEP 2: SPOTTING THE BLACK

Establish the darkest shadows.

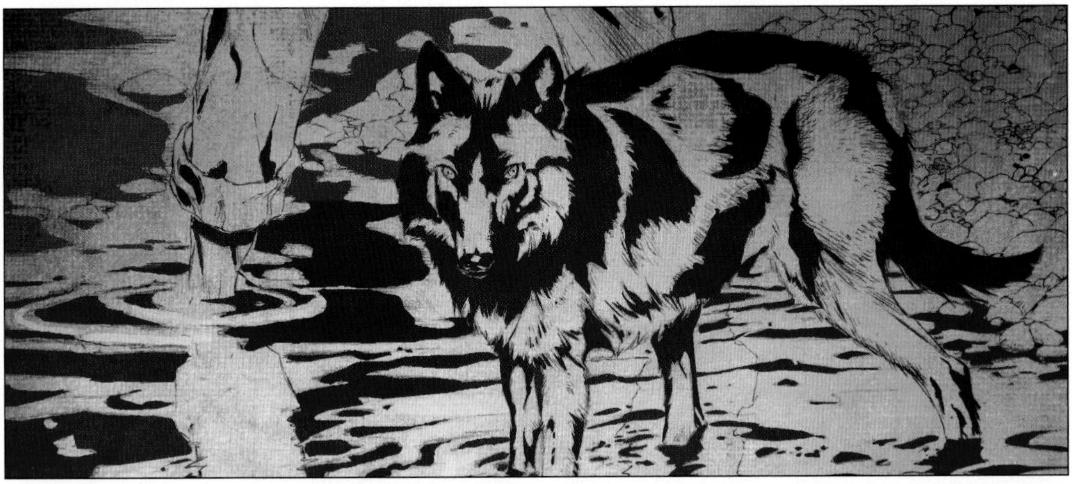

STEP 3 AND 4: RENDERING

Start to blend the lights and darks to create the impression of volume and texture.

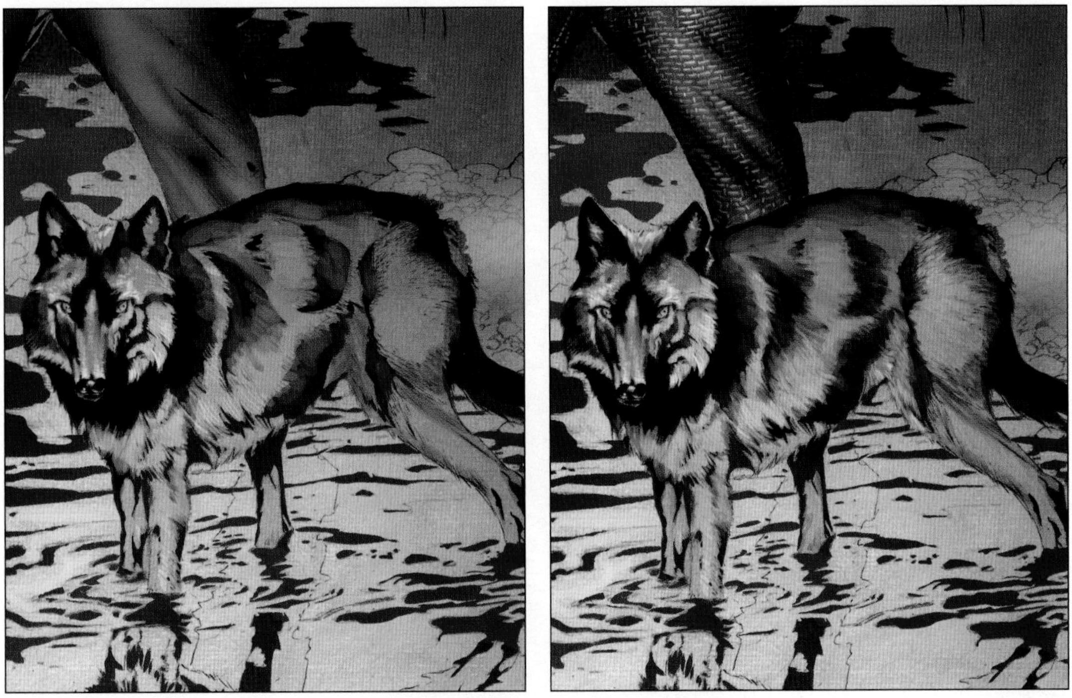

STEP 5: THE REFLECTION

Flip the result and paste it, replacing the black by a dark brown to make the figures less tangible.

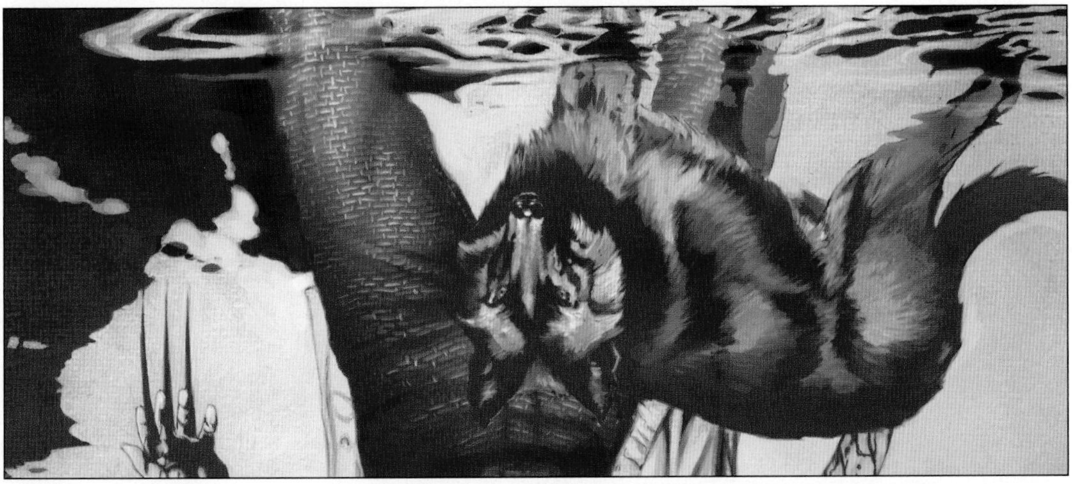

STEP 6: FINE-TUNING

This takes longer than all the other steps combined. Lighten up certain areas and darken others to separate background from foreground; add highlights to accentuate the volumes and create the water effect; fade the remaining line art into the "painting."

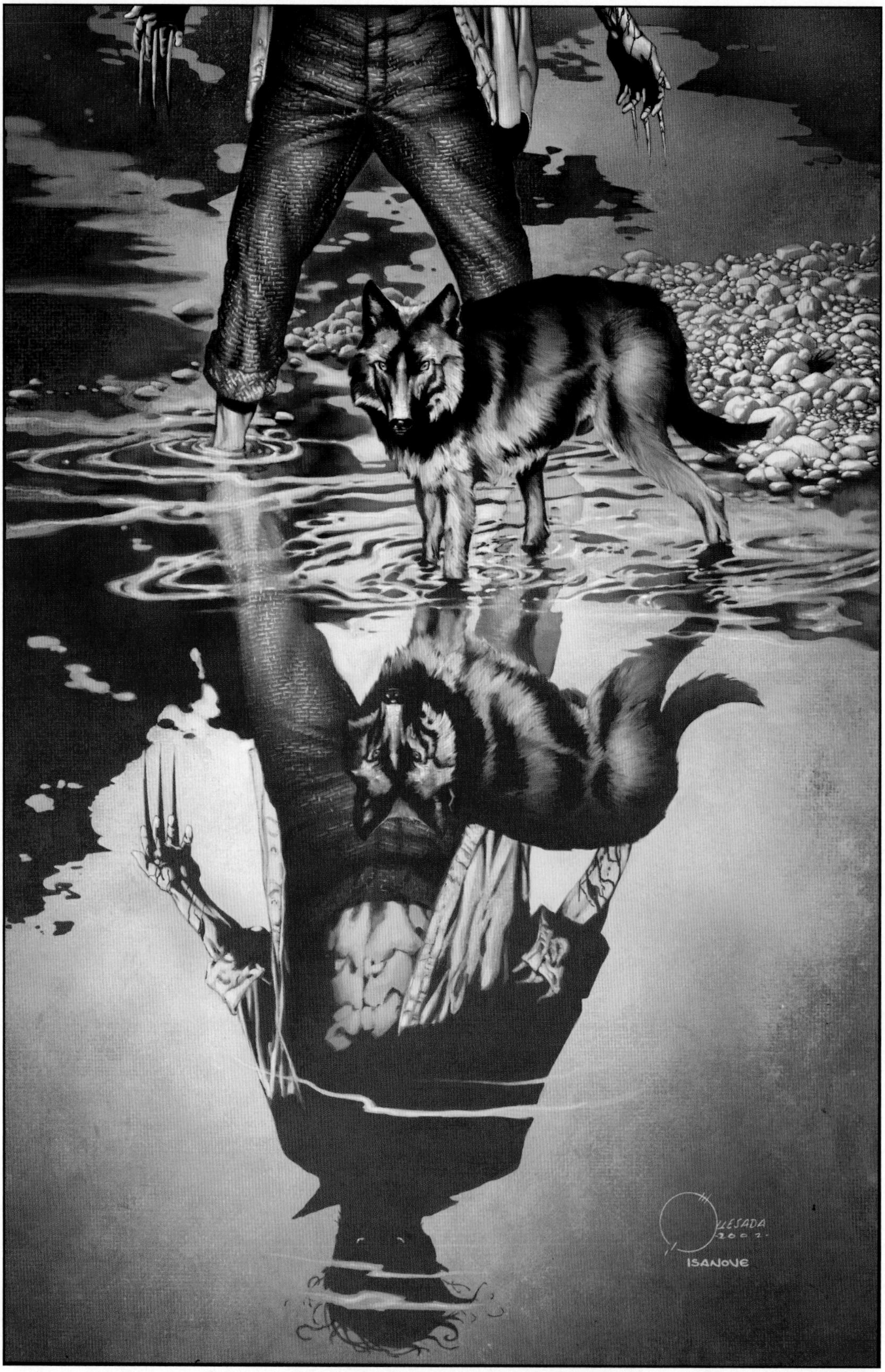
QUESADA
2002.
ISANOVE

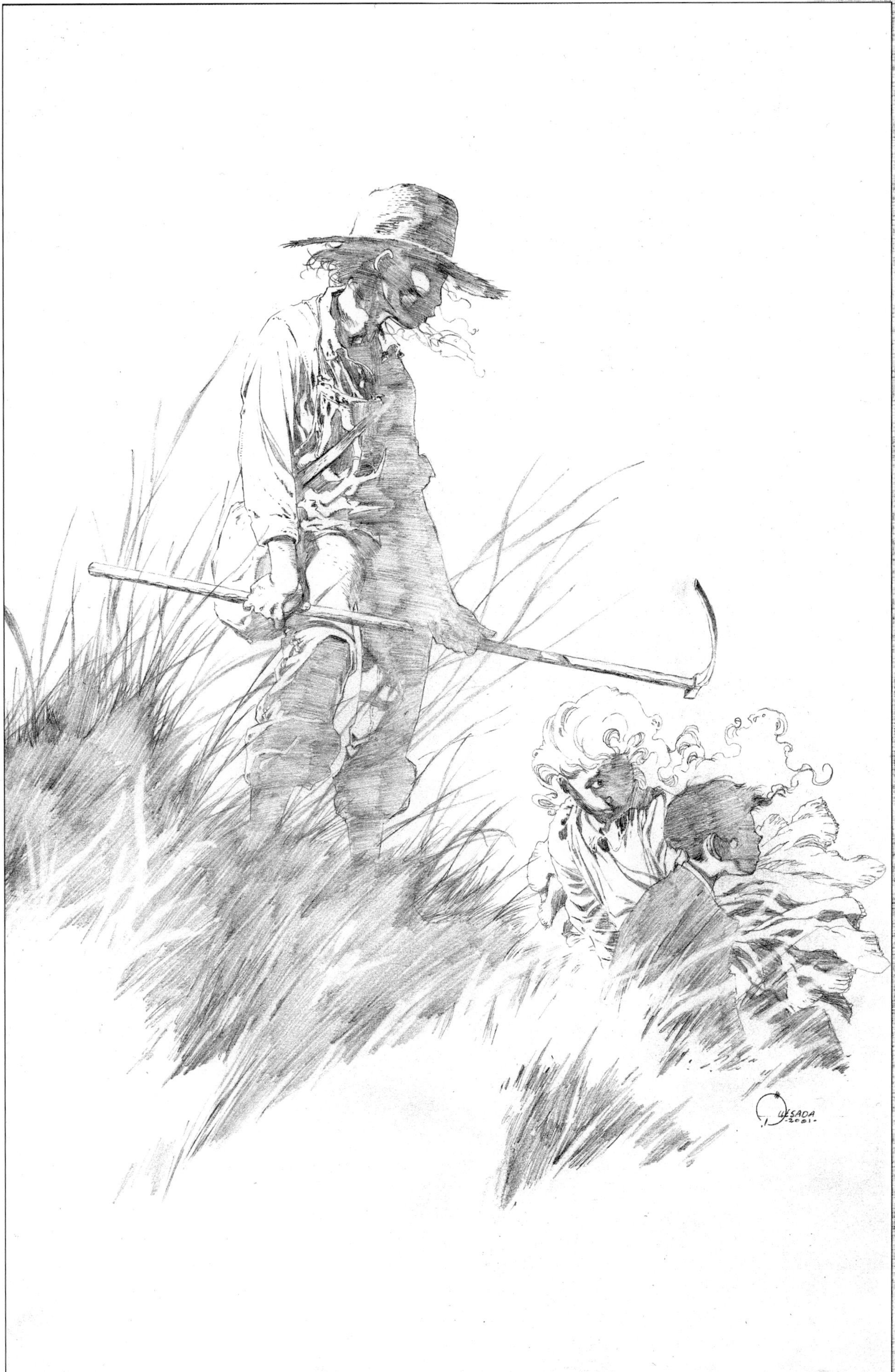
QUESADA
2001

**ORIGIN #1** COVER PENCILS

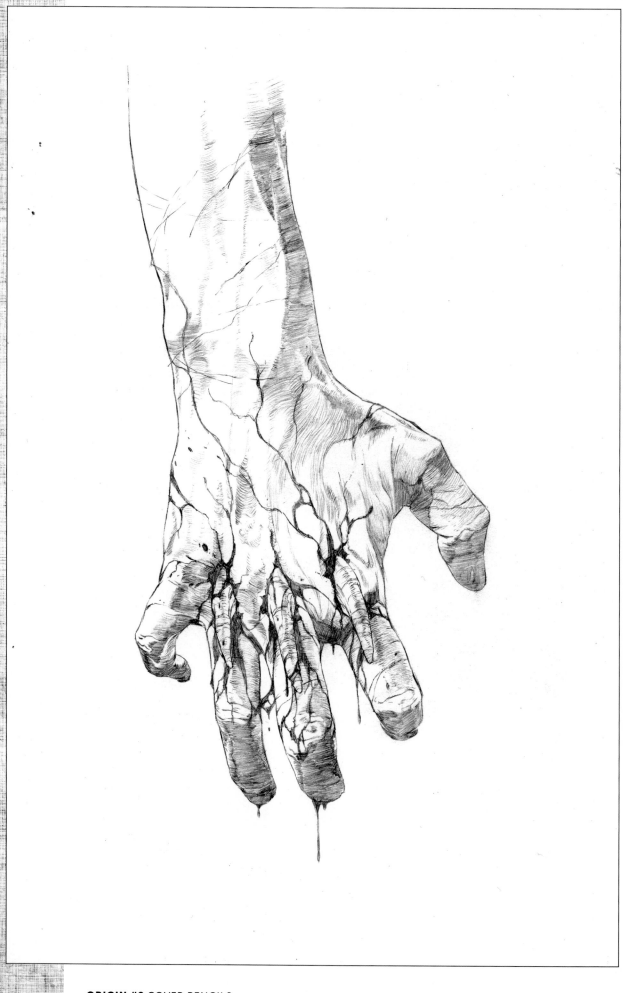

**ORIGIN #2** COVER PENCILS

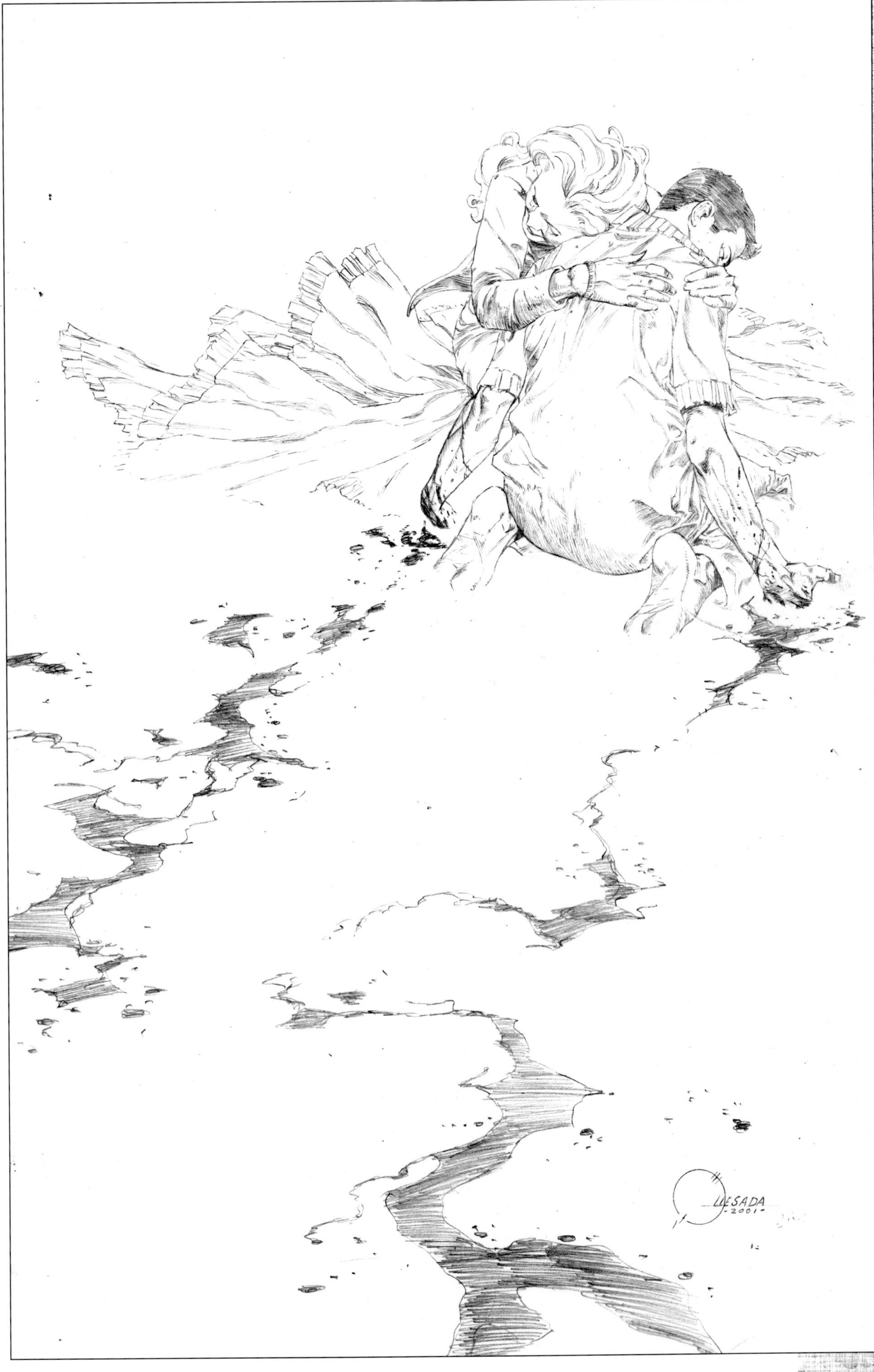
QUESADA
-2001-

**ORIGIN #3** COVER PENCILS

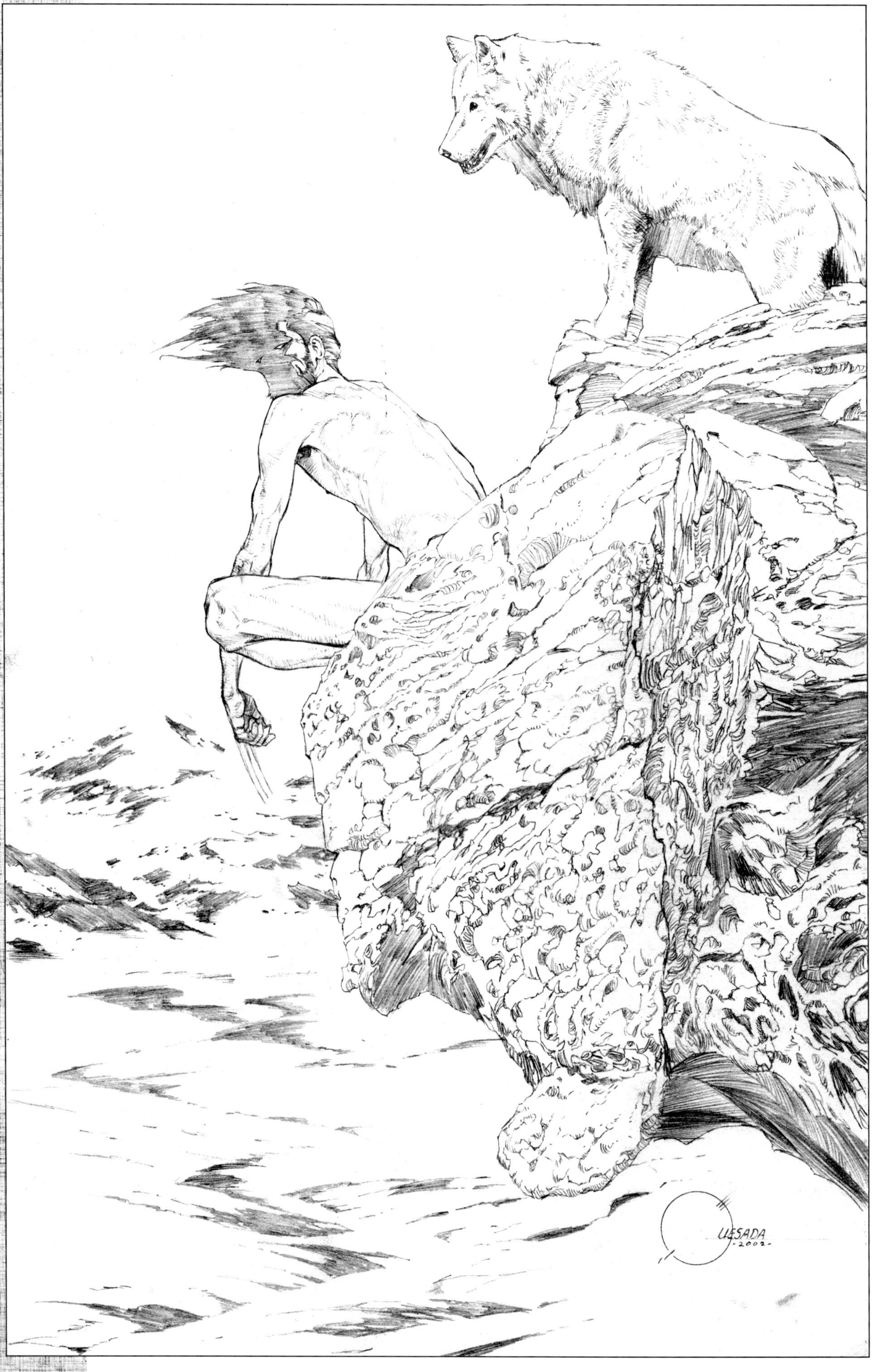
QUESADA
2002

**ORIGIN #6** COVER PENCILS

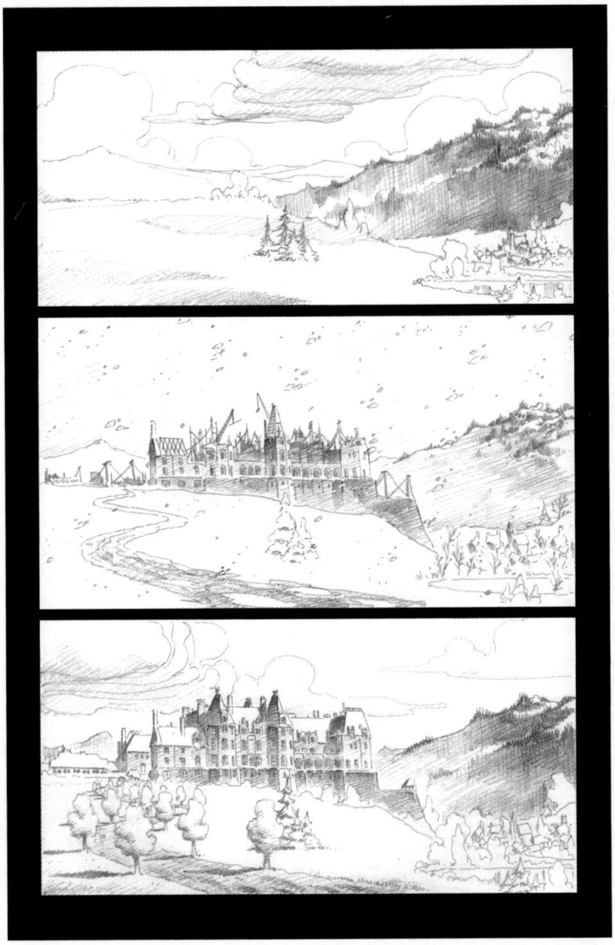
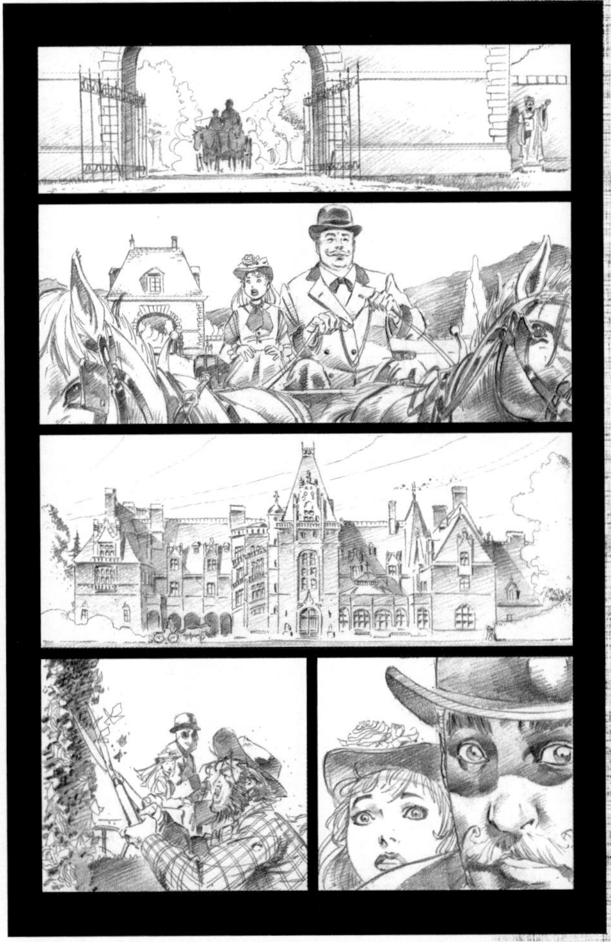
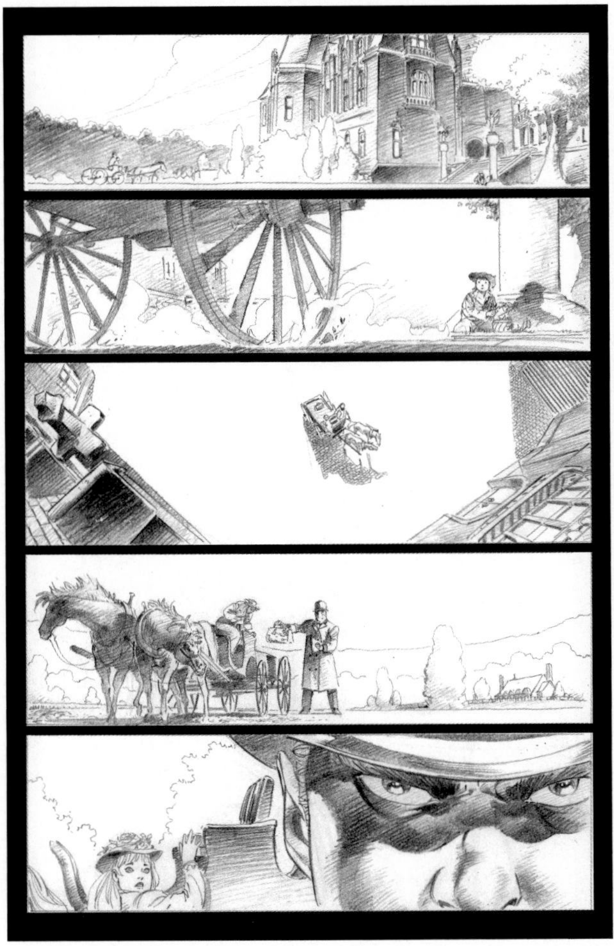
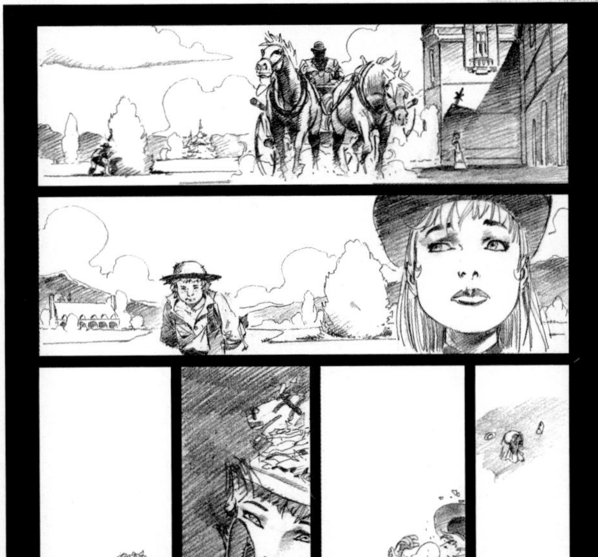

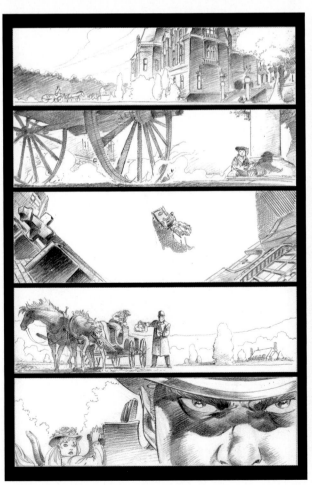

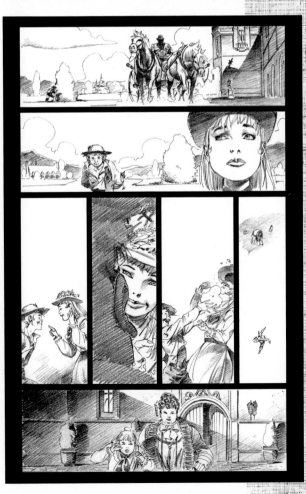

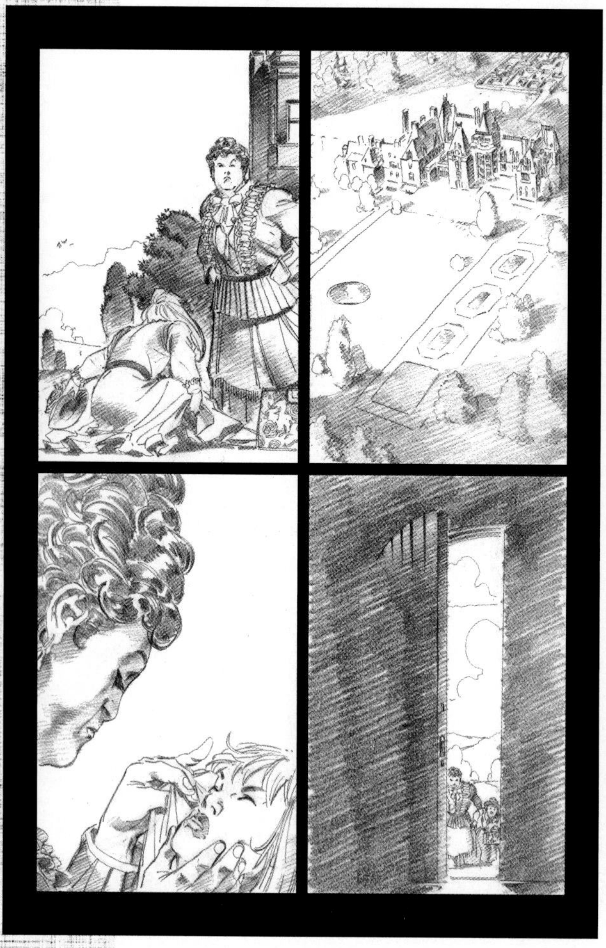

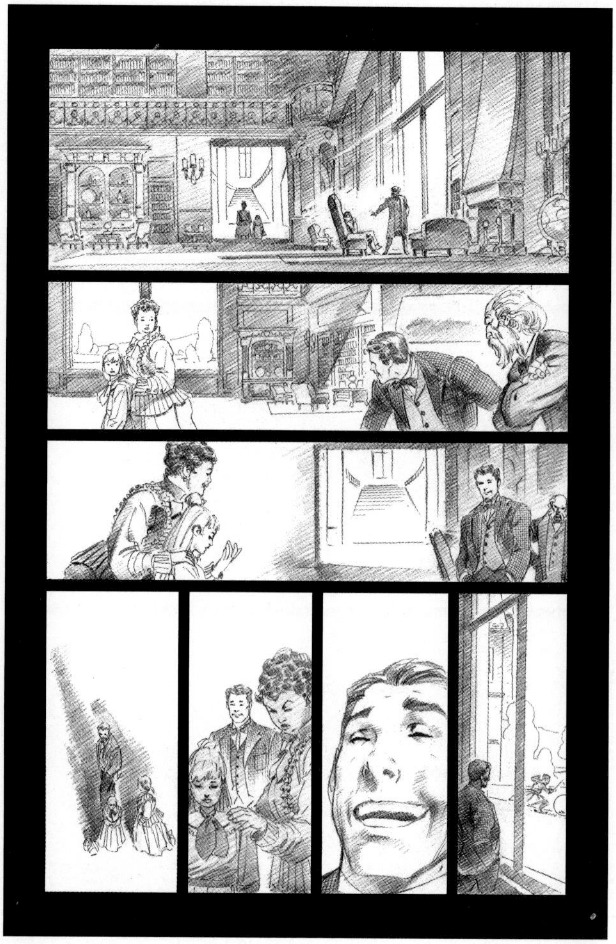

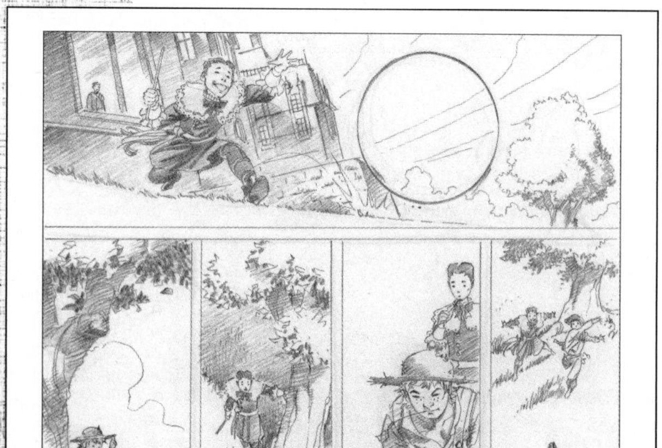

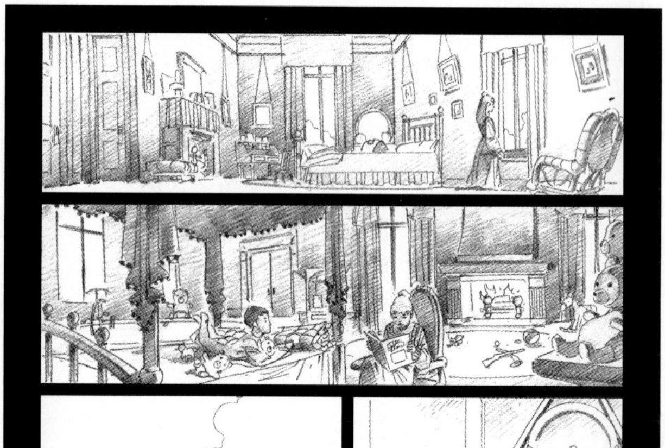

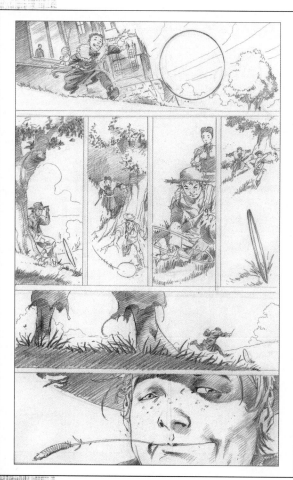

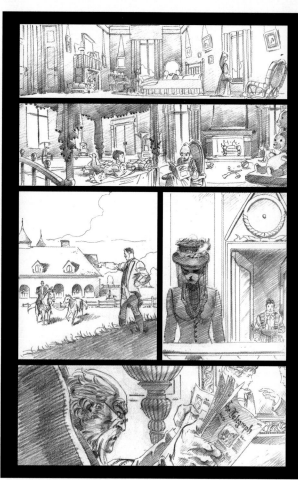

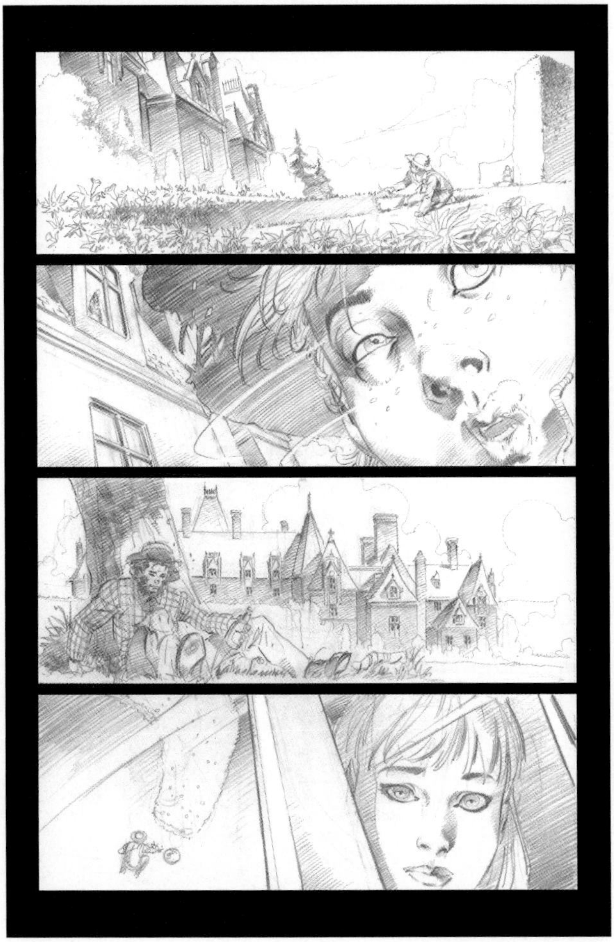
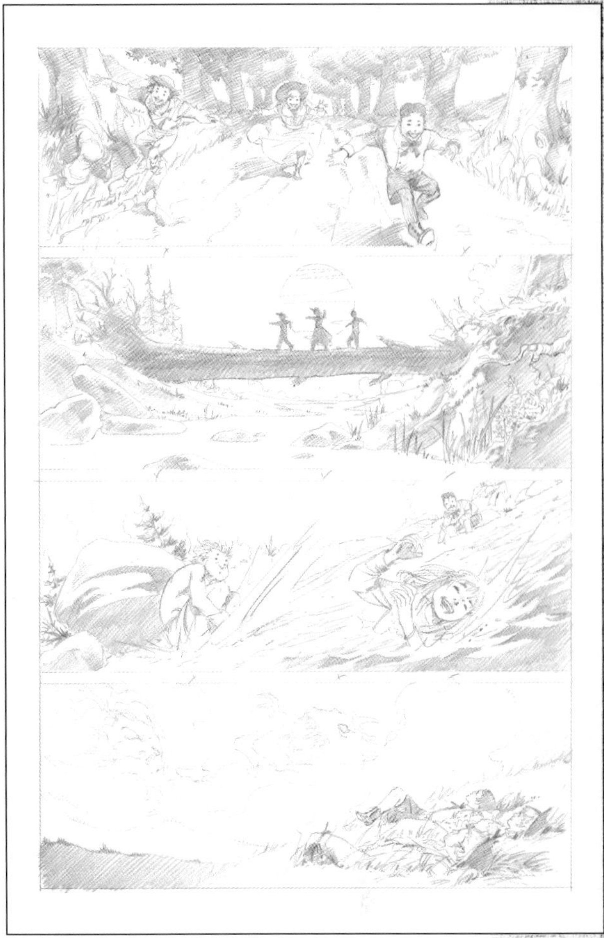
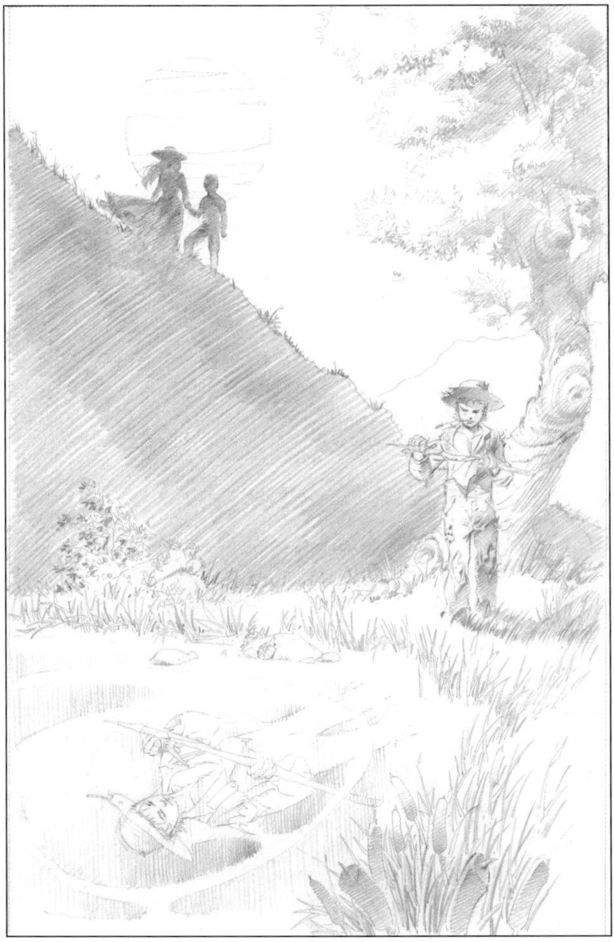
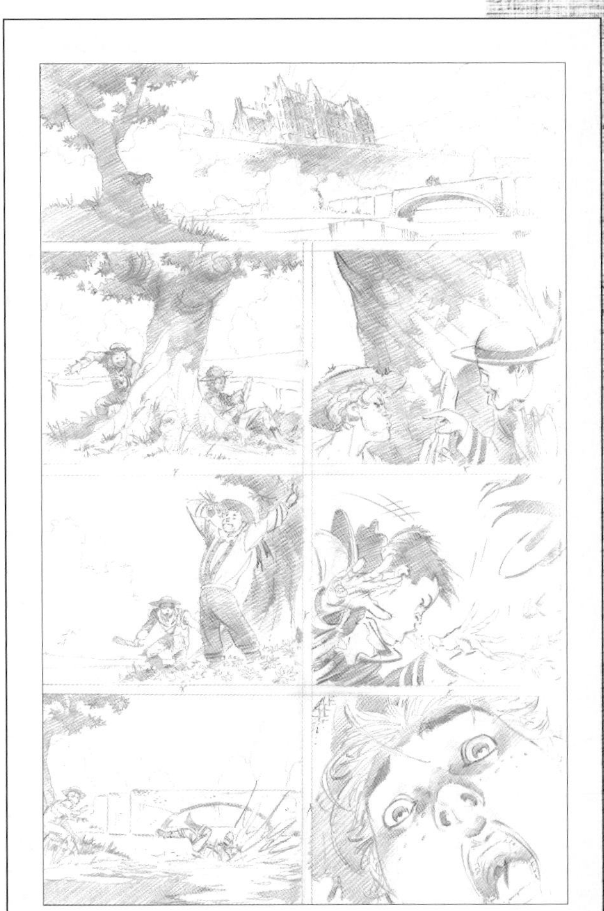

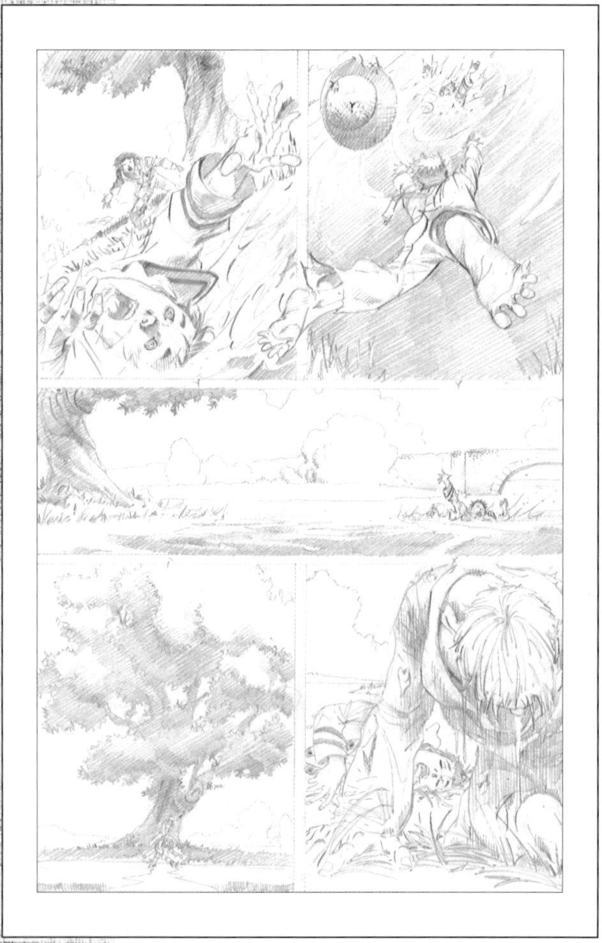
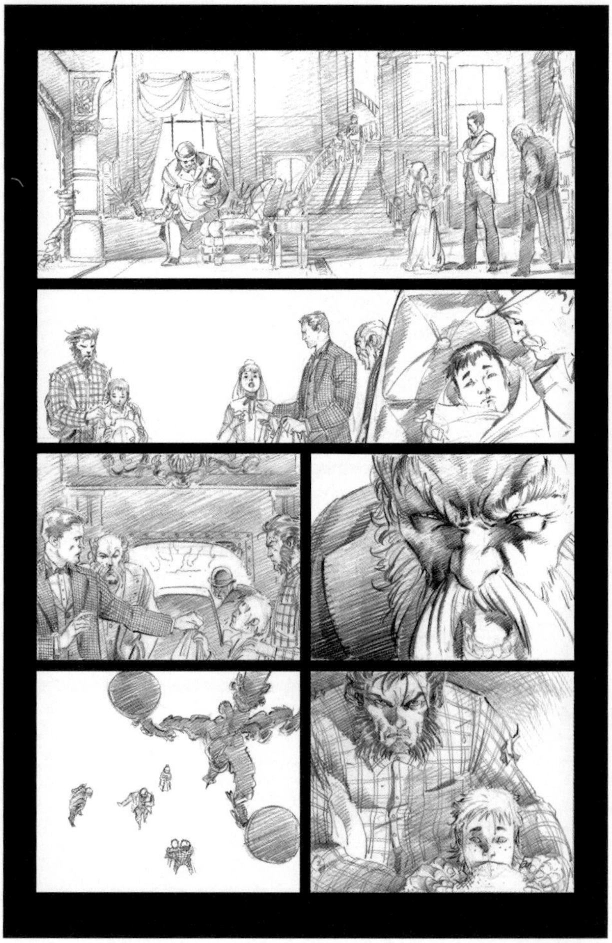
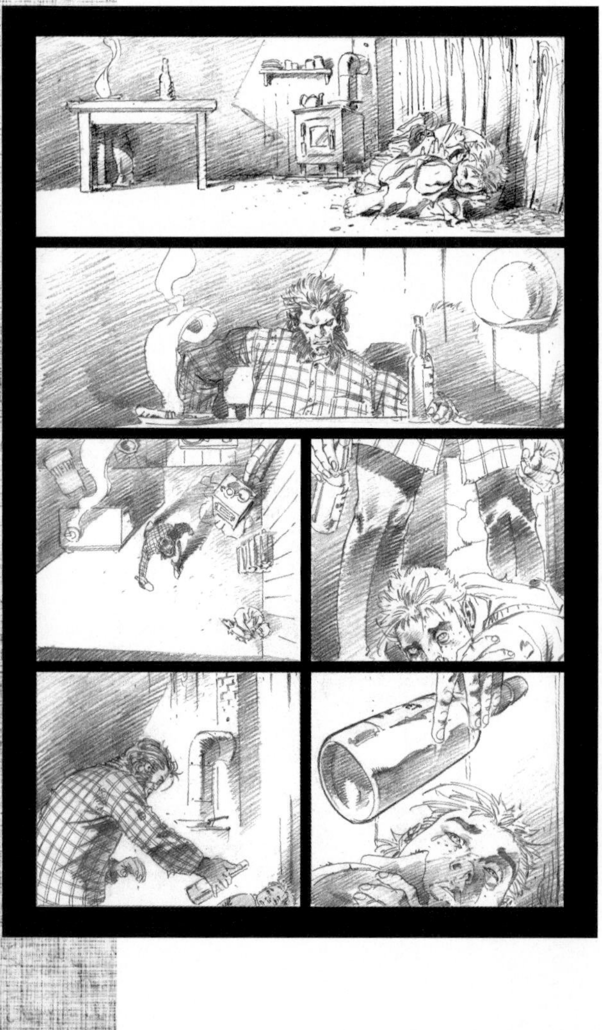
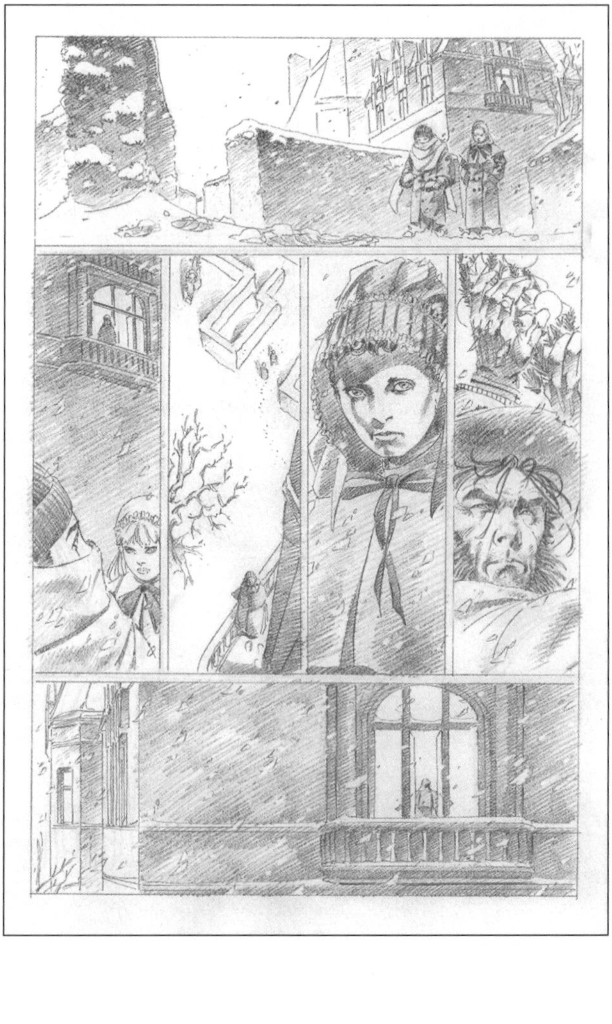

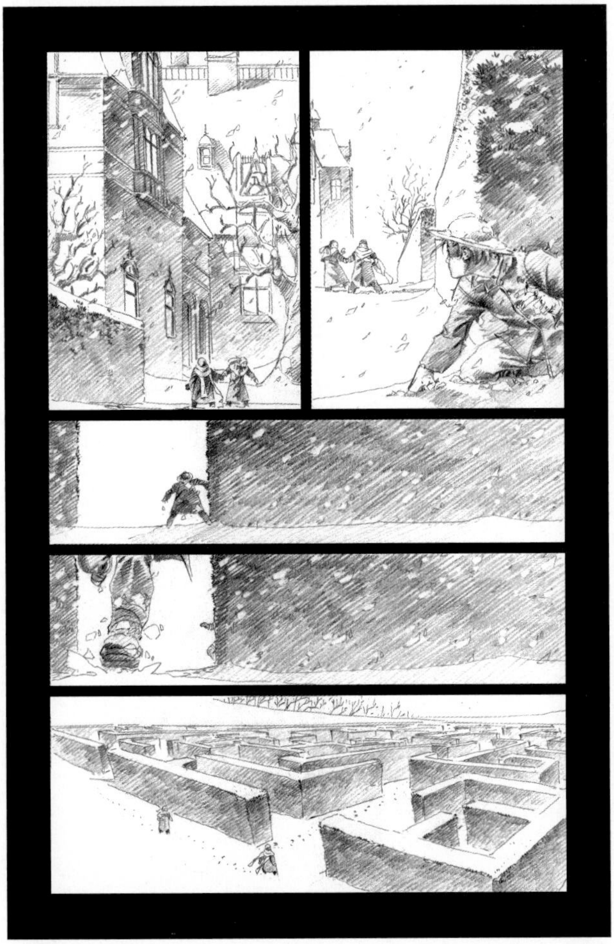

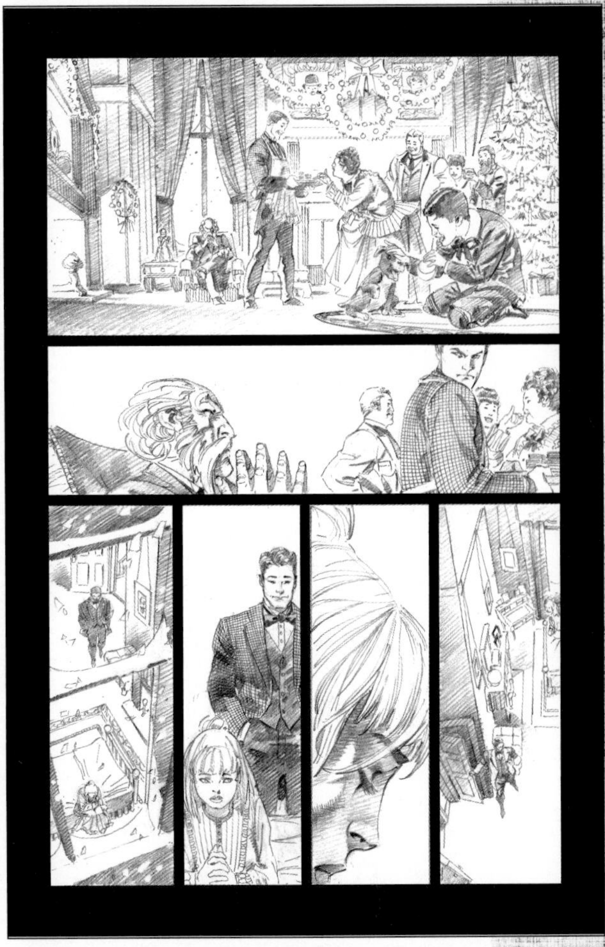

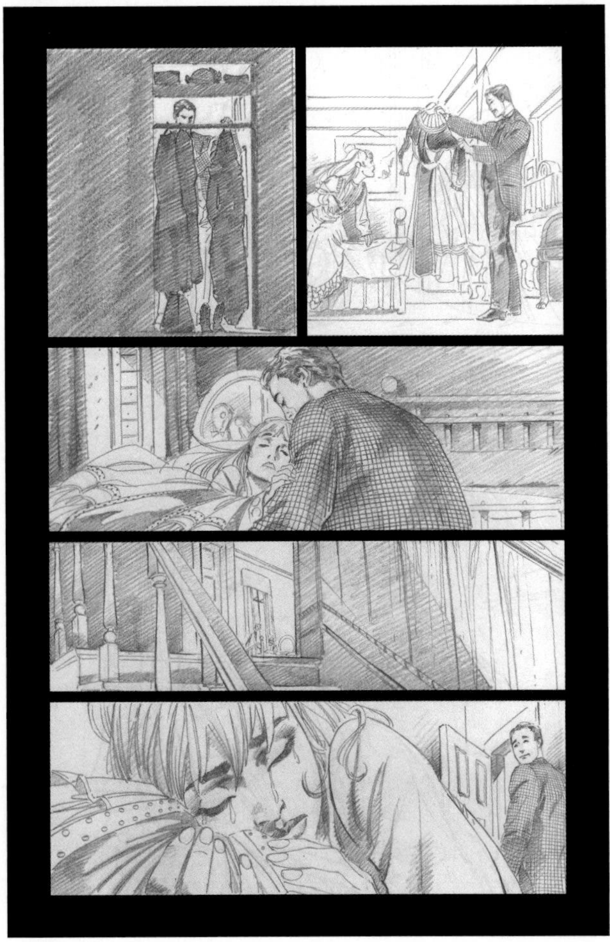

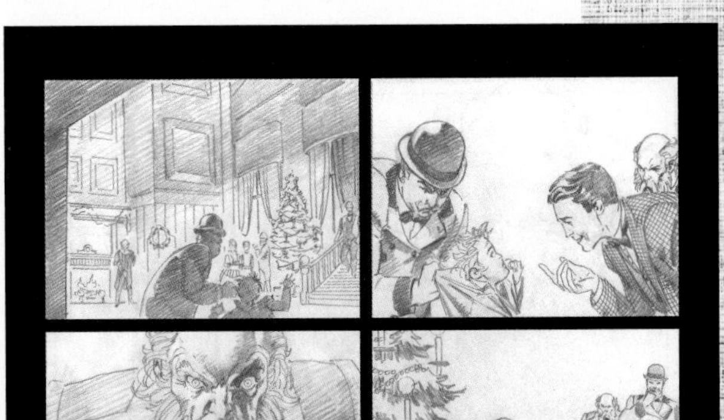

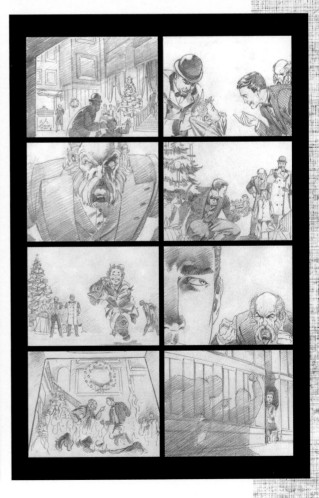

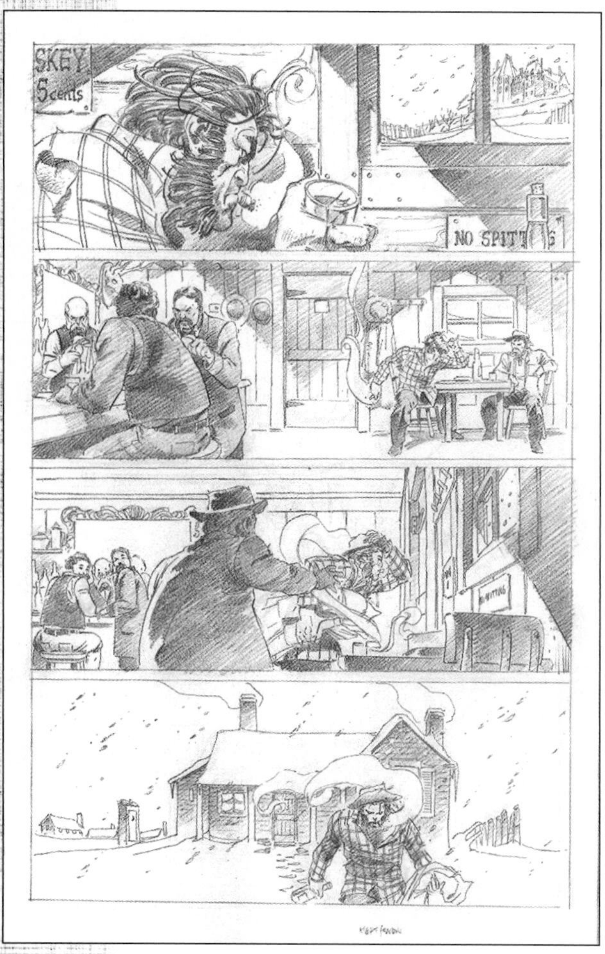
SKEY!
5 cents
NO SPITT

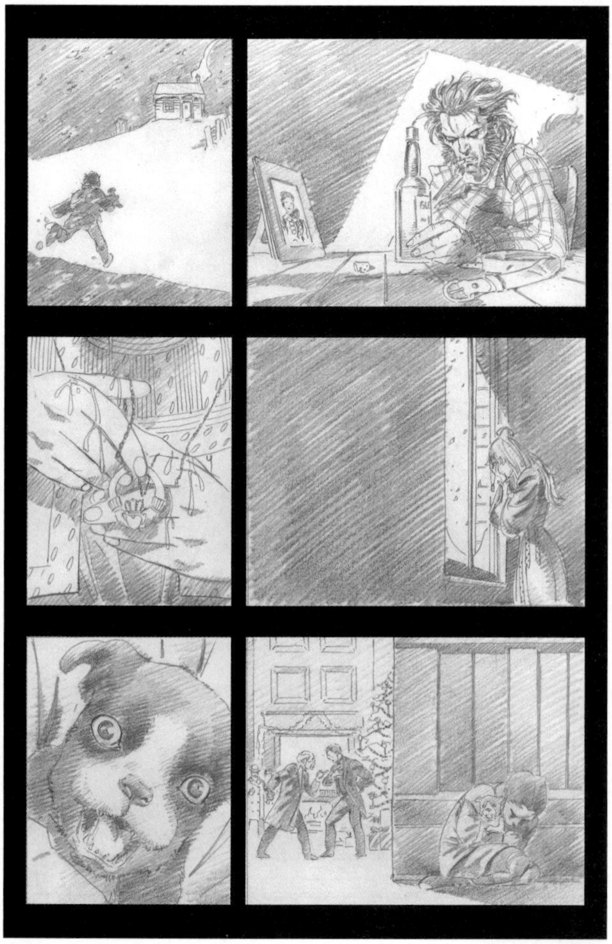

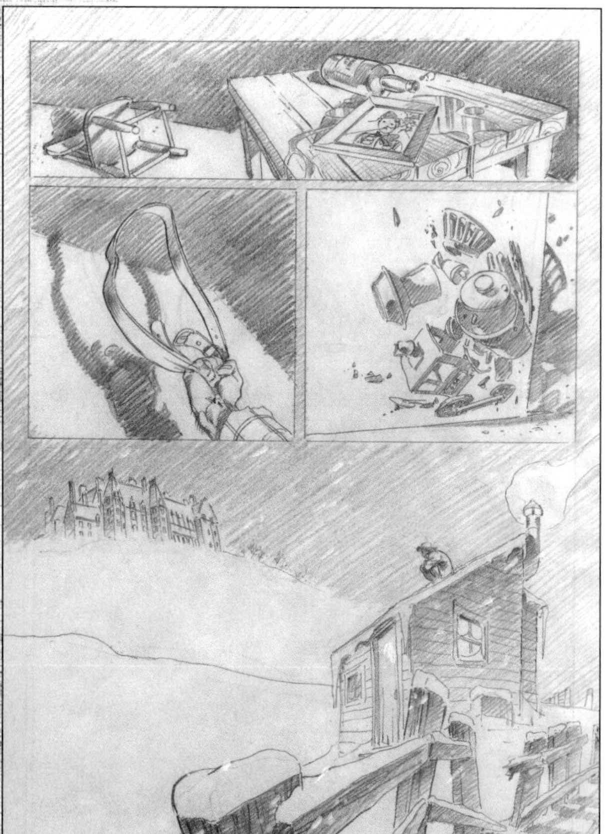

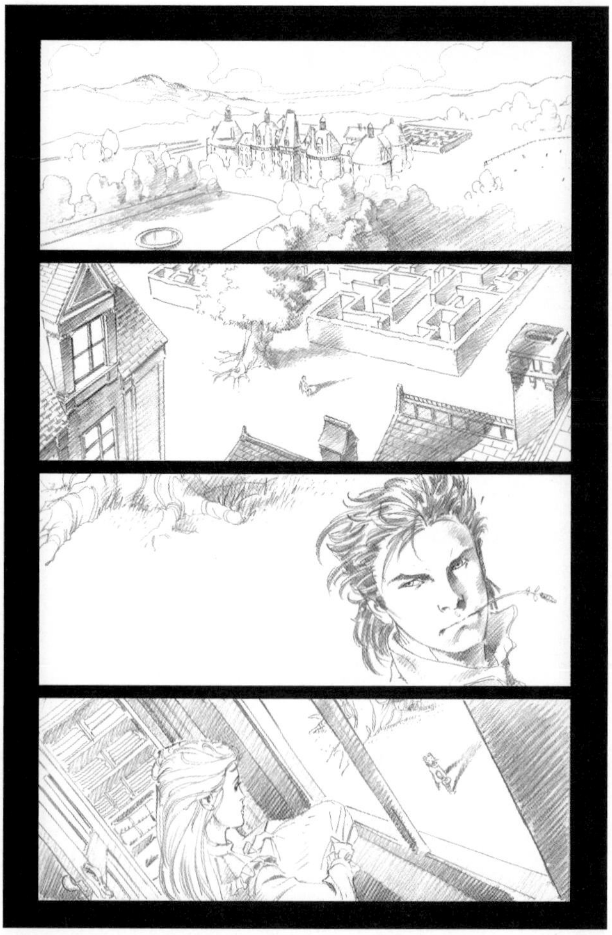

**ORIGIN #2**, PAGE 1 PENCILS

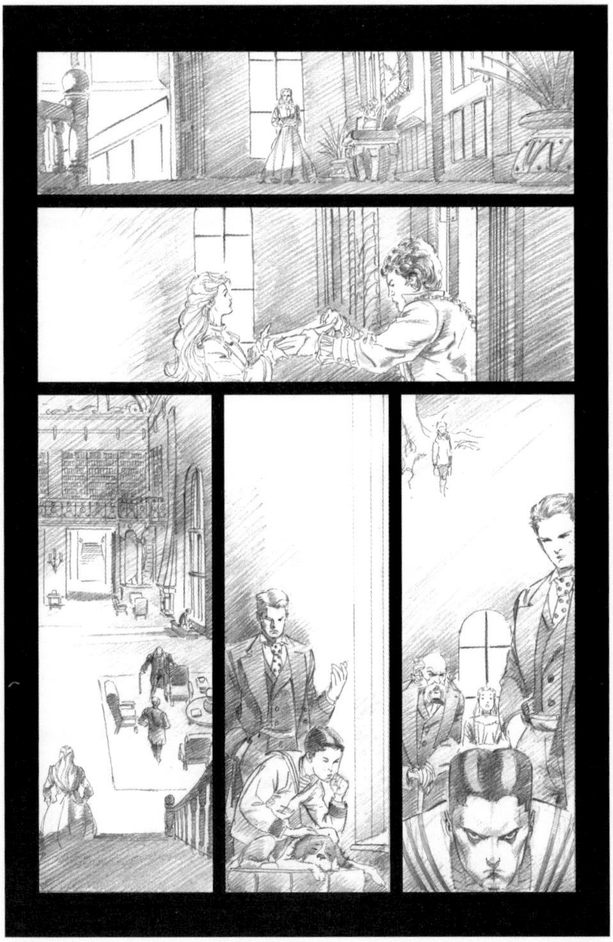
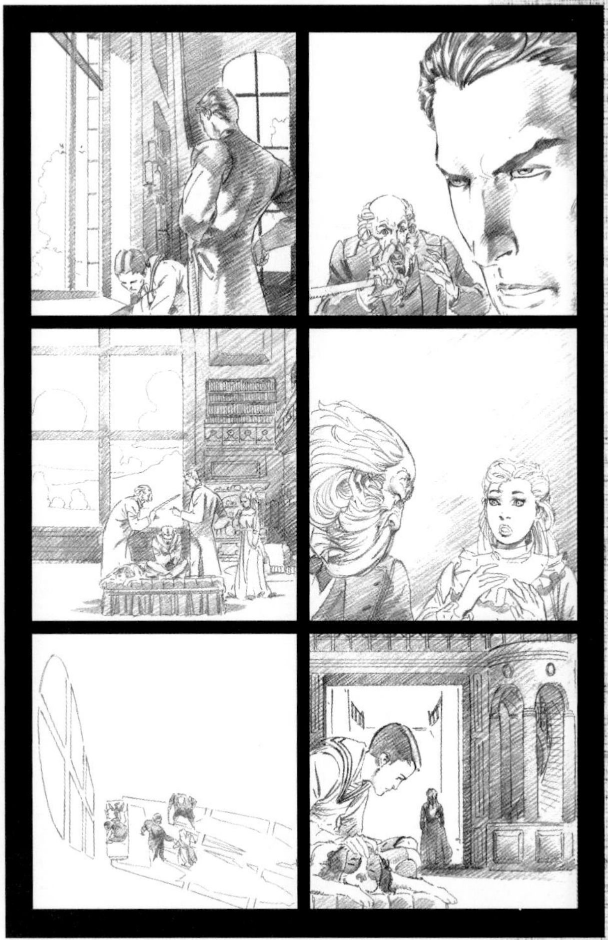
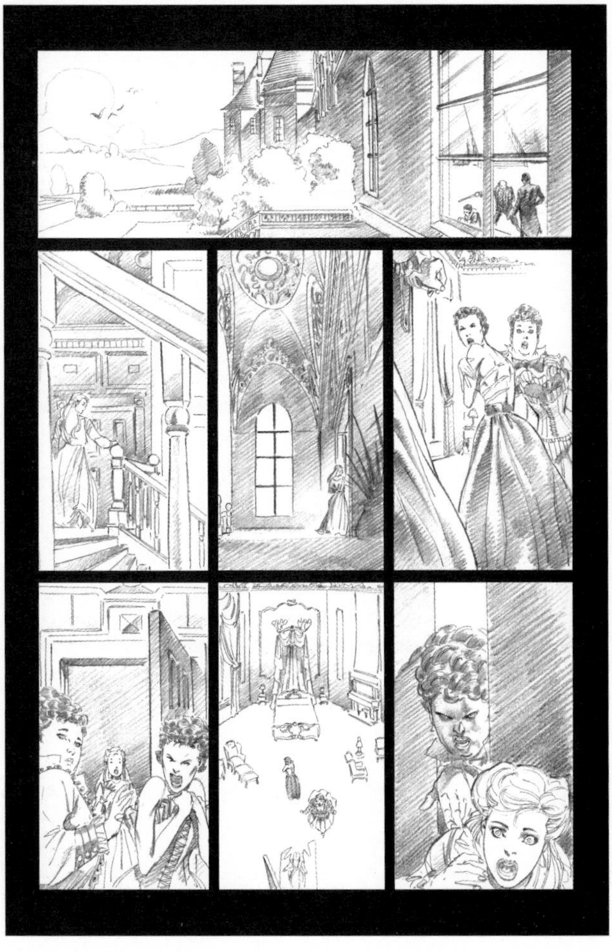
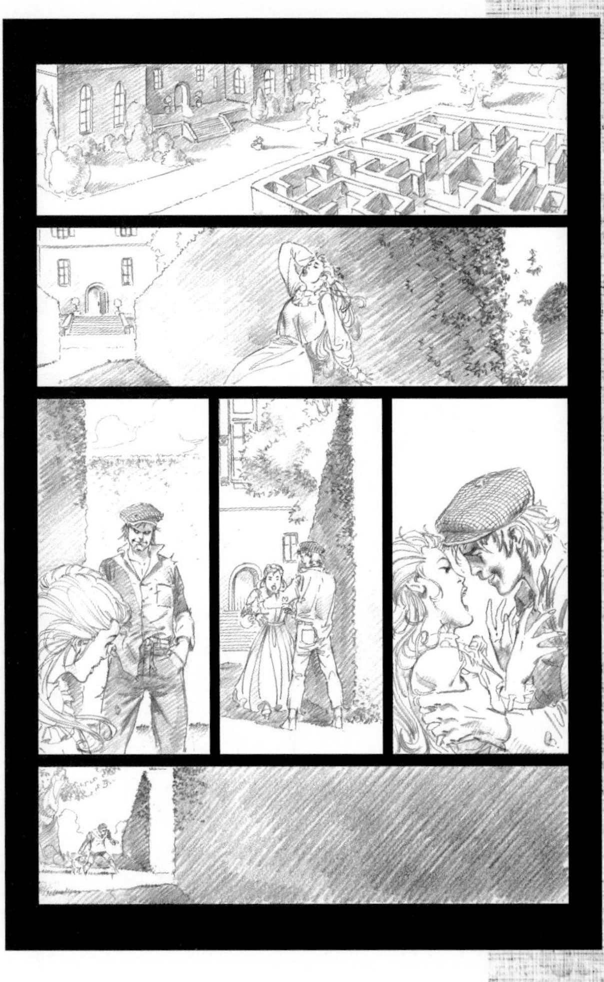

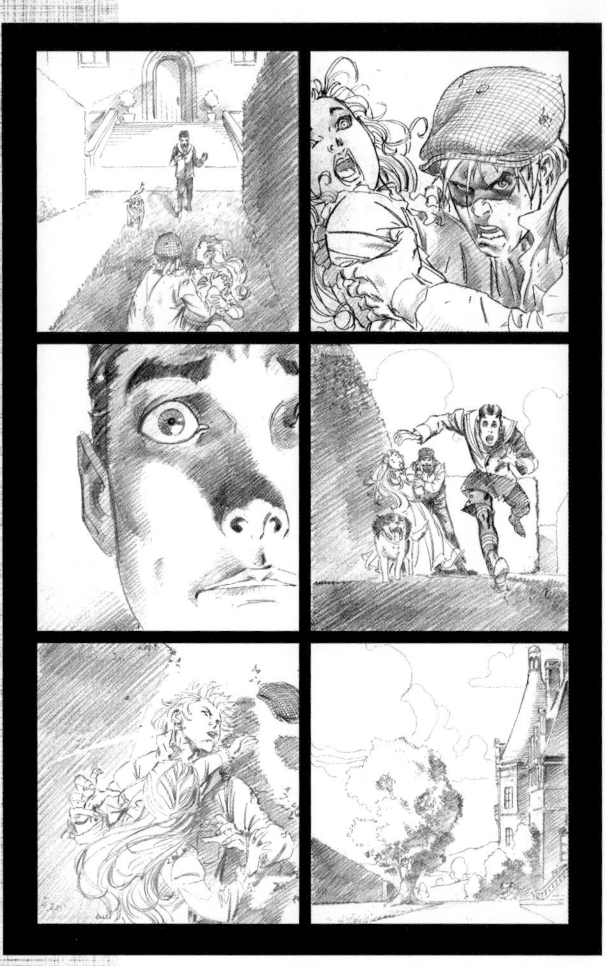

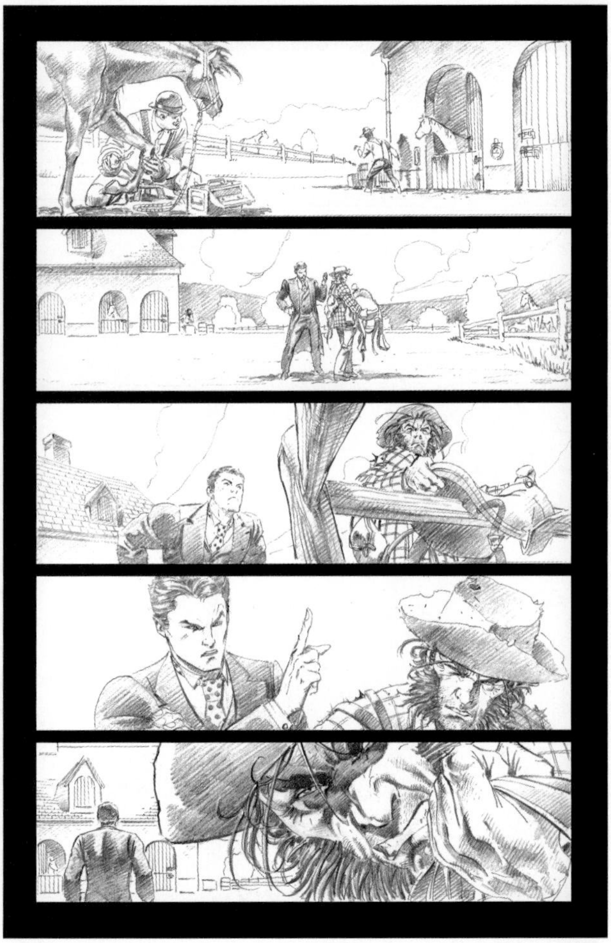

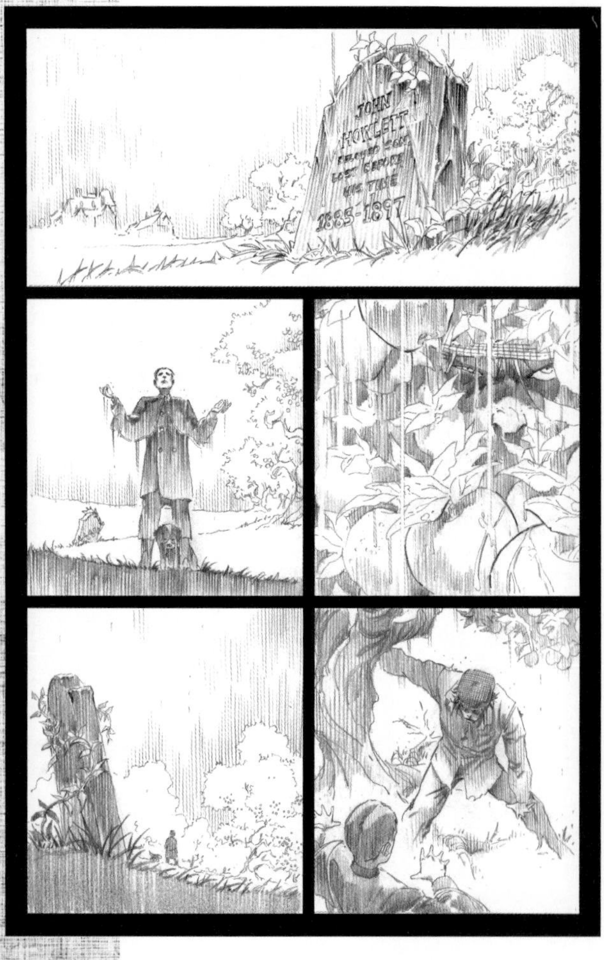
JOHN
HOWLETT
BELOVED SON
LOST BEFORE
HIS TIME
1885-1897

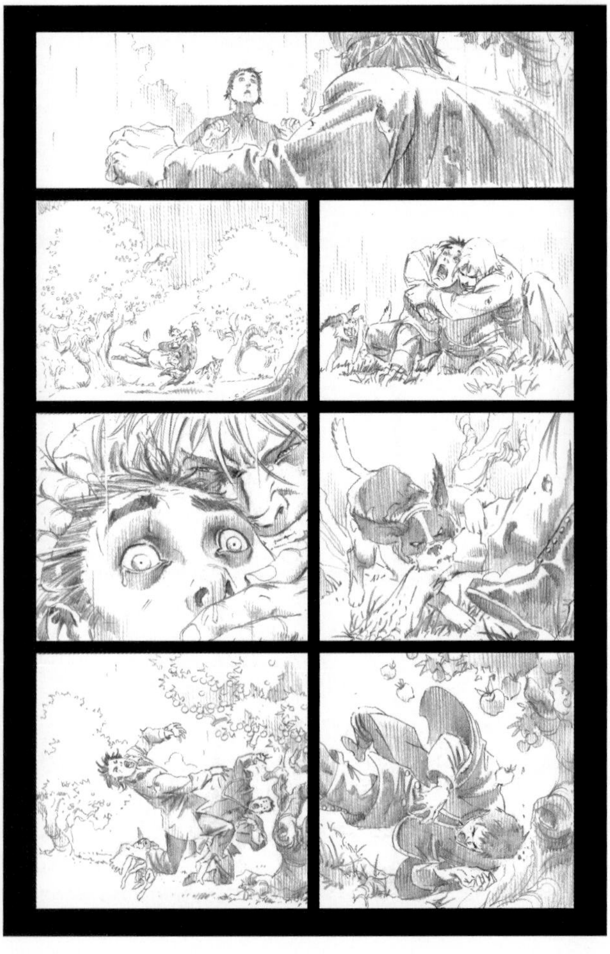

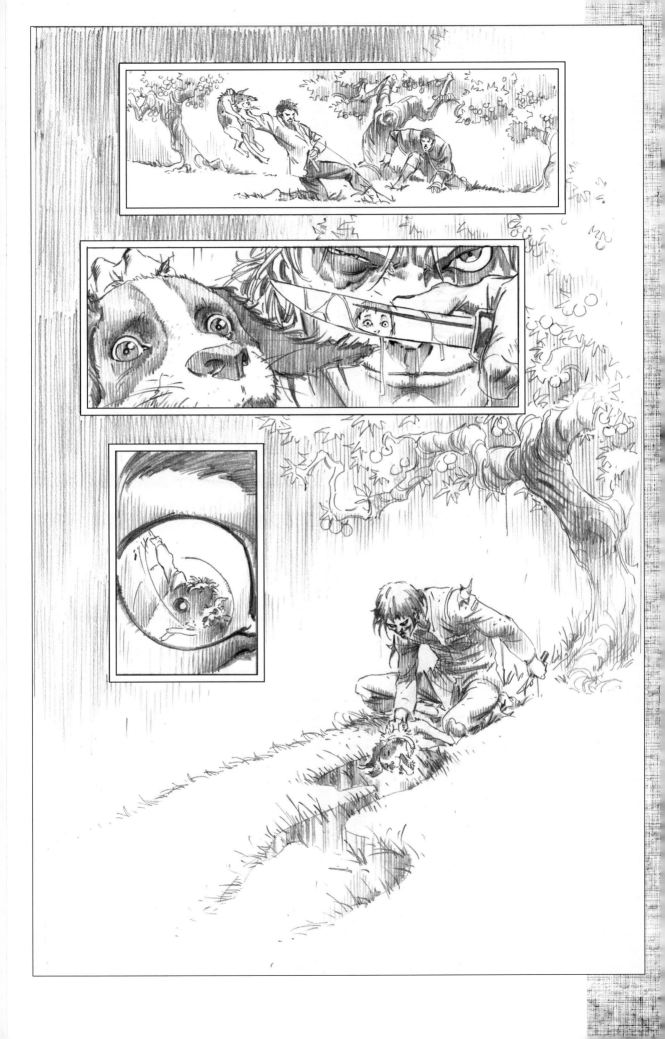

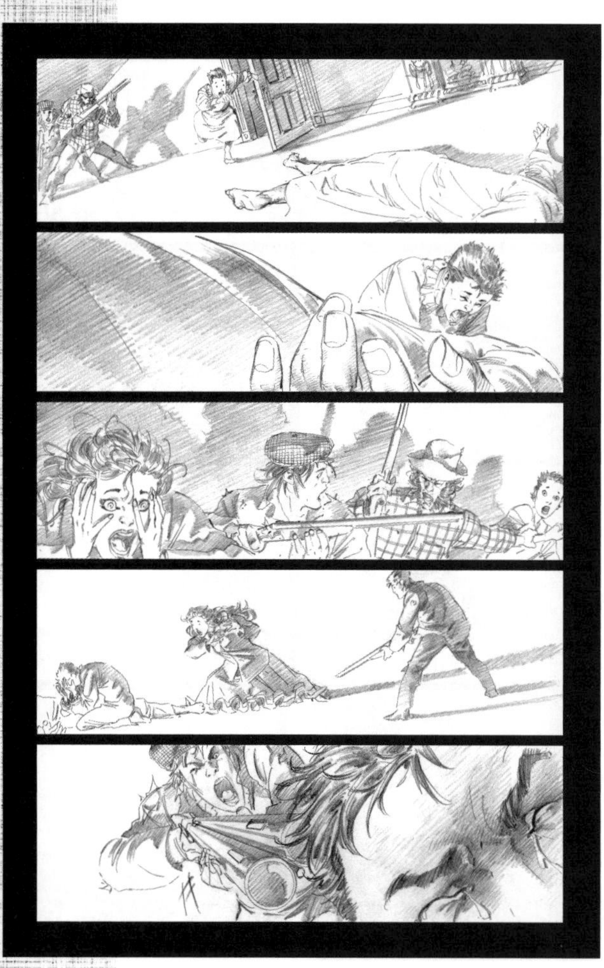
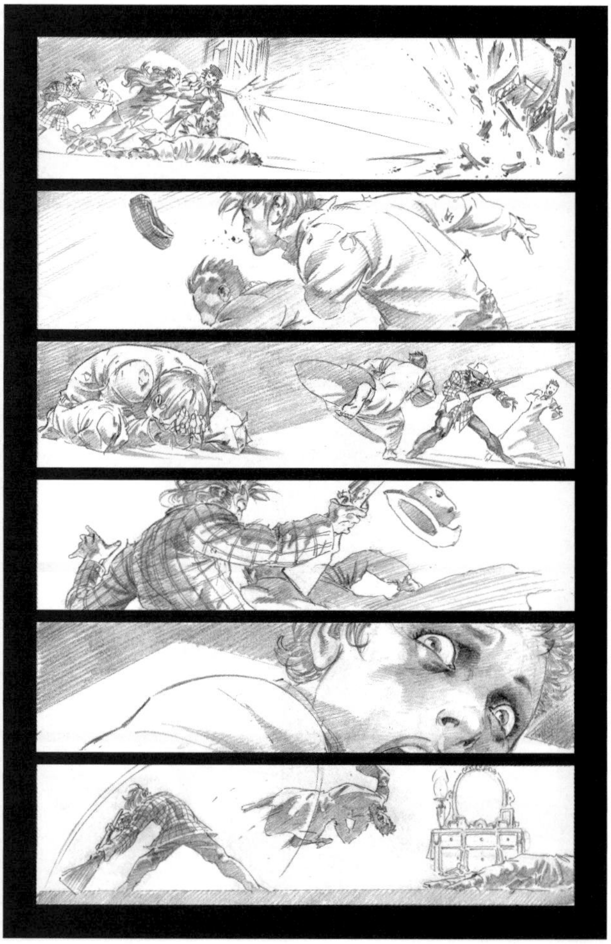
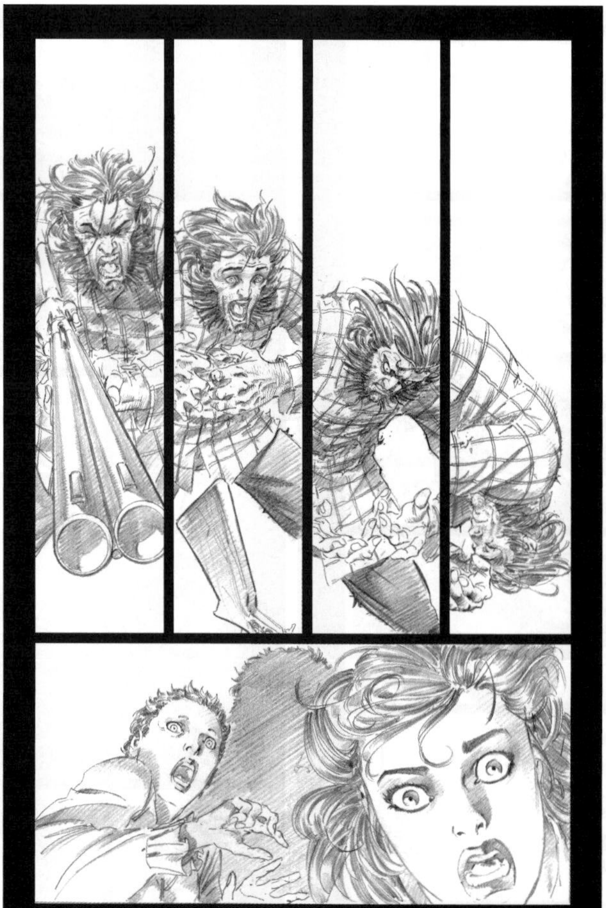

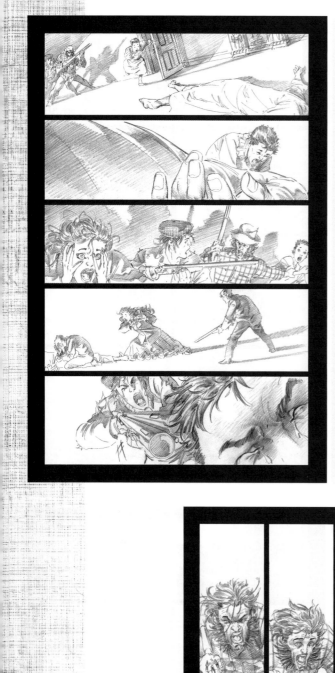

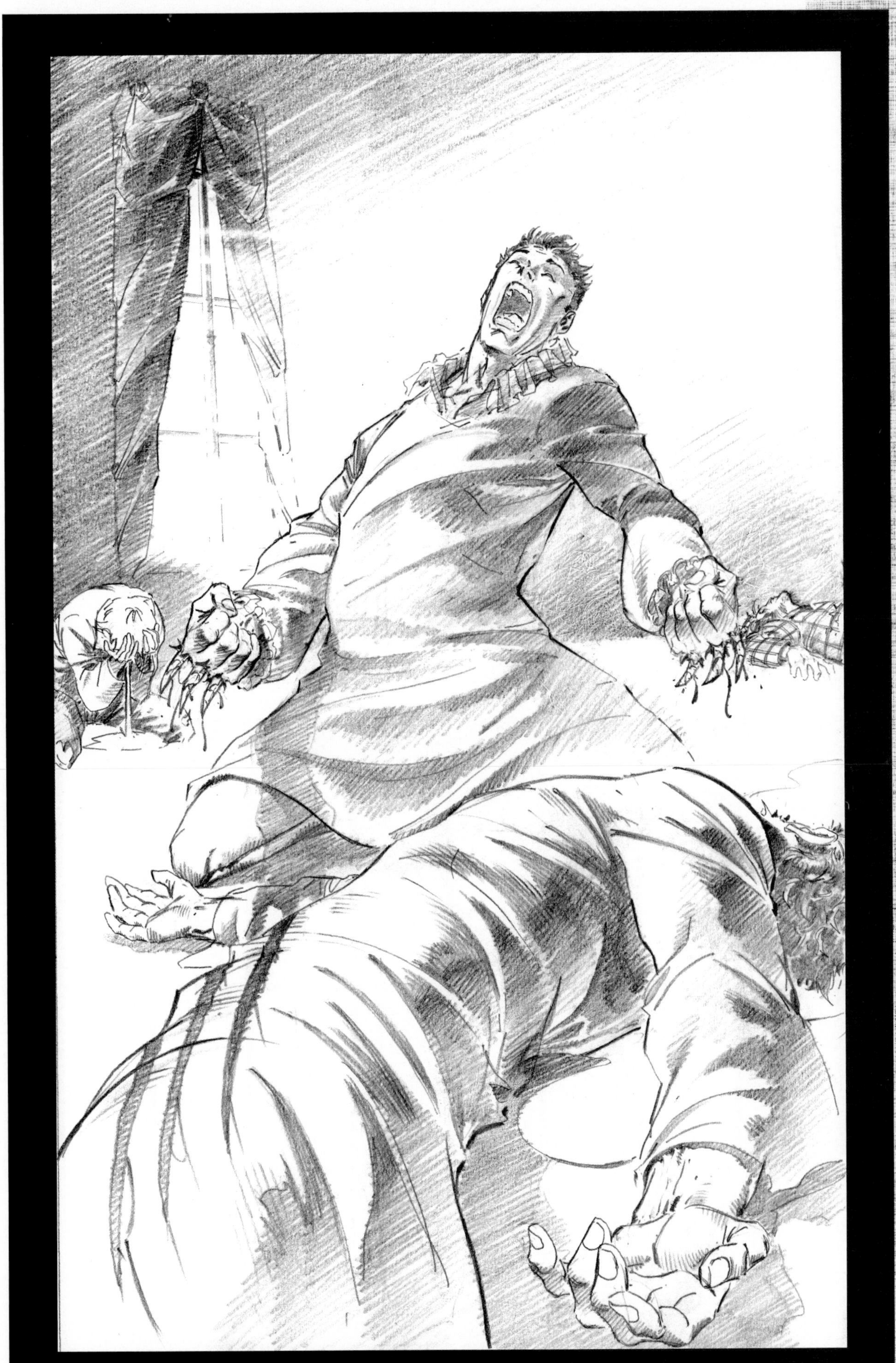

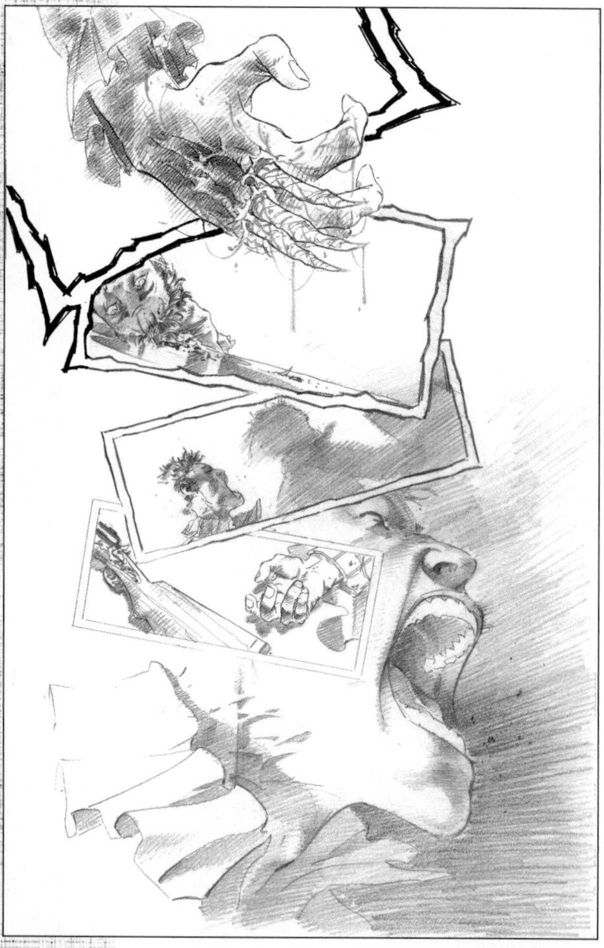

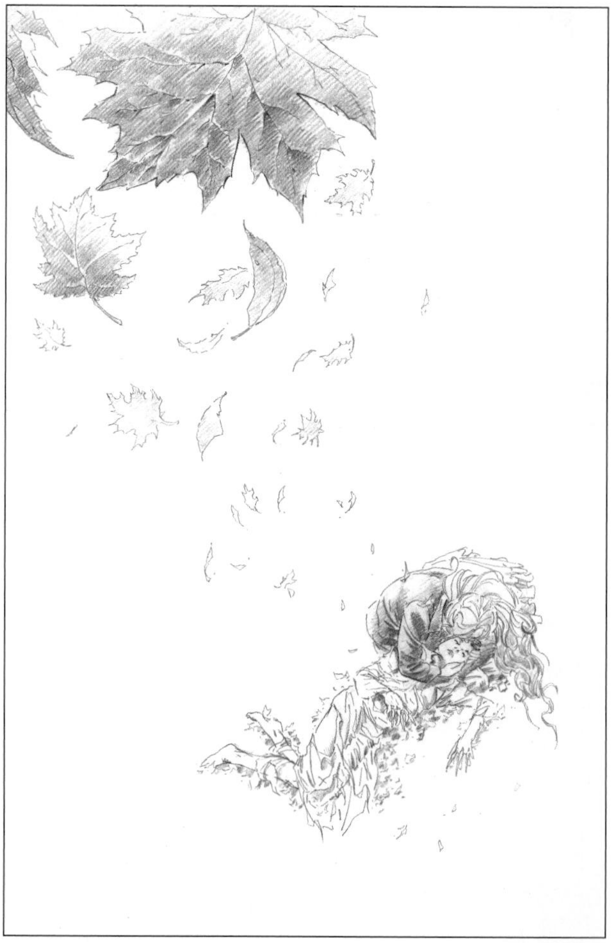

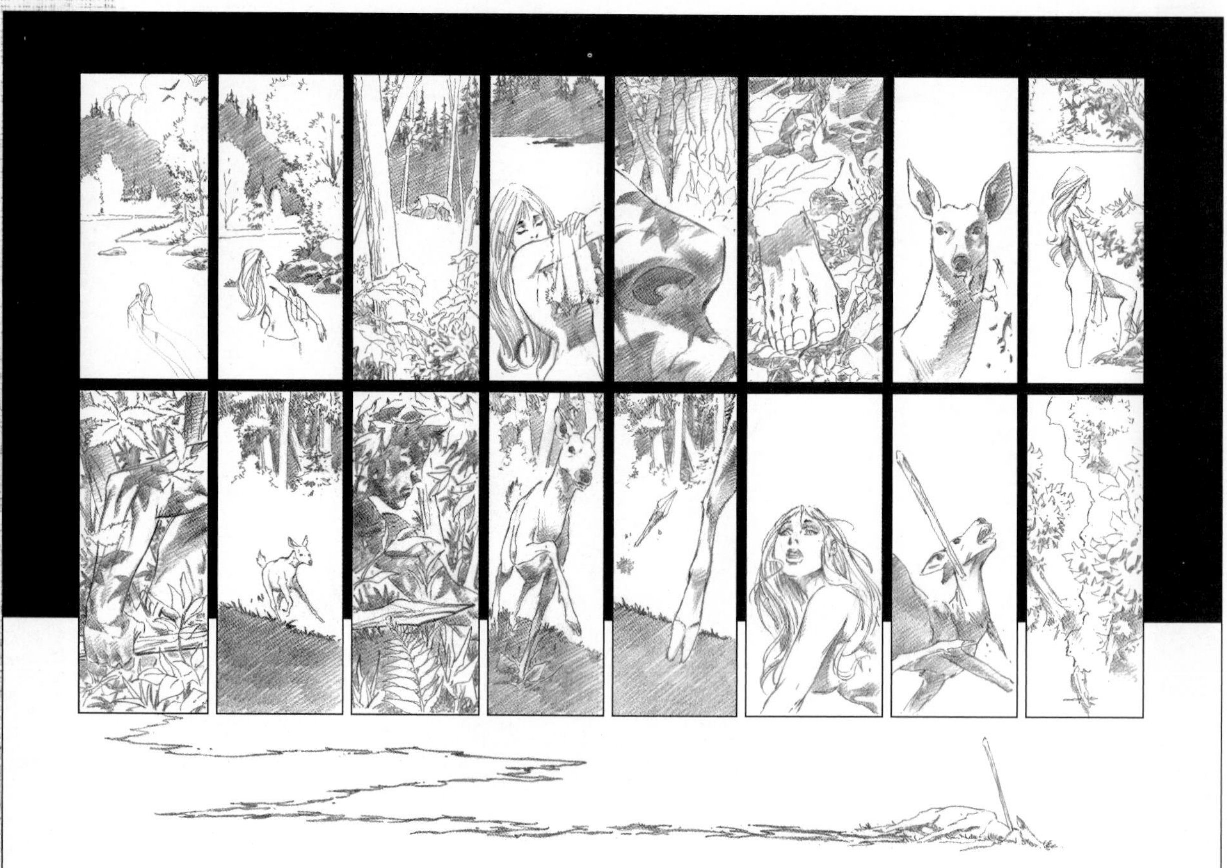

**ORIGIN #3**, PAGES 1 & 9; **ORIGIN #4**, PAGES 12-13

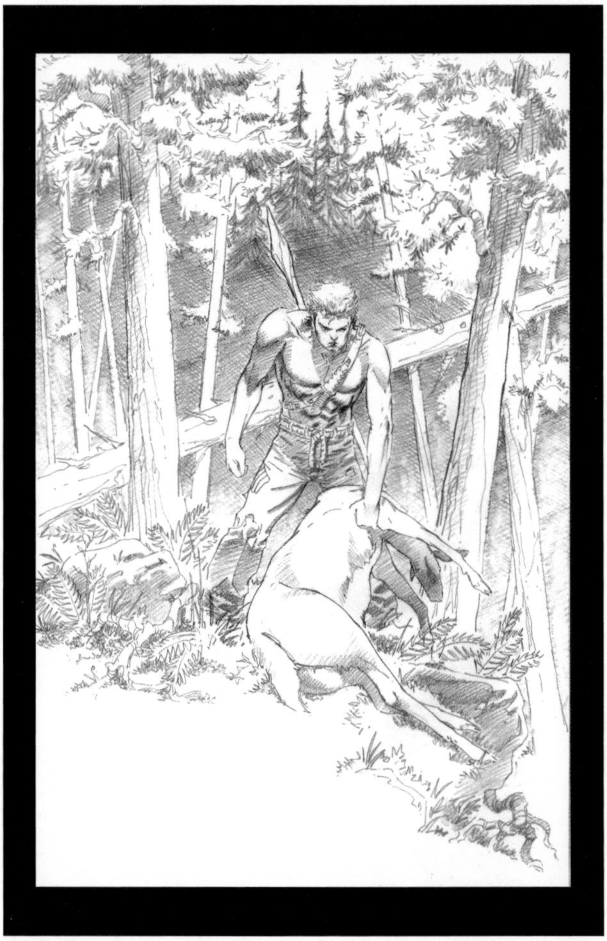
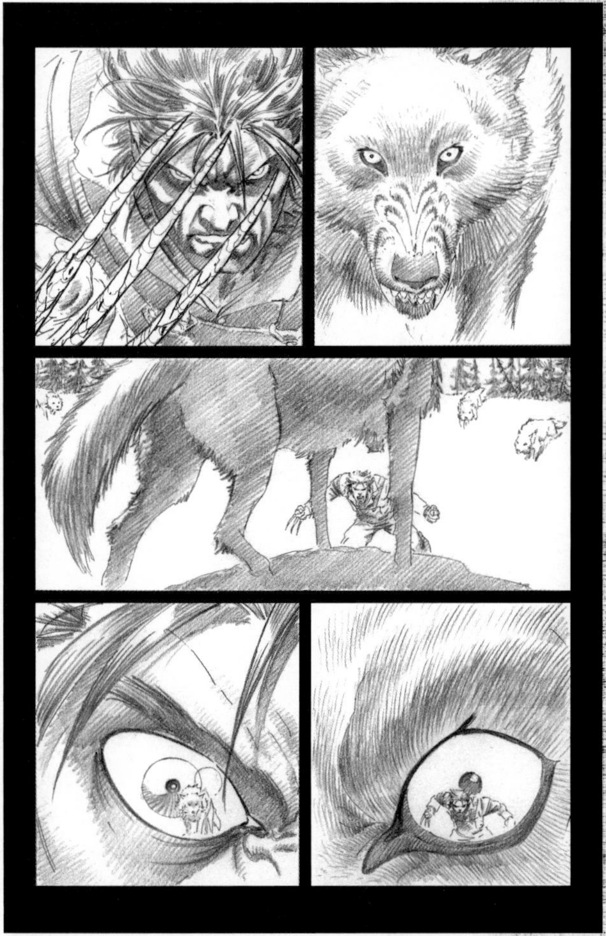
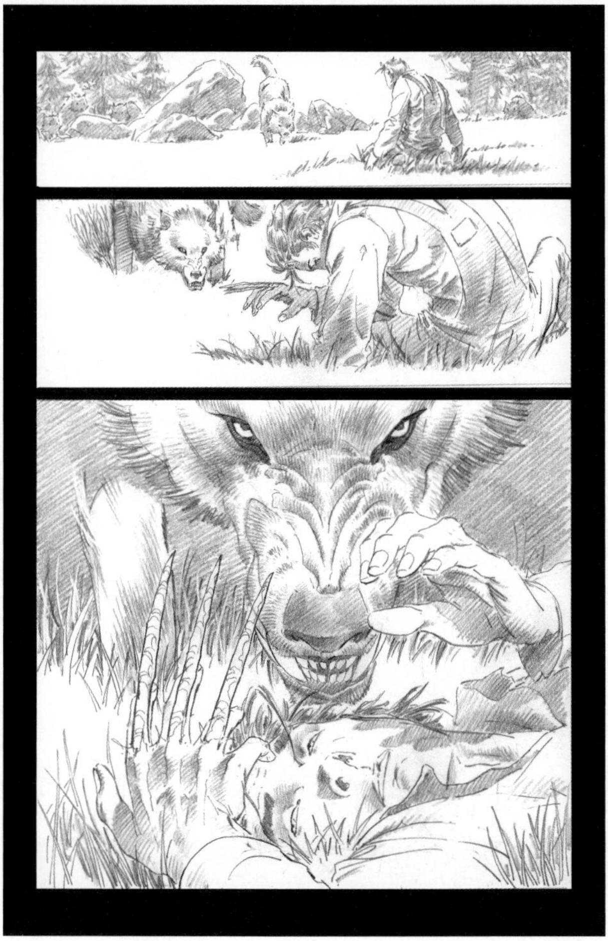
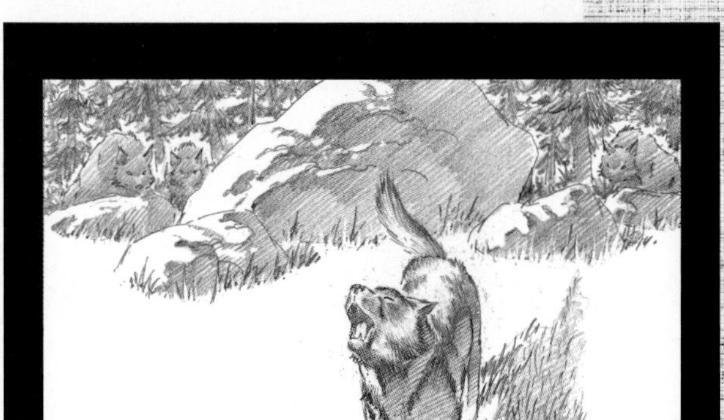

**ORIGIN #4**, PAGES 15 & 26-28

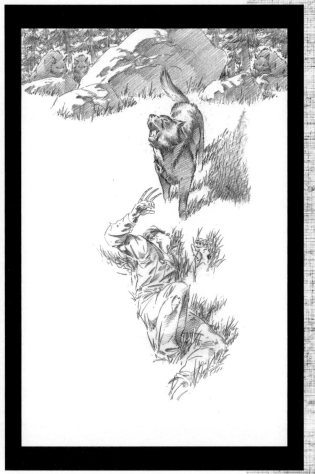

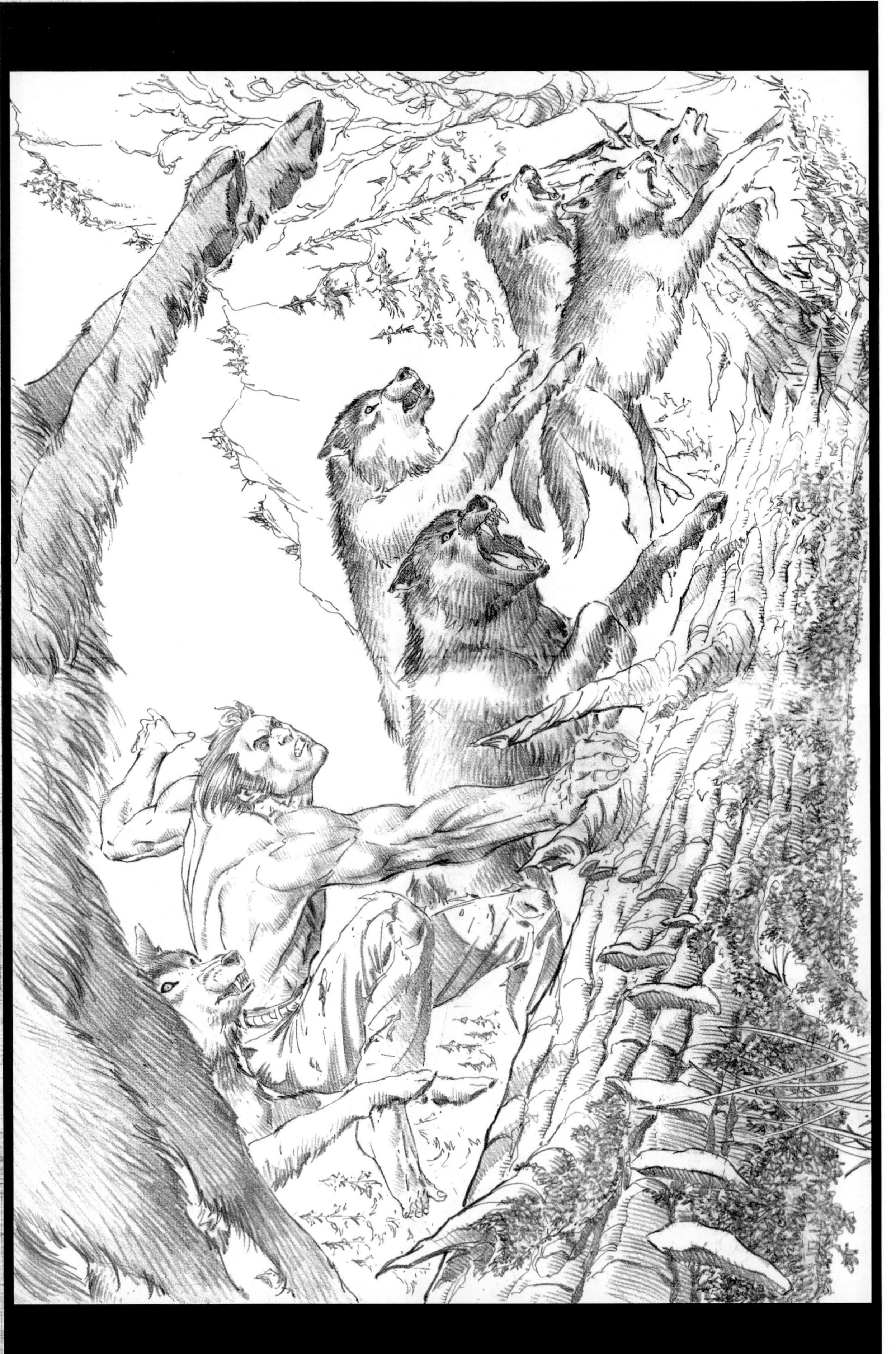

**ORIGIN #5**, PAGES 2-3

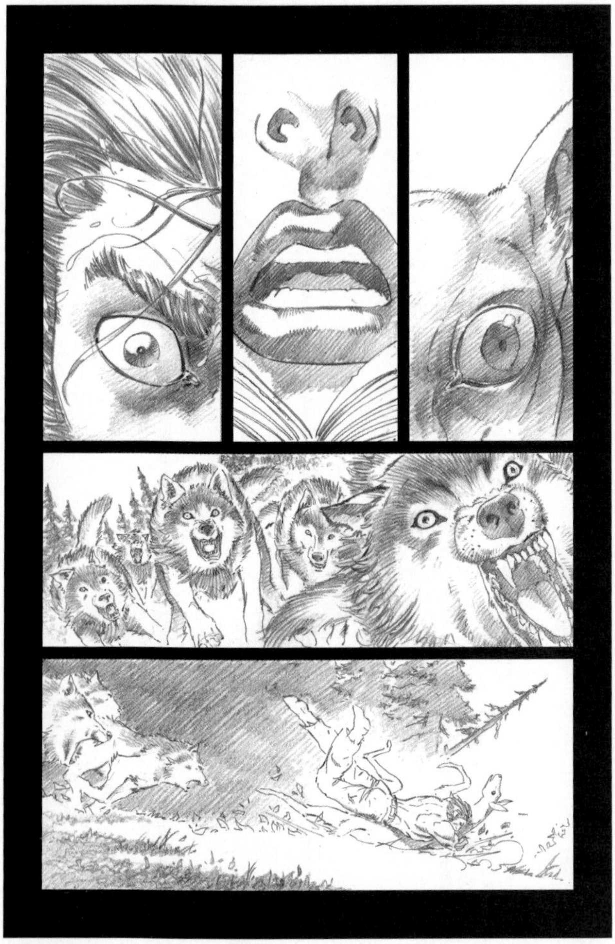
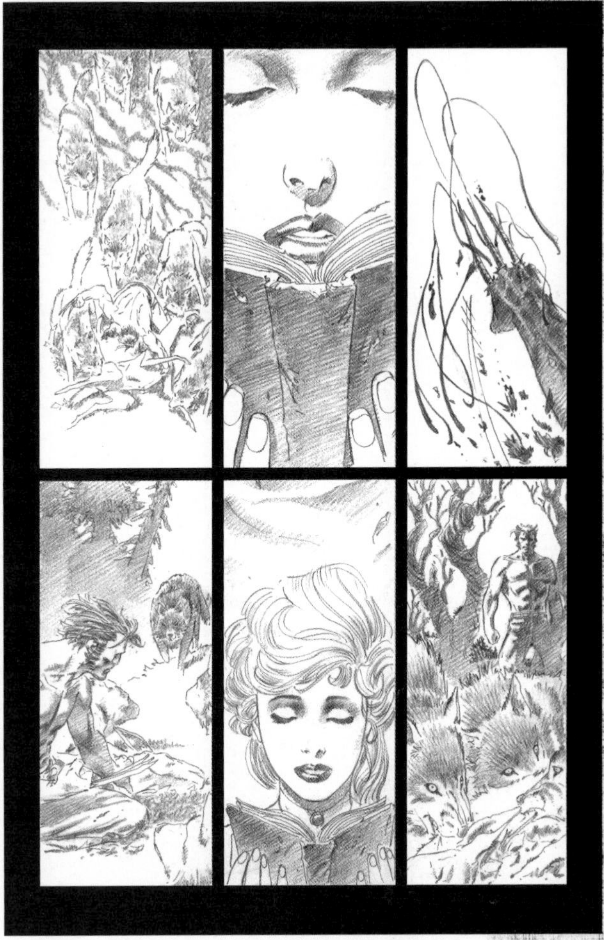
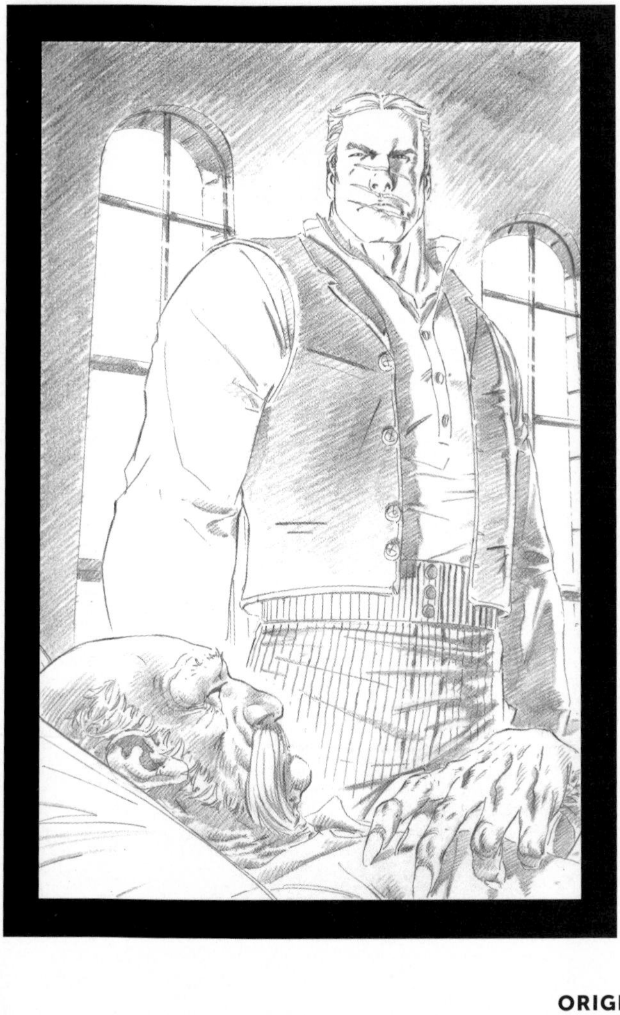
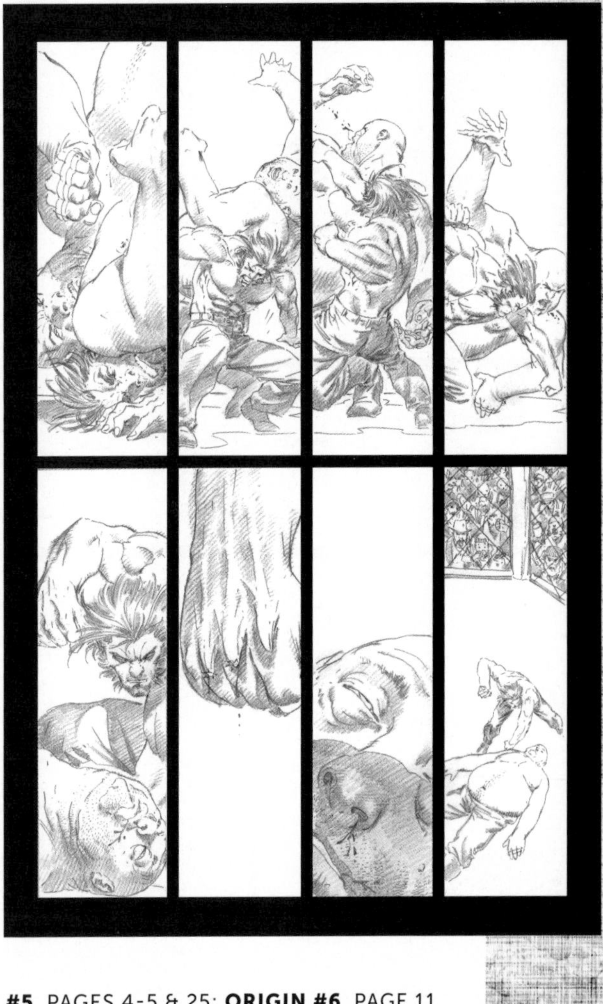

**ORIGIN #5**, PAGES 4-5 & 25; **ORIGIN #6**, PAGE 11